American Civil Procedure

KLUWER LAW INTERNATIONAL

American Civil Procedure

A Guide to Civil Adjudication in US Courts

John B. Oakley
Vikram D. Amar

This book was originally published as a monograph in the International Encyclopaedia of Laws/Civil Procedure.

Wolters Kluwer
Law & Business

AUSTIN BOSTON CHICAGO NEW YORK THE NETHERLANDS

Published by
Kluwer Law International
PO Box 316
2400 AH Alphen aan den Rijn
The Netherlands
Website: www.kluwerlaw.com

Sold and distributed in North, Central and South America by
Aspen Publishers, Inc.
7201 Mckinney Circle
Frederick, MD 21704
United States of America
E-mail: customer.care@aspenpubl.com

Sold and distributed in all other countries by
Turpin Distribution Services Ltd
Stratton Business Park
Pegasus Drive, Biggleswade
Bedfordshire SG18 8TQ
United Kingdom
E-mail: kluwerlaw@turpin-distribution.com

ISBN 978-90-411-2872-0

The Authors

John B. Oakley is Distinguished Professor of Law at the University of California at Davis. From 1991 to 1996, by appointment of the Chief Justice of the United States, he served as the Reporter for the United States Judicial Conference's Committee on Federal-State Jurisdiction. From 1997 to 2001, by appointment of the Chief Justice of California, he was a member of the State of California's Appellate Process Task Force. From 1996 to 1998, Professor Oakley was a member of the Board of Directors of the American Judicature Society. In 2006-2007, he chaired the system-wide Academic Senate of the University of California.

Professor Oakley received his B.A. in History from the University of California at Berkeley in 1969, with Honors and with Distinction, and his J.D. from Yale University in 1972, where he served as an editor of the *Yale Law Journal* and, in his final year, as an Assistant in Instruction. Before joining the Davis Faculty in 1975, he served for one year as a law clerk for the Chief Judge of the US District Court for the District of Connecticut, and for two years as a law clerk for the Chief Justice of the California Supreme Court. In 1979-1980, he was the Scholar in Residence in the Civil Rights Division of the US Department of Justice, in Washington, DC, participating in litigation across the United States as a Senior Trial Attorney. In 1982-1983, he was a visiting scholar at University College, Oxford. From 1984 to 1996, he served by appointment of the California Supreme Court as appellate counsel for a condemned California prisoner. Professor Oakley remains an active member of the State Bar of California who often serves as a consultant on matters of jurisdiction and procedure to lawyers conducting complex civil litigation in state and federal courts throughout the United States. From 1994 to 2004, he served as Reporter for the American Law Institute's Federal Judicial Code Revision Project. He has taught as a Visiting Professor at the University of California, Berkeley, and at the University of Tennessee. In 2005, he was given the title Distinguished Professor of Law by the University of California, Davis. From 2005 to 2007, he served as Faculty Representative on the Board of Regents of the University of California.

Professor Oakley is the author of many books and articles, dealing principally with variations in civil procedure and the allocation of jurisdiction among the state and federal court systems of the United States, as well as the process of judicial decision-making. Among his publishers are Aspen Publishers, Foundation Press, the

University of California Press, and West Publishing. His articles have appeared in the *Annals of the American Academy of Political and Social Science*, the *Arizona State Law Journal*, the *Brigham Young University Law Review*, the *California Law Review*, the *Duke Law Journal*, the *Hastings Constitutional Law Quarterly*, the *Indiana Law Review*, the *Journal of Appellate Practice and Procedure*, the *Southern California Law Review*, the *Texas Law Review*, the *U.C. Davis Law Review*, the *Washington Law Review*, and the *Yale Law Journal*, among other periodicals. His newspaper articles and editorials on legal and political topics have been published in the *Los Angeles Times*, *Newsday*, *The Sacramento Bee*, and *The Sunday Times* of London.

Vikram D. Amar is Professor of Law and Associate Dean for Academic Affairs of the School of Law of the University of California at Davis. He joined the law faculty at Davis in 1993, becoming Professor of Law in 1997. He has also taught in a regular or visiting capacity at the other three University of California law schools: at Berkeley, Hastings (in San Francisco), and Los Angeles. Professor Amar received his A.B. in 1985 from the University of California at Berkeley, and his J.D. in 1988 from the Yale Law School, where he served as an Articles Editor of the Yale Law Journal. After law school, he spent one year clerking for Judge William Norris of the US Court of Appeals for the Ninth Circuit, and another year clerking for US Supreme Court Justice Harry Blackmun.

Before entering academia, Professor Amar practiced complex civil and criminal litigation in California at the law firm of Gibson, Dunn & Crutcher. During his academic career, Professor Amar has taught either as a regular or Visiting Professor at each of the four University of California law schools.

Professor Amar's scholarship focuses on the public law fields, especially Constitutional Law, Civil Procedure, and Remedies. He is a co-author, along with Jonathan Varat of UCLA and William Cohen of Stanford, of a widely used constitutional law casebook, and also a co-author of several volumes of the Wright & Miller Federal Practice and Procedure Treatise. He has published on a variety of topics in many leading law reviews, including *Constitutional Commentary*, the *California Law Review*, the *Cornell Law Review*, the *Hastings Constitutional Law Quarterly*, the *Hastings Law Journal*, the *Stanford Law Review*, the *U.C. Davis Law Review*, the *Vanderbilt Law Review*, the *Virginia Law Review*, the *William & Mary Law Review*, and the *Yale Law Journal*. He authors a bi-weekly column on constitutional matters for the website findlaw.com and has written scores of op-ed pieces in many leading American newspapers, including *The New York Times*, *The Washington Post*, and the *Los Angeles Times*.

Table of Contents

List of Abbreviations

AAA	American Arbitration Association
ABA	American Bar Association
ADEA	Age Discrimination in Employment Act
ADR	Alternative Dispute Resolution
ADRA	Administrative Dispute Resolution Act
ALI	American Law Institute
AOUSC	Administrative Office of the United States Courts
CCJ	Conference of Chief Justices
CJRA	Civil Justice Reform Act
ENE	Early Neutral Evaluation
FAA	Federal Arbitration Act
Fed. R. App. P.	Federal Rules of Appellate Procedure
Fed. R. Civ. P.	Federal Rules of Civil Procedure
FEHA	Fair Employment and Housing Act
FJC	Federal Judicial Center
FRE	Federal Rules of Evidence
FSIA	Foreign Sovereign Immunities Act
GSA	Government Services Agency
JPML	Judicial Panel on Multidistrict Litigation
LOA	Last Offer Arbitration
LSC	The Legal Services Corporation
LSP	Legal Services Program
MEDALOA	Mediation And Last Offer Arbitration
NCSC	National Center for State Courts
NIDR	National Institute for Dispute Resolution
NJC	Neighborhood Justice Center
PMPA	Petroleum Marketing Practices Act
RICO	Racketeer Influenced and Corrupt Organizations Act
S. Ct.	Supreme Court Reporter
SJI	State Justice Institute
SJT	Summary Jury Trial
TRO	Temporary Restraining Order
UAA	Uniform Arbitration Act
US	United States

Preface

Dean Kevin R. Johnson of the School of Law of the University of California at Davis, as well as his predecessors, Deans Emeriti Rex R. Perschbacher and Bruce A. Wolk, have each generously supported this project through their funding of student research assistants. Those named below are all graduates, or graduates-to-be, of the U.C. Davis Law School, in the year indicated after each name.

We acknowledge with thanks the research assistance of Suzanne Ayers '96, Peter Vladimir '97, and Kirk Mylander '99 in the early phases of the writing of this work. We especially appreciate the research and editorial assistance of David Austin '01 during the summer of 1999, and Brett Davis '02 during the summer of 2000. Both were indispensable in our completion of this work as first published in 2001. In preparing the revised 2008 edition of this work, we have greatly benefited from and gratefully acknowledge the research assistance of Holly Carmichael '09 and Lani Todd '10.

It has been a daunting task trying to describe in reasonably succinct fashion the historical foundations, present rules, general policies, normative principles, and future trends of the civil procedure of the United States – a country with (seemingly) almost as many legal systems as other countries have lawyers. We hope we have succeeded in our efforts to summarize without false simplification.

General Introduction

§1. General Background

1. Although it is commonplace today to refer to "the United States" as a single entity and as the subject of statements that grammatically employ singular verbs, it is important to remember that "the United States" remains in many important ways a *collective* term. The enduring legal significance of the fifty states that together constitute the United States, and their essential dominion over most legal matters affecting day-to-day life within the United States, vastly complicates any attempt to summarize the law of civil procedure within the United States.

Within the community of nations, the United States is a geopolitical superpower that acts through a federal government granted constitutionally specified and limited powers. The organizing principle of the federal Constitution,[1] however, is one of popular sovereignty, with governmental powers distributed in the first instance to republican institutions of government organized autonomously and uniquely in each of the fifty states. Although there are substantial similarities in the organization of state governments, idiosyncracies abound.

1. We follow conventional practice by capitalizing "Constitution" when referring to the Constitution of the United States as opposed to the constitution of one of its fifty states. *See* Bryan A. Garner, *A Dictionary of Modern Legal Usage*, 2nd edn (1995), 208.

2. Every state has its own constitution, establishing a legislative branch of government, generally but not universally consisting of a bicameral legislature in which the representatives in the lower house are greater in number and serve for shorter terms of office than their counterparts in the upper house, an executive branch headed by an officer denominated as "governor", and a judicial branch organized into tiers of trial and appellate courts headed by a court of last resort of five to nine judges – generally but by no means universally designated the "Supreme Court" of the state in question. State legislators are elected by and accountable to the voters of particular districts, generally drawn with reference to particular counties, cities, and other municipal subdivisions of the state, each such district consisting of a set of precincts in which the ideal of popular sovereignty is made real by the casting and collection of votes at local polling places. By a long process of constitutional development culminating in the ratification in 1971 of the 26th Amendment to the federal Constitution, the right to vote in state and federal elections extends to all citizens of the age of eighteen or older. In practice, however, the exercise of universal adult suffrage is limited by the requirement that voters register in their particular precincts of residence at a specified time prior to an election, and personally, or by prescribed absentee-voting procedure, cast their votes at the time and in the manner specified. Depending upon the local political culture and the issues of the day, the majority of votes cast at a particular election may be only a small percentage of those registered to vote, and an even smaller percentage of those eligible to vote.[1]

State governors are universally elected by statewide vote, and in many states the judiciary (or at least some judges within it) is also elected either by direct popular vote or is subject to electoral confirmation by popular vote subsequent to executive appointment. Most state constitutions also permit legislation to be enacted independently of conventional legislative processes by direct popular vote when an "initiative" measure is placed on the statewide ballot by the petition of an often quite small percentage of the state's registered voters. In recent years, it has become commonplace in the states to enact state constitutional limits, called "term limits", that restrict the maximum tenure in office of elected state legislators and governors. Combined with the initiative process, this has increased the volatility of the content of the state law. Except where state law is challenged as violative of federal constitutional restrictions of state authority, issues of the construction and application of state law – including, of course, issues relating to the civil procedure of the several states – are governed by the decisions of each state's court of last resort.

1. *See* Bill Winders, "The Roller Coaster of Class Conflict: Class Segments, Mass Mobilization, and Voter Turnout in the U.S., 1840-1996," Soc. Forces 77 (1999): 833; *see also* Jonathan E. Davis, "The National Voter Registration Act of 1993: Debunking States' Rights Resistance and the Pretense of Voter Fraud," Temp. Pol. & Civ. Rts. L. Rev. 6 (1997): 117 (noting that voter turnout in the US ranks twenty-third among Western, industrialized nations).

3. As a matter of federal constitutional law, the population of the districts which elect all state legislators, whether seated in the lower or upper house of a state legislature, must be substantially similar in size to the districts electing all other legislators of similar rank in that state. This is commonly referred to as the principle of "one person, one vote."[1] When this became federal constitutional doctrine in the 1960s, it ended the domination of state legislatures by rural voters entrenched within disproportionately small electoral districts.

1. "The conception of political equality from the Declaration of Independence, to Lincoln's Gettysburg Address, to the Fifteenth, Seventeenth, and Nineteenth Amendments can mean only one thing – one person, one vote." *Gray v. Sanders*, 372 U.S. 368, 381 (1963).

4. There are important similarities and differences between the typical organization of a state government and that of the federal government. Article I of the federal Constitution vests the legislative power in the Congress, consisting of the House of Representatives and the Senate. The "one person, one vote" principle extends to the election of legislators to the lower house of the federal Congress, called the "House of Representatives," subject to the constraint that each state is entitled to elect at least one representative. Representatives serve two-year terms. The number of representatives is set by Congress, not by the Constitution, and since 1910 has been fixed at 435. A national census is conducted decennially, on the basis of resident population without regard to eligibility to vote. The total population of the United States, according to the 2000 census,[1] was about 281.4 million and each representative is thus accountable to a population of approximately 647,000, subject to minor variation because no state may elect a fractional number of representatives.

The upper house of the federal legislature, the Senate, is not subject to the "one person, one vote" principle. In a compromise of pure popular sovereignty with the rival idea that the states themselves should retain residual sovereignty within a federal union that established a national government of limited rather than plenary power – a compromise essential to the successful drafting of the federal Constitution in 1787 and its ratification in 1788 – each state, regardless of population, has equal suffrage in the Senate, there being two senators per state. Senators serve six-year terms.

Executive power is vested by Article II in the president of the United States, elected to a four-year term by the so-called "electoral college", an anachronistic body in which the electors from each state usually are picked by popular majority on a winner-take-all, state-by-state basis.[2] Generally, but not necessarily, the winner of a presidential election has received a plurality of the votes cast nationwide. This mechanism of presidential election by majority vote of the members of the electoral college, with each state getting the number of electors equal to the number of its representatives in both houses of Congress, is a further manifestation – along with the equal suffrage of states in the Senate – of the federal system's qualification of direct popular democracy. The independent political significance of the states is reinforced by the powers vested in them as political entities without regard to their relative populations.

1. *See* <www.census.gov/main/www/cen2000.html> (last visited 24 Jun. 2008). The precise count of US population as of 1 Apr. 2000, was 281,421,906.
2. *See* generally Christopher Anglim, "A Selective, Annotated Bibliography on the Electoral College: Its Creation, History, and Prospects for Reform," Law Libr. J. 85 (1993): 297.

5. The practical scope of state sovereignty within the federal union has remained a contentious issue throughout the history of the United States. By and large, the historical trend has been toward a centripetal concentration of power in the national government, resulting in part from judicial deference to the federal legislature when it has chosen to intrude on state sovereignty, but ultimately reflecting profound social and political changes within the nation as a whole. The Civil War of 1861-1865 was fought over the twinned issues of slavery and the prerogative of states to secede from the union in order to protect their sovereign power to perpetuate slavery. The victory of that war by the federal government, and the industrial revolution which that war accelerated, caused a profound shift of power from the states to the national government. This practical change in the political center of gravity was accompanied by a series of "Civil War Amendments", the Thirteenth, Fourteenth, and Fifteenth Amendments to the Constitution. The most important of these has been the Fourteenth Amendment, which imposed on states vague obligations to accord all their inhabitants both "due process of law" and "the equal protection of the laws", and vested Congress with authority to protect these new civil liberties through appropriate legislation. Another important political change was the adoption in 1913 of the Seventeenth Amendment, which substituted a system of direct popular election of each state's two senators for the original system by which senators were elected by, and thus accountable to, the state legislatures. Despite these developments, state governments retain fundamental importance in the regulation of daily life within the United States. The allocation of governmental competence as between the state and federal levels of government is ultimately the business of the federal courts through their power to interpret the federal Constitution, and in a series of recent decisions the US Supreme Court has vigorously reaffirmed the residual sovereignty of the states by striking down overreaching federal legislation.[1]

1. *See, e.g., United States v. Morrison*, 529 U.S. 598 (2000).

6. The constitutional principle of "federalism" that the US Supreme Court has deployed to protect state sovereignty from undue federal incursion coexists with the equally important constitutional principle of the "separation of powers" of the federal government into distinct legislative, executive, and judicial departments. Although a similar principle is enforced to some extent by the constitution of each state as interpreted by its court of last resort, the federal Constitution's separation of powers applies only to the structure of the federal government. It is that separation of powers, however, that has vested in the federal courts a preeminent role in determining the meaning and application of the federal Constitution, and thus has often made the federal courts the arbiters of the relative powers of the state and federal levels of government.

The famous case of *Marbury v. Madison*,[1] decided by the US Supreme Court in 1803, conclusively resolved that it is the responsibility of the federal judiciary to interpret and apply the federal Constitution, with the consequence that legislative or executive action, if determined to be violative of the Constitution, may be nullified by the federal judiciary. The federal courts thus have the power of "judicial review" of the constitutionality of actions by coordinate branches of the federal government, and by virtue of the "Supremacy Clause" of Article VI of the federal Constitution that makes a federal law supreme over any conflicting state law, this power of judicial review extends to all questions of state law that implicate the federal Constitution's limits on state power. Federal courts thus are the fulcrum for resolution of disputes not only of the relative powers of the branches of the federal government but also of the relative powers of the national government vis-à-vis the states and their subordinate entities of local sovereignty. This exceptional power extends to the construction and application not only of the structural provisions of the original Constitution but also of the scheme of constitutional rights of individuals enforceable against the national and state governments under various amendments to the original Constitution, most notably the first ten amendments (i.e., the "Bill of Rights") adopted in 1791, and the Fourteenth Amendment adopted in 1868 as a consequence of the Civil War. These structural provisions and constitutional rights significantly limit the conduct of the state and federal governments in prosecuting crimes, but also, and quite commonly, may be invoked in the course of ordinary civil litigation. This invests the rules of civil procedure with constitutional significance, whether or not those rules and the forum to which they apply are the creature of the federal or a state government.

The constitutional structure of the federal courts is sensitive to the political ramifications of their decisions construing and applying federal law, including federal constitutional law. Many state judges gain or retain judicial office by popular election. Article III gives judicial officers of the United States extraordinary immunity from political accountability once the political process of appointment has been completed. The president nominates judges of the lower federal courts and justices of the US Supreme Court, subject to the advice and consent of the Senate, which must confirm the appointment of a judge or justice by majority vote. The appointment and confirmation of federal judges is most overtly political when the president and a majority of the Senate are members of opposing political parties. Once confirmed in office, judges hold office for life on good behavior, to be removed only by impeachment for the most serious misconduct, and may not have their compensation reduced while in office – although this protection has not been extended to prohibit such diminution of income as flows from the effect of inflation.

Only the Supreme Court is required to exist by dint of Article III itself, and the extent and jurisdiction of the lower federal court system is the prerogative of Congress to decide, subject to the general authority of Article III limiting the jurisdiction of federal courts to cases arising under federal law, to cases to which the United States government is a party, to admiralty and maritime cases, and to cases between citizens of different states or between domestic citizens and foreign states or their citizens and subjects. The first Congress created a system of lower federal courts in 1789, and this system has since been considerably expanded, especially in a series of post-Civil War statutes that by 1875 had established the lower federal courts as the principal trial courts for cases arising under federal law.

1. *Marbury v. Madison*, 5 U.S. (1 Cranch) 137 (1803).

§2. Delimitation of the Subject Matter

I. Definition of the Term "Civil Procedure"

7. Within American law, "civil procedure" consists of the rules governing the presentation of civil disputes for adjudication by courts, the presentation of disputed issues by appropriate pleadings, the marshaling of the facts relevant to the dispute by a process of reciprocal discovery from the parties, the resolution by pretrial motion of the legal sufficiency of claims if the facts alleged are assumed to be true, trial of disputed facts respecting legally sufficient claims, and the enforcement of the ensuing judgment. In principle, civil procedure extends to questions of the jurisdiction of courts, the competency of evidence, and the procedures for the appeal of adverse judgments, although in American parlance these incorporated matters are generally segregated doctrinally into distinct sets of rules governing the jurisdiction and venue of particular courts, rules of evidence, and rules of appellate procedure that are distinct from the rules of "civil procedure," which are typically confined under that rubric to the rules relating to the operation only of trial courts.

II. Distinction from Other Types of Procedure

8. The prosecution of crimes by state or federal prosecutors is universally subject to a separate and distinct system of "criminal procedure," which reflects often intricate state and federal constitutional provisions that give individuals extraordinary protection against the loss of liberty by conviction of a crime.[1]

There is a vast array of regulatory agencies created by state and federal law which operates under generally autonomous rules of administrative procedure, although here there is greater congruence with the general rules of civil procedure for the adjudication of civil disputes by courts of record.[2] Although the distinction between judicial adjudication of civil disputes and administrative adjudication of civil disputes is often nebulous, and in theory many administrative tribunals might be viewed simply as civil courts of particularly narrow subject-matter jurisdiction, the defining characteristic of administrative agencies as distinct from courts is that the same agency may play both a legislative and a judicial role. Thus, on the one hand, the agency promulgates substantive regulations according to a highly general delegation of legislative power from the state or federal legislature, and, on the other, it resolves disputes about compliance with those very regulations.[3]

The field of "administrative law" has developed within the general scheme of American law independently of, although influenced by, the rules of civil procedure governing trial courts of general jurisdiction. Administrative proceedings are generally conducted in a spirit of less formality, and within an administrative orientation towards the effectuation of public policy rather than the enforcement of private rights.[4] Almost all administrative adjudication is subject, as a final step before enforcement of the order in question, to the opportunity for judicial review which then proceeds by ordinary processes of civil and appellate procedure, but with the focus of judicial attention generally being limited to questions of law as to administrative power rather than to review of findings of fact by the administrative tribunal whose judgment is subject to review.

There is a similar, but much more complex, congruence of criminal and civil procedure insofar as the lower federal courts have the capacity by the nominally civil writ of habeas corpus to review the constitutionality of state court criminal judgments.[5] Such habeas corpus proceedings are the source of considerable conflict between state governments and the federal judiciary, especially with respect to state judgments imposing capital punishment, and are subject to an autonomous set of rules and statutes outside the general scope of the rules of civil procedure otherwise applicable in federal courts.[6]

1. *See generally* Wayne R. LaFave, *Criminal Law*, 4th edn (2003), §1.1, at 1; *compare with* 1 B.E. Witkin et al., *California Criminal Law*, 2nd edn (1988), Preface.
2. *See* 13 Charles Alan Wright et al., *Federal Practice and Procedure*, 2nd edn (1984), §3528, at 265-266 (noting that in *Crowell v. Benson*, 285 U.S. 22 (1932), the Supreme Court approved of an administrative tribunal's award of money by likening the procedure of the tribunal to that of federal commissioners, masters, or assessors).
3. *See* id., §3528.
4. *See* id., §3528, at 267.
5. 28 U.S.C. §2241.
6. While habeas corpus litigation is outside the scope of this article, there is an extensive literature describing such litigation and its relationship to standard American civil and criminal litigation. *See, e.g.*, Randy Hertz & James S. Liebman, *Federal Habeas Corpus: Practice and Procedure*, 5th edn (2005).

§3. Sources of Civil Procedure Law

9. All of the states, with one exception, have a procedural system derived basically from the common law of Great Britain at the time of the American Revolution, and as further developed by the common law of both British and American courts up to the time of the admission to statehood of the state in question.[1] The one exception is the state of Louisiana, whose courts were organized according to French civil law, and which retained many civil law characteristics even after statehood.

There was a general divide in British law between courts of "common law" jurisdiction and courts of "equitable" jurisdiction; following this tradition, it was commonplace in the nineteenth century for American courts to have separate rules of "legal" procedure for suits "at law" (that is, triable in a court of common-law jurisdiction) and of "equitable" procedure for suits "in equity."[2] In 1848, the state of New York adopted an innovative and vastly influential new Code of Civil Procedure that merged and simplified legal and equitable procedure. Drafted by one of the nation's leading lawyers, David Dudley Field, the so-called "Field Code" was widely adopted by other states. Within thirty years, "code pleading" had become the dominant model of civil procedure within the United States.

1. *See* Geoffrey C. Hazard, Jr & Michele Taruffo, *American Civil Procedure: An Introduction* (1993), 1-22.
2. *See* id.; *see also* 4 Wright, *supra*, §1002.

10. The next great wave of procedural reform commenced when the Federal Rules of Civil Procedure went into effect in 1938. Until then, the federal courts had generally sought to conform their civil procedure to that of the state in which a particular federal court was located.[1] The federal rules made the civil procedure of the federal courts essentially uniform nationwide, and sought to reform the emphasis on "fact pleading" under the Field Code with a "notice-pleading" system that looked to discovery rather than pleading as the principal means of identifying the core issues in dispute between the parties to civil litigation.[2]

The federal rules have been widely emulated by the states, and many states have adopted virtual replicas of the federal rules as their own state rules of civil procedure.[3] But some states – including many of the larger ones – retain state systems of civil procedure which are derived from the Field Code and which depart in important ways from the operation of the federal system under the Federal Rules of Civil Procedure.[4]

Recent tinkering with the Federal Rules of Civil Procedure for a time allowed particular federal district courts to adopt local rules at variance with the national scheme, leading to something of a crisis of disuniformity in civil procedure even at the federal level.[5] (See Part VIII, paragraph 266.) It is a regrettable fact that in some respects there is not a truly national set of rules of civil procedure within American law, and it is crucially important to take account of the particular rules of civil procedure applied by a particular court – state or federal – to the concrete circumstances of the litigation at hand. But these discrepancies and matters of detail can be exaggerated, and the general course of litigation can for the most part be understood by reference to the Federal Rules of Civil Procedure, with occasional parenthetical references to significant departures from federal procedure that may be encountered in the courts of important states.

1. *See* Hazard & Taruffo, *supra*, at 26-27 (explaining that while it was always assumed that the federal courts would have their own procedural system, the Conformity Act of 1789 required federal courts to follow the common law procedure of the state in which they sat); *see also* 4 Wright, *supra*, §1002, for a brief history of federal courts under the Conformity Act of 1789.
2. *See* Hazard & Taruffo, *supra*, at 28.
3. For exhaustive treatment of the extent to which states have modeled their civil procedure after the Federal Rules, *see* John B. Oakley & Arthur F. Coon, "The Federal Rules in State Courts: A Survey of State Court Systems of Civil Procedure," Wash. L. Rev. 61 (1986): 1367. *See also* John B. Oakley, "A Fresh Look at the Federal Rules in State Courts," Nev. L. J. 3 (2003): 354; Carl Tobias, "The Past and Future of the Federal Rules in State Courts," Nev. L. J. 3 (2003): 400, 402-403.
4. *See* Oakley & Coon, *supra*, at 1426-1427 (arguing that while a majority of states follow some form of the Federal Rules, if the population of the divergent jurisdictions is measured, more people are subject to civil procedure systems incongruent with the Federal Rules).
5. *See, e.g.*, Alfred W. Cortese, Jr, "Mandatory Disclosure Rule 26(a)(1): Variety Reigns," *Practicing L. Inst. Litig.* 498 (1994): 425 (discussing the sundry approaches taken by district courts that have "opted out" of mandatory disclosure rules found in Fed. R. Civ. P. 26).

§4. General Features of the Administration of Justice in Civil Matters

I. Characteristics of the Procedure

11. The American system of civil procedure is primarily an adversarial one, in which parties with opposing interests vie to persuade the judge and the trier of fact as to the merits of their conflicting contentions of law and fact.[1] At the outset of the twenty-first century, this adversary system of adjudication is not as perfectly realized as it may have been a century before. The American political tradition, the litigious quality of American culture, and recent developments in American constitutional law have made commonplace the use of civil litigation to challenge the operation of social institutions. Such suits against school boards, prisons, and other prominent governmental and corporate entities, including major employers, property holders, and investors, use tactical legal claims as the means to achieve strategic social goals.[2] Because the impact of such "public law litigation" extends far beyond the clash of the personal interests of the particular (often nominal) litigants, judges have assumed a more active role in the litigation – not really an "inquisitorial" role, but at least a "managerial" one.

The rise of the "managerial judge" within an otherwise adversarial system of procedure is also associated with nominally private litigation involving "mass torts," where a large number of claimants allege injury under similar circumstances, e.g., arising from the collapse of a structure, the destruction of an aircraft, or exposure to a toxic substance such as asbestos.[3] The rising cost of modern complex litigation – including lawyers" fees, expert-witness expenses, and fierce battles over discovery issues – gives litigants an incentive to achieve economies of scale by joining together related claims and parties. But this tendency to aggregate claims into larger and larger lawsuits produces "megacases" that are unmanageable without aggressive judicial control.[4] In such litigation, parties tend to be viewed as representatives of constituencies beyond the court, and judges act as trustees of the public interest and not merely as referees in a private dispute.

These "managerial" aspects of modern American judging are changes more of style than of substance. American civil procedure remains basically adversarial down to the root. Judges play a very small role in the determination of what claims to submit and how such claims are to be proved.[5]

Although particular judges may make more extensive use of oral procedure, and every judge will rule from the bench on minor matters (such as objections to evidence in the course of a trial or a hearing) and accept oral stipulations in the course of a proceeding, the general emphasis in important litigation, especially in the federal courts, is to proceed at every turn by written submission and written judicial response. This builds as comprehensive a record as possible for purposes of subsequent appellate review.[6]

1. *See* Hazard & Taruffo, *supra*, at 19-22.
2. For more on the litigious nature of American society, *see generally* Marlene Adler Marks, *The Suing of America* (1981) (discussing the use of litigation to protest, harass, effect social change and vindicate, inter alia, dignity, grief, and perceived wrongs).
3. *See* Frances E. McGovern, "An Analysis of Mass Torts for Judges," Tex. L. Rev. 73 (1995): 1821.
4. *See generally* John C. Coffee, Jr, "Class Wars: The Dilemma of the Mass Tort Class Action," *Colum. L. Rev.* 95 (1995): 1343 (discussing the changing nature of mass torts, class actions and the lawyers who litigate such actions).
5. As suggested by the managerial role that a judge is often required to assume in mass torts, there may be an exception to this general rule in such cases. *See* McGovern, *supra*, at 1838-1839.
6. For a discussion of the judge's limited role in an adversary system, *see* Hazard & Taruffo, *supra*, at 89-90. *See generally* Barry R. Schaller, "Managerial Judging: A Principled Approach to Complex Cases in State Court," Conn. B. J. 68 (1994): 77; Judith Resnik, "Managerial Judges," Harv. L. Rev. 96 (1982): 374.

II. Fundamental Guarantees

12. The guarantee of due process of law made applicable against the federal government by the Fifth Amendment to the Constitution, and to the states by the Fourteenth Amendment, enforces the familiar minimum criteria for a civilized system of civil justice.[1] "Due process of law" requires, of course, that courts be established by law, and any act by a judge in excess of his or her prescribed jurisdiction is void as a violation of due process.[2] Judicial *impartiality*, in the sense of freedom from personal bias or a personal conflict of interest, is surely included within the constitutional guarantee of due process.[3] Less certain is the scope of the judicial *independence* required by constitutional principles of due process, in the sense of insulation from political pressure. The independence of federal judges is guaranteed structurally by Article III's provision of life tenure without diminution of salary, discussed above (paragraph 6). States courts vary greatly, however, in the political independence of their judges. (This is one major reason why sophisticated lawyers generally prefer the federal courts, absent some strong suspicion that less predictable state courts will strain in one's favor.)[4] The federal Constitution does not address directly the politics of state judiciaries, but it does permit federal courts to review state judgments that turn on issues of federal law – either by direct review in the

United States Supreme Court or, in criminal cases, by writ of habeas corpus in the lower federal courts.

Although many specific guarantees of the federal Constitution's Bill of Rights have been made applicable to the states as a component of the due process guaranteed by the Fourteenth Amendment, one such specific guarantee remains applicable only to the federal government. That is the Seventh Amendment's preservation of the right to jury trial in civil cases at common law where more than a trivial amount is at stake. The federal courts have construed the scope of this right by reference to British jury trial practice in 1791, the date of ratification of the Seventh Amendment.[5] The states are not subject to this federal constitutional guarantee of jury trial in civil (as opposed to criminal) cases. As a matter of state law, every state provides a right to jury trial in at least some civil cases, but the circumstances and content of this non-federal right vary greatly from state to state.[6]

Appeal is widely valued and liberally exercised in American civil litigation, but is a privilege extended by tradition rather than by constitutional mandate.[7] It is generally recognized that there should be at least one level of appeal of decisions made by a judge in the first instance, but it has never been held that the unavailability of appeal in a particular case conflicts with the federal constitutional guarantee of due process of law. In the federal system, appeal is permitted as of right from all final judgments by trial courts, with most interlocutory orders subject to earlier review only in exceptional circumstances.[8] A general, plenary right of appeal is also recognized in virtually every state at some point in virtually all litigation, but the procedures for making appeals vary greatly. Some states, notably California and New York, are more liberal than the federal courts in permitting interlocutory review of particular orders before the main litigation has progressed to a final judgment in the trial court.[9]

1. *See* Hazard & Taruffo, *supra*, at 37.
2. *See* Rex R. Perschbacher & Debra Lyn Bassett, "The End of Law," B.U. L. Rev. 84 (2004): 1, n. 1 (suggesting causes for the recent, explosive rise of litigation in the United States); *see* also 16B Am. Jur. 2nd *Constitutional Law* §905 (1998).
3. *See* David A. Martland, "Justice Without Favor: Due Process and Separation of Executive and Judicial Powers in State Government," Yale L. J. 94 (1985): 1675, 1676-1679.
4. *See generally* Thomas B. Marvell, "The Rationales for Federal Question Jurisdiction: An Empirical Examination of Student Rights Litigation," Wis. L. Rev. 1984 (1984): 1315, 1350-1366 (discussing the factors influencing federal versus state courts forum selection in student rights cases).
5. *See generally Chauffeurs, Teamsters and Helpers, Local No. 391 v. Terry*, 494 U.S. 558 (1990) (United States Supreme Court's analysis of how to determine whether the Seventh Amendment right to jury trial has been preserved for a particular cause of action).
6. *See* Hazard & Taruffo, *supra*, at 128.
7. *See* Harlon Leigh Dalton, "Taking the Right to Appeal (More or Less) Seriously," Yale L. J. 95 (1985): 62.
8. 28 U.S.C. §1291 (appeal from final judgment) and §1292 (when interlocutory appeal is available).
9. *See, e.g.*, David Scheffel, "Interlocutory Appeals in New York – Time Has Come for a More Efficient Approach," Pace L. Rev. 16 (1996): 607 (decrying the confusion extant within New York courts due to the parties' right to appeal virtually any order prior to judgment).

Selected Bibliography

BOOKS

Abraham, Henry J., *Justices, Presidents, and Senators*. Rev. edn. Lanham, Maryland: Rowman & Littlefield Publishers, Inc., 1999.

American Law Institute, *Federal Judicial Code Revision Project*. Philadelphia: The American Law Institute, 2004.

American Law Institute, *Restatement (Second) of Judgments* §24. Philadelphia: The American Law Institute, 1980.

American Law Institute, *Restatement (Third) of Foreign Relations Law* §481(1). Philadelphia: The American Law Institute, 1986.

American Law Institute/UNIDROIT, *Transnational Rules of Civil Procedure*. Cambridge: Cambridge University Press, 2006.

Bodenheimer, Edgar, John Bilyeu Oakley & Jean C. Love, *An Introduction to the Anglo-American Legal System*. 4th edn. St. Paul: West Publishing Co., 2004.

Carp, Robert A. & Ronald Stidham, *The Federal Courts*. 4th edn. Washington: CQ Press, 2001.

Epstein, David et al., *International Litigation: A Guide to Jurisdiction, Practice and Strategy*. 3rd edn. New York: Transnational Publishers, Inc., 1999.

Faigman, David et al., *Modern Scientific Evidence: The Law and Science of Expert Testimony*. St. Paul: West Publishing Co., 1997.

Fallon, Jr, Richard H., Daniel J. Meltzer & David L. Shapiro, *Hart and Wechsler's The Federal Courts and the Federal System*. 5th edn. New York: Foundation Press, 2003.

Flamm, Richard E., *Judicial Disqualification: Recusal and Disqualification of Judges*. 2nd edn. Berkeley: Banks & Jordan Law Publishing Co., 2007.

Friedman, Lawrence M., *A History of American Law*. 3rd edn. New York: Simon & Schuster, 2005.

Gerhardt, Michael J., *The Federal Impeachment Process*. 2nd edn. Chicago: University of Chicago Press, 2000.

Gilmore, Grant & Charles Lund Black, *The Law of Admiralty*. 2nd edn. New York: The Foundation Press, 1975.

Graham, Michael H., *Modern State and Federal Evidence: A Comprehensive Reference*. Notre Dame: National Institute for Trial Advocacy, 1989.

Green, Eric D., "Avoiding the Legal Logjam – Private Justice, California Style." In *Corporate Dispute Management*. Edited by Center for Public Resources. New York: Matthew Bender, 1982.

Hazard, Jr, Geoffrey C. et al., *Cases and Materials on Pleading and Procedure: State and Federal*. 9th edn. New York: Foundation Press, 2005.

Hazard, Jr, Geoffrey C. & Michele Taruffo, *American Civil Procedure: An Introduction*. New Haven: Yale University Press, 1993.

Hazard, Jr, Geoffrey C. & Deborah L. Rhode, *The Legal Profession: Responsibility and Regulation*. 3rd edn. New York: Foundation Press, 1994.

Hertz, Randy & James S. Liebman, *Federal Habeas Corpus: Practice and Procedure*. 5th edn. Charlottesville: Michie Co., 2005.

Holtzmann, Howard M. & Donald Francis Donovan, "United States." In *International Handbook on Commercial Arbitration*. Edited by Pieter Sanders. Deventer: Kluwer Law and Taxation, 1998.

James, Jr, Fleming et al., *Civil Procedure*. 5th edn. New York: Foundation Press, 2001.

Lacey, Frederick B. & Jay G. Safer, "The Authority, Roles, Responsibilities and Utilization of Magistrate Judges." In *Business and Commercial Litigation in Federal Courts*, vol. 2. Edited by Robert L. Haig. Chicago: American Bar Association, 1998.

LaFave, Wayne R., *Criminal Law*. St. Paul: West Publishing Co., 2003.

Lookofsky, Joseph M., *Transnational Litigation and Commercial Arbitration: A Comparative Analysis of American, European, and International law*. 2nd edn. Huntington, New York: Juris Publications, 2004.

Madison, James, Alexander Hamilton & John Jay, *The Federalist Papers*. Edited by Issac Kramnick. London: Penguin, 1987.

Meador, Daniel John, *American Courts*. 2nd edn. St. Paul: West Publishing Co., 2001.

Meador, Daniel John, *Appellate Courts in the United States*. 2nd edn. St. Paul: West Publishing Co., 2006.

Moore, James W. et al., *Moore's Federal Practice*. 3rd edn. New York: Mathew Bender, 1997-2000 (date varies by volume).

Rivkin, David W., "International Arbitration." In *Commercial Arbitration for the 1990's*. Edited by Richard J. Medalie. Chicago: American Bar Association, 1991.

Saari, David J., *American Court Management: Theories and Practices*. Westport, CO: Quorum Books, 1982.

Smith, Christopher E. *Judicial Self Interest: Federal Judges and Court Administration*. New York: Praeger, 1995.

Teply, Larry L. & Ralph U. Whitten, *Civil Procedure*. 2nd edn. New York: Foundation Press, 2000.

Wheeler, Russell R. & Howard R. Whitcomb, *Judicial Administration: Text and Readings*. Englewood Cliffs, NJ: Prentice-Hall, 1977.

Wigmore, John Henry, *A Treatise on the System of Evidence in Trials at Common Law*. Boston: Little, Brown & Co., 1905.

Wright, Charles Alan et al., *Federal Practice and Procedure*. 2dn & 3rd edn. St. Paul: West Publishing Co., 1982-1998 (date and edition varies by volume).

Wright, Charles Alan, John B. Oakley & Debra Lyn Bassett, *Federal Courts: Cases and Materials*. 12th edn. New York: Foundation Press, 2008.

Selected Bibliography

ARTICLES

Abel, Richard L., "Law Without Politics: Legal Aid under Advanced Capitalism," UCLA L. Rev. 32 (1985): 474.

Amar, Akhil Reed & Vik Amar, "President Quayle?," Va. L. Rev. 78 (1992): 913.

Amar, Vik D., "The Senate and the Constitution," Yale L. J. 97 (1988): 1111.

Amar, Vikram David, "Jury Service as Political Participation Akin to Voting," Cornell L. Rev. 80 (1995): 203.

Amar, Vikram David, "The Truth, the Whole Truth, and Nothing But the Truth About 'High Crimes and Misdemeanors' and the Presidential Impeachment Process," Const. Comment. 16 (1999): 403.

Anglim, Christopher, "A Selective, Annotated Bibliography on the Electoral College: Its Creation, History, and Prospects for Reform," Law Libr. J. 85 (1993): 297.

Arfin, Miriam R., "The Benefits of Alternative Dispute Resolution in Intellectual Property Disputes," Hastings Comm/Ent L. J. 17 (1995): 893.

Arnold, Tom, "A Vocabulary of ADR Procedures," ALI-ABA C976 (1994): 19.

Baker, Lynn A., "Unnecessary and Improper: The Judicial Councils Reform and Judicial Conduct and Disability Act of 1980," Yale L. J. 94 (1985): 1117.

Baker, Thomas E., "A Primer on the Jurisdiction of the U.S. Courts of Appeals," Federal Judicial Center Education and Training series (1989).

Bone, Robert G., "The Process of Making Process: Court Rulemaking, Democratic Legitimacy, and Procedural Efficacy," Geo. L. J. 87 (1999): 887.

Bermant, Gordon & Russell R. Wheeler, "Federal Judges and the Judicial Branch: Their Independence and Accountability," Mercer L. Rev. 46 (1995): 835.

Brewer, Jr, Wilburn, "Due Process in Lawyer Disciplinary Cases: From the Cradle to the Grave," S.C. L. Rev. 42 (1991): 925.

Brickman, Lester, "ABA Regulation of Contingency Fees: Money Talks, Ethics Walks," Fordham L. Rev. 65 (1996): 247.

Brickman, Lester, "Contingent Fees without Contingencies: Hamlet without the Prince of Denmark?," UCLA L. Rev. 37 (1989): 29.

Brunet, Edward, "The Timing of Summary Judgment," F.R.D. 198 (2001): 679.

Burbank, Stephen, "Procedure, Politics and Power: The Role of Congress," Notre Dame L. Rev. 79 (2004): 1677.

Cahn, Naomi R., "Family Law, Federalism and the Federal Courts," Iowa L. Rev. 79 (1994): 1073.

Campbell, Jr, Robert S. et al., ABA Committee on Federal Civil Procedure, "The Importance of the Twelve-Member Jury in Federal Courts," F.R.D. 205 (2003): 247.

Chayes, Abram, "The Role of the Judge in Public Law Litigation," Harv. L. Rev. 89 (1976): 1281.

Coffee, Jr, John C., "Class Wars: The Dilemma of the Mass Tort Class Action," Colum. L. Rev. 95 (1995): 1343.

Colagiovanni, Joseph & Thomas W. Hartmann, "Enforcing Arbitration Awards," Disp. Resol. J. 50-Jan (1995): 14.

Dalton, Harlon Leigh, "Taking the Right to Appeal (More or Less) Seriously," Yale L. J. 95 (1985): 62.

Deja, Daniel R., "How Judges are Selected: A Survey of the Judicial Selection Process in the United States," Mich. B. J. 75 (1996): 904.
Delgado, Richard, et al., "Fairness and Formality: Minimizing the Risks of Prejudice in Alternative Dispute Resolution," Wisc. L. Rev. 1985 (1985): 1359.
Developments, "The Paths of Civil Litigation," Harv. L. Rev. 113 (2000): 1752.
Devlin, Mary M., "The Development of Lawyer Disciplinary Procedures in the United States," Geo. J. Legal Ethics 7 (1994): 911.
Dubois, Philip L., "Accountability, Independence, and the Selection of State Judges: The Role of Popular Judicial Elections," Sw. L. J. 40 (1986): 31.
Edwards, Harry T., "Alternative Dispute Resolution: Panacea or Anathema," Harv. L. Rev. 99 (1986): 668.
Eisenberg, Theodore, et al., "Juries, Judges and Punitive Damages," Cornell L. Rev. 87 (2002): 743.
Fairman, Christopher M., "The Myth of Notice Pleading," Ariz. L. Rev. 45 (2003): 987.
Fletcher, William A., "The 'Case or Controversy' Requirement in State Court Adjudication of Federal Questions," Calif. L. Rev. 78 (1990): 263.
Freer, Richard, "The Cauldron Boils: Supplemental Jurisdiction, Amount in Controversy and Diversity of Citizenship Class Actions," Emory L. J. 53 (2004): 55.
Friedenthal, Jack & Joshua Gardner, "Judicial Discretion to Deny Summary Judgment in the Era of Managerial Judging," Hofstra L. Rev. 31 (2002): 91.
Galanter, Mark, "The Vanishing Trial: An Examination of Trials and Related Matters in State and Federal Courts," J. Empir. Legal Stud. 1 (2004): 459.
Gerhardt, Michael J., "Panel II: The Appointment Power: Putting Presidential Performance in the Federal Appointments Process in Perspective," Case W. Res. L. Rev. 47 (1997): 1359.
Hadfield, Jilian, "Where Have All the Trials Gone?," J. Empir. Legal Stud. 1 (2004): 705.
Hale, Kathryn L., "Nonbinding Arbitration: An Oxymoron?," U. Tol. L. Rev. 24 (1993): 1003.
Harges, Bobby Marzine, "The Promise of the Mandatory Summary Jury Trial," Temp. L. Rev. 63 (1990): 799.
Ifill, Sherrilyn A., "Racial Diversity on the Bench: Beyond Role Models and Public Confidence," Wash. L. Rev. 57 (2000): 405.
Johnson, Kevin R. & Luis Fuentes-Rohwer, "A Principled Approach to the Quest for Racial Diversity on the Bench," Mich. J. Race & L. 10 (2004): 5.
Josselyn, Janet Eve, "The Song of the Sirens – Sanctioning Lawyers Under 28 U.S.C. §1927," B.C. L. Rev. 31 (1990): 477.
Keeling, Byron C., "Toward a Balanced Approach to 'Frivolous' Litigation: A Critical Review of Federal Rule 11 and State Sanctions Provisions," Pepperdine L. Rev. 21 (1994): 1067.
Kerbeshian, Lynn A., "ADR: To Be Or . . . ?," N.D. L. Rev. 70 (1994): 381.
Kerekes, Robert J., "The Crisis of Congested Courts: One Potential Solution," Seton Hall Legis. J. 18 (1994): 489.
Kessler, Gladys & Linda J. Finkelstein, "The Evolution of a Multi-Door Courthouse," Cath. U. L. Rev. 37 (1988): 577.

Kirgis, Paul F., "The Right to a Jury Decision on Questions of Fact under the Seventh Amendment," Ohio St. L. J. 64 (2003): 1125.

Kritzer, Herbert M., "The Wages of Risk: The Returns of Contingency Fee Legal Practice," DePaul L. Rev. 47 (1998): 267.

Lambros, Thomas D., "The Summary Jury Trial and Other Alternative Methods of Dispute Resolution: A Report to the Judicial Conference of the United States Committee on the Operation of the Jury System," F.R.D. 103 (1984): 461.

Leute, Sheila A., "The Effective Use of Summary Judgment: A Comparison of Federal and Texas Standards," Baylor L. Rev. 40 (1988): 617.

Lilly, Graham, "The Decline of the American Jury," U. Colo. L. Rev. 72 (2001): 53.

Longan, Patrick E., "Congress, the Courts, and the Long Range Plan," Am. U. L. Rev. 46 (1997): 625.

Macey, Jonathan R. & Geoffrey P. Miller, "The Plaintiffs" Attorney's Role in Class Action and Derivative Litigation: Economic Analysis and Recommendations for Reform," U. Chi. L. Rev. 58 (1991): 1.

Marcus, Richard, "Only Yesterday: Reflections on Rulemaking Responses to E-Discovery," Fordham L. Rev. 73 (2004): 1.

Marella, Fabrizio, "Emerging Dilemmas in International Economic Arbitration: Unity and Diversity in International Arbitration: The Case of Maritime Arbitration," Am. U. Int'l L. Rev. 20 (2005): 1055.

Martland, David A., "Justice without Favor: Due Process and Separation of Executive and Judicial Powers in State Government," Yale L. J. 94 (1985): 1675.

Marvell, Thomas B., "The Rationales for Federal Question Jurisdiction: An Empirical Examination of Student Rights Litigation," Wis. L. Rev. 1984 (1984): 1315.

McGovern, Frances E., "An Analysis of Mass Torts for Judges," Tex. L. Rev. 73 (1995): 1821.

Mengis, Warren L., "Professional Responsibility," La. L. Rev. 49 (1988): 487.

Menkel-Meadow, Carrie, "When Dispute Resolution Begets Disputes of its Own: Conflicts among Dispute Professionals," UCLA L. Rev. 44 (1997): 1871.

Meyer, Judith P., "The Pros and Cons of Mediation," Disp. Resol. J. 52-Sum (1997): 8.

Mullenix, Linda S., "The Counter-Reformation in Procedural Justice," Minn. L. Rev. 77 (1992): 375.

Nihan, Charles W., "A Study in Contrasts: The Ability of the Federal Judiciary to Change Its Adjudicative and Administrative Structures," Am. U. L. Rev. 44 (1995): 1693.

Note, "The Courts' Inherent Power to Compel Legislative Funding of Judicial Functions," Mich. L. Rev. 81 (1983): 1687.

Note, "Registration of Federal Judgments," Iowa L. Rev. 42 (1957): 284.

Oakley, John B., "A Fresh Look at the Federal Rules in State Courts," Nev. L. J. 3 (2003): 354.

Oakley, John B., "Federal Jurisdiction and the Problem of the Litigative Unit: When Does What "Arise Under" Federal Law?", Tex. L. Rev. 76 (1998): 1829.

Oakley, John B., "Integrating Supplemental Jurisdiction and Diversity Jurisdiction: A Progress Report on the Work of the American Law Institute," Ind. L. J. 74 (1998): 25.

Oakley, John B., "Memorandum on Divisional Organization of the United States Court of Appeals for the Ninth Circuit," Working Papers For the Commission on Structural Alternatives for the Federal Courts of Appeal (1998): 146.

Oakley, John B., "Reporter's Memorandum on the Claim-Specific Nature of the Original Jurisdiction of the District Courts." In Federal Judicial Code Revision Project. Philadelphia: The American Law Institute, 2004.

Oakley, John B. & Arthur F. Coon, "The Federal Rules in State Courts: A Survey of State Court Systems of Civil Procedure," Wash. L. Rev. 61 (1986): 1367.

Patterson, Roger J., "Dispute Resolution in a World of Alternatives," Cath. U. L. Rev. 37 (1988): 591.

Perschbacher, Rex R. & Debra Lyn Bassett, "The End of Law," B.U. L. Rev. 84 (2004): 1.

Peterson, Todd D., "Controlling the Federal Courts Through the Appropriations Process," Wis. L. Rev. 1998 (1998): 993.

Pitt, Steven & Joshua D. Rogers, "Charting a Course for Federal Removal Through the Abstention Doctrine: A Titanic Experience in the Sargasso Sea of Jurisdictional Manipulation," DePaul L. Rev. 56 (2006): 107.

Ponte, Lucille M., "Putting Mandatory Summary Jury Trial Back on the Docket: Recommendations on the Exercise of Judicial Authority," Fordham L. Rev. 63 (1995): 1069.

Primm, Edith B., "The Neighborhood Justice Center Movement," Ky. L. J. 81 (1993): 1067.

Rau, Alan Scott & Edward F. Sherman, "Tradition and Innovation in International Arbitration Procedure," Tex. Int'l L. J. 30 (1995): 89.

Redlich, Allen, "Who Will Litigate Constitutional Issues for the Poor?," Hastings Const. L. Q. 19 (1992): 745.

Rehnquist, William H., "L. Ralph Meacham & Federal Courts Administration: A Decade of Innovation and Progress," Am. U. L. Rev. 44 (1995): 1477.

Resnik, Judith, "Managerial Judges," Harv. L. Rev. 96 (1982): 374.

Reynolds, William L., "The Iron Law of Full Faith and Credit," Md. L. Rev. 53 (1994): 412.

Robreno, Eduardo C., "Learning to do Justice: An Essay on the Development of the Lower Federal Courts in the Early Years of the Republic," Rutgers L. J. 29 (1998): 555.

Rosenberg, David, "Individual Justice and Collectivizing Risk-Based Claims in Mass-Exposure Cases," N.Y.U. L. Rev. 71 (1996): 210.

Rosenstein, David D., "For Whom the Bill Tolls: Quantity, Not Quality, Becomes the Goal When Hourly Fees Prevail," A.B.A. J. 81-Nov (1995): 120.

Sabatino, Jack M., "ADR as "Litigation Lite": Procedural and Evidentiary Norms Embedded Within Alternative Dispute Resolution," Emory L. J. 47 (1998): 1289.

Sander, Frank, "Varieties of Dispute Precessing," F.R.D. 70 (1976): 111.

Schaller, Barry R., "Managerial Judging: A Principled Approach to Complex Cases in State Court," Conn. B. J. 68 (1994): 77.

Shaman, Jeffery M., "Judicial Ethics," Geo. J. Legal Ethics 2 (1988): 1.

Shaman, Jeffery M. et al., "The 1990 Code of Judicial Conduct: An Overview," Judicature 74 (1990): 21.

Snyder, Lloyd B., "Rhetoric, Evidence, and Bar Agency Restrictions on Speech by Attorneys," Creighton L. Rev. 28 (1995): 357.

Stempel, Jeffrey, "A Distorted Mirror: The Supreme Court's Shimmering View of Summary Judgment, Directed Verdict, and the Adjudication Process," Ohio St. L. J. 49 (1988): 96.

Stuart, Kenneth K. & Cynthia A. Savage, "The Multi-Door Courthouse: How It's Working," Colo. Law. 26-Oct (1997): 13.

Thier, Whitney, "In a Dignified Manner: The Bar, The Court, and Lawyer Advertising," Tulane L. Rev. 66 (1991): 527.

Tobias, Carl, "The Past and Future of the Federal Rules in State Courts," Nev. L. J. 3 (2002): 400.

Twitchell, Mary, "The Myth of General Jurisdiction," Harv. L. Rev. 101 (1988): 610.

Vargo, John F., "The American Rule on Attorney Fee Allocation: The Injured Person's Access to Justice," Am. U. L. Rev. 42 (1993): 1567.

Wennihan, Angela, "Let's Put the Contingency Back in the Contingency Fee," SMU L. Rev. 49 (1996): 1639.

Winders, Bill, "The Roller Coaster of Class Conflict: Class Segments, Mass Mobilization, and Voter Turnout in the U.S., 1840-1996," Soc. Forces 77 (1999): 833.

Wolfram, Charles W., "The Constitutional History of the Seventh Amendment," Minn. L. Rev. 57 (1973): 639.

Woodley, Ann E., "Strengthening the Summary Jury Trial: A Proposal to Increase Its Effectiveness and Encourage Uniformity in Its Use," Ohio St. J. on Disp. Resol. 12 (1997): 541.

Woolley, Patrick, "The Sources of Federal Preclusion Law after *Semtek*," U. Cin. L. Rev. 72 (2003): 527.

Yamamoto, Eric, Katherine G. Leonard & Shawna Sodersten, "Summary Judgment at the Crossroads: The Impact of the Celotex Trilogy," Univ. Haw. L. Rev. 12 (1990): 1.

WEBSITES/REPORTS

American Bar Association, The ABA Standing Committee on Federal Judiciary: What It Is and How It Works, <www.abanet.org/scfedjud/federal_judiciary07.pdf> (1991, updated 2007).
American Bar Association, Model Code of Judicial Conduct, <www.abanet.org/judicialethics/ABA_MCJC_approved.pdf> (2007).
American Bar Association, Section of Legal Education and Admissions to the Bar, <www.abanet.org/judicialethics/approved_MCJC.html> (2008).
American Judicature Society, AJS Model Code of Conduct for Non-Judicial Court Employees, <www.ajs.org/ethics/eth_non-judic-employ.asp> (1989).
American Law Institute, <www.ali.org/>.
Georgia State Courts, <www.georgiacourts.org/courts/index.html>.
National Center for State Courts, <www.ncsconline.org/>.
National Conference of Bar Examiners & American Bar Association, *Comprehensive Guide to Bar Admissions 2008*, <www.ncbex.org/fileadmin/mediafiles/downloads/Comp_Guide/CompGuide.pdf>.
US Census Bureau, <www.census.gov/main/www/cen2000.html>.
US Courts, <www.uscourts.gov>.

Part I. Judicial Organization

Chapter 1. The Courts and Their Members

§1. Courts

I. Structure of the Federal Court System

13. The Constitution forms the basis for the US federal court system. Article III of the Constitution provides, "The judicial Power of the United States, shall be vested in one supreme Court, and in such inferior Courts as the Congress may from time to time ordain and establish."[1] Congress quickly added federal trial courts through the Judiciary Act of 1789.[2] In 1891, Congress established the first intermediate courts with the sole purpose of hearing appeals.[3] Since 1891, the basic organization of the federal judiciary has remained unchanged. The federal court system's organization can be conceptualized as a triangle. At the base of the triangle are the trial courts (usually called "district courts"). The middle of the triangle represents a smaller number of courts of appeal, organized into "circuits." At the pinnacle of the triangle resides the US Supreme Court.[4]

1. US Const. Art. III, §1.
2. *See generally* Eduardo C. Robreno, "Learning to do Justice: An Essay on the Development of the Lower Federal Courts in the Early Years of the Republic," Rutgers L. J. 29 (1998): 555 (presenting a historical look at the creation and growing pains of the lower federal courts).
3. *See* Murray M. Schwartz, "The Exercise of Supervisory Power by the Third Circuit Court of Appeals," Vill. L. Rev. 27 (1982): 506, 517.
4. *See* Daniel John Meador, *American Courts,* 2nd edn (2006), 20.

A. District Courts

14. Congress has divided the United States into ninety-one "districts." A district can encompass an entire state or only a portion of it, depending on the state's population. In states with large populations there are numerous districts, while in lesser populated states there may be only a single district. Every state contains at least one district, and only two districts cross state lines.[1] Federal districts are named for the state (and portion of that state) in which they sit.[2] Each of the ninety-one districts contains a US district court "for" that district, established as a court exercising federal judicial power under Article III of the Constitution. Three more districts (not established under Article III but exercising similar functions) have been established in federal territories, bringing the total number of federal district courts to ninety-four.[3] The number of judges of each federal district court varies from two to more than twenty judges, depending on the population of the district.[4]

In civil cases where the plaintiff seeks money damages, either party enjoys the right under the Seventh Amendment to the US Constitution to request a jury trial.[5] In other types of cases, statutes provide the right to a jury trial.[6] If a case does not implicate a constitutional or statutory right to a jury trial, or if any such right has been waived by the parties, the district-court judge acts as the trier of fact and law.[7] All criminal defendants facing serious charges also have a constitutional right to a jury trial.[8]

Magistrate judges are civil employees who assist the district courts in managing cases. Unlike district-court judges, who are appointed by the president and confirmed by the Senate as described below, magistrate judges serve only for a fixed term of years, and are selected by the district-court judges in each district. Magistrate judges are particularly helpful in resolving pretrial disputes between the parties and other procedural matters concerning, among other things, the civil discovery process – the exchange of relevant information between the parties.[9]

1. The district of Wyoming includes within its territory all of Yellowstone National Park, small parts of which are in the states of Idaho and Montana. The district of Hawaii does not include any territory within another state, but does include federally administered islands that are not within any state. *See* 28 U.S.C. §91 (Hawaii); §131 (Wyoming).
2. *See* Meador, *supra*, at 20-21. It should be noted that the district of the District of Columbia and the district of Puerto Rico, although in every other way equivalent to the districts within the fifty states, are not themselves within any state.
3. These latter three federal district courts – sometimes called "territorial courts" to distinguish them from the ninety-one "constitutional" federal district courts created under Article III rather than under Congress's power under Articles I and IV to administer federal territories – have been established in territories outside of the United States that are subject to the sovereignty of the United States. They are not "United States District Courts" but rather are the District Court of Guam, the District Court for the Northern Mariana Islands, and the District Court of the Virgin Islands. *See* 48 U.S.C. §1424 (Guam); §1612 (Virgin Islands); §1821 (Northern Mariana Islands). Although these three district courts differ slightly in their jurisdiction as well as their legal status from the US District Courts "for" the ninety-one districts established in the fifty states, Puerto Rico, and the district of Columbia, for most practical purposes all ninety-four of the district courts of both types operate in similar fashion. For a discussion of the anomalous status of territorial courts within the federal judicial system, see American Law Institute, *Federal Judicial Code Revision Project* (2004), 239-252. *See generally* 13 Wright, *supra*, §§3508, 3528.
4. *See* Meador, *supra*, app. C at 93-96.
5. *See* Fed. R. Civ. P. 38.
6. *See, e.g.*, 28 U.S.C. §1873 (granting the right to trial by jury upon demand of either party in admiralty or maritime actions).
7. *See* Hazard & Taruffo, *supra*, at 128-129; for a discussion of the modern approach to jury trial guarantees, *see* 9 Wright, *supra*, §2302.1.
8. U.S. Const. amend. VI; Hazard & Taruffo, *supra*, at 63.
9. *See generally* Frederick B. Lacey & Jay G. Safer, *The Authority, Roles, Responsibilities and Utilization of Magistrate Judges*, in 2 *Business and Commercial Litigation in Federal Courts* §26.3 (1998).

B. Courts of Appeals

15. By statute, Congress has established thirteen federal judicial circuits, each of which includes a US Court of Appeals. Eleven of these courts of appeals are identified by the number ("First" through "Eleventh") of the regional "circuit" in which each court has been established; the other two are known as the US Court of Appeals for the District of Columbia Circuit and the US Court of Appeals for the Federal Circuit, respectively, and both are based in the federal capital, Washington DC.[1] With the exception of the US Court of Appeals for the Federal Circuit, each Federal Court of Appeals hears civil and criminal cases appealed from the district courts within the geographic region covered by the circuit. The size of each of the regional circuits varies a great deal, in terms of area and population and in the number of judges. Each regional circuit consists of at least three judges. The US Court of Appeals for the First Circuit, for example, consists of six judges and hears cases appealed from the US district courts in Maine, Massachusetts, New Hampshire, Puerto Rico, and Rhode Island; the US Court of Appeals for the Ninth Circuit consists of twenty-eight judges and hears cases appealed from the US district courts in Alaska, Arizona, California, Hawaii, Idaho, Montana, Nevada, Oregon, Washington, as well as Guam and the Northern Mariana Islands.[2]

The US Court of Appeals for the District of Columbia Circuit hears only cases that originate in Washington, DC. Although all of the federal courts of appeals have jurisdiction to review rulings of administrative agencies, most of this agency review occurs in the DC Circuit.[3]

The US Court of Appeals for the Federal Circuit is unique among the federal courts of appeals in that it hears appeals based on the subject matter of a case, rather than the location of the district court from which appeal is taken. The court has jurisdiction over appeals from all ninety-four districts in cases arising under the patent laws and in certain damage suits against the federal government. Additionally, it has jurisdiction over appeals from two special federal trial courts that lie outside the geographical district system: the US Claims Court and the US Court of International Trade.[4]

While the number of judges on each of the thirteen federal courts of appeals varies in rough proportion to the size of the population within the circuit,[5] each case is heard and decided by a randomly-selected panel of three judges. The panel reviews questions of law and fact stemming from the proceedings of the trial court, but the review of purely factual matters is very deferential. The composition of the panels is continually changed across cases, so that judges sit in different threesomes. Should two panels of a circuit adopt conflicting conclusions about a matter of law, or if there is a question of unusual importance, each federal Court of Appeals has the authority to rehear a case "en banc" – that is, with all the active judges of the whole circuit on a single panel – to resolve the intracircuit conflict or other important question.[6] (See also Part IV, paragraph 206.)

1. The capital city of Washington has grown to be coextensive with the federal district, the District of Columbia.
2. *See* 28 U.S.C. §41 (states within circuits); 28 U.S.C. §44 (judges per circuit) 48 U.S.C. §1821(a) (placing US District Court for the Northern Mariana Islands within the Ninth Circuit).

3. Id., at 25.
4. Id.; 9 Wright, *supra*, §3903.1.
5. The First Circuit has the fewest judges (six) and the Ninth Circuit the most (twenty-eight). The other circuits have between eleven and seventeen judges.
6. *See* Meador, *Appellate Courts in the United States*, 2nd edn (2006), 25-26; *see generally* Thomas E. Baker, A Primer on the Jurisdiction of the U.S. Courts of Appeals, Fed. Judicial Center Education and Training Series (1989). Because a full en banc panel of all twenty-eight active judges would be extremely unwieldy, the Ninth Circuit generally convenes a "limited en banc court" of eleven judges for rehearings en banc. *See* Ninth Circuit Rule 35-3, as revised 1 Jul. 2007.

C. The Supreme Court

16. The US Supreme Court has jurisdiction to review decisions of all the federal courts of appeals. Additionally, the US Supreme Court has the power to review the decisions of the highest state court in any state when a question of federal law has determined the outcome of the case.[1] Whereas the federal courts of appeals must hear the cases appealed from the federal district courts in their circuit, the US Supreme Court's jurisdiction is almost entirely discretionary. With rare exceptions, it can pick and choose which cases appealed from the federal courts of appeals, or from state courts, that it wants to hear.[2]

The US Supreme Court has nine justices, one of whom is designated as "Chief Justice." The Chief Justice has important administrative and case-assignment duties, but once review has been granted all cases are decided by majority vote of the entire court sitting en banc. (Some cases are decided by fewer than nine justices when one or more justices have recused themselves.) Four justices must vote to hear a case in order for the court to take it up for decision. A litigant asking the court to hear a case does so by petitioning the court for a writ of *certiorari*. When fewer than four justices wish to hear a case, the ruling of the lower court is left standing, and *certiorari* is denied. If four justices vote to hear the case, the court grants the writ, directing the court from which the case is appealed to send it up. All participating justices then consider the parties' briefs and listen to oral argument. Written opinions are issued reflecting the views of the various justices or groups of justices. An opinion signed by a majority of justices is considered the opinion of the US Supreme Court and is binding on all lower courts, state and federal, until overturned by a subsequent opinion of that court. Concurring and dissenting opinions are common, and some cases result only in a judgment of the court justified on different grounds by the divergent opinions of several justices or groups of justices. In such cases, the opinion joined by the most justices is called the "plurality" opinion, but is not considered the opinion of the court. Plurality opinions may be influential on lower courts, but do not constitute binding precedent.[3]

Denial of *certiorari* does not mean that the US Supreme Court necessarily agrees with the lower court's decision. The court may turn down a case for many other reasons. For example, the court's docket may already be full, the issue raised may have been incorrectly decided but lacks national importance, or the justices may want to wait until other lower courts have also considered the issue.[4]

1. This will typically be the supreme court of the state in question, but depending on the structure of the state-court system, this may be an inferior state court in states in which the jurisdiction of higher

courts is limited, or in which higher courts have discretionary control of their dockets. See Meador, *Appellate Courts, supra*, at 27.
2. *See* Meador, *American Courts, supra*, at 25-26.
3. *See generally* Hazard & Taruffo, *supra*, at 184-187.
4. Generally, this practice is known as judicial discretion. *See* 16B Wright, *supra*, §4004.1.

II. Structure of the States' Court Systems

17. Each of the fifty states is free to organize its courts as it sees fit. Accordingly, no two states have identical court structures. Generally, however, the states have a trial court of general jurisdiction, an intermediate appeals court, and a court of last resort, often called a "supreme court."[1] In all cases, the state constitution determines the composition of the courts.[2]

The lowest level of state courts is the inferior courts, or courts of limited jurisdiction. As the name implies, these courts typically deal with minor matters, either in subject matter or amount in controversy. For example, California's inferior courts adjudicate only controversies worth less than 50,000 United States dollars (USD). Other states may subdivide the inferior courts by subject matter. Georgia has no less than six types of inferior courts that deal with juvenile, probate, and small civil matters in particular counties.[3] The judges who preside over these tribunals are known by a variety of titles. In nonurban areas, the judge may be called a justice of the peace whereas in metropolitan areas, she may have the title of magistrate judge.[4] Aside from the names of the parties and the attorneys and the verdict, inferior courts usually do not keep thorough records of the proceedings; they are not typically "courts of record." Appeal from judgment is usually available but involves a trial de novo[5] in the next highest level of trial courts.

The next level of trial courts is the courts of general jurisdiction. The jurisdiction is general because the states have authorized these fora to adjudicate all civil and criminal matters, regardless of subject matter.[6] While most commonly known as "superior courts," there are many variations that are often confusing. New York, for example, calls its courts of general jurisdiction "supreme courts," a term typically reserved for the court of last resort in other states.[7] In contrast, Florida has named its courts of general jurisdiction "district courts," causing some confusion with the federal district courts.[8] At any rate, these tribunals are the workhorses of the American justice system. More suits are filed in California's courts of general jurisdiction each year than in the federal district courts nationwide.[9] As discussed below (paragraph 52), the federal district courts are courts of limited jurisdiction and complex hurdles must be cleared in order to bring suit therein. By contrast, the state trial courts of general jurisdiction almost always have concurrent jurisdiction with the federal courts as well as exclusive jurisdiction over some state matters, leading to much higher caseloads.

The final level of state courts is the appellate level. All states have a court of last resort, usually known as the "Supreme Court" of that state. Forty states each have an intermediate appellate court, often called the "Court of Appeal."[10] These intermediate courts of appeal are organized in different ways. First, they may be organized into geographical districts and an essentially separate court is set up for each district, much like the federal circuit system. Second, they may be unitary courts, meaning that the intermediate appeals court may review the decisions of any trial court in the state.

The unitary method may be further refined by allowing review in panels of at least three appellate judges or en banc.[11] En banc proceedings consist of all appellate judges sitting together to hear cases of first impression or to resolve issues on which panels have split.[12] Six states have chosen to organize intermediate appellate courts by subject matter. The courts are typically divided between civil and criminal matters, with each intermediate appeals court having independent and exclusive jurisdiction over their discrete subject matter.[13]

Courts of last resort are the final arbiters of the interpretation and application of state regulatory, common, statutory, and constitutional law.[14] Typically, the courts of last resort consist of five to nine members and review the cases that come before them en banc.[15] Only two states, Texas and Oklahoma, have more than one court of last resort. In both states, each high court entertains appeals based on subject matter, namely criminal and civil matters respectively.[16] While the decisions of the courts of last resort are final as to state matters, questions of federal law decided by the courts are reviewable in the federal courts, since the US Supreme Court is the final authority on federal law. However, if a decision by a state's highest tribunal is premised on "adequate and independent" state grounds, federalism concerns prevent the federal courts from reviewing the decision. The US Supreme Court will not find an "adequate and independent" state ground where it fairly appears on the face of the decision that the holding is based on federal law.[17] A state court of last resort may, however, decide that its laws and constitution provide its citizens more protections than the laws and Constitution of the United States, but not less.[18]

1. *See* Edgar Bodenheimer, John Bilyeu Oakley & Jean C. Love, *An Introduction to the Anglo-American Legal System*, 4th edn (2004), 62-63.
2. *See* Hazard & Taruffo, *supra*, at 47.
3. *See* <www.georgiacourts.org/courts/index.html> (last visited 17 Jul. 2008) (listing state, juvenile, magistrate, civil, probate, and municipal courts).
4. Bodenheimer, *supra*, at 56.
5. "De novo" is a term of art meaning that the appeal consists of a completely new trial in the higher court, so that the appeal proceeds as if the previous trial in the lower court had never occurred.
6. *See* Bodenheimer, *supra*, at 56.
7. Id.
8. *See* Meador, *supra*, at 10.
9. Id., at 31-32.
10. States without intermediate appellate courts include Delaware, Maine, Montana, Nevada, New Hampshire, Rhode Island, South Dakota, Vermont, West Virginia and Wyoming. *See* John B. Oakley, *Memorandum on Divisional Organization of the United States Court of Appeals for the Ninth Circuit*, Working Papers For the Commission on Structural Alternatives for the Federal Courts of Appeal 146 (1998).
11. Id., at 146-147. *See* Meador, *Appellate Courts, supra*, at 12-16.
12. Meador, *American Courts, supra*, at 24. For a discussion of the mechanics of en banc proceedings, *see* Oakley, *Memorandum, supra*, at 147-148. The practice in some states of having intermediate appellate courts hear important cases of first impression en banc, bypassing an initial hearing of the appeal by a three-judge panel of the court, differs from the federal en banc practice discussed above (para. 15).
13. *See* Oakley, *Memorandum, supra*, at 147.
14. *See* Hazard & Taruffo, *supra*, at 49.
15. *See* Meador, *supra, Appellate Courts*, at 10.
16. *See* Oakley, *Memorandum, supra*, at 147.
17. *See Michigan v. Long*, 463 U.S. 1032, 1042 (1983).

18. *See generally PruneYard Shopping Center v. Robins*, 447 U.S. 74 (1980) (holding that the California Supreme Court may interpret the free speech provision of its constitution more broadly than the First Amendment would allow).

III. Administration of the Courts

18. The three legs of the federal judiciary's administrative apparatus are: (1) the Judicial Conference of the United States, which engages in policy-making and general oversight of administration; (2) the Administrative Office of the United States Courts (AOUSC), which is the bureaucracy that runs the day-to-day operations of the court system, pays the bills, contracts with the Government Services Agency (GSA) and others for physical plant, office and courtroom space, paperclips, etc.;[1] and (3) and the Federal Judicial Center (FJC), whose mission revolves around research and education.[2] Insofar as research about what judges, marshals, prosecutors and others do affects how court administration is optimized and what legislation is desired or feared, the FJC and the AOUSC are sometimes rivals who occasionally bump into each other.[3] The State Justice Institute (SJI) is a conduit for federal funds to support state-court improvements: It is essentially a grant-disbursement agency.[4] It is a major source of support for the National Center for State Courts (NCSC) and the Conference of Chief Justices (CCJ). The NCSC performs an FJC-like education and research function for state courts collectively.[5] The CCJ performs for the Chief Justices of the fifty states' high courts a policy-making role analogous to that of the Judicial Conference within the federal system. The CCJ frequently deals with the effect of federal policy on state courts. Each state has an Administrative Office of the Courts or similarly named entity.[6]

1. *See generally* Charles W. Nihan, "A Study in Contrasts: The Ability of the Federal Judiciary to Change Its Adjudicative and Administrative Structures," Am. U. L. Rev. 44 (1995): 1693, 1707-1716 (describing the AOUSC and praising it as one of the most efficient administrative agencies in the federal government); *see also* William H. Rehnquist, "L. Ralph Meacham & Federal Courts Administration: A Decade of Innovation and Progress," Am. U. L. Rev. 44 (1995): 1477.
2. *See* Robert A. Carp & Ronald Stidham, *The Federal Courts*, 4th edn (2001), 34.
3. *See* id., at 34-35; *see generally* Christopher E. Smith, *Judicial Self Interest: Federal Judges and Court Administration* (1995), 15-25 (discussing the role of federal court administrative agencies as "judicial lobbying" apparatuses to advance the political interests of federal judges).
4. *See* 42 U.S.C. §§10702-10713; Francis J. Larkin, "The State Justice Institute: An Investment in Justice that must Continue," Judges' J. 31, no. 2, (1992): 1, 3.
5. *See* National Center for State Courts, 2005 Annual Report, *available at* <www.ncsonline.org/D_Comm/NCSCAnnlRpt_Archives/AnnlReport05.pdf> (last visited 31 Mar. 2008).
6. National Center for State Courts, Courts Website, <http://ncsconline.org/d_kis/info_court_web_sites.html> (last visited 31 Mar. 2008).

A. Administrative Offices

19. As noted above, both federal and state courts have administrative offices running the day-to-day operations of the courts. Within either system, the busiest individual courts may each have their own court executive or administrator. Together, administrative offices and court executives handle such pretrial and trial matters as selecting potential jurors from the citizenry, managing court records and case scheduling. Administrative offices also take care of the more mundane matters of a court, such as budgets, support staff, equipment, and maintenance of the courthouse itself.[1]

1. For traditional analyses of court management, *see* Meador, *supra*, at 61-63; Russell R. Wheeler & Howard R. Whitcomb, *Judicial Administration: Text and Readings* (1977), 85-92; for a business management analysis, *see generally* David J. Saari, *American Court Management: Theories and Practices* (1982).

B. Judicial Councils

20. The federal government and most states have a judicial council or conference.[1]

1. *See generally* Bureau of Justice Statistics, *Office of Justice Programs, U.S. Dep't of Justice, State Court Organization 1993* (1995), 120-129; Federal Judicial Center, *Organizing and Using a Council of State and Federal Judges* (1993); John B. Oakley, "Proceedings of the Western Regional Conference on State-Federal Judicial Relationships," F.R.D. 155 (1993): 233.

C. Court Funding

21. The judicial branch depends on the executive and legislative branches of government for its funding, and ultimately has no formal role in the budgetary process. Federal courts are at the mercy of the legislature when in need of funding.[1] State-court funding, however, comes from a variety of sources. Both state and local government contribute monies to the courts. The courts themselves also generate revenue through fees, fines and bail forfeitures. Additionally, federal funds come to state courts by way of the SJI, as noted above (paragraph 18).[2]

1. *See* Patrick E. Longan, "Congress, the Courts, and the Long Range Plan," Am. U. L. Rev. 46 (1997): 625, 654; *but cf.* Note, "The Court's Inherent Power to Compel Legislative Funding of Judicial Functions," Mich. L. Rev. 81 (1983): 1687, 1688 (noting that every state court that has addressed the issue has found an inherent power in the courts to demand monies of the legislature for essential judicial functions). For a discussion of the influence that Congress may assert via judicial appropriations *see generally* Gordon Bermant & Russell R. Wheeler, "Federal Judges and the Judicial Branch: Their Independence and Accountability," Mercer L. Rev. 46 (1995): 835; Todd D. Peterson, "Controlling the Federal Courts Through the Appropriations Process," Wis. L. Rev. 1998 (1998): 993.
2. *See generally* Bureau, *supra*, at 136-165.

IV. "Ministère Public"

22. In the United States there is no ministère public as such who is considered a member of the court system. However, similar functions are performed by the US Attorney General in the federal system, or the state attorney general for each state system.

V. Appointment of Judges

A. Selection of Federal Judges

1. Appointment and Confirmation

23. A federal judgeship is essentially a political appointment, often based on whether the president agrees with the legal philosophy and views of the potential judge.[1] This is especially true for appointments to the US Supreme Court.[2] The appointments clause of the US Constitution gives the president the power to nominate the judges of the Supreme Court and all other officers of the United States with the advice and consent of the US Senate.[3] Once confirmed by the Senate, all judges of federal courts established under Article III of the US Constitution enjoy lifetime tenure – an idea Article III of the Constitution captures by saying federal judges "shall hold their Offices during good Behaviour."[4] Also, Article III guarantees that compensation for a federal judge "shall not be diminished during" his or her continuance in office.[5] These provisions are designed to insulate federal judges after they are appointed from political pressures, to enable them to decide their cases free from concern about personal implications.[6]

In filling each federal judicial vacancy, the president narrows a list of possible nominees and chooses one person to nominate for Senate confirmation. The president delegates much of the selection process of most lower federal judges to officials within the Department of Justice, taking a much more personal role in US Supreme Court nominations.[7] Senators – especially those of the president's party – have considerable influence over the nomination of judges to the federal district courts within their states, and (to a lesser degree) over the nomination of judges of the federal courts of appeals.

The American Bar Association (ABA) maintains a Standing Committee on the Federal Judiciary. This committee has no formal role in the appointment of judges. However, the committee evaluates the qualifications of nominees to the federal bench, and submits an informal report to the Department of Justice for each person considered. The committee categorizes each potential nominee as "exceptionally well qualified," "well qualified," "qualified," or "not qualified."[8]

After the president has made his nomination and the ABA Standing Committee has submitted its report, the final step is Senate confirmation. The Senate Judiciary Committee evaluates the president's nominee prior to a plenary vote by the entire Senate. The Judiciary Committee considers the ABA report, the nominee's publications and – if he or she was ever a judge before – any earlier judicial opinions. The Judiciary Committee also questions the nominee in person. This is often the time when the senators try to elicit a nominee's position on contentious legal issues of the day, and determine how the nominee might rule if a case presenting such an issue were to come before him in the future. This kind of scrutiny is most pronounced during the confirmation of US Supreme Court justices, and to a lesser degree for nominees to the federal courts of appeals. After evaluating the president's nominee, the Judiciary Committee passes on its recommendation to the full Senate, where the nominee is either confirmed or denied by a majority vote. There have been periods throughout history during which the Senate generally deferred to the president, confirming whoever was nominated without serious scrutiny. At other times, the Senate has been more forceful. Indeed, some senators would like to expand their presently informal role in providing the president with recommendations and advice on judicial nominations ex ante, that is, before the president has formally nominated anyone.[9]

1. *See* Henry J. Abraham, *Justices, Presidents and Senators*, Rev. edn (1999), 1-7.
2. Id.
3. US Const. Art. II, §2, cl. 2.
4. US Const. Art. III, §1.
5. Id.
6. *See* The Federalist No. 78 (Alexander Hamilton, 1788), reprinted in James Madison et al., The Federalist Papers, ed. Issac Kemnick (1987).
7. Carp, *supra*, at 83; *see generally* Michael J. Gerhardt, "Panel II: The Appointment Power: Putting Presidential Performance in the Federal Appointments Process in Perspective," Case W. Res. L. Rev. 47 (1997): 1359 (reassessing the president's role in federal appointments in light of an expanded executive branch).
8. *See* Carp, *supra*, at 87-88; *see generally* American Bar Association, The ABA Standing Committee on the Federal Judiciary: What It Is and How It Works (2007), *available* at <www.abanet.org/scfedjud/federal_judiciary07.pdf> (ABA-produced pamphlet roughly sketching the role of its Standing Committee in federal judicial appointments).
9. Carp, *supra*, at 88-92.

24. Many reasons exist for the Senate's rejection of a nominee. The nominee's political and legal views may coincide with the president's, but differ from a majority of the senators. This is particularly likely when the nominating president and the confirming Senate majority are from different political parties. If the Senate continually rejects nominees, the president will be forced to eventually nominate someone with views more like the senators', or else let the position go unfilled. Keeping the position unfilled may be exactly what the senators are trying to do if the president is at the end of his term, and someone with views more like those of the majority of senators may become the next president.[1]

Interest groups may also pressure the Senate to reject the president's nominee. This occurs not only when the nominee's views are in opposition to the views of the interest group, but also when the nominee's views are unclear or unknown.[2]

One method of effectively scuttling a federal district-court nomination is through "senatorial courtesy." The Senate recognizes the special importance of the district-court judgeships to the senators who represent the state in which the district is located. Senatorial courtesy is the unofficial custom of giving the two home-state senators veto power over the appointment. If either of the home-state senators disapproves of the nominee, the Senate will often withhold confirmation – generally by keeping the nomination "in committee" so that it never proceeds to a formal vote of either the Judiciary Committee or the Senate as a whole. Since judges on the Federal Court of Appeals hear cases from more than one state, the interests and influence of any single senator in the nomination of judges of the federal courts of appeal (called "circuit judges") is reduced. This gives the president more leeway to nominate a person of his liking to be a circuit judge without particular deference to the senators from the states within the relevant circuit – but this leeway is by no means unbounded, and circuit-judge nominations are often the product of political compromises wholly unrelated to the position or individual in question. The president has the most freedom from parochial (but not political) concerns in making nominations of justices of the US Supreme Court. However, the president must still take the views of the confirming Senate majority into account, especially if they differ from the president's own.[3]

1. For an informative and thorough analysis of at least eight reasons why the Senate has refused to confirm twenty-eight of 142 Supreme Court nominees, *see* Abraham, *supra*, 39-48.
2. Id., at 30.
3. Id., at 48.

2. Appointment without Confirmation

25. The recess-appointment clause in Article II of the US Constitution[1] gives the president the power to appoint temporary government officers without prior Senate approval. Federal judgeships are subject to the recess-appointment clause, making it possible for the president to appoint a federal judge (but only temporarily) without prior Senate confirmation. Any such appointment expires at the end of the next legislative session, however, and risks angering senators whose voice in the appointment process has thus been silenced. Recess appointments of federal judges are chiefly used (and then only rarely) to force a confirmation vote for a nominee generally favored by the Senate, whose confirmation has been blocked only by an isolated opponent's exercise of senatorial courtesy.

1. US Const. Art. II, §2, cl. 3.

3. Background of Federal Judges

26. As in the British judicial system, American judges are drawn from the ranks of experienced lawyers and legal scholars. Unlike the British and European civil legal systems, however, American judges can enter the judiciary at the appellate level, or even as a member of the Supreme Court. One need not accumulate experience as a trial judge first.

Although a nominee to the US Supreme Court need not have any prior judicial experience, in recent history the president's nominees have usually come from the judges of the Federal Court of Appeals. A few have been nominated from positions on a state's highest court. Most modern justices of the US Supreme Court have graduated from the nation's elite law schools.

Nominees to the federal courts of appeals and district courts come from a wide variety of backgrounds. Recently, judges, practitioners, and scholars have spoken out about the need for greater gender and ethnic diversity on the bench. Scholars have suggested diversity among judges would improve judicial decision-making and improve the public perception of the impartiality of judicial decision-making.[1] Today, 37.3 percent of all federal judges are "nontraditional" appointments. Women hold nearly twenty-five percent of all federal judgeships. Representation of Asian-Americans is at less than one percent; no Native Americans sit on the federal bench and none has sat since 2001.[2] Many federal appellate-court nominees have been federal trial judges, or (more rarely) state judges. But many federal circuit judges and district judges come to the federal judiciary directly from careers as litigators, business lawyers, or law professors. Among those appointed district judges, many have served as federal prosecutors or as counsel to federal agencies, or have served as state trial judges. Many federal judges not drawn from the state bench were actively engaged in organized political activity before their judicial appointments. This should not be surprising, given the frankly political nature of the appointment process as a function of the executive and legislative branches.[3]

1. *See* Sherrilyn A. Ifill, "Racial Diversity on the Bench: Beyond Role Models and Public Confidence," Wash. L. Rev. 57 (2000): 405; Kevin R. Johnson & Luis Fuentes-Rohwer, "A Principled Approach to the Quest for Racial Diversity on the Bench," Mich. J. Race & L. 10 (2004): 5.
2. *See* Marcia Coyle, "Diversity Pool for High Court Justices Too Shallow?" The Nat'l L. J. (26 Sept. 2005): 1.
3. *See* Abraham, *supra*, at 68-106; Carp, *supra*, at 68-106.

B. Selection of State Judges

27. The method of selecting state judges is usually quite different from the federal system, and varies a great deal from state to state. Some states employ elections to select their judiciary. Other states use an appointment process, or a system combining appointments and elections. Finally, a few states use a merit plan to select judges. These merit plans can be used in isolation, or in conjunction with the election and appointment systems.[1]

1. *See generally* Daniel R. Deja, "Feature: Judicial Selection: How Judges are Selected: A Survey of the Judicial Selection Process in the United States," Mich. B. J. 75(1996): 904.

1. Elections

28. There are three basic types of elections used by states to select judges. The first is a partisan election. A partisan election is the same type used to elect a politician to office. Candidates for the judiciary in a partisan election may be endorsed by party leaders, candidates for other judgeships or candidates for other offices.[1] A second type is the "nonpartisan" election. In nonpartisan elections, candidates run without party affiliation. Usually there are restrictions on the type of campaigns that may be waged. Retention elections are the third type of election, which are often used in combination with the appointment method. In states where retention elections are used, the governor initially appoints the judge to the bench. Periodically thereafter the people must vote to retain the judge, or else a new judge will be appointed. Generally, once a judge is appointed to the bench he or she is retained, except in cases where the judge has received extremely negative publicity.[2]

Elections pose a number of problems when used to select judges. The process of campaigning to attain and retain judicial office may adversely affect judicial independence. A judge faced with an unpopular decision that the law nonetheless calls for may be forced to choose between following the law or getting re-elected. Also, many well-qualified people are discouraged from seeking judicial office because they do not want to engage in politics, particularly the process of campaigning. Longer terms in office, such as ten to fifteen years, can offset the negative effects of elections.

Judges with longer terms are less likely to be swayed by popular sentiment and retain a higher degree of judicial independence insofar as the next election may be far enough off for popular passions to cool.[3]

As mentioned above, some states place restrictions on judicial campaigning. Some prohibit candidates from personally soliciting or accepting campaign contributions. Instead, judicial candidates may establish committees to solicit and accept reasonable contributions on their behalf. Candidates are prohibited from making pledges or promises regarding their conduct once in office. They are allowed to promise only the faithful and impartial performance of judicial duties. Any statement that commits or appears to commit the candidate to a position regarding a case, controversy, or issue that is likely to come before the court is expressly forbidden.[4]

In two states, Virginia and South Carolina, judges are elected not by the citizenry, but by the legislature. Legislative election of judges often means that the result depends upon partisan political factors. Yet, at least the judicial candidates themselves are spared the expense of raising money for a statewide campaign.[5]

1. Id., at 906.
2. Id., at 905-906.
3. *See generally* Philip L. Dubois, "Accountability, Independence, and the Selection of State Judges: The Role of Popular Judicial Elections," Sw. L. J. 40(1986): 31.
4. *See, e.g.*, Nicole C. Allbritain, "One Step Closer to Merit-Based Judicial Selection: Ohio's New Limitations on Judicial Campaign Contributions and Expenditures," U. Cin. L. Rev. 64 (1996): 1323.
5. *See generally* Martin Scott Driggers, Jr, "Judiciary: South Carolina's Experiment: Legislative Control of Judicial Merit Selection," S.C.L. Rev. 49 (1998): 1217.

2. Appointments

29. Selecting judges by a system of *gubernatorial* appointment is usually used in conjunction with either general confirmation elections or legislative confirmation. As with elections, appointments for longer terms better protect the judicial independence of the new judge. In some states, the governor gets to appoint only a portion of the state judiciary. The background and experience of state judges can vary, depending on the criteria that each successive governor uses. State judges are frequently experienced litigators. They may have represented private businesses or the interests of the state as prosecuting attorneys. As is true with federal nominees, many appointees to a state bench often have political experience.[1]

1. *See* Hazard & Taruffo, *supra*, at 64-68.

3. Merit Selection

30. Another type of system used to select state judges is called "merit selection," or a "merit plan." Merit selection employs a judicial nominating commission, which can consist of members of the state bar, the judiciary and the public.[1] The nominating commission requires that anyone seeking judicial office submit an extensive application. The required application delves deeply into the background of potential judges. Personal experiences, educational and professional histories are all examined. Some commissions require those seeking judgeships to submit a personal statement.[2]

The commission then evaluates all the applicants, seeking to select the most highly qualified for recommendation to the governor. The criteria of the nominating commission usually include integrity and moral courage, impartiality, a judicial temperament, knowledge and understanding of substantive and procedural law, communication skills, attentiveness, docket management skills, administrative skills, punctuality and effectiveness in working with other participants in the judicial process. Taking all of these factors into account, the commission presents a short list of four to six names to the governor for consideration for each vacancy. The governor then applies his or her own criteria to those on the commission's list and appoints one person. In some states, an elective element is brought into the merit plan system; after a specified time the appointee may have to be affirmed by the voters through a retention election.[3]

1. *See generally* Jona Goldschmidt, "Selection and Retention of Judges: Is Florida's Present System Still the Best Compromise?: Merit Selection: Current Status, Procedures, and Issues," U. Miami L. Rev. 49 (1994): 1.
2. *See* id., at 26.
3. *See generally* Allan Ashman et al., *The Key to Judicial Merit Selection: The Nominating Process* (1974).

§2. Members of the Judiciary

I. Incompatibilities

A. Recusal

31. As noted below in Part V's discussion of judicial disqualification (paragraphs 207-210), "recusal" refers to a judge voluntarily abstaining from the adjudication of a case in which the judge may have, or may appear to have, a personal interest.[1] Despite the political nature of the selection of American judges, the American legal system – especially with respect to the federal courts – places a high value on the independence and impartiality of judges as necessary to ensure all parties in a trial receive a fair and impartial hearing in court.[2] Anything that adversely affects a judge's impartiality in hearing a case can be grounds for recusal.[3]

The US Judicial Code (Title 28 of the overall US Code) describes the circumstances in which recusal may be proper in federal courts. Section 455(a) of the US Judicial Code allows recusal upon a motion filed at any time by any party (including the judge) on the grounds that a judge's impartiality may reasonably be questioned.[4] Doubt of a judge's impartiality sufficient to require recusal may be established by demonstrating that a judge has personal bias stemming from extrajudicial sources, has personal knowledge of disputed evidentiary facts, at an earlier time served as a lawyer in the matter in controversy, or has been connected with the proceeding in another capacity. Recusal is also required under §455 when the judge, judge's spouse, or other family member is a party in the case, is acting as a lawyer for either party, is likely to be a material witness, or has a financial interest in the proceeding.[5]

Additionally, a nonfinancial interest that could be substantially affected by the outcome of the case may justify recusal.[6]

1. For a leading authority on recusal and judicial disqualification, *see* Richard E. Flamm, *Judicial Disqualification: Recusal and Disqualification of Judges*, 2nd edn (2007) (covering both state and federal disqualification practices).
2. Id., §3.1 at 54.
3. Id., §3.1 at 54.
4. 28 U.S.C. §455(a).
5. Id. §455(b)(4)-(5).
6. Id. §455(b)(4) ("... or any other interest that could be substantially affected by the outcome of the proceeding").

B. 2007 Model Code of Judicial Conduct

32. The ABA's 2007 Model Code of Judicial Conduct (Model Code) provides guidelines and limits on all judges in order to ensure impartiality and reinforce public confidence in the judiciary.[1] The Model Code requires judges to "act at all times in a manner that promotes public confidence in the integrity and impartiality of the judiciary."[2] Certain types of speech are prohibited in the third section of the Model Code. Rule 2.10 prohibits judges from making statements about pending cases "that might reasonably be expected to affect its outcome or impair its fairness." While the Model Code does prohibit judges from making such comments about proceedings "pending or impending in any court," it does not keep judges from commenting publicly on prior cases. Judges are actually encouraged to speak publicly, so long as their comments do not affect the outcome or impartial hearing of present or future cases. Rule 3.1 of the Model Code suggests that judges "speak, write, lecture, teach, and participate in other extrajudicial activities concerning the law, the legal system, the administration of justice, and nonlegal subjects." Such activities must not, however, "demean the judicial office," or "interfere with the proper performance of judicial duties." The Model Code acknowledges the unique ability of judges to improve "the law, the legal system, and the administration of justice," and thus encourages them to play an active role in the civic life both in and out of the courtroom.

At the same time, however, partisan political activity by judges is discouraged, even with regard to their own election. As mentioned earlier, judges cannot make any campaign promises regarding their duties on the bench aside from the faithful and impartial performance of the duties of the office.

The Model Code also suggests that a judge not hold membership in any organization that "practices invidious discrimination on the basis of race, sex, religion, or national origin."[3] Membership in such clubs raises the potential for public misperception of the judge's views, even if the club's restrictions do not reflect a judge's true prejudices. A club's exclusionary policies may suggest bias on the part of a judge who belongs to such a club, particularly by implying a lack of sensitivity and concern by the judge for those types of people who are excluded.[4]

Judges and their families are limited in what kinds of gifts they can accept, and what sort of business they can pursue. Rule 3.13 of the Model Code prohibits the acceptance of gifts, favors, or loans by a judge or members of his or her family who reside in the same household from anyone whose interests are likely to come before the judge in court. The spouse and children of a judge are discouraged from engaging in business activities with persons who may come before the judge's court, or under circumstances that may appear to exploit the judge's office.[5] A judge's position may also constrain his family's activities in the political arena. When family members of a judge engage in partisan political activities, it may create the same suspicion of political bias as if the judge had actually engaged in the political activity.[6]

1. American Bar Association, *Model Code of Judicial Conduct* (2007).
2. Id., at Preamble.
3. Id., at Rule 3.6.
4. Id., commentary at 2; *see also* Robert J. Alberts & Kenneth C. Fonte, "Is Section 2C of the Model Code of Judicial Conduct Justified? An Empirical Study of the Impropriety of Judges Belonging to Exclusive Clubs," Geo. J. Legal Ethics 8 (1995): 597, 602-603.
5. Model Code, Rule 3.11; *see generally* Jeffery M. Shaman et al., "The 1990 Code of Judicial Conduct: An Overview," Judicature 74 (1990): 21, 24-25.
6. Model Code, Rule 4.2(A)(1).

II. End of Functions

A. *Federal Judges*

33. The tenure of most federal judges ends with their death, retirement, or (occasionally) impeachment. By virtue of their guarantee of tenure during "good behavior," federal judges can remain on the bench well into their elderly years. Retirement may be elected due to declining health, a disability, or simply because of personal circumstances. Judges can opt for senior status after attaining the scheduled statutory age with the requisite years of service.[1] Senior judges receive a full salary and continue to hear cases as long as they remain qualified. Another way a judge's career on the bench may end is by impeachment and Senate conviction,[2] discussed below (paragraph 35).

1. *See* 28 U.S.C. §371.
2. *See* Carp, *supra*, at 111-114.

B. *State Judges*

34. The judicial career of some state judges can end as it began, through a contested election. Although less frequent, an uncontested retention election can also end a judge's time on the bench. As with federal judges, death, retirement, and impeachment also bring state judges' careers to a close.[1]

1. *See generally* Mary L. Volcansek, *Judicial Impeachment: None Called for Justice* (1993); Jeffery M. Shaman, "Judicial Ethics," Geo. J. Legal Ethics 2 (1988): 1 (discussing the methods short of impeachment by which judges may be disciplined).

III. Discipline

A. *House Impeachment and Senate Conviction of Federal Judges*

35. Impeachment is the most severe disciplinary action judges can face in connection with their official duties.[1] In Article II, section 4, the Constitution gives Congress power to impeach "the President, Vice President, and all civil officers of the United States."[2] An offence must involve abuse of the public trust in order to justify impeachment.

According to Article I of the Constitution, judgment in cases of impeachment cannot extend further than removal from office and disqualification to hold and enjoy any office of honor or trust.[3] However, impeachment addresses only the question of whether the judge's breach of the public trust justifies removal from office. It does not settle questions regarding the judge's criminal or civil liability for any offence. Federal judges can be prosecuted and tried – both in civil and criminal proceedings – for their conduct.[4] Judges do enjoy immunity from lawsuits that stem from their official acts as judges; but members of the judiciary are not immune from actions arising out of their private conduct, or any act which is not a part of their official duties.

In cases where a federal judge has committed an offence breaching the public trust, the Judicial Conference considers whether impeachment is warranted. Should the Judicial Conference determine that impeachment is warranted, the House of Representatives will draft and vote on articles of impeachment. In drafting the articles, the House reviews the record of investigations compiled by the Judicial Conference. If a majority of the members of the House determine that the accused judge's conduct warrants impeachment, the articles are approved. In most instances the House's vote follows the recommendation of the Judicial Conference.

After the articles of impeachment – the indictment, if you will – have been approved by the House, they are referred to the Senate, where the Senate conducts a trial of the accused judge. During this trial the House of Representatives acts as the prosecutor of the judge. A Senate committee often hears the case in the first instance, compiling a record of the proceedings for presentation to the full Senate. Based on the evidence, the full Senate votes on whether to convict the judge. Should two-thirds of the Senate vote to convict the judge on any of the articles of impeachment, the judge is officially convicted and removed from office. He may also, depending on the Senate's discretion, be disqualified from holding future office in the United States.[5]

1. *See generally* 15 James W. Moore et al., *Moore's Federal Practice*, 3rd edn (1999), §100.04.
2. US Const. Art. II, §4.
3. Id., Art. I, §3, cl. 7.
4. Id.
5. *See generally* Michael J. Gerhardt, The Federal Impeachment Process, 2nd edn (2000).

B. *Judicial Conduct Act*

36. The Judicial Conduct and Disability Act of 1980 permits anyone to file a complaint against a district judge or circuit judge for "conduct prejudicial to the effective and expeditious administration of the business of the courts."[1] An allegation can also be made that a judge is unable to fulfill the requirements of his office due to a mental or physical disability.[2]

The complaint must be filed with the appropriate circuit court. The Chief Judge of the circuit reviews the complaint and sends a copy to the accused judge. If the complaint merits further consideration, the Chief Judge sends it on to a special investigative committee. The special committee then conducts an investigation and reports its findings either to the judicial council for the circuit or Congress' Judicial Conference.[3]

The judicial council for the circuit is charged only with curtailing judicial misbehavior that falls short of an impeachable offence, and is denied the power to remove a judicial official.[4] However, many of the actions the judicial council can take result in the accused judge stepping down from the bench. While the council cannot remove a judge directly, it can urge the judge to retire voluntarily, certify the disability of the judge, or temporarily freeze the judge's caseload.[5] Should a case given to the judicial council for a circuit decide that the offence committed by the judge in question does merit impeachment, the council can refer the complaint to Congress' Judicial Conference.[6] The Judicial Conference then handles the complaint as previously discussed under "House Impeachment and Senate Conviction of Federal Judges."

1. 28 U.S.C. §372(c)(1).
2. Id.
3. Id., §372(c)(2)-(7).
4. Id., §372(c)(7)(B).
5. Id., §372(c)(6).
6. Id., §372(c)(7); *see* Lyn A. Baker, "Unnecessary and Improper: The Judicial Councils Reform and Judicial Conduct and Disability Act of 1980," Yale L.J. 94 (1985): 1117 (arguing that the procedures established by the Judicial Conduct Act are unconstitutional).

C. *Informal Sanctions*

37. The court system can also discipline judges through informal sanctions. Denying a judge a promotion to a higher court, reducing court budgets, freezing a judge's salary level, and judicial review, including mandamus,[1] all function as unofficial actions of discipline for judicial misconduct.[2]

1. The writ of mandamus permits appellate review of a trial court's abuse of discretion outside of the normal channels and constraints of review as of right from a final judgment of the trial court. For the scope of the writ of mandamus and other extraordinary writs in the federal system, *see* 16 Wright, *supra*, §3932. Such writs are also generally available – and are often more liberally available – in state judicial systems.
2. *See* 15 Moore, *supra*, §100.04[3][a]; Carp, *supra*, at 111-114.

D. Certification as Disabled

38. Under 28 U.S.C. §372(a), a judge or justice who becomes permanently disabled may retire and receive the salary of the office if she has served at least ten years or half the salary of the office if she has served less than ten years. Should a permanently disabled judge decline to retire voluntarily, §372(b) provides that the judge may be certified as disabled by a majority of the circuit judicial panel, which may then lead to a removal of cases from that judge.[1]

1. 28 U.S.C. §§372(a-b); *see also* Carp, *supra*, at 111-116.

Chapter 2. The Bar

§1. Exercise of the Legal Profession

I. Conditions for Admission

A. *Membership in the Bar*

39. During the presidency of Andrew Jackson (1829-1837), a strong anti-elitist ethos led to the elimination of the requirement that someone have formal training before being able to practice law.[1] This lasted until the 1870s, when the legal profession became increasingly concerned about the lack of professionalism among lawyers and the need for better legal education.[2]

In the latter part of the nineteenth century, local organizations of practicing lawyers began to exert more influence on regulation of the profession and to assist in the creation of formal legal training programs at universities and colleges.[3] These local bar organizations helped establish the ABA – which remains the most important lawyer body – in 1878. Fifteen years later, in 1893, the ABA set up the Section of Legal Education, a body designed to regulate the increasing number of law schools founded during this period. Another thirty years later, in 1923, the ABA's Council of the Section to the Admissions to the Bar published a list of law schools officially approved and accredited by the ABA. ABA accreditation served its intended function well; the quality of US legal education improved. Today there are more than 200 ABA-approved law schools in the United States.[4]

Eligibility to practice law in each state depends upon the laws of that state. Each state requires that one be admitted to its bar in order to engage in the full range of lawyering activities within its boundaries. But the admission requirements vary a great deal from state to state. To become admitted to the bar, most states require – in addition to the payment of annual dues – graduation from an ABA-approved law school and passage of a state-administered bar examination, which may last two or three days. Some states will also allow a person to sit for the bar exam who is not a graduate of an ABA-approved law school, provided the person has attended a school that has received approval from that state though not the ABA. And a very few states will waive the requirement of a bar examination for persons who graduate from certain ABA-approved schools within that state. No one contends that a standardized bar examination, which tests national and local legal principles, is a perfect way to measure knowledge of or ability to successfully practice law. But no clearly preferable alternative has been presented.[5]

As a general matter, admission to practice in a federal court turns on eligibility to practice in the state courts in which the federal court is located. A federal court ordinarily admits applicants who are members of the bar of the highest court of the state in which the federal court exists.[6] In some instances, federal courts permit lawyers to be admitted who are not members of the local state bar but who are employees of the federal government – such as lawyers in the United States Attorneys' (regional federal criminal and civil prosecutors) offices. Admission in these circumstances may last only as long as the federal employment.[7]

1. Mary M. Devlin, "The Development of Lawyer Disciplinary Procedures in the United States," Geo. J. Legal Ethics 7 (1994): 911, 918.
2. *See* Lawrence M. Friedman, *A History of American Law*, 3rd edn (2005), 500.
3. *See* id., at 495-500.
4. *See* Am. Bar Assoc., Section of Legal Education and Admissions to the Bar, <www.abanet.org/legaled/approvedlawschools/approved.html> (last visited 29 Jul. 2008).
5. *See generally* American Bar Association, *Comprehensive Guide to Bar Admission Requirements* (2008); *Martindale Hubbell Law Directory* (2008).
6. *See* Fed. R. App. P. 46(a); 32 Am. Jur. 2nd *Federal Courts* §631 (1995).
7. *See generally* Don C. Keenan, *Out-of-State Practice of Law* (1981).

II. Rights and Duties

40. Membership in the bar of a state entitles one to practice law only in that state (and, as noted above, may provide a basis for practicing in federal courts located in that state.) But what if a lawyer needs to represent a client located in, and embroiled in a controversy in, another state? Localized admission presents especially serious problems for lawyers whose clients are multistate companies. These lawyers have a strong interest in being able to represent their clients in many states and, not surprisingly, are not eager to take a number of different three-day bar examinations. There are a few possible answers to this problem, although none has fully solved it. One is the device of reciprocity, whereby State A agrees to admit members of State B's bar without insisting on an applicant taking State A's bar exam, provided State B affords the same courtesy to members of State A's bar. Many states do grant reciprocity, at least for experienced out-of-state lawyers, but many – including California, the largest state – do not.[1] Another potential solution is the device of *pro hac vice* – or special appearance. This is a mechanism by which out-of-state lawyers can appear in a court in which they are not admitted by making a special request for accommodation to that court, limited to the purposes for which they are appearing. Such requests are not always granted, and may also require out-of-town counsel to affiliate with local counsel. Moreover, the *pro hac vice* device allows an unadmitted lawyer only to appear in court, not to engage in other out-of-court lawyer's work, which may be more time consuming and important. And although many states do not rigidly enforce their criminal and civil prohibitions on practicing law without a valid state license, very few out-of-state lawyers want to run the risk.[2]

1. *See generally* American Bar Association, *Comprehensive Guide to Bar Admissions* (2008) (detailing bar admission requirements in each American jurisdiction and the ability of an out-of-state bar-admitted attorney to practice in other jurisdictions); Charles W. Wolfram, "Sneaking Around in the Legal Profession: Interjurisdictional Unauthorized Practice by Transactional Lawyers," S. Tex. L. Rev. 36 (1995): 665 (bemoaning the inability of bar-admitted attorneys to practice in every state and advocating the creation of a true national bar).
2. *See generally* Keenan, *supra*.

III. Discipline and Regulatory Organizations

41. Shakespeare could have been describing the future sentiment of the American public toward the legal profession when he wrote in *Henry VI*, "[t]he first thing we do, let's kill all the lawyers.'[1] The general climate of distrust and dislike of lawyers began early in the United States.[2] In an effort to establish public trust in the profession, the nationwide ABA and state bar associations are trying to curb abuses by lawyers through more effective disciplinary methods.[3] Bar associations also hope effective discipline of lawyers will keep legislatures from regulating attorneys' conduct.[4]

1. William Shakespeare, *The Second Part of Henry the Sixth Act 4*, eds G. Blakemore Evans et al. (1997), sc. 2.
2. *See* Friedman, *supra*, at 94-96.
3. *See generally* American Bar Association, Model Rules of Professional Conduct, <www.abanet.org/cpr/mrpc/e2k_chair_intro.html> (2008) [hereinafter Model Rules]; American Bar Association, *Survey on Lawyer Discipline Systems* (1996) (providing state statistics regarding mode and frequency of lawyer discipline).
4. *See generally* Geoffery C. Hazard, Jr & Deborah L. Rhode, *The Legal Profession: Responsibility and Regulation*, 3rd edn (1994), 108-134.

42. Throughout American history various methods for disciplining lawyers have been used. Up to the 1870s, judges controlled the discipline of lawyers. Attorneys were subject to discipline by the courts in which they practiced, for their professional conduct both inside and outside of the courtroom. According to *Ex Parte Wall*,[1] judges could exercise discipline over lawyers *sua sponte*, so long as the charge was specific and the accused lawyer received due process. If the judge found the lawyer guilty of professional misconduct, the judge could strike the lawyer from the rolls, effectively barring the attorney from practicing in that court. But this method gave rise to obvious concerns about the judge performing both the role of accuser and trier.[2]

Many states adopted clearer standards shortly after the turn of the century. In 1908, the ABA published the "Canons of Legal Ethics," largely based on the Alabama State Bar's code.[3] Twenty-two additional states adopted the Canon of Legal Ethics, which came to define the legal profession's ethical norms.[4] Although the ABA Canon of Legal Ethics was widely adopted, different states used different types of procedures when enforcing the rules. The varying procedures confused members of the public who sought disciplinary action for attorney misconduct. Widespread public distrust of attorneys and the methods used to discipline them continued.[5]

1. *Ex Parte Wall*, 107 U.S. 265 (1882).
2. *See, e.g.*, Wilburn Brewer, Jr, "Due Process in Lawyer Disciplinary Cases: From the Cradle to the Grave," S.C.L. Rev. 42 (1991): 925.
3. *See* Model Rules, *supra*, at vii.
4. *See* Devlin, *supra*, at 919.
5. *See* id., at 919-921.

43. To counteract negative public sentiment, in 1970 the ABA commissioned the Clark Committee to investigate disciplinary enforcement. The committee reported that in many jurisdictions disciplinary action was nonexistent. Frequently, disciplinary agencies of local bars had little or no real power to discipline attorneys. Public distrust of the bar increased. The Clark Committee made three recommendations based on their findings. First, the judiciary should increase the use of its inherent power to supervise the disciplinary process of lawyers. Second, disciplinary actions should be centralized in a state's highest court. Third, the committee emphasized the need to hire a full-time professional staff to handle disciplinary procedures for the bar.[1]

The Clark Committee also produced a comprehensive plan for resolving the conflicts created by having many different procedures for attorney discipline. The Model Uniform Procedure for Discipline spells out specific steps for effectively handling allegations of misconduct against lawyers. First, allegations must be submitted to the bar's professional staff for investigation. Second, after investigation, any matters that cannot be dismissed as unfounded or resolved with a simple warning letter are sent on to an inquiry committee. If the inquiry committee itself does not dismiss the charges, the issue is sent to a formal hearing committee. The state bar governing board and then the state's highest court will consider the issue on the basis of the record presented by the formal committee and oral arguments.[2]

During the 1970s, the ABA adopted the Clark Committee recommendations but added that members of the public should be included in the disciplinary agencies of the bar. By 1982, thirty-two states had members of the public on their disciplinary agencies – largely as an effort to regain the public trust. By the end of the 1980s, most of the Clark Committee recommendations had been adopted by the states' bar associations.[3]

In 1989 another committee, the McKay Commission, evaluated the functioning of the bar associations' systems for disciplining lawyers. The McKay Commission found that while nearly every state bar had professional disciplinary counsel, inadequate funding kept the disciplinary counsel from effectively enforcing the rules. Controversy continues over the issue of when a complaint against an attorney should be made public. In addition, due to the lack of enforcement funds lawyers who commit minor infractions are frequently not disciplined at all.[4]

Some commentators criticize the increasing use of formal rules and disciplinary procedures for attorneys. Formal rules and procedures undermine the basic tenets of law as a profession as distinct from a trade, they argue.[5] Supreme Court Justice Sandra Day O'Connor presented this view in one case.[6] She argued that law is a learned profession, and self-regulation is crucial to professionalism. Unlike a vocational trade, the practice of law comes with great privileges and responsibilities. According to O'Connor, there is "an ethical obligation to temper one's selfish pursuit of economic success by adhering to standards of conduct" that cannot be enforced by legal fiat or through formal disciplinary rules.[7] Critics of formal disciplinary rules call for the bar, the judiciary and law schools to promote professional and ethical conduct. Law schools, it is argued, have a special obligation to teach ethics as a part of each and every course.

Other critics attack the ABA and its disciplinary procedures as elitist. The rise of the ABA's power, they argue, was due to the organization's desire to serve America's expanding corporate interests throughout the late nineteenth century. Pointing to the ABA's hostility toward advertising and solicitation by lawyers, they claim that the ABA is run by commercial lawyers for commercial lawyers, who do not need to advertise as do other less well-heeled practitioners. These critics also point out that lawyers in large commercial firms are rarely subjected to discipline.[8] Based on these concerns, there is a fair bit of local skepticism of the ABA's claim that the model rules are based on the high-minded ideal of protecting the public.[9]

1. *See* id., at 921-926.
2. *See* id., at 926-927.
3. *See* id., at 928.
4. *See* id., at 930-933.
5. *See generally* Warren L. Mengis, "Professional Responsibility," La. L. Rev. 49 (1988): 487.
6. *Shapero v. Kentucky Bar Ass'n.*, 486 U.S. 466, 490 (1988) (O'Connor, J., dissenting).
7. Id., at 488-489.
8. *See generally* Lloyd B. Snyder, "Rhetoric, Evidence, and Bar Agency Restrictions on Speech by Attorneys," Creighton L. Rev. 28 (1995): 357, 360-364 (noting that the rules governing ethical conduct were developed by attorneys more concerned with representing their corporate clients like gentlemen than providing an ethical service to the public); Whitney Thier, "In a Dignified Manner: The Bar, The Court, and Lawyer Advertising," Tulane L. Rev. 66 (1991): 527, 528-539 (arguing that the Canons governing lawyer advertising ought to be liberalized in order to allow broader access to legal services).
9. *See generally* "Proceedings of the Ninety-Fourth Annual Meeting of the North Dakota State Bar Association," N.D.L. Rev. 70 (1994): 743, 744 (discussing what a local bar association can do to counteract "lawyer bashing").

Chapter 3. Bailiffs and Other Non-Judicial Court Employees

§1. ETHICS

44. The services of many different people are essential for a fair and efficient court system. In addition to judges and lawyers, both federal and state courts employ court clerical workers to handle administrative tasks and paperwork, bailiffs and marshals to provide security in the courtroom and sometimes assist in the serving of process and executing court judgments, and "elbow clerks" who assist the judge in carrying out their judicial duties. All court employees must treat the public fairly.[1] Court administrators must not select cases to move forward on the calendar in order to benefit themselves or others.[2] Bailiffs and especially elbow clerks are privileged to a great deal of information, including the judge's impressions of any given case. Elbow clerks may know how a judge will rule on a case before the ruling is officially announced. Consequently, confidentiality on the part of court employees is paramount.[3] A breach of confidentiality can jeopardize the public's trust in the court system and the fair administration of justice.[4]

Court employees must also prevent conflicts between their personal interests and the duty they owe the public of impartially carrying out their duties.[5] For example, partisan political activity on the job should be avoided by elbow clerks. Political activity can lead to favoring some people appearing before the court over others, thereby compromising the duty of fairness.[6] In response to these concerns, the American Judicature Society developed a Model Code of Conduct for Non-Judicial Court Employees.[7] The code limits the kinds of activities that court employees can engage in, while stressing the confidential nature of much of their work.

1. AJS Model Code of Conduct for Non-Judicial Court Employees §5(b) available at <www.ajs.org/ethics/eth_non-judic-employ-employ.asp> (last visited 2 Jul. 2008).
2. Id., §§1(A)-1(C).
3. Id., §1(A).
4. *See generally* David T. Ozar et al., "Ethical Conduct of Nonjudicial Court Employees: A Proposed Model Code," Judicature 73 (1989): 126.
5. AJS Model Code, *supra*, §3(A).
6. Ozar, *supra*, at 126.
7. AJS Model Code, *supra*.

Part II. Jurisdiction

Chapter 1. Domestic Jurisdiction

§1. SUBJECT-MATTER JURISDICTION

I. Factors to be Taken into Account

45. All American court systems are divided into separate levels of trial and appellate courts. In some states the trial courts of general jurisdiction also exercise appellate jurisdiction over trial courts of inferior jurisdiction. The same is functionally true in the federal system, which assigns adjudicatory responsibility in some cases to subordinate tiers of federal "magistrate judges" and "bankruptcy judges" who serve as adjuncts to federal district judges.[1] Decisions of federal magistrate judges and bankruptcy judges are subject in principle to review by the federal district judges to whom they report, but in practice most decisions of federal magistrate judges and federal bankruptcy judges are adopted without change by federal district judges. They are then subject to review by federal appellate courts in the same manner as any other decisions of the federal district courts.[2]

Many regulatory disputes under state and federal law must be litigated in the first instance before administrative tribunals through essentially trial-like proceedings. These tribunals function in effect as a highly variegated set of state and federal trial courts of specialized subject-matter jurisdiction, rendering judgments that are then reviewable in the formal state and federal court systems. Generally, judicial review of administrative rulings is assigned to the state and federal trial courts of general jurisdiction. In some cases the trial courts conduct trial de novo of any disputed facts, but in most such cases the trial courts are bound by reasonable factual findings of the administrative tribunal, and exercise an essentially appellate jurisdiction.

1. *See generally* US Courts Web Page, <www.uscourts.gov> (last visited 10 Apr. 2008).
2. *Id.*

46. For cases triable in the first instance in conventional courts, the most common basis for allocating subject-matter jurisdiction is the value of the claim. It is always difficult to assign a value to claims for specific relief (such as an injunction) rather than money damages. Most states that assign low-value cases to trial courts of inferior jurisdiction avoid this problem by routing any claim for specific relief to their trial courts of general jurisdiction. Some states retain formal trial courts of specialized subject-matter jurisdiction, but there is a general trend toward the consolidation of the trial courts of each state, with even the value of the claim becoming a criterion only for administrative assignment of petty cases to particular divisions within a single trial court of general jurisdiction.

The value of the claim remains an important factor in federal subject-matter jurisdiction only with respect to federal diversity jurisdiction, as discussed below (paragraphs 55-63). In such cases jurisdiction often depends on the application of problematic and unsettled rules for assigning value to claims for specific relief. Diversity cases of insufficient value are triable only in state courts.

There are a number of trial courts of specialized jurisdiction within the federal system that operate independently of the federal district courts, such as the US Tax Court, the US Court of Federal Claims, and the US Court of International Trade.[1] Decisions of these courts are reviewed by the same system of federal courts of appeals that reviews decisions of the federal district courts.

1. *Id.*

II. Main Claims and Ancillary Claims

47. In the state courts it is rarely problematic when the main claim routes litigation to a trial court of inferior jurisdiction, and an ancillary claim is later filed that is beyond the jurisdiction of the inferior court. If it is not practicable to sever the ancillary claim for transfer to the trial court of general jurisdiction, the entire case is transferred.

Ancillary claims are a much greater problem for the federal courts. Although the federal district courts are the trial courts of "general" jurisdiction *within* the federal system, the overall federal court system's jurisdiction is inherently limited by the Constitution, and further limited by statute. For many years the federal courts dealt with this problem improvisationally through court-created doctrines of "pendent" and "ancillary" jurisdiction. These doctrines have recently been superseded by a comprehensive statute, discussed below (paragraphs 69-72), that in most cases grants federal district courts "supplemental jurisdiction" of ancillary claims to the broadest extent permitted by the federal Constitution.

III. Overview of the Jurisdiction of the Different Courts

48. The overwhelming preponderance of American litigation, of both a criminal and a civil nature, is heard by state rather than federal courts. Even as to civil suits based on federal law, state courts generally share jurisdictional competence with the federal court system. This is referred to as "concurrent jurisdiction," and it is presumed that any right to sue created by federal law lies within the concurrent jurisdiction of the state courts unless Congress has by statute expressly declared the right to sue to be exclusively within the jurisdiction of the federal courts.

Although federal courts are courts of limited jurisdiction that hear only a small fraction of all litigation brought in American courts, the nature of their jurisdiction leads to a concentration in federal courts of litigation brought by or against foreign nationals and foreign corporations. This concentration justifies extended treatment of the rather complex structure of federal subject-matter jurisdiction within the American legal system.

IV. Subject-Matter Jurisdiction of State Courts

A. Trial Courts

49. Although idiosyncracies may still be found in most states, and the jurisdictional structure of such an important state as New York remains particularly complex, the general trend among state courts has been one of consolidation and simplification at the trial-court level. The most common basis for a formal division of jurisdictional competence between trial courts in a given state is the amount in controversy. Lawsuits seeking relief valued at below the jurisdictional threshold, which is rarely more than USD 25,000, must be heard in an inferior court. The names of such courts are legion, but their importance to any litigation of substance is diminishing. Every state has a statewide system of trial courts of general jurisdiction in which virtually any suit of significance may be brought. Liberal transfer provisions generally permit a suit filed in a state trial court that lacks subject-matter jurisdiction to be transferred without prejudice to the proper court.

The court system of the state of California exemplifies the modern trend of simplification and consolidation. Historically, California's trial courts were bifurcated county-by-county into a "superior court" of general jurisdiction and inferior courts called either "municipal" or "justice" courts depending on the population of the districts served by such courts. Municipal courts served urban areas and justice courts served rural areas. The distinction dated from a time when only municipal courts were courts of record whose judges were professional lawyers. Justice courts at one time were presided over by nonlawyer "justices of the peace." But this system was struck down by the California Supreme Court in 1974 as violative of the mandate of the federal Constitution's Fourteenth Amendment that states conduct judicial proceedings with "due process of law."[1] Since that time the functions and operations of municipal and justice courts were identical, but the terminological distinction was retained because the trial courts were the creatures of local county governments despite their statewide responsibilities. Whether called "municipal" or "justice" courts, these inferior courts conducted petty criminal trials and heard civil suits seeking money damages of up to USD 25,000. In 1998, California consolidated its trial courts into a statewide system of superior courts that are operated by the counties but funded by the state itself. As an administrative matter, but not as a jurisdictional matter, the superior court for each county is organized into divisions that specialize in particular types of civil and criminal proceedings. Every judge is qualified to hear every type of proceeding, enhancing administrative flexibility and ending the possibility of a judgment being invalidated because it was conducted in the wrong state court.

By contrast, the New York state-court system retains a compartmentalized jurisdictional structure. Its trial court of general jurisdiction is called, idiosyncratically, the "Supreme Court." But some types of cases, such as those involving decedent's estates or domestic-relations issues, must be heard by specialized courts such as the "Surrogate's Court" and the "Family Court." While New York's court of last resort, the "Court of Appeals," has been reluctant to invalidate judgments rendered by the wrong court within this unduly complicated structure,[2] there remains a standing risk in New York that a case within the jurisdiction of some state court may be litigated in the wrong state court.

Other states have court systems that fall along a spectrum between the complexity of New York's and the simplicity of California's. But there is one feature common to all states, New York and California included. Regulatory disputes must generally be litigated first in administrative tribunals, which in effect function as courts of limited and specialized subject-matter jurisdiction, before formal judicial review of the resulting administrative determination may be had by a new proceeding commenced in a state trial court – generally but not always its trial court of general jurisdiction. The procedures for such judicial review of administrative orders vary greatly, sometimes featuring trial de novo of disputed facts in the state trial court, but more commonly limited to de novo review only of questions of law as framed by the binding factual determinations of the administrative tribunal. When state trial courts thus review administrative orders on the basis of the factual findings of a state administrative tribunal, they are essentially acting in an appellate capacity.

1. *See Gordon v. Justice Court*, 12 Cal.3d 323, 525 P.2d 72 (Cal. 1974).
2. *See Nuernberger v. State*, 41 N.Y.2d 111, 359 N.E.2d 412 (N.Y. 1976).

B. Appellate Courts

50. Appeal as of right to at least one higher court, the procedural incidents of which are described below (paragraphs 199-206), is virtually a universal feature of American law although it has never been held to be required as part of the federal constitutional guarantee of "due process of law." Every state provides for appeal as of right from decisions of trial courts to at least one higher court, even when the trial court is exercising the essentially appellate function of judicial review of an administrative order. At present, forty-one of the fifty states have an intermediate appellate court system in which appeal as of right lies from the decisions of the trial court of general jurisdiction. In general, decisions of trial courts of inferior jurisdiction are appealable as of right only to the trial court of general jurisdiction, acting in such cases as an appellate court. Decisions of trial courts of general jurisdiction are appealable as of right to the courts of last resort in those states lacking an intermediate appellate court. Decisions of intermediate appellate courts are generally subject only to discretionary review in the court of last resort of those states that have an intermediate appellate system. The US Supreme Court has discretionary appellate jurisdiction of any judgment of the highest state court in which (according to state appellate procedure) review may be had, but only to the extent that the judgment turns on an issue of federal rather than state law.

V. Subject-Matter Jurisdiction of Federal Courts

A. Trial Courts

1. Overview of the Jurisdiction of the Federal District Courts

51. The federal "trial court of general jurisdiction" is the federal district court. The term is somewhat of a misnomer, since it follows from the limited jurisdiction of federal courts that no federal court truly has "general" jurisdiction. Nonetheless it is true that the district court is the federal trial court that generally has jurisdiction of such cases as the federal courts may hear. There are, however, subordinate tiers of inferior federal judges, called "magistrate judges" and "bankruptcy judges," whose decisions are nominally subject to review by federal district judges. Magistrate judges try petty criminal cases and, by consent of the parties, some petty civil cases. Bankruptcy judges preside over bankruptcy courts that formally operate as adjuncts to district courts but functionally operate with nearly complete autonomy from the district courts, although they are subject as well to appellate review by the federal courts of appeals, which often delegate such review to special "bankruptcy appellate panels."

The distinguishing characteristic of federal district judges, as opposed to federal magistrate judges and bankruptcy judges, is that district judges exercise federal judicial power under Article III of the Constitution. As such, federal district judges hold office for life, subject to removal only by impeachment, once they have been appointed by the president and confirmed by the Senate. Although all Article III federal judges are significantly underpaid by the standards of their colleagues at the bar – a problem resulting from the regrettable and unnecessary linkage of judicial salaries to those of members of Congress – accession to such a judgeship remains the capstone achievement of an American lawyer. It is difficult to underestimate the allure and prestige of an Article III federal judgeship. The distinction in the quality of the state and federal judiciaries is palpable, as is the extent of office and staff resources that federal judges enjoy in comparison to their state counterparts. Federal district judges decide, on average, one-third to one-fifth the number of cases per year as their counterpart judges of state courts of general jurisdiction. Yet federal district judges are equipped with full law libraries, virtually unlimited access to electronic legal databases, personal secretaries, and the services of two or three law clerks, who are generally among the top echelon of recent graduates of American law schools. While the quality of justice in federal district courts is not perfect, it is not for lack of supporting resources.

52. These resources (except for judicial salaries) are provided to district judges in support of their subject-matter jurisdiction to hear (in addition to the trial of serious crimes under federal law) civil cases that for the most part fall into one of three categories:

(1) "federal-question" cases arising under federal law;

(2) "diversity" cases between citizens of different states, or between state citizens and aliens, providing that in such cases more than USD 75,000 is in controversy; and
(3) "admiralty" cases arising under federal maritime law.

It should be noted that these three basic categories are discussed here in the context of the three basic jurisdictional statutes conferring subject-matter jurisdiction on the federal district courts. The limited nature of the subject-matter jurisdiction of the federal courts is attributable ultimately to Article III of the federal Constitution, which specifies that federal judicial power may be extended only to certain categories of cases and controversies. With the exception of the US Supreme Court, no federal court is vested with jurisdiction directly by the Constitution itself. All inferior federal courts have only such jurisdiction as has been granted to them by statute. By and large, the constitutional categories of "Article III" jurisdiction have been broadly construed, affording Congress a generous degree of discretion in determining how much litigation is to be directed into the federal court system or left for adjudication by state courts.

This scheme of potentially sweeping federal jurisdiction – permitted by the Constitution but dormant until authorized by Congress – is referred to as the "Madisonian compromise," after James Madison, the principal draftsman and creative genius of the Constitution. There is a standing danger, from the perspective of those concerned about "states' rights," that too expansive a scope of federal jurisdiction will overshadow the role of the states and their courts within the federal system. Under the Madisonian Compromise, the scope of federal jurisdiction is left primarily to the political judgment of Congress. As previously discussed (paragraphs 4-6), Congress itself is a compromise between popular democracy (the House of Representatives) and representatives of the states themselves (the Senate). Thus it is unlikely that the jurisdictional statutes enacted by Congress will blindly serve federal interests at the expense of state autonomy.

Although there are many jurisdictional statutes of limited application that expand federal jurisdiction over particular cases up to, or close to, the constitutional limits of Article III, the vast majority of cases heard by federal district courts fall within the three general jurisdictional statutes that vest the federal district courts with the three categories of jurisdiction mentioned above (paragraph 52). These three statutes are successive sections of the Judicial Code, which is Title 28 of the United States Code. The general federal-question statute is 28 U.S.C. §1331; the general diversity statute is 28 U.S.C. §1332; and the general admiralty statute is 28 U.S.C. §1333. These three statutory grants of subject-matter jurisdiction to the federal district courts are discussed in sequence below, followed by discussion of a fourth statute of special significance to foreign litigants, 28 U.S.C. §1330; a fifth statute, 28 U.S.C. §1367, dealing with lawsuits that feature a mixture of claims (only some of which fall within federal jurisdiction under the preceding statutes); and finally a related set of federal statutes, parasitic on the five jurisdictional statutes previously discussed, permitting the removal to federal court of certain suits filed in state courts.

53. The federal district courts have express statutory discretion to decline to exercise their subject-matter jurisdiction only with respect to the "supplemental" jurisdiction conferred by 28 U.S.C. §1367. In addition, there are several court-created doctrines of "abstention" in which the Supreme Court has permitted, and in some circumstances required, federal district courts – despite the "virtually unflagging obligation" to exercise such subject-matter jurisdiction as they have been given by statute – to invoke the inherent discretion of a court of equitable jurisdiction to decline to exercise that jurisdiction upon a showing of "exceptional circumstances" creating a serious risk of conflict with state governmental authority or of premature adjudication of an unsettled issue of federal constitutional law.[1] There is also a somewhat amorphous doctrine of "justiciability" – grounded in part in the language of Article III of the federal Constitution limiting federal judicial power to actual "cases" or "controversies," and in part on related "prudential" rules of self-restraint adopted by the US Supreme Court – that may prohibit the adjudication of a case otherwise within the statutory subject-matter jurisdiction of a federal district court.[2]

Although the US Supreme Court's cases on justiciability are legion and the topic is one of perennial and often heated dispute within federal constitutional law, the number of cases in which justiciability concerns actually limit the exercise of jurisdiction by federal district courts is quite low. The abstention doctrines are much more frequently asserted by defendants seeking to escape from the jurisdiction of a federal district court, but overall their range of application is also quite limited.[3] The vast majority of cases that qualify for federal subject-matter jurisdiction will, if filed in or removed to a federal district court possessed of both proper venue and territorial jurisdiction over the parties, proceed to judgment in that court. As discussed below, in some instances a change of venue may be granted to another district court within the federal system (paragraph 85), and in rare circumstances a federal district court may relinquish its jurisdiction to permit adjudication in a foreign court under the doctrine of *forum non conveniens* (paragraph 123).

1. *Quackenbush v. Allstate Ins. Co.*, 517 U.S. 706, 716-728 (1996).
2. *See, e.g.*, *Lujan v. Defenders of Wildlife*, 504 U.S. 555, 560 (1992).
3. *See* Steven Pitt & Joshua D. Rogers, "Charting a Course for Federal Removal through the Abstention Doctrine: A Titanic Experience in the Sargasso Sea of Jurisdictional Manipulation," DePaul L. Rev. 56 (2006): 107.

2. Federal-Question Jurisdiction (28 U.S.C. §1331)

54. Under 28 U.S.C. §1331, federal district courts are literally vested with jurisdiction over all cases "arising under" federal law, but the US Supreme Court has construed this general statutory grant of "federal-question" jurisdiction much more narrowly than its literal terms would suggest. At the level of greater detail, the rules governing the federal-question jurisdiction of the federal district courts under 28 U.S.C. §1331 are highly complex and difficult to apply in marginal cases, but the basic principles may be simply stated.

If the right to sue has been created by federal law, the federal district courts have jurisdiction. If federal law provides merely a defense to a right to sue created by state law, the federal district courts lack jurisdiction (absent the diversity of citizenship discussed below), even if the federal defense is dispositive of the suit and is the only issue in contention between the parties. This situation is frequently presented in cases in which the defendant claims an immunity from some state-imposed obligation by virtue of a "preemptive" federal law. The governing principle is often referred to as the "well-pleaded complaint rule," which requires the determination of whether a case arises under federal law to be based only on the well-pleaded allegations of the plaintiff's complaint, without reference to any anticipation by the plaintiff of the reason for the defendant's resistance to the plaintiff's claim of right.[1]

There are three primary sources of complexity in the application of these basic principles for determining when a case arises under federal law so as to fall within the general federal-question jurisdiction of the federal district courts.

First, there are a few cases in which a suit on a state-created right to sue has been held nonetheless to "arise under" federal law when state law has incorporated some element of federal law as the basis for liability under state law. This situation most clearly arises when state law provides a remedy for the breach of some federally created duty. In a leading case, a federal statute imposed certain standards for the labeling of pharmaceutical products sold in interstate or foreign commerce. Enforcement of this duty was left solely to federal administrative proceedings; however, there was no accompanying federal statutory remedy by which a private party harmed by a violation of the labeling standards could sue for damages as a matter of federal law. Private parties sued for damages under state tort law on the ground that the defendant's violation of the federal labeling statute constituted actionable negligence as a matter of state tort law. The US Supreme Court applied a frankly pragmatic standard to determine that, in this instance, the issue of federal law (whether the defendants had violated the federal labeling statute) was not a sufficiently "substantial" element of the state-law tort claim to bring the case within the federal-question jurisdiction of the federal district courts.[2] But the Supreme Court acknowledged that similar cases had been differently decided, and left these decisions undisturbed – thus preserving the confused and unsatisfactory condition of this corner of the law of federal jurisdiction.[3]

Second, there are a few cases that depart from the usual rule that the possible federal preemption of a state-created right to sue raises merely a defensive issue of federal law, and thus is not the kind of issue that brings a case within the federal-question jurisdiction of the federal district courts. In these exceptional cases the sweep of a federal statute has been found to be so broad that any parallel state power to regulate the activity in question has been cut off or "completely preempted." Although the lower courts have applied the "complete preemption" doctrine more broadly, only three federal statutes have been given this sweeping construction by the US Supreme Court: §301 of the Labor-Management Relations Act, §502 of the Employees Retirement Income Security Act, and §86 of the National Bank Act.[4] It follows from the construction of these provisions that any lawsuit seeking to enforce the rights they create is a suit upon a federally created right, even if the plaintiff by "artful pleading" seeks to characterize the suit as one to enforce only parallel rights under state law. Because this doctrine of "complete preemption" results in the re-characterization of the putative state-law right to sue invoked by the plaintiff as inherently a federal right, it is most frequently encountered in the context of the "removal" of a case from a state trial court to a federal district court. The right of defendants to remove cases from state to federal courts is discussed below (paragraphs 74-75).

Third, the advent of a new form of judicial relief, the "declaratory judgment" that resolves disputes of law without ordering coercive relief, has unsettled the jurisdictional categories created by the "well-pleaded complaint rule." Under that rule federal issues of a defensive nature are not sufficient to bring a case within the federal-question jurisdiction of the federal district courts. But the enactment in 1934 of the Federal Declaratory Judgment Act permitted a lawsuit to be filed for the express purpose of resolving a concrete controversy between opposing parties about any issue of federal law. Many states have enacted similar laws authorizing suits for declaratory judgments.

Suppose, for instance, that party A has a contract with party B, enforceable under state law, calling for some kind of performance that may have been rendered illegal by a new federal statute. It was held in the *Mottley* case that if A sues B on the contract, the "well-pleaded complaint rule" bars federal-question jurisdiction under 28 U.S.C. §1331 even though the only dispute between the parties is whether the new federal statute preempts state law, thus providing B with a federal defense to A's state-law suit to compel performance of the contract.[5] By invoking either the federal Declaratory Judgment Act or one of its state-law counterparts, either A or B could instead sue for purely declaratory relief. An essential element of the well-pleaded complaint for such declaratory relief would of course be the issue of federal law about which the parties are in dispute. The US Supreme Court has twice decided, however, that the availability of declaratory relief does not change the jurisdictional posture of such a suit. Instead, the suit must be analyzed as if it were, hypothetically, a suit for whatever coercive relief would be available but for the new procedural option of seeking only declaratory relief.[6]

Although this convoluted reasoning borders on nonsense, the US Supreme Court has justified it on the ground that the legislative history of the federal Declaratory Judgment Act did not demonstrate the sort of political decision to expand the scope of federal jurisdiction that is required by the Madisonian Compromise. Thus, until Congress expressly changes the jurisdictional rules as they pertain to suits for declaratory relief as to issues of federal law, the Supreme Court has mandated that the pre-existing rules of federal-question jurisdiction be applied as if suits for declaratory relief did not exist.

1. *See, e.g., Louisville & Nashville R.R. v. Mottley*, 211 U.S. 149 (1908), the contract case discussed below as a leading example of the well-pleaded complaint rule.
2. *See Merrell Dow Pharmaceuticals Inc. v. Thompson*, 478 U.S. 804, 814 (1986).
3. The Supreme Court reaffirmed the pragmatic approach of *Merrell Dow*, and again "disclaimed the adoption of any bright-line rule," in *Grable & Sons Metal Products, Inc. v. Darue Engineering & Manufacturing*, 545 U.S. 308, 317 (2005). The court declared: "the question is, does a state-law claim necessarily raise a stated federal issue, actually disputed and substantial, which a federal forum may entertain without disturbing any congressionally approved balance of federal and state judicial responsibilities." Id., at 314.
4. *See Beneficial National Bank v. Anderson*, 539 U.S. 1 (2003).
5. *Louisville & Nashville RR. Co. v. Mottley*, 211 U.S. 149 (1908).
6. *See Franchise Tax Board v. Construction Laborers Vacation Trust*, 463 U.S. 1 (1983); *Skelly Oil Co. v. Phillips Petroleum Co.*, 339 U.S. 667 (1950).

3. Diversity Jurisdiction (28 U.S.C. §1332)

55. In principle, federal diversity jurisdiction is simple enough. Suits between citizens of different states, or between a citizen of a state and an alien, may be brought in the federal district courts if the amount in controversy exceeds a stated sum, currently USD 75,000. This avoids the risk that litigation significantly implicating interstate or international interests might be affected by the local bias of a state rather than a national court system.

It is well established that Article III of the Constitution permits federal courts to hear such cases if there is any degree of diversity between opposing litigants. That is, if just one of several plaintiffs is of diverse citizenship from just one of several defendants, the Constitution permits the suit to be heard by a federal court. Congress has authorized the federal district courts to hear suits when such "minimal diversity" exists only in three special contexts: when the suit involves the "interpleader" of rival claimants to the same property, suits under the Multiparty, Multiforum Trial Jurisdiction Act of 2002, and suits under the Class Action Fairness Act of 2005.[1] Under the general diversity statute, 28 U.S.C. §1332, however, it is well established that the federal district courts lack jurisdiction unless "complete diversity" exists.[2] This means that if any plaintiff is a co-citizen of any defendant, federal diversity jurisdiction is lacking.

1. The federal interpleader statute is 28 U.S.C. §1335. It was held to require only "minimal diversity" in *State Farm and Casualty Co. v. Tashire*, 386 U.S. 523 (1967). The Class Action Fairness Act (CAFA) added a series of complex and rather ragged provisions – greatly broadening federal subject-matter jurisdiction in the class-action context, but also making it partially discretionary – in the form of sprawling new subsection (d) of the general diversity statute, 28 U.S.C. §1332. CAFA also enacted a parallel expansion of federal removal law relating to class actions. *See* 28 U.S.C. §1453. *See generally* 7A Wright, *supra*, §1756.2 (Supp. 2008). The net effect of CAFA is to allow any class action in which there is minimal diversity of citizenship between any plaintiff class member and any defendant, and the aggregate value of the claims asserted on behalf of the plaintiff class exceeds USD five million, to be either commenced in or removed to federal court. Congress's apparent intent was to avoid perceived abuses of the class-action device that had allegedly occurred in the courts of some states, by concentrating such litigation in federal court where it could be administered according to nationally uniform standards of practice and rules of procedure under the ultimate supervision of the US Supreme Court. It is too early to tell how effective CAFA will be, and whether the new burdens it imposes upon federal judges to manage large, interstate class actions will impair the effective functioning of the federal courts in other types of litigation. The earlier and less ambitious Multiparty, Multiforum Trial Jurisdiction Act added 28 U.S.C. §§1369, 1441(e), and miscellaneous other provisions to the federal Judicial Code. The Act deals with mass torts in which at least seventy-five people have died at a single location, permitting resulting litigation to be commenced in or removed to federal court unless the mass tort is essentially localized, involving events in and parties from only one state. *See generally* 7 Wright, *supra*, §1659 (Supp. 2008). For analysis of the expansion of federal diversity jurisdiction in both the mass-tort and class-action contexts, see James E. Pfander, "Protective Jurisdiction, Aggregate Litigation, and the Limits of Article III," Calif. L. Rev. 95 (2007): 1423; C. Douglas Floyd, "The Limits of Minimal Diversity," Hastings L. J. 55 (2004): 613.
2. *See Strawbridge v. Curtiss*, 7 U.S. (3 Cranch) 267 (1806).

56. In principle, the same rules of substantive law apply whether a lawsuit is litigated in a state or federal court. State courts are bound by the Supremacy Clause of Article VI of the federal Constitution to follow federal substantive law whenever it applies. Under the "*Erie* doctrine," federal courts are required by the Rules of Decision Act, 28 U.S.C. §1652, to apply state substantive law whenever it applies,[1] as it generally does when federal courts possess jurisdiction only by virtue of the diversity of citizenship of the parties. But federal and state procedural rules often vary in ways that may affect the outcome of litigation; federal venue rules (discussed below, paragraph 84) and the size of federal districts may affect the demographics and hence the voting patterns of juries in civil cases, and there may indeed be a tendency of local bias in at least some cases if tried in state courts. These factors give parties an incentive in many cases to manipulate the rules of federal diversity jurisdiction in order to secure, or avoid, trial in federal court. The practical application of the requirements of complete diversity and a sufficient amount in controversy generates many complexities designed to deal with these incentives for manipulation.

The federal court is not bound to accept the litigation as it has been structured by the plaintiff or plaintiffs. The doctrine of "fraudulent joinder" requires that the federal court determine its jurisdiction without regard to claims asserted in the complaint by or against nondiverse parties who are not subject to the territorial jurisdiction (discussed below, paragraphs 86-109) of the state in which suit has been brought, or against whom no legally substantial claim has been asserted. The doctrine of "realignment" permits federal courts to treat nominal plaintiffs as functional defendants, and nominal defendants as functional plaintiffs, according to their true alignment of interests in the litigation.[2]

Quite aside from any issues of the improper joinder or alignment of certain parties, the determination of the parties' citizenship can pose difficult questions in particular cases.

1. *See Erie R. Co. v. Tompkins*, 304 U.S. 64 (1938).
2. *See United States Fidelity & Guar. Co. v. A & S Mfg. Co.*, 48 F.3rd 131, 132 (4th Cir. 1995) (citing the circuit split). *See also*, e.g., *United States Fidelity & Guar. Co. v. Thomas Solvent Co.*, 955 F.2nd 1085, 1088-1091 (6th Cir. 1992); *Employers Ins. of Wausau v. Crown Cork & Seal Co.*, 942 F.2nd 862, 864-867 (3rd Cir. 1991); *Continental Airlines, Inc. v. Goodyear Tire & Rubber Co.*, 819 F.2nd 1519, 1523 n.2 (9th Cir. 1987).

57. Natural persons domiciled in a state are deemed citizens of that state if they are either citizens of the United States or are aliens admitted to the United States for permanent residence. "Domicile" in this sense is a term of art within the law of federal jurisdiction. The domicile of a minor is deemed to be that of the child's parents, or of the custodial parent. At the age of eighteen, the child gains the capacity to change his or her domicile. No person's previous domicile is ever lost until that person has established a new domicile, and this can be accomplished only by establishing residence in the place of new domicile with the intention of making this one's home for the indefinite future. Because the jurisdictionally significant act of establishing a new domicile depends upon two facts, one objective in nature (residence in the new state of domicile) and one subjective in nature (intent to remain resident there indefinitely), the party whose domicile is in question has an obvious opportunity – and frequently an equally obvious incentive – to report whatever state of mind will serve that party's litigative interests. For this reason federal courts will often look beyond the self-serving testimony of interested parties to whatever objective evidence may exist of intent to reside in the new state indefinitely, or merely temporarily. The results of such analysis are predictably unpredictable.

For example, take the case of a student who was born and raised in the state of Kansas and at the age of eighteen briefly enrolled in a state university in Kansas. After an illness for which the student received treatment from a physician in Kansas, the student transferred to a state university in Colorado. Before doing so the student obtained under false pretenses a Colorado driver's license purporting to show his residence in Colorado, and used this license to avoid paying out-of-state tuition at the university in Colorado. The student remained enrolled at the university in Colorado for only a few months, but during this time brought a federal diversity suit in Kansas against the doctor who had treated him (or, as the student alleged, mistreated him) for his earlier illness. In this suit the student, as plaintiff, claimed to be a citizen of Colorado, and hence of diverse citizenship from the defendant doctor, who was indisputably a citizen of Kansas. After several temporary jobs in Colorado in the ski industry, the former student returned to his parents' home in Kansas for medical treatment of a skiing injury, and later enrolled again in a state university in Kansas. The federal district court in Kansas refused, however, to dismiss the student's long-pending lawsuit for lack of diversity jurisdiction. The court held correctly that the relevant diversity need exist only at the time of suit. At the time of suit the plaintiff was a first-year college student with a false driver's license listing him as resident at a friend's house where he had never resided, and in fact the student was residing in temporary quarters in a college dormitory. The district court held, quite doubtfully in the view of the present writers, that at this time the student had indeed established (as he testified) a new domicile in Colorado.[1]

1. *See Bair v. Peck*, 738 F. Supp. 1354 (D. Kan. 1990).

58. The riddle of domicile need be resolved only for aliens who have the immigration status of permanent residents of the United States. Such an alien is deemed to be a citizen of the state in which he or she is domiciled. It follows from the literal text of the diversity-jurisdiction statute, 28 U.S.C. §1332, that such an alien could, as a state citizen, invoke federal diversity jurisdiction in a suit brought against another alien. Most federal courts that have considered this question have soundly concluded that such a suit, although within the scope of §1332's grant of jurisdiction, is constitutionally impermissible since the judicial power authorized by Article III of the federal Constitution contains no provision permitting suit by one alien against another alien. The idea that some aliens may be deemed citizens of the states in which they are domiciled is purely a statutory notion, and no statute can grant federal jurisdiction beyond that authorized by Article III of the Constitution.

For all aliens not admitted to the United States for permanent residence, their place of domicile is irrelevant for federal jurisdictional purposes. Federal diversity jurisdiction, sometimes referred to in this specific application as "alienage jurisdiction," extends to a suit by an alien against a citizen of a state, or to a suit by a citizen of a state against an alien, provided in both instances that the requisite amount is in controversy, and further (for the constitutional reasons discussed above) that the citizen of a state is for international purposes a citizen of the United States rather than a permanent resident alien domiciled in a state.

The statutory rule of complete diversity previously discussed (paragraph 55) applies to suits to which aliens are party, with one exception. Two plaintiffs, one a citizen of France and one a citizen of Germany, may invoke diversity jurisdiction in a suit against a United States citizen domiciled in, and hence a citizen of, any state. But two plaintiffs, one a citizen of France and one a citizen of Kansas, may not invoke diversity jurisdiction in a suit they jointly bring against a citizen of Germany. However, by a special statutory provision (28 U.S.C. §1332(a)(3)) that draws on the broader constitutional authority to grant jurisdiction to federal district courts where merely minimal diversity exists, federal district courts do have jurisdiction of a suit between citizens of different states (e.g., a suit by a citizen of Kansas against a citizen of Colorado) even if aliens are joined both as additional plaintiffs and additional defendants.

A citizen of the United States who is domiciled outside of the United States, and hence not in any state, occupies a quite anomalous position for purposes of federal diversity jurisdiction. Such a person is neither an alien nor, for lack of domicile in any state, a citizen of a state. Such a person is thus ineligible for federal diversity jurisdiction, whether bringing suit as a plaintiff or being sued as a defendant. A famous case illustrates this point.[1] The American actress Elizabeth Taylor and the British actor Richard Burton began a notorious affair while under contract with an American movie studio to perform the leading roles in the film "Cleopatra." The production of the film was repeatedly delayed, at great expense, while the stars were absent from the set. The studio later sought to invoke federal diversity jurisdiction in a suit brought jointly against both Ms. Taylor and Mr. Burton. The suit was held to qualify for federal diversity jurisdiction with respect to Mr. Burton, since the studio was a citizen of California (see the discussion below of corporate citizenship, paragraph 60) and Mr. Burton was an alien. But the suit was dismissed as to Ms. Taylor, because at the time the suit was filed she had established a new domicile in London, England, where she was then living with Mr. Burton. As such, she was an American citizen but not the citizen of any state.

1. *Twentieth Century Fox Films Corp. v. Taylor*, 239 F. Supp. 913 (S.D.N.Y. 1965).

59. Unincorporated entities such as partnerships and labor unions are transparent for federal diversity purposes. They have no citizenship status independent of their members, and are thus deemed to have the collective citizenship of all of their members. Together with the rule of complete diversity, this makes it difficult to invoke federal diversity jurisdiction of any suit by or against large unincorporated entities, since it is likely that such entities will have at least one member who is a co-citizen or fellow alien of at least one opposing party. Although some partnerships are organized in ways that mimic the organization of corporations, shielding some forms of partnerships from liability for the general activities of the partnership – generally investors, rather than managers, who hold merely "limited" partnerships – the US Supreme Court has held that under the current provisions of 28 U.S.C. §1332 these partnerships are still to be treated as having the collective citizenship of all of their partners, regardless of their class of partnership or the functional similarity of the partnership to a corporation.

60. A corporation, on the other hand, does have a citizenship status that is independent of its shareholders. The distinct treatment of corporations as citizens of their state of incorporation dates from the decisions of the United States Supreme Court in the nineteenth century, but since 1958 has been codified by 28 U.S.C. §1332(c). Under this statute, corporations may be citizens of multiple states: any state in which they are incorporated (generally only one state) and also of the one state (if not a state of incorporation) in which the corporation maintains its "principal place of business." The determination of the principal place of business of a corporation with activities in several states has been much litigated in lower-court cases in which federal diversity jurisdiction has been contested, but to date the Supreme Court has not rendered an authoritative decision.

Nonetheless, most cases can be resolved by application of a three-step test. First, the principal place of business should be that state in which the preponderance of corporate business is conducted. Second, if there is no such preponderant concentration of corporate business in one state, the principal place of business is that state in which the corporation conducts a significant amount of business activity and also maintains its administrative headquarters. Third, if the corporation maintains its administrative headquarters in a state in which no significant business activity otherwise occurs, the principal place of business is that state in which the corporation is most frequently sued. Depending on the nature of the corporation's activities, this may be either the state in which the corporate headquarters is located, or the state in which the corporation conducts the largest proportion of its far-flung business activities.

Alien corporations are generally treated simply as citizens of the foreign state by which they have been incorporated, but a foreign corporation that has its *worldwide* "principal place of business" in a state of the United States will also be deemed to be a citizen of that state.

Suppose, for example, Greek corporation A operates cruise ships from ports in Athens, Greece, Miami, Florida, US, and Sydney, Australia. Passengers B, C, and D are injured in Miami in a traffic accident while traveling in A's bus from their hotel to A's terminal for embarkation on A's ship. B is a citizen of the United States domiciled in Florida, and C is a citizen of the United States domiciled in California. Whether B can invoke federal diversity jurisdiction to sue A in a federal district court depends on whether A is a citizen not only of Greece, where it is incorporated, but also of Florida, where it may have its principal place of business. If A is deemed to be a citizen of both Greece and Florida, B's suit is disqualified from diversity jurisdiction because a citizen of Florida would be both a plaintiff and a defendant. There would thus be no "diversity of citizenship."

Although Florida is the only state in which A conducts business in the United States, that fact alone does not make Florida A's "principal place of business" for diversity purposes. The three-step test discussed above must be applied to determine whether Florida is also A's worldwide principal place of business. If a clear majority of A's revenues are generated by cruises operated from its port in Florida, it is likely that under the first step of the three-step test Florida would be deemed to be A's principal place of business, worldwide. A would thus be deemed a citizen of Florida as well as Greece, and B could not invoke diversity jurisdiction to sue A in a federal district court. If A's operations are more evenly dispersed, and if A's corporate headquarters are located in Athens, from which it also operates cruises, then it is likely that under the second step of the three-step test Athens would be deemed to be A's principal place of business, worldwide. A would thus be deemed a citizen only of Greece, and B's suit against A would qualify for the diversity jurisdiction of a federal district court.

Whether A was deemed to be a citizen of Greece only, or of both Greece and Florida, would be irrelevant to the eligibility for diversity jurisdiction of the suit against A by C. Since C is a citizen of California, diversity will exist whether or not A is deemed to be a state citizen of Florida as well as an alien citizen of Greece. A's possible state citizenship in Florida is also irrelevant to the jurisdictional posture of D's suit against A. D is a citizen of Great Britain, and hence an alien. Whether or not A is deemed to be a citizen of the state of Florida on account of having its worldwide principal place of business there, A is indisputably also a citizen of Greece, and hence, like D, an alien. Although A and D are citizens or subjects of different foreign sovereigns, this is not the sort of "diversity of citizenship" to which federal diversity jurisdiction extends. Except in the special situation discussed above (paragraph 58) where aliens may join as additional parties to a suit between citizens of different states under 28 U.S.C. §1332(a)(3), an alien may not invoke diversity jurisdiction to sue another alien.

61. One further complexity is introduced into the law of federal diversity jurisdiction by the requirement, independent of the requisite diversity of citizenship between the parties, that the lawsuit involve a sufficient amount in controversy. No jurisdictional amount is required as a condition of the federal-question or admiralty jurisdiction of the federal district courts, but diversity jurisdiction requires that the amount in controversy exceed a stipulated sum, exclusive of interest added to the judgment, and exclusive of the costs of suit.

In a simple diversity suit for damages brought by a single plaintiff against a single defendant, the rules for determining the amount in controversy are relatively uncomplicated. The amount claimed "in good faith" by the plaintiff is the measure of the amount in controversy, so a plaintiff desiring to invoke federal diversity jurisdiction need only demand a sum of damages in excess of the statutory threshold. That threshold, which is stated in the first sentence of 28 U.S.C. §1332(a), has been frequently raised in recent years. As of 2008, it is set at USD 75,000. It should be noted that the amount in controversy required for diversity jurisdiction is an amount *in excess* of the statutory figure. Thus a suit seeking *exactly* USD 75,000 would not presently qualify for federal diversity jurisdiction by the slim but legally significant margin of a single cent.

The frequent references in caselaw to the "good faith" standard for determining the amount in controversy are somewhat misleading. While it is true that the sum of damages claimed in good faith by the plaintiff is presumptively accepted as determinative of the amount in controversy, this presumption may not be overcome simply by challenging the *subjective* "good faith" of the plaintiff. The standard is in fact an *objective* one, requiring that the defendant who challenges the amount claimed by the plaintiff establish to a "legal certainty" that as a matter of law the plaintiff cannot recover a sum in excess of the statutory threshold. For example, a plaintiff who seeks damages for personal injuries and is entitled by law to recover noneconomic damages for "pain and suffering" incident to the injury can with virtual impunity claim damages in excess of the USD 75,000 threshold for diversity jurisdiction.[1] But in some circumstances only certain types of damages may be legally recoverable for a certain type of injury. In one leading case, the plaintiff's shipment of goods to a customer was wrongfully detained by a competitor. The plaintiff sued the competitor not only for the value of the goods (concededly less than the required jurisdictional amount) but also for consequential damages to the value of the plaintiff's business, which raised the value of the plaintiff's claim above the jurisdictional threshold. Because it was established to a "legal certainty" that the applicable substantive law did not allow recovery of consequential damages, the plaintiff's reliance on such damages was unavailing, and the case was dismissed for lack of jurisdiction.[2] The "legal certainty" rule has important ramifications in cases in which punitive damages are legally recoverable. Even a plaintiff who has suffered only slight personal injury can easily claim sufficient punitive damages to satisfy the jurisdictional amount required for diversity jurisdiction.

1. *But cf. Burns v. Anderson*, 502 F.2nd 970 (5th Cir. 1974).
2. *See Vance v. W.A. Vandercook*, 170 U.S. 468 (1898).

62. More difficult problems are presented when a plaintiff seeks specific relief, such as an injunction or the abatement of a nuisance. The diversity statute provides no guidance on how to value such controversies, and the Supreme Court merely restated the problem by declaring in a famous case that "the value of the object" must govern the determination of the amount in controversy.[1] In that case, the alleged nuisance of the defendant's railroad-bridge piers across the Mississippi River impeded the plaintiff's riverboat business, and the plaintiff sought abatement of the nuisance. It was obvious that the cost of removing or relocating the bridge would exceed the required amount, but it was not obvious that the value of the plaintiff's business, or at least of its diminution in value should the plaintiff's suit be unsuccessful, would exceed that amount. In upholding diversity jurisdiction the Supreme Court failed to specify just which of these calculations it had in mind as "the value of the object" of the litigation. The general rule followed by the lower courts is that specific relief may be valued from either party's perspective, as measured either by the loss to the plaintiff in the absence of relief, or by the cost to the defendant should the requested relief be granted.

1. *See Mississippi and Mo. R.R. Co. v. Ward*, 67 U.S. 485 (1862).

63. The final area of controversy relating to the determination of the amount in controversy concerns the aggregation of multiple claims that have been joined together in a single lawsuit under the liberal rules of joinder of claims and parties followed by the federal courts, as discussed below (paragraphs 151-152). Aggregation of the amount of damages has traditionally been permitted only in two circumstances.[1] First, a particular plaintiff may rely on the aggregate value of all claims asserted by that plaintiff against a particular defendant. Second, multiple plaintiffs can aggregate the value of their individual claims against a common defendant, and a single plaintiff can aggregate the value of multiple claims asserted against a group of defendants, in the relatively unusual circumstance where the right or liability at issue is "joint" rather than "several".

An example of the first exception is where plaintiff A of Texas asserts two claims against defendant B of Georgia for B's breach of two distinct contracts. If plaintiff A claims in good faith a right to damages of USD 50,000 resulting from B's breach of the first contract and a right to damages of USD 30,000 resulting from B's breach of the second contract, the two claims may be aggregated, and since their aggregate value of USD 80,000 exceeds the current threshold of USD 75,000, A may invoke diversity jurisdiction to sue B in a federal district court. This is true even though neither claim standing alone is of sufficient value, and, oddly enough, even if the claims are completely unrelated except that each is between the same pair of claiming and defending parties.

An example of the second exception is where negligent driver C of Oregon causes an automobile accident that damages the property of A of Texas and B of Georgia. If the damage to A and B consists of the total destruction of two automobiles, one owned by A and worth USD 50,000, the other owned by B and worth USD 30,000, A and B cannot jointly invoke diversity jurisdiction to sue C in a federal district court. A and B's ownership interests in their respective automobiles are "several" and not "joint," and aggregation of the amount of damages each may claim is not permitted. But suppose instead that C's negligence caused the complete destruction of a race car worth USD 80,000 and owned jointly and in equal shares by A and B. Aggregation of their joint claims for damages is permitted, even though neither A nor B has suffered more than USD 40,000 in harm, and their aggregated claims for a total of USD 80,000 in damages permit them to invoke diversity jurisdiction to sue C in a federal district court.

A variant of the "aggregation" problem is presented when a single plaintiff asserts a claim for damages presently owed that does not exceed the jurisdictional amount, but the judicial establishment of that claim will as a matter of law create the virtual certainty that in due course the plaintiff will become entitled to additional damages that, aggregated over time, will exceed the jurisdictional amount. As noted above, the first exception to the general rule of nonaggregation of multiple claims to meet the jurisdictional amount permits such aggregation when a single plaintiff asserts multiple claims against a single defendant. But it is well established that only multiple claims that are presently ripe for adjudication may thus be aggregated. The value of future claims may not be aggregated to the value of such claims as the plaintiff has a present right to enforce in court, even if the future ripening of those claims is a virtual certainty, and even if the outcome of that future litigation will be foreordained by the preclusive effect of the current litigation under the doctrine of res judicata, discussed below (paragraphs 279-284).

This situation frequently arises in cases involving the breach of an obligation to make periodic payments, as under an insurance contract or a lease. In such cases, the computation of the amount presently in controversy is controlled by the applicable substantive law. In some installment-payment cases, the substantive law will permit an immediate action of "anticipatory breach" of the entire series of contractual obligations. If so, the plaintiff's legally permissible present claims for such contract damages as have accrued to date may be aggregated to the plaintiff's legally permissible present claim for future damages resulting from the anticipatory breach of future obligations of payment. But absent some such substantive legal doctrine that accelerates the plaintiff's right to sue for contractual performances not yet due from the defendant, aggregation is not permitted.[2]

1. In *Exxon Mobil Corp. v. Allapattah Services, Inc.*, 545 U.S. 546 (2005), the Supreme Court of the US authorized what amounts to a third type of aggregation by holding that claims for less than the jurisdictional amount by additional plaintiffs in a diversity case are within the "supplemental" jurisdiction of the federal district court under 28 U.S.C. §1367, provided that (1) the additional plaintiffs are joined under either Rule 20 (permissive joinder of parties) or Rule 23 (class actions), (2) the additional plaintiffs do not destroy the "complete diversity" required for the district court to exercise original jurisdiction under 28 U.S.C. §1332, and (3) the claims of the additional plaintiffs arise out of the same case or controversy as the claims over which the district court has jurisdiction under §1332. Supplemental jurisdiction under §1367 is discussed below (paras 69-72).
2. *See Town of Elgin v. Marshall*, 106 U.S. 578 (1883); *also see Beaman v. Pacific Mutual Life Ins. Co.*, 369 F.2nd 653 (4th Cir. 1966).

4. Admiralty Jurisdiction (28 U.S.C. §1333)

64. Federal courts have jurisdiction without regard to the amount in controversy of all actions to redress maritime torts and to enforce maritime contracts. Maritime torts are defined by a locality test, which has recently been narrowed by the additional requirement that the allegedly tortious conduct be related to traditional maritime activity. Maritime contracts are defined by their subject matter. In general, all contracts that deal with maritime activity qualify as maritime contracts, but with some surprising exceptions. Federal admiralty jurisdiction is nominally exclusive; state courts lack concurrent jurisdiction to act as admiralty courts in the strict sense of courts competent to grant certain forms of relief that historically were the exclusive province of the British admiralty courts before the American Revolution, most notably the seizure of a vessel as a means of asserting jurisdiction over the owners of the vessel in connection with a suit upon a maritime tort or contract, or, conversely, the limitation of the liability of vessel owners to the value of the vessel that caused certain forms of maritime torts. But the "saving to suitors" clause of 28 U.S.C. §1333, which dates back to the first Federal Judiciary Act of 1789, has always preserved the right of plaintiffs to seek the classic common-law remedy of money damages by suing upon a maritime tort or contract in a nonadmiralty court, i.e., a state court or a federal court exercising diversity jurisdiction.

65. The "saving to suitors" clause vastly complicates analysis of the effectively concurrent jurisdiction of state and federal courts to adjudicate claims for damages caused by maritime torts or breaches of maritime contracts. At the outset it should be noted that the substantive law to be applied in determining whether a maritime tort has been committed, or a maritime contract has been created and breached, is exclusively federal in nature. This raises the immediate question whether any lawsuit premised on a maritime tort or contract is not, ipso facto, a case arising under federal law and hence within the federal-question jurisdiction conferred upon the federal district courts by 28 U.S.C. §1331, discussed above (paragraph 54). In the famous *Romero* case, the US Supreme Court sternly answered "no," for reasons of both history and policy.[1] An understanding of this decision requires elaboration of the special features of a federal court when acting as an admiralty court.

Cases adjudicated by a federal district court on the basis of the admiralty jurisdiction conferred by 28 U.S.C. §1333 are said to be litigated on "the admiralty side" of that court, as opposed to "the law side." In cases on "the admiralty side" the federal district court follows certain modes of procedure associated with pre-revolutionary British admiralty courts; in cases on "the law side," where its jurisdiction is conferred by 28 U.S.C. §1331 (federal-question cases) and 28 U.S.C. §1332 (diversity cases) the federal district court follows the different procedures associated with the pre-revolutionary British common-law courts. Although most procedural differences between admiralty and common-law procedure have been eliminated by the 1966 merger of the Admiralty Rules with the Federal Rules of Civil Procedure, one difference of vast importance remains. The right of jury trial in common-law actions, guaranteed in federal courts by the Seventh Amendment to the United States Constitution and independently guaranteed in all state courts as a matter of state law, is inapplicable to cases tried "in admiralty," which is another way of saying "on the admiralty side" of a federal district court.

The historic role of the "saving to suitors" clause has been to preserve the right of jury trial for suitors who do not need to take advantage of the exclusive power of an admiralty court to seize a vessel and to exercise in rem jurisdiction against that vessel whether or not it can exercise in personam jurisdiction over the owners of the vessel. A federal district court exercising admiralty jurisdiction can grant money damages, but in order to have their cases tried to a jury, most plaintiffs who seek only money damages will take advantage of the "saving to suitors" clause to file suits based on maritime torts and contracts in state court, or on "the law side" of a federal district court. Historically, the right to file a "saving to suitors" action "on the law side" of a federal district court has been limited to cases in which the parties are of complete diversity of citizenship, and the requisite amount is in controversy. In this sense, "saving to suitors" cases are treated like any other case within the jurisdiction of state courts: if, and only if, there is complete diversity of citizenship and a sufficient sum is in controversy, the plaintiff has the option of filing the suit in a federal district court instead of a state court.

The original versions of both 28 U.S.C. §1332 (diversity jurisdiction) and 28 U.S.C. §1333 (admiralty jurisdiction) were first enacted in 1789. The original version of 28 U.S.C. §1331 (federal-question jurisdiction) was not enacted until 1875. Thus this system by which "saving to suitors" actions could be brought on the law side of a federal court (instead of in state court) only if diversity existed, was well established when federal courts were given general federal-question jurisdiction in 1875. In the *Romero* case the US Supreme Court found no evidence that Congress intended to upset the settled jurisdictional rules governing "saving to suitors" actions when it enacted the predecessor to 28 U.S.C. §1331 in 1875. Had the Supreme Court ruled to the contrary, state courts would have been almost totally excluded from adjudication of "saving to suitors" cases because a plaintiff seeking only money damages on account of a maritime tort or contract could always have brought suit "on the law side" of a federal district court by invoking federal-question jurisdiction even if diversity jurisdiction were unavailable. Given the choice, most maritime-law plaintiffs would elect a federal forum if one were available without sacrifice of the right to jury trial, because as previously noted (paragraph 64) the applicable substantive law is federal law, in which federal judges have particular expertise. While this might logically justify giving federal courts plenary jurisdiction of all "saving to suitors" actions, it would not only diminish the importance of state courts but would also add substantially to the caseloads of the federal district courts.

The *Romero* case thus reaffirmed the existing system by which maritime plaintiffs can have the best of both worlds – federal judges but jury trials – only when a "saving to suitors" action qualifies for diversity jurisdiction under 28 U.S.C. §1332. A maritime claim does not "arise under" federal law for purposes of federal-question jurisdiction under 28 U.S.C. §1331.

1. *Romero v. Int'l Terminal Operating Co.*, 358 U.S. 354 (1959). *See also* Fabrizio Marella, "Emerging Dilemmas in International Economic Arbitration: Unity and Diversity in International Arbitration: The Case of Maritime Arbitration," Am. U. Int'l L. Rev. 20 (2005): 1055.

66. There are many cases, especially those between commercial interests, in which the plaintiff is quite happy to forego jury trial in order to proceed in a federal forum. If the suit involves a maritime tort or contract, the admiralty jurisdiction conferred on federal district courts by 28 U.S.C. §1333 provides access to a federal court that might not otherwise exist under 28 U.S.C. §§1331-1332, and in addition provides access to the unique admiralty remedies previously mentioned – principally in rem jurisdiction over vessels and orders limiting the liability of shipowners. Even when the plaintiff chooses to bring a nonadmiralty suit for damages in a state court or (when diversity exists) on the law side of a federal district court, thereby invoking the "saving to suitors" clause, the conclusion that a maritime tort or contract is in issue triggers the application of federal maritime law rather than the substantive state law that would otherwise apply. Thus the classification of a particular tort or contract claim as involving a distinctly "maritime" tort or contract has profound significance not only for the place and mode of trial, but also for the rules by which liability will be determined.

In the early years of the federal court system, federal admiralty courts followed the British conception of the maritime tort locality as embracing not only torts on the high seas and in coastal waters, but also as far up navigable rivers as could be detected the "ebb and flow" of salt-water tides. This test conveniently extended the jurisdiction of the British admiralty courts to the London docks, but proved unduly restrictive when applied to American lakes and rivers – such as the Mississippi River – that served as highways of maritime commerce far from any intrusion of tidal waters. By the mid-nineteenth century, a new and distinctly American locality test had emerged, under which the maritime tort jurisdiction of the federal courts was extended to any body of water navigable in interstate or foreign commerce. By the middle of the twentieth century, this locality test had become too inclusive, however, making maritime torts of pleasure-boat and waterskiing accidents, as well as aviation accidents occurring on or over navigable waters. In one such aviation case, the US Supreme Court qualified the locality test by adding, as an additional criterion for a tort to be deemed a maritime tort, that the activity in question bear a substantial relationship to traditional maritime activity.[1] This "maritime nexus" rider to the locality test for maritime torts has been applied literally rather than by analogy. Thus aviation accidents occurring on navigable waters generally do not have the required nexus,[2] even though the aviation industry today performs much the same function of transporting goods, mail, and persons that once was the function of the shipping industry. But accidents occurring on navigable waters involving recreational watercraft[3] or conventionally land-based industrial equipment temporarily mounted on a barge[4] have been held to constitute maritime torts because of the standing potential that the hazards caused by such vessels will disrupt traditional maritime activity.

There has been less volatility in the definition of maritime contracts, and for the most part common sense is a reliable guide. The occasional odd exception, such as those by which contracts to build ships or to procure maritime insurance have been held not to be maritime contracts, have gained sufficient notoriety to be conspicuous to knowledgeable practitioners of admiralty law, and to serve as familiar cautions against relying entirely on common sense to classify a particular contract as a maritime contract without confirming that conclusion by study of the applicable caselaw.[5] One interesting area at the definitional margins of maritime tort and contract law concerns "product liability" suits. Such suits are generally prosecuted on a combination of legal grounds, featuring both tort-like allegations that the defective product was negligently manufactured or designed, and contract-like allegations that the maker or vendor of the product warranted it to be free of defects. In one such case, which serves more to exemplify than to clarify the continuing definitional confusion, the US Supreme Court recently held that a claim for purely economic injury (rather than personal injury) arising from installation of a defective ship's engine was neither a maritime tort claim nor a maritime contract claim, and as such could not be adjudicated by a federal district court exercising only the admiralty jurisdiction granted by 28 U.S.C. §1333.[6]

1. *Executive Jet Aviation, Inc. v. City of Cleveland*, 409 U.S. 249 (1972).
2. *See* id.
3. *See Foremost Ins. Co. v. Richardson*, 457 U.S. 668 (1982).
4. *See Jerome B. Grubart, Inc. v. Great Lakes Dredge & Dock Co.*, 513 U.S. 527 (1995).
5. *See* Grant Gilmore & Charles L. Black, Jr, *The Law of Admiralty* (1975), 22-30.
6. *East River Steamship Corp. v. Transamerica Delaval, Inc.*, 476 U.S. 858 (1986).

5. Suits Against Foreign Sovereigns (28 U.S.C. § 1330)

67. Until the enactment in 1976 of the Foreign Sovereign Immunities Act (FSIA), suits by private parties against foreign states were within the jurisdiction of the federal district courts only as one category of diversity litigation, pursuant to 28 U.S.C. §1332(a)(4). As such, federal jurisdiction of these often sensitive suits was subject to the limitations of the "complete diversity" and jurisdictional-amount requirements of federal diversity litigation, discussed above (paragraph 55). The result was that much of such litigation was confined to state courts, with resulting uncertainty and unpredictability in the application of international legal principles of foreign sovereign immunity.

The FSIA resolved this unsatisfactory situation by amending 28 U.S.C. §1332(a)(4) to apply only to suits brought against citizens of states by foreign states acting as *plaintiffs*. A new jurisdictional statute enacted by the FSIA, 28 U.S.C. §1330, vests the federal district courts with jurisdiction of all suits brought by private parties against foreign states as *defendants*. Although this jurisdiction is concurrent with the jurisdiction of state courts, the FSIA also enacted a very liberal removal provision, 28 U.S.C. §1441(d), discussed below (paragraphs 73-75). This new removal statute gives foreign states a virtually unlimited right to remove from state courts any suits in which any party asserts a claim against a foreign state.

68. The linchpin of this new jurisdictional system by which foreign states always have access to a federal forum in which to assert the defense of foreign sovereign immunity – which the FSIA codified as a matter of federal substantive law rather than customary international law – is 28 U.S.C. §1330. It is sweeping in its scope. No jurisdictional amount is required, and there is no requirement of diversity of citizenship. Moreover, the FSIA statutorily defines a "foreign state" to include any alien corporation a majority of whose shares are owned by a foreign state – thus bringing within its compass many national airlines and other essentially commercial enterprises. Even though these commercial enterprises are likely to be found ineligible for foreign sovereign immunity, a federal district court remains vested with jurisdiction under 28 U.S.C. §1330 to adjudicate to final judgment even a suit against a nonimmune foreign state (as defined to include a state-owned alien corporation).

The sweeping nature of the jurisdiction thus granted by 28 U.S.C. §1330 raised obvious questions as to its constitutionality. While in many instances suits by US citizens against foreign states or state-owned corporations could be justified under the language of Article III of the federal Constitution permitting Congress to confer federal judicial power on federal courts to adjudicate controversies between a citizen of a state and foreign states or their citizens or subjects, on its face 28 U.S.C. §1330 permits even an alien to bring suit in a federal court against a foreign state or state-owned alien corporation, and as previously discussed (paragraph 58) the constitutional grant of federal judicial power does not extend to suits by one alien against another except when joined to a claim to which a citizen of a state is party. Thus it was significant that the US Supreme Court chose, as its vehicle for reviewing the constitutionality of 28 U.S.C. §1330, just such a suit – in which an alien was the plaintiff and a state-owned alien corporation was the defendant.[1]

In this case the US Supreme Court upheld the constitutionality of 28 U.S.C. §1330 as a special form of federal-question jurisdiction that drew upon the full constitutional power of Congress, pursuant to the previously discussed Madisonian Compromise (paragraph 52), to vest the federal district courts with jurisdiction of any case that may turn on a question of federal law. The general federal-question jurisdictional statute is 28 U.S.C. §1331, discussed above (paragraph 54). It does not draw upon the full constitutional power of Congress under Article III of the Constitution to confer federal-question jurisdiction on federal district courts, excluding from their jurisdiction under 28 U.S.C. §1331 cases in which the federal question arises only as a defensive matter. But Congress sought to exhaust its jurisdictional power under Article III when it enacted 28 U.S.C. §1330, and thus went beyond the jurisdiction previously granted by 28 U.S.C. §1331 to vest federal district courts with the broadest scope of jurisdiction that was constitutionally permissible. In every suit against a foreign sovereign or a state-owned alien corporation, the newly codified federal defense of foreign sovereign immunity might be applicable. The Supreme Court held that because this potentially dispositive federal defense *might* arise in every such suit, *all* such suits arose under federal law within the broad meaning of the power granted to Congress by Article III of the federal Constitution to vest federal courts with jurisdiction of any suit "arising under" federal law.

1. *Verlinden B.V. v. Central Bank of Nigeria*, 461 U.S. 480 (1983).

6. Supplemental Jurisdiction (28 U.S.C. §1367)

69. If every lawsuit consisted merely of the adjudication of a single claim asserted by a single plaintiff against a single defendant, there would be no need to add to the foregoing a discussion of supplementary forms of jurisdiction. In such a simple litigative world, whether the limited jurisdiction of the federal district courts extended to a particular lawsuit would be determined solely by reference to that single bipolar dispute. Does the claim arise under federal law in the sense required for jurisdiction to exist under 28 U.S.C. §1331? Is it a maritime claim of the sort that qualifies for federal maritime jurisdiction under 28 U.S.C. §1333? Is the citizenship of the parties and the value of the claim such that jurisdiction exists under 28 U.S.C. §1332 regardless of the federal basis of the claim? While these questions might not yield mutually exclusive answers – federal jurisdiction might exist on multiple grounds – they would yield an unambiguous answer: either the lawsuit would qualify for federal jurisdiction, or it would not.

But in fact such a simple lawsuit has become rare in modern American civil litigation. As discussed below, liberal joinder rules (paragraphs 151-152) and broad preclusion doctrines (paragraphs 279-284) encourage and sometimes compel multiple claims to be asserted simultaneously in one complex lawsuit, often involving multiple parties. Judicial resources are scarce and the cost of litigation is high, both for the public that funds the institutions of adjudication and for the private parties that submit disputes to those institutions. The resulting concern for efficient operation of courts and economies of scale in litigation places great pressure on parties to combine a whole array of intersecting and overlapping claims into one litigative event, in which a single judgment will consistently and uniformly determine the rights and liabilities of the universe of persons and entities interested in or affected by a particular out-of-court transaction or occurrence.

In this environment even a lawsuit that begins with the assertion of a single claim by one plaintiff against one defendant may, and likely will, soon grow into a cluster of claims asserted by multiple parties. The defendant may have a claim against the plaintiff, and as discussed below (paragraph 156), if this "counterclaim" arises out of the same transaction or occurrence as the plaintiff's original claim against the defendant, it will be forfeited unless joined to the litigation commenced by the plaintiff. The defendant may have other, unrelated claims against the plaintiff, and it will often be convenient for the defendant to assert them in the existing litigation even when not compelled to do so. And once an unrelated counterclaim is thus permissively asserted by the defendant, that may trigger the obligation of the plaintiff (now placed in a defensive posture with respect to the permissive counterclaim) to assert any related and hence compulsory counterclaims to the defendant's counterclaim. Third parties may have interests that will be affected by the litigation, and to protect them their joinder may be mandatory. Even if their joinder is not required for the litigation to proceed fairly and efficiently, they may on their own initiative intervene in the litigation as additional plaintiffs or defendants. Some of the parties, although similarly aligned as plaintiffs or defendants with respect to some claims, may have conflicting interests or levels of responsibility that result in "cross-claims" between coparties.

And some parties against whom claims have been asserted will wish to seek contribution or indemnity by "impleading" third-party defendants who by law or contract may bear ultimate responsibility for the liability asserted against some existing party to the litigation. Thus, once a single claim is placed upon the litigative Petri dish by the commencement of even the simplest lawsuit, that litigation may grow into a tangled and sometimes fuzzy cluster of organically related claims among multiple parties.

70. Modern multi-claim, multi-party litigation poses considerable challenges of jurisdictional analysis when it proceeds in a court system, such as the federal district courts, that has an inherently limited jurisdiction dependent upon the citizenship of particular parties and the nature and value of particular claims. For much of their history the federal courts were forced to invent their own rules to determine which additional claims and parties could be brought into pending federal litigation without exceeding the limits of federal jurisdiction. Two overlapping and rather complex doctrines resulted. The doctrine of "pendent" jurisdiction was confined to cases within the federal-question jurisdiction restrictively granted by 28 U.S.C. §1331, as extended to the limits of federal judicial power by 28 U.S.C. §1330 when a foreign state was involved as a defendant. It permitted additional nonfederal claims to be joined in the complaint if transactionally related to a qualifying federal-question claim. The doctrine of "ancillary" jurisdiction applied to all cases within federal jurisdiction, whether federal-question, diversity, or maritime litigation. It permitted most forms of reactive claims of the sort previously mentioned – counterclaims, cross-claims, third-party claims, and claims asserted by or against interveners – to be joined to the litigation and adjudicated by the federal district court if they, too, were transactionally related to other claims in the litigation that qualified in their own right for the federal jurisdiction expressly conferred by 28 U.S.C. §§1330-1333.

A crisis arose in May of 1989 when the US Supreme Court called into question the constitutional legitimacy of these court-created doctrines of pendent and ancillary jurisdiction.[1] It is a measure of the contemporary public interest in reducing overall the number of lawsuits by increasing the scope and complexity of each particular lawsuit that by December of 1990 Congress had enacted a sweeping new statute that not only codified the old judicial doctrines, but in general extended them. In this new statute, 28 U.S.C. §1367 – as in 28 U.S.C. §1330, discussed above (paragraph 67) – Congress drew upon the maximum extent of the federal judicial power permitted by Article III of the Constitution. This sweeping new form of statutory jurisdiction conferred upon the federal district courts is called "supplemental jurisdiction."

1. *See Finley v. United States*, 490 U.S. 545 (1989).

71. There are three major components of the 1990 supplemental-jurisdiction statute. The first subsection of the statute, 28 U.S.C. §1367(a), expressly confers on the federal district courts as much supplemental jurisdiction as the Constitution will permit. In any civil lawsuit in which any claim qualifies for federal jurisdiction under 28 U.S.C. §§1330-1333 (or under any other federal jurisdictional statute of more specialized application), a federal district court is vested with supplemental jurisdiction of every other claim asserted in the same lawsuit, including claims by or against additional parties, if that claim is part of the same constitutional "case or controversy" as the qualifying claim that is within federal jurisdiction without resort to supplemental jurisdiction.

It is difficult to overstate the breadth of the supplemental jurisdiction thus globally conferred upon the federal district courts by 28 U.S.C. §1367(a). Congress both expressly invoked, and to the limit of its constitutional power expressly ratified, the constitutional theory that the Supreme Court had developed in support of the now superseded doctrines of pendent and ancillary jurisdiction. According to the first part of this theory, once some claim within a lawsuit is found to be either a "case" or a "controversy" to which federal judicial power may extend under Article III of the Constitution, and is further found to be within some statutory implementation of that federal judicial power (such as 28 U.S.C. §§1330-1333), the federal jurisdiction that attaches to the statutorily qualifying claim extends beyond it to all other claims that are part of the same "case or controversy" of which the qualifying claim is just one part. According to the second part of this theory, a single "case or controversy" in this constitutional sense includes every claim, by whomever asserted, that arises from the same out-of-court transaction or occurrence.

Had Congress stopped here, the 1990 supplemental-jurisdiction statute would have revolutionized the allocation of jurisdiction between state and federal courts. In 28 U.S.C. §1367(b), however, Congress substantially qualified the scope of supplemental jurisdiction in diversity cases. And in 28 U.S.C. §1367(c), Congress conferred on the federal district courts substantial discretion to decline to exercise their supplemental jurisdiction as to particular claims in particular cases.

72. The obvious aim of Congress in restricting the application of supplemental jurisdiction in diversity cases was to preserve the traditional limitations of 28 U.S.C. §1332 – the rule of complete diversity and the general prohibition of the aggregation of claims for purposes of determining the amount in controversy – while preserving the power of federal courts to adjudicate in diversity cases what used to be called "ancillary" claims: transactionally related counterclaims, cross-claims, third-party claims, and claims involving interveners. By and large this aim was accomplished, but it is generally acknowledged that the statute suffered from certain drafting defects that conflicted with this aim. This led to a division among lower federal courts as to whether the statute should be given its intended effect, or rather the effect that is literally commanded by certain of the imperfectly drafted qualifications of 28 U.S.C. §1367(b).[1] In 2005, the US Supreme Court resolved the division among the lower courts in the *Allapattah* case.[2] The Supreme Court held that supplemental jurisdiction extends to claims for less than the jurisdictional amount by some plaintiffs in a diversity case, if at least one plaintiff asserts claims that exceed the required amount. As discussed above (paragraph 63), the supplemental-jurisdiction statute, so construed, permits a new form of "aggregation" of claims for purposes of determining the amount in controversy.

The US Supreme Court has yet to resolve a less dramatic division as to the proper construction of the provisions of 28 U.S.C. §1367(c) that authorize the federal district courts to decline in some circumstances to exercise their supplemental jurisdiction. Some courts construe the statute as codifying without change the broad discretion that the Supreme Court had previously extended to federal district courts to decline to adjudicate pendent claims, and extending this broad discretion to ancillary claims as well. Other courts read the statute more narrowly as cutting back on the discretion of the federal district courts to decline to exercise supplemental jurisdiction except in the specific circumstances specified by the statute.[3]

1. *See Meritcare Inc. v. St. Paul Mercury Ins. Co.*, 166 F.3rd 214 (3rd Cir. 1999); *Leonhardt v. W. Sugar Co.*, 160 F.3rd 631 (10th Cir. 1998); *Stromberg Metal Works, Inc. v. Press Mechanical Inc.*, 77 F.3rd 928 (7th Cir. 1996); *In re Abbott Labs*, 51 F.3rd 524 (5th Cir. 1995) (affirmed by an equally divided court in *Free v. Abbott Labs Inc.*, 529 U.S. 333 (2000)). The influential American Law Institute (ALI) has proposed an amended supplemental-jurisdiction statute that would, in general, codify the "literal" reading of the present statute. Thus the ALI's proposal would expand the circumstances in which supplemental jurisdiction could be used in diversity cases to aggregate claims in order to satisfy the jurisdictional amount, and would restrict the circumstances in which federal district courts would be permitted to decline supplemental jurisdiction. *See* John B. Oakley, *Reporter's Memorandum on the Claim-Specific Nature of the Original Jurisdiction of the District Courts*, in American Law Institute, Judicial Code Project, *supra*, at 599-656. The ALI, founded in 1923, seeks "to promote the clarification and simplification of the law and its better adaptation to social needs, to secure the better administration of justice, and to encourage and carry on scholarly and scientific legal work." This elective organization of leading lawyers, judges and law professors has a substantial endowment which it uses to fund and publish intensive studies and proposed reforms of problematic areas of American law. The Institute's members have carried out its goals by debating and publishing an extensive series of Restatements of Law (proposing clarification and reform of principles of common law) and statutory projects. *See generally* American Law Institute, *About the American Law Institute*, <http://www.ali.org/ ali/thisali.htm> (visited 28 Apr. 2008).
2. *Exxon Corp. v. Allapattah Servs. Inc.*, 545 U.S. 546 (2005).
3. *See* Charles Alan Wright, John B. Oakley & Debra Lyn Bassett, *Federal Courts: Cases and Materials*, 12th edn (2008), 346.

7. Right of Removal (28 U.S.C. §§1441-1447)

73. There is an important reason, hitherto touched on only briefly, why even a summary account of American civil procedure must deal extensively with the subject-matter jurisdiction of the federal court system. The plaintiff's decision to bring suit in state rather than federal court is not necessarily controlling. Even when the plaintiff's choice is unquestionably sound, the state court's jurisdiction being indisputable, the defendant will often have the right of removing the case from one proper forum (the state court) to another (the federal district court). The opportunity defensively to shift the litigation from a state court to the federal system is obviously important to defending parties, as it is very frequently exercised. The standing likelihood that the defendant can and probably will remove litigation from state to federal court casts a broad shadow over American civil procedure. For one thing, removal acts as a ratchet, moving cases in only one direction. If the plaintiff elects to file suit in federal court in the first place, the defendant has no parallel right of reverse removal to state court; the plaintiff's choice of a federal forum in the first instance is irrevocable. This one-way system of removal tends to concentrate cases in the federal court system despite their seemingly limited jurisdiction vis-à-vis the state court system. Offsetting this ratchet-like effect, but only to some extent, is the incentive given to a plaintiff who is anxious to remain in state court to structure the litigation in a way that will impede or prevent the removal of the case to federal court.

Federal removal law is necessarily complicated, given the important interests at stake – the relative roles and standing of the state and federal court systems, the general public interest in processes of adjudication that are both fair and efficient, and the welter of private interests at stake when either state or federal law is applied coercively in court. It is unnecessarily confused, with important principles hidden by vague or opaque statutory language and a hodgepodge of interpretive caselaw. As such, it stands sorely in need of further statutory attention. In parallel with its proposal of a revised supplemental-jurisdiction statute, discussed above (paragraphs 69-72), the American Law Institute has proposed a comprehensive revision of the removal statutes that would clarify, if not wholly uncomplicate, the shopworn legislation currently in effect.[1] The following summary of removal law as it presently stands is necessarily confined only to the highlights of this intricate corner of the law of federal jurisdiction.

1. *See* American Law Institute, Judicial Code Project, *supra*, at 325-597.

74. The basic right of removal conferred on defendants by 28 U.S.C. §1441(a) is not itself a grant of subject-matter jurisdiction to the federal district courts. Rather it permits removal only of cases that independently qualify for federal jurisdiction under 28 U.S.C. §§1330-1333 or some other federal jurisdictional statute of specialized application, as supplemented by 28 U.S.C. §1367. The underlying principle is that, if the plaintiff could have filed the case in a federal court to begin with, the choice between a federal and state forum should also be extended to the defendant. If the defendant is content with the state court chosen by the plaintiff, the case remains in state court, and the waivable nature of the basic right of removal is reinforced by a strict thirty-day time limit in which the right of removal must be exercised.

There is no right of partial removal. The entire case is removed when the right of removal is exercised, not just particular claims in cases. In general this means that removal operates on an "all or nothing" basis: unless every claim asserted in the complaint qualifies for federal jurisdiction, the case as a whole is nonremovable. In most instances any claim not independently within federal subject-matter jurisdiction under 28 U.S.C. §§1330-1333 will be sufficiently related to some other such claim in the same action as to be within the supplemental jurisdiction conferred on federal district courts by 28 U.S.C. §1367, but it is possible in most state courts for a plaintiff to file a single lawsuit that joins together two or more entirely unrelated claims against the same defendant. In a case in which the plaintiff has thus joined a claim within federal jurisdiction to an entirely unrelated claim not within federal jurisdiction, a special removal statute may apply: 28 U.S.C. §1441(c). This permits the entire case to be removed (subject to the prerogative of the district court to remand back to state court any claim "as to which state law predominates"), but only if the part of the case that (standing alone) would qualify for federal jurisdiction does so because it involves a claim within the federal-question jurisdiction of 28 U.S.C. §1331. The underlying principle is that a defendant who faces judicial coercion as a matter of federal law should not lose the right to remove the case to a federal court because the plaintiff has contrived to join to the federal-question claim an entirely unrelated, nonremovable claim. If none of the unrelated claims is based on federal law, however, and some but not all qualify for federal jurisdiction merely on the basis of diversity jurisdiction, there is no such powerful reason to ensure that the defendant can bring nonfederal claims before a federal court.

This more stringent attitude towards the desirability of removal when the basis for federal jurisdiction is merely the diversity of citizenship of the parties is also manifested by 28 U.S.C. §1441(b), which forbids removal if any defendant properly joined and served is a citizen of the state in whose courts the plaintiff has filed suit. The rationale for this restriction on removal is that the joinder of any "forum-state" defendant is sufficient to reduce the risk of biased adjudication by the courts of that defendant's home state, and thus there is no need to afford the further protection from local bias that diversity jurisdiction is intended to provide. The "properly joined and served" caveat means that the joinder to the litigation of a removal-defeating forum-state defendant will be disregarded if the claim against that defendant is so baseless as to amount to "fraudulent joinder," discussed above (paragraph 56), or if that defendant will not actually participate in the state court proceedings because the plaintiff has not or cannot be effectively served with process. (The effective scope of a state court's process is discussed below (paragraphs 86-87) in connection with the territorial jurisdiction of state courts.)

Another impediment to removal is created by 28 U.S.C. §1445, which expressly makes certain cases nonremovable. These are cases in which the plaintiff has asserted any of four types of claims. Two of these types of claim are fairly arcane and infrequently litigated. The other two – claims under the federal statutes giving railroad and maritime workers special rights to sue their employers for job-related injuries (which would otherwise always be removable as federal-question claims under 28 U.S.C. §1331), and claims under state worker-compensation laws (which would otherwise be removable only on diversity-jurisdiction grounds under 28 U.S.C. §1332) – are standard fare for litigation. The purpose of these restrictions on removal is to give a unilateral choice of forum, state or federal, to favored classes of plaintiffs.

There are also favored classes of defendants. The basic right of removal is subject to a "rule of unanimity" that requires all properly joined and served defendants to join in the removal. But there are several special removal statutes that allow certain defendants to remove certain cases unilaterally.

One of these, 28 U.S.C. §1441(d), was discussed above in connection with the FSIA (paragraph 67). It confers upon foreign states a right of removal that differs importantly from the basic right of removal. In addition to permitting unilateral removal by a foreign state, it allows the federal district court to which the case is removed to suspend the normal time limits on removal. It also allows a foreign state to remove a case even if it was not originally named as a defendant, and was brought into the case only as a "third-party defendant" to a counterclaim or a claim for indemnity or contribution filed against it by one of the original defendants.

There are a number of other statutes that grant special rights of removal. Most of these are scattered throughout the United States Code as part of legislation that does not otherwise deal with removal, but three appear side-by-side with the basic removal statutes as 28 U.S.C. §§1442-1444. These three special provisions confer a unilateral right of removal on the defendants to whom they refer: federal officers or agencies sued for official acts (28 U.S.C. §1442), a very narrow class of private defendants sued for activities protected by federal civil rights laws (28 U.S.C. §1443), and the United States when it is a party to certain actions involving title to real property (28 U.S.C. §1444).

Removal presents unique problems in cases that qualify for federal admiralty jurisdiction under 28 U.S.C. §1333. As discussed above (paragraph 65), any suit based on a maritime tort or contract may be filed by the plaintiff "on the admiralty side" of a federal district court, but as an admiralty case will be tried to the court rather than to a jury. If the plaintiff seeks only money damages, the "saving to suitors" clause protects the plaintiff's right to jury trial by allowing such a suit to be filed instead in a state court, or "on the law side" of a federal district court if the suit qualifies for federal diversity jurisdiction. This protection of the right to jury trial would be nullified if any case based on federal maritime law could be removed to "the admiralty side" of a federal district court. Although the removal statutes do not speak directly to this point, it is settled as a matter of caselaw that a maritime case filed in state court under the "saving to suitors" clause may be removed only if it qualified for federal diversity jurisdiction, and thus could have been filed by the plaintiff on "the law side" rather than "the admiralty side" of a federal district court. Removal in such a case brings it to "the law side" of a federal district court, where the plaintiff's right to jury trial will be protected.

75. The procedures for exercising and challenging the right of removal are set forth in 28 U.S.C. §§1446-1447. The removal of a case is effected by the simple act of filing a notice of removal in the federal district court for the district in which the state court is located where the case is pending. A copy of the notice of removal must promptly be served on opposing parties and the state court from which the action was removed. The removal of the case is a self-executing act solely within the control of the defendant or defendants; no prior judicial assent is required. But this does not mean that there is no judicial control over the removal process; a case that has been improperly removed, or that is not within federal jurisdiction, is subject to remand back to the state court from which it was removed. Any defect in removal procedure – such as an untimely removal (paragraphs 74-75), the removal of a diversity case in which one or more proper defendants is a forum-state citizen (paragraphs 74-75), or a removal in which all proper defendants have failed to join as required by the "rule of unanimity" (paragraph 74) – is waived unless the removal is challenged by a motion to remand made within thirty days of the filing of the notice of removal. No such time limit applies, however, if the federal district court determines at any time before final judgment that it lacks subject-matter jurisdiction of a removed case; such a case must be remanded forthwith to the state court from which it was removed, whether or not any party has contested the federal court's jurisdiction. If some claim in an otherwise properly removed case depends upon the federal district court's exercise of its discretionary supplemental jurisdiction, that claim alone may be remanded at any time even though the rest of the case remains in federal court.[1]

The general rule is that a removal is untimely if the removal does not occur within a thirty-day period. The issue of just when this thirty-day period begins has been much litigated. The US Supreme Court has recently clarified some of these problems by holding that the thirty-day period commences only when the defendant is formally served with process; the date on which a case is filed in state court, or on which the defendant is informally notified of the commencement of state court litigation, is not controlling.[2]

Other timing problems continue to divide the lower courts. The statute that imposes the general thirty-day requirement for timely removal, 28 U.S.C. §1446(b), also provides that, if a case is not initially removable, the time limit does not begin to run until the case later becomes removable. Only certain subsequent events will suffice to convert an initially nonremovable case into one that may later be removed; in general what is required is that the plaintiff must voluntarily dismiss any claims that prevented the removal of the lawsuit as originally commenced. If the only jurisdictional basis for the removal of a lawsuit is the diversity of citizenship of the parties, 28 U.S.C. §1446(b) imposes an absolute time limit that bars removal more than one year after the lawsuit was commenced in state court. Most lower courts have held that this one-year limit applies only to cases that were not initially removable, as otherwise a plaintiff may frustrate the right of removal simply by filing suit in state court and withholding service of process on the defendant until the one-year period has elapsed.

1. *See Carnegie-Mellon Univ. v. Cohill*, 484 U.S. 343 (1988).
2. *Murphy Bros., Inc. v. Michetti Pipe Stringing, Inc.*, 526 U.S. 344 (1999).

B. Appellate Courts

76. Final decisions of the federal district courts, and some interlocutory decisions, are appealable as of right to the federal courts of appeals, described above (paragraph 50). Interlocutory decisions not appealable as of right may be certified to the courts of appeals by the district courts, in which case the courts of appeals have discretionary jurisdiction.

The US Supreme Court has discretionary appellate jurisdiction to review any case in a Federal Court of Appeals, either before or after judgment. The power to review cases before judgment in the Court of Appeals is rarely exercised – roughly about once a decade – and only then in cases of the most pressing public importance. In a very narrow category of cases, principally those involving electoral matters, special statutes require the district court to sit as a court of three judges, including one judge of the Court of Appeals embracing that district. Decisions of such three-judge district courts are appealable as of right to the Supreme Court rather than the courts of appeals.

The US Supreme Court also has discretionary appellate jurisdiction of any final judgment of a state court on an issue of federal law, provided two requirements are met. First, the judgment must turn on the disputed issue of federal law and not on an "independent and adequate state ground." Second, the judgment must be that of the highest court within the state system in which review of the federal issue could be had. Generally this means that the US Supreme Court reviews only judgments of state courts of last resort, although occasionally the court reviews judgments of lower state courts when review of the federal issue was unavailable in, or was denied by, the state court of last resort.

The US Supreme Court exercises its discretionary appellate jurisdiction by granting or denying petitions for a writ of *certiorari*. Each year about 7,000 such petitions are filed in the US Supreme Court, and only about 70-80 are granted.[1] The court exercises "institutional review" rather than "review for correctness," limiting its grant of petitions of *certiorari* principally to cases in which the issues have broad public significance extending beyond the interests of the parties to the suit. The court is most likely to grant review in cases to which the United States is itself a party, or in which the Solicitor General of the United States (the chief appellate attorney for the United

States) represents that there is a strong federal interest. Generally the Supreme Court will not review an issue of federal law unless the next lower level of courts – the federal courts of appeals and state courts of last resort – have previously rendered conflicting decisions on that issue. Often the court will allow such conflicting decisions to accumulate. This practice of delaying review until there is a diversity of opinion among lower courts benefits the court when it ultimately decides to resolve the disputed issue, but it also leads to disuniformity in the application of federal law by the lower courts, sometimes for prolonged periods.

1. *See* <www.scotusblog.com/wp/wp-content/uploads/2008/05/statpack_5-28.pdf> (last visited 1 Jul. 2008).

§2. Territorial Jurisdiction and Venue

I. Factors to be Taken into Account

77. Although the doctrines of territorial jurisdiction and venue both serve to allocate cases geographically among courts of equivalent subject-matter jurisdiction, and both are sensitive to the convenience of the defendant, the political structure of the American court system invests rules of territorial jurisdiction with a constitutional significance that rules of venue lack. This makes the rules of territorial jurisdiction far more significant within American law than the rules of venue, and requires here that they be given separate elaboration.

The important differences between territorial jurisdiction and venue are particularly manifest when dealing with state courts. The law of venue operates internally to divide every state-court system into geographically distinct districts, but from a national perspective the first level of geographical organization is between the states themselves. This is the level at which the law of territorial jurisdiction comes into play, and because states are themselves political entities, the exercise of territorial jurisdiction by any one state has always had constitutional ramifications.

Because territorial jurisdiction acts upon individual defendants, modern American constitutional law regulates state-court territorial jurisdiction principally by enforcing the Fourteenth Amendment to the federal Constitution, which, inter alia, prevents any state from depriving a natural or corporate person of property without "due process of law." But even though the constitutional law of state-court territorial jurisdiction thus has the character of enforcing an individual right – so that states may occasionally exercise greater territorial jurisdiction than the Constitution would otherwise permit, because the individual has waived that right – structural issues of the limits of state power within a federal system of mutually independent sovereign states are never far from the surface when the constitutional limits of state-court territorial jurisdiction are disputed.

This does not mean, however, that the rules of state-court territorial jurisdiction allocate litigation exclusively to one state. Often the plaintiff may choose among multiple states that share territorial jurisdiction to adjudicate particular claims against a particular defendant. Here again the political character of the states themselves endows the allocation of territorial jurisdiction with political significance, because each state has substantial independence in its choice of the substantive law applicable to a given lawsuit. The disuniformity of state substantive law promotes the pervasive American practice of "forum-shopping" for the state whose law will be most favorable to the party choosing the forum. The defendant's right to object on constitutional grounds to the territorial jurisdiction of the plaintiff's chosen state court is often asserted principally to resist the application of unfavorable law rather than to avoid trial in an inconvenient forum.

78. The Fifth Amendment to the federal Constitution parallels the Fourteenth Amendment by imposing on the federal government and its courts the same obligation it imposes on state courts to respect individual defendants' right to due process of law. The constitutional law of federal territorial jurisdiction has a distinctly international perspective, however, because it operates not to allocate cases among the different federal district courts, but as a limit on the jurisdictional power of the national system of federal courts vis-à-vis the court systems of other nations. This international perspective sometimes spills over to questions of state-court territorial jurisdiction, when alien defendants are involved. This occurs when the point of a due-process objection is not to force reallocation of the case to the courts of another state, but rather to challenge the scope of American territorial jurisdiction in general as applied to a foreign litigant.

79. Venue rules, as opposed to rules of territorial jurisdiction, are treated within American law as the internal prerogative of each state's court system, and of the federal system. While the general similarity of basic venue rules in all American courts reflects a strong legal tradition of respect for the convenience of defendants, the lack of any constitutional basis for challenging a particular venue rule has allowed many local idiosyncracies to develop.

II. Main Claims and Ancillary Claims

80. Federal constitutional standards limiting the territorial jurisdiction of both state and federal courts are sensitive to the connection between the defendant's forum-related activities and the particular claim asserted against the defendant. In some cases this may result in a court having territorial jurisdiction of some but not all of the claims asserted in that case against a particular defendant. There is no general doctrine of "ancillary territorial jurisdiction" to cure such problems, but if the main claim and an ancillary claim arise out of the same transaction or occurrence, it is likely that the two will be sufficiently related so that the court's territorial jurisdiction over a defendant with respect to the main claim will extend as well to an ancillary claim against the same defendant.

If the ancillary claim is asserted against a different defending party, the territorial jurisdiction of the court with respect to that party must be independently established. A court will always have territorial jurisdiction to adjudicate a true ancillary claim – that is, a claim arising out of the same transaction or occurrence as one of the main claims asserted in the complaint – when such an ancillary claim is asserted against a plaintiff. Having invoked the jurisdiction of the court to adjudicate the main claim, the plaintiff is deemed to have submitted to the court's territorial jurisdiction with respect to any claims against the plaintiff that are related to the main claim and are asserted in the course of the litigation of the main claim.

Although the federal courts are a national system whose territorial jurisdiction may constitutionally extend nationwide, by statute and court rule the territorial jurisdiction of a particular federal district court extends in most cases no more broadly than does the territorial jurisdiction of the courts of general jurisdiction of the state in which the federal district court sits. (See the discussion below, paragraph 83.) In certain cases, however, Congress has by statute specially conferred nationwide territorial jurisdiction on the federal district courts. The US Supreme Court has yet to rule on the issue, but the virtually unanimous view of the lower federal courts is that the federal district courts do have "ancillary territorial jurisdiction" in such cases with respect to ancillary claims that are related to a main claim against the same defendant, who thereby becomes subject to nationwide federal territorial jurisdiction. By court rule, such "ancillary territorial jurisdiction" may also be asserted over a very limited class of additional defendants whose joinder is necessary, even in ordinary cases in which the territorial jurisdiction of the federal courts is otherwise restricted by reference to state law.

Statutes specially conferring nationwide territorial jurisdiction on federal district courts often provide for special venue rules that afford the plaintiff a greater choice among federal district courts than would be allowed under the normal federal venue rules. The general view in such cases is that such special venue rules apply as well to ancillary claims related to a qualifying main claim, so that the federal district court has "ancillary venue" as well as "ancillary territorial jurisdiction". The situation is less clear when only the normal federal venue rules apply and venue is based on the location of events giving rise to some, but not all, of the claims asserted in the complaint. It is generally thought, however, that any claim within the supplemental subject-matter jurisdiction of the federal courts may not be resisted on venue grounds. These points have been infrequently litigated, and until there is persuasive authority to the contrary it should be assumed that if a federal district court is a proper venue for the litigation of a main claim, that court will also have "ancillary venue" over any additional claims related to that main claim. If there is more than one main claim and their relationship is such that venue is proper as to some but not all, only the claim as to which the district court lacks venue will be dismissed upon timely assertion of the defendant's venue objection.

81. Most state courts have special rules for dealing with a multi-claim lawsuit in which different venue rules apply to different main claims in that lawsuit; generally these rules require the more restrictive venue rule to be applied to the entire lawsuit. Once the venue of a state court has been upheld with respect to the main claims, there is generally no further restriction of venue with respect to ancillary claims. From a functional perspective "ancillary venue" may thus be said to be a standard feature of state practice.

III. Overview of the Different Rules

82. The constitutional standard for the assertion of territorial jurisdiction by either a state or a federal court is the existence of "minimum contacts" between the defendant and the forum. With respect to state courts, "minimum contacts" must exist between the defendant and the particular state in question. With respect to federal courts, "minimum contacts" need exist only between the defendant and the United States as a whole.

83. Not every state asserts in every case the full scope of the territorial jurisdiction it may constitutionally possess. Thus the scope of state-court territorial jurisdiction must in every case be determined by reference to the scope of the local state law authorizing the assertion of territorial jurisdiction – generally called the state's "long-arm statute" – as well as by reference to the federal constitutional limits on such territorial jurisdiction. In many cases, state law simply incorporates federal constitutional law by reference, asserting territorial jurisdiction as broadly as the federal Constitution will permit. In these cases, the determination of the scope of territorial jurisdiction as a matter of state law is subsumed within the constitutional determination whether the defendant has the requisite "minimum contacts" with the state in question. But in other cases, the constitutional "minimum contacts" issue need never be reached because solely as a matter of state law it may be determined that the relevant state long-arm statute does not give the state court territorial jurisdiction over the defendant in question.

In most cases, the territorial jurisdiction of a federal district court is confined as a matter of federal statutory law (as implemented by court rule) to the territorial jurisdiction of the courts of general jurisdiction of the state in which the federal district court sits. This requires federal district courts to follow the same bifurcated process of analysis as state courts, looking first to the scope of territorial jurisdiction authorized by the local state long-arm statute, and then applying the constitutional "minimum-contacts" test only if that has been incorporated by reference as the state-law test, or if the scope of the territorial jurisdiction otherwise authorized by the state's long-arm statute is challenged by the defendant as exceeding the "minimum contacts" standard of federal constitutional law as applied to the particular state in question. In some cases, however, federal district courts are authorized by statute to exercise nationwide territorial jurisdiction. In such cases, the defendant may resist the federal court's territorial jurisdiction on constitutional grounds only by establishing that the defendant lacks "minimum contacts" with the United States as a whole.

84. Federal venue rules generally allocate venue on either residential or transactional grounds. In the federal courts, residential venue requires that all defendants live in the same state. Some states have more than one (and as many as four) federal districts. When all defendants reside in such a multidistrict state, venue is proper in any district in the state in which any one defendant resides. Of far broader applicability is the transactional venue of the federal district courts, which requires only that a substantial part of the events or property relating to the litigation have a locus in the district in question. This may permit litigation involving interstate transactions to be filed in any one of several different districts. In some cases the federal venue requirement is suspended altogether, permitting a case to be filed in any district that has territorial jurisdiction over the defendant.

Most state venue rules are also residential or transactional in nature, sometimes combining these two characteristics so that residential venue is permitted only when certain types of transactions are the subject of the litigation. Residential venue, when available, may be invoked in some states on the basis of the residence of any defendant rather than all defendants. Rules of transactional venue often differ according to the nature of the transaction at issue, with different rules pertaining to lawsuits involving torts as opposed to breaches of contract.

Both state and federal courts follow the "local action" rule, which requires lawsuits involving title or injury to real property to be brought in the judicial district in which the property is located. This rule was once widely thought to be a nonwaivable rule of subject-matter jurisdiction, and it is still so regarded in some states that permit a judgment in a local action to be collaterally attacked as invalid if rendered by a court other than that in which the real property is located. But in most states and the federal system the local action rule is now treated merely as a venue rule, subject to waiver by the parties and qualified by the power of the trial court to transfer cases by ordering a change of venue.

85. In most states, trial courts have broad discretion to transfer any lawsuit, including a "local action," to any other judicial district within the state in which the lawsuit might be more conveniently or efficiently adjudicated – whether or not the transferee district is one in which venue would have been proper absent transfer. No state has formal power to transfer a case for trial in another state, although the discretionary doctrine of *forum non conveniens*, discussed below (paragraph 112), can be used as an informal mechanism for interstate transfer of litigation between state courts. When so applied, the state in which the case was initially filed grants a stay or conditional dismissal terminating the litigation, reserving power to resume the litigation if it cannot be litigated to judgment in the courts of a more convenient state. Defendants anxious to facilitate such a de facto interstate transfer thus have an incentive to make and honor commitments not to assert waivable objections, such as a lack of territorial jurisdiction or the running of the statute of limitations, that might otherwise bar the litigation from proceeding when refiled in the alternative state.

Although the transfer power of a federal district court can and often does permit formal transfer of a case to a federal district court in another state, in another important respect it is more limited than the transfer power of most state courts. A case may be transferred from one federal district court to another – either to cure an initial lack of proper venue (28 U.S.C. §1406) or on general convenience and efficiency grounds (28 U.S.C. §1404) – only if the transferee district is one in which venue would originally have been proper, and in which the plaintiff may assert territorial jurisdiction over the defendant without reliance on the defendant's consent.[1] This restriction does not apply to transfers ordered by the Judicial Panel on Multidistrict Litigation (JPML), a standing body of seven federal judges appointed by the Chief Justice of the US Supreme Court. The JPML can consolidate in any federal district court all factually related lawsuits pending throughout the federal system (28 U.S.C. §1407), and this power is frequently exercised in "mass-tort" cases such as aviation disasters or suits arising from exposure to toxic substances such as asbestos. But such consolidation extends only to pretrial proceedings, principally consisting of discovery of evidence and related motions for summary judgment. Unless the parties agree to keep the case in the transferee district, any case (other than certain antitrust cases) not settled or disposed of by pretrial motion must be retransferred for trial in the district in which it was commenced.[2]

1. *Hoffman v. Blaski*, 363 U.S. 335 (1960). The purpose of the *Hoffman* rule is to prevent the defendant, by offering to waive objection to either venue or territorial jurisdiction, from having a broader choice of forum upon moving to transfer the case than the plaintiff had in selecting the forum initially.
2. *Lexecon Inc. v. Milberg Weiss Bershad Hynes & Lerach*, 523 U.S. 26 (1998). The different rule for certain antitrust cases is provided by 28 U.S.C. §1407(g).

IV. Federal Constitutional Regulation of State Court Territorial Jurisdiction

A. Full Faith and Credit Standards

86. The term "territorial jurisdiction" within American law is a modern amalgam of the two types of judicial jurisdiction over particular cases that were historically exercised by common-law courts. Jurisdiction in personam was based on the power of a court over the person of a defendant brought before it by service of process summoning that defendant to appear and defend against the claim of the plaintiff. Jurisdiction in rem was based on the power of a court over particular property brought before it by a writ of attachment or similar process asserting judicial control over the property incident to the claim of the plaintiff.

For the first ninety years after the current government of the United States was formed by the ratification of the federal Constitution in 1788, individual states were free to fashion their own rules of territorial jurisdiction as they saw fit, subject only to the constraint that a judgment of one state might be denied recognition by other states, or by the federal courts, if the judgment was predicated on some theory of jurisdictional power that went beyond customary standards. This constraint arose from Article IV of the US Constitution and a parallel statute first enacted in 1789, 28 U.S.C. §1738. These provisions require any valid state-court judgment to be given "Full Faith and Credit" by every other state and federal court, and gave the US Supreme Court the authority to determine in disputed cases whether or not a particular state-court judgment was indeed valid and hence binding on other American courts.

By definition, a judgment in rem is enforceable only against the property against which the judgment is directed – the very property already within the control of the court rendering the judgment. Thus, in rem judgments could rarely if ever become the basis for a Full Faith and Credit challenge to the enforceability of that judgment in some other court. But in personam judgments are enforceable against the defendant personally by means of a writ of execution ordering the seizure and judicial sale of the defendant's property wherever it may be found. During this initial ninety-year period, the US Supreme Court would occasionally be called upon to decide whether an in personam judgment from state A had wrongfully been denied enforcement by the courts of state B, the state B courts having refused enforcement on the grounds that state A had improperly asserted in personam jurisdiction over the defendant. But no such dispute over the validity of a particular state-court judgment could arise unless the occasion arose for it to be enforced or otherwise given some legal recognition by some court external to the state in which the judgment was rendered. The US Supreme Court had no authority on Full Faith and Credit grounds to declare a state-court judgment invalid and unenforceable even within the state whose courts had rendered the judgment.

B. Initial Due-Process Standards

87. The status of state-court territorial jurisdiction under the federal Constitution, and the role of the US Supreme Court in elaborating the constitutional standards for state-court territorial jurisdiction, changed dramatically in 1878. In the famous *Pennoyer* case, the Supreme Court ruled that the ratification of the Fourteenth Amendment in 1868 had given it authority to determine the validity of every state-court judgment, whether enforced within the rendering state or elsewhere.[1] The Fourteenth Amendment prohibits any state from depriving persons of their property without "due process of law." In *Pennoyer*, the Supreme Court held that no judgment constituted "due process of law" unless it was a valid judgment according to the standards established by its previous "Full Faith and Credit" caselaw.

Because these Full Faith and Credit precedents had been concerned exclusively with in personam judgments, the constitutional standards for state-court territorial jurisdiction laid down in *Pennoyer* were incomplete, and have since been much revised. *Pennoyer* said little about in rem jurisdiction, other than to point out that no judgment could be justified on in rem grounds unless the property in question had been brought before the court by appropriate process before the judgment was rendered. *Pennoyer* dealt primarily with the power of particular states to exercise in personam jurisdiction over residents of other states. It framed the issue in terms of the mutually exclusive territorial sovereignty of the various states. A state could validly assert personal jurisdiction over a nonresident defendant only if that defendant had first been personally served with process while physically present within the territory of the state in question. This rule was subject to an important qualification, however. A defendant resident in one state might voluntarily submit to the jurisdiction of the courts of another state either by appointing an agent in that state upon whom process might be served, or by voluntary appearance in the courts of that state despite the lack of proper service of process on the defendant or an agent within that state.

This scheme of territorial jurisdiction had a decidedly "pro-defendant" tilt. Plaintiffs with claims against residents of other states generally faced the burden of filing suit in the home state of their adversaries. This became increasingly intolerable for two reasons. First, modern means of communication and transportation brought citizens of different states into virtually daily contact, often without either party to a transaction leaving his or her state of residence, and even when there was personal contact, it was often for only a fleeting encounter. Second, the business landscape changed to one in which the dominant form of commercial enterprise was the corporation, a legally fictitious "person" whose "presence" in a particular state at a particular time was a legal and metaphysical construct rather than an objective fact of physical reality. After many efforts to adapt the *Pennoyer* standards to modern realities, primarily by extremely loose applications of the idea that process might be served within a particular state on some putative "agent" of the defendant, in 1945 the US Supreme Court adopted a new standard for determining the constitutionality of state-court assertions of territorial jurisdiction.[2]

1. *Pennoyer v. Neff*, 95 U.S. (5 Otto) 714 (1877).
2. *International Shoe Co. v. Washington*, 326 U.S. 310 (1945).

C. *Reformulation of Due-Process Standards as Requiring "Minimum Contacts"*

88. In the *International Shoe* case, the Supreme Court declared that due process demanded only that the state asserting personal jurisdiction over a nonresident have "certain minimum contacts with it such that the maintenance of the suit does not offend "traditional notions of fair play and substantial justice."[1] In 1977, the US Supreme Court extended the "minimum-contacts" test to all assertions of state-court territorial jurisdiction, whether premised on in personam or in rem jurisdiction.[2]

The "minimum-contacts" test of *International Shoe* has been much criticized, from its inception to the present day, as unduly vague and hence productive of too much threshold litigation over the jurisdictional power of a particular state to adjudicate a particular lawsuit. Nonetheless it remains, as interpreted and in part reformulated by a long series of subsequent US Supreme Court cases applying it to the facts of particular cases, the touchstone for constitutional analysis of the permissible scope of state-court territorial jurisdiction.

Modern "minimum-contacts" analysis will be summarized below. It consists of a set of questions that do not always yield determinate answers, and that deploy subtle and sometimes unsettled legal concepts. But it is important to note at the outset that these questions remain grounded in the same fundamental rule of constitutional law expressed by *Pennoyer*. States are entities defined in territorial terms, and the power of a particular state to adjudicate a particular lawsuit depends, on a fundamental level, on some connection between that lawsuit and the territory of that state. It is the nature of the qualifying connection that has changed since *Pennoyer*, and that continues to evolve as the analytical framework of *International Shoe* is reviewed and applied in subsequent cases. But the twists and turns of that evolution should not obscure the obvious: "territorial" jurisdiction must ultimately be justified in territorial terms.

Pennoyer took the qualifying connection to be a legally subordinate relationship between the defendant and the forum state at the time the litigation takes place. That relationship might arise from the standing power of a state to determine the legal rights and liabilities of its residents, the contingent power of a state to determine the legal rights and liabilities of any nonresident summoned before its courts while present in the state or otherwise voluntarily submitting to the jurisdiction of its courts, or from legal title to any property within the state that by appropriate process had been brought within the control of its courts. *International Shoe* recognized that the qualifying connection had gradually been expanded, as cases took account not only of the defendant's relationship to the forum state, but also of the litigation's relationship to that state – what had happened and where, that was alleged by the plaintiff as the basis for coercive judicial action against the defendant.

1. Id., at 316.
2. *Shaffer v. Heitner*, 433 U.S. 186 (1977).

89. This concern for some territorial connection between a particular state and the facts giving rise to a particular lawsuit might have led to dispensing with any concern for some additional territorial connection between that state and the defendant against whom the lawsuit was directed, such that a sufficient legal relationship between the forum state and the plaintiff would suffice to bring a lawsuit within that state's territorial jurisdiction. Such a test has frequently been proposed, by which any state would have territorial jurisdiction of suits brought by its own residents for injuries wherever received against defendants wherever found. But the US Supreme Court has rejected such a test, which surely rests on a slippery slope leading to the end of any genuine territorial limitation on state-court jurisdiction. For if the plaintiff's territorial connection to the forum state alone suffices, no limiting principle is obvious. Must the plaintiff have resided in the forum state before being injured, or may the plaintiff invoke the territorial jurisdiction of a state by moving there after injury but before bringing suit? And if the latter, how could it be determined whether the change of residence was genuine or merely a pretext? Why ought it not suffice as an adequate legal relationship between the plaintiff and the forum state that the plaintiff has chosen merely to file suit in that state, thereby submitting to that state's authority to determine whether the plaintiff has suffered any legal injury at all?

Although with scant elaboration, the US Supreme Court has resisted this collapse of its constitutional regulation of state-court territorial jurisdiction into a simple plaintiff's option rule. Instead, the Supreme Court has frequently repeated the threshold requirement that the requisite minimum contacts must be found by analysis of the "relationship among the defendant, the forum, and the litigation."[1] If such minimum contacts exist from the perspective of the defendant, the plaintiff's stake in the litigation and the interests of the forum state that may be entailed by its relationship to the plaintiff will be considered as bearing on the "reasonableness" of the assertion of the jurisdictional power that results from those minimum contacts. This leads to a two-tiered process of analysis that first asks whether such contacts as may exist "between the defendant, the forum, and the litigation" amount to "minimum contacts," and only if this first question is answered affirmatively proceeds to ask whether the exercise of jurisdiction would circumstantially be fair and reasonable and thus, in the words of *International Shoe*, be "consistent with traditional notions of 'fair play and substantial justice.'"[2]

1. Id., at 204. *See, e.g., World-Wide Volkswagen Corp. v. Woodson*, 444 U.S. 286, 313 (1980) (quoting *Shaffer v. Heitner*, 433 U.S. 186, 204 (1977)).
2. *International Shoe*, 326 U.S. at 316.

D. Six-Step Approach to Minimum-Contacts Analysis

90. Although the caselaw expressly provides only for this rather fuzzy, two-tiered process of analysis,[1] it is best understood as implying a more detailed set of six successive steps for determining whether a particular defendant is subject to the territorial jurisdiction of a particular state, either generally or only with respect to some specific lawsuit. This six-step mode of analysis is the writers' construct, but it reliably takes into account every relevant issue identified in cases from *International Shoe* to the present date.

1. *See Asahi Metal Indus. Co. v. Superior Court*, 480 U.S. 102 (1987); *Burger King Corp. v. Rudzewicz*, 471 U.S. 462 (1985).

1. Contact

Has the defendant had any contact of any kind with the forum state?

91. This question has great formal significance, although rarely if ever is it practically dispositive. Given the demand for at least "minimum contacts" between the defendant and the forum state, plaintiffs rarely will bring suit in a forum utterly foreign to the defendant. But posing this question at the outset of the analysis not only underscores that the present régime does not give the plaintiff an unlimited choice of forum, but also encourages consideration of any possible contact of any kind that a defendant may have had with particular states. This contact might or might not have anything to do with the particular lawsuit in question. The best way to avoid prematurely overlooking some potentially relevant form of contact is to look for any kind of contact at all.

2. Purposefulness

If there are contacts between the defendant and the forum state, do any of them constitute "purposeful" contacts?

92. Of course if the first analytical step yields a negative answer, analysis stops. If there has been no contact whatsoever between the defendant and the forum state, the requisite "minimum contacts" cannot possibly exist and the forum state cannot constitutionally exercise territorial jurisdiction over the defendant. But in virtually any case brought under the present rules by a rational plaintiff, a broad net cast for contacts between the defendant and the forum state will produce at least some form of contact. This leads to the next question. Are these contacts the right kind of contacts, in the sense that they result from the voluntary and self-serving acts of the defendant?

This "purposefulness" criterion is one of the subtle and unsettled areas of minimum-contacts analysis that awaits definitive elaboration by the US Supreme Court. A full account cannot be given here of the many strands of authority that highlight the need to distinguish between contacts in general and those contacts that are purposeful enough to bring the defendant within the territorial jurisdiction of a particular state.

In business cases, the purposefulness criterion has been used to distinguish between contacts generated by the unilateral activity of a business partner, client, or customer in moving or traveling to a different state where the relationship with the defendant continues or the defendant's product is used, the question being phrased as whether the defendant has "purposefully avail[ed] itself of the privilege of conducting activities within the forum State," thereby enjoying the "benefits and protection" of forum law.[1] This has led to great controversy in so-called "stream of commerce" cases, in which a product manufactured or sold in one state is carried by the "stream of commerce" to some other state where it eventually causes injury, often after passing down a chain of distribution or use and resale before some injury occurs that is remote in time and place from the defendant's last involvement with the product. In the leading case on this topic, no majority of the nine Justices of the US Supreme Court could agree on whether the purposefulness criterion could be satisfied in "stream of commerce" cases by the defendant's "mere awareness" of the likelihood of injury in the forum state, or whether some form of "purposeful direction" of the product towards the forum state was required.[2]

The "purposefulness" debate has not been confined to the business context. In another leading case involving domestic relations and liability for child support, the US Supreme Court rejected as insufficiently purposeful certain obvious contacts between the defendant and the forum state because they had been undertaken, however voluntarily and deliberately, "in the interests of family harmony" rather than from some self-serving desire to benefit from the law of the forum to which the defendant parent had allowed his child to move.[3]

1. *World-Wide Volkswagen*, 444 U.S. at 297; *Hanson v. Denckla*, 357 U.S. 235, 253 (1958).
2. *Asahi*, 480 U.S. at 122.
3. *Kulko v. Superior Court*, 436 U.S. 84, 94 (1978).

3. Tag Jurisdiction

Is the defendant a natural person whose purposeful contact with the forum state includes voluntary presence within the forum state at the time of service of process, resulting in "tag jurisdiction" over that defendant limited to the particular lawsuit with whose process the defendant was thus served?

93. As explained later in this section (paragraph 102), it is controversial whether "tag jurisdiction" is properly viewed as a species of "minimum-contacts" jurisdiction or as justified by a form of essentially historical due-process analysis that is distinct from minimum-contacts analysis. Although unable to agree on why "tag jurisdiction" is constitutional, the US Supreme Court has made clear that in almost all cases "tag jurisdiction" will be held consistent with the defendant's right to due process of law. In this context the "purposefulness" inquiry is limited to ascertaining whether the defendant was voluntarily present in the forum state at the time of service of process.

4. General Jurisdiction

Are the defendant's purposeful contacts with the forum state so substantial that the defendant is subject to that state's "general jurisdiction?"

94. Despite its many references to a seemingly three-sided "relationship between the defendant, the forum, and the litigation," the US Supreme Court has always recognized that a particular defendant's purposeful contacts with a particular state may be so pervasive that the defendant may be sued in that state on any cause of action whatsoever – thus eliminating any need for the showing of some relationship between the forum and the litigation that is distinct from the defendant's status as a party to that litigation. Within American law, this form of territorial jurisdiction has come to be called "general jurisdiction."

General jurisdiction is directly rooted in the premises of *Pennoyer*, which never suggested that its rules limiting the assertion of territorial jurisdiction over nonresidents applied as well to residents of the forum state, so as to forbid the rendering of a personal judgment against a defendant who happened to be absent from the state when summoned to defend against a lawsuit in the courts of that defendant's state of residence. Residence in a state, or more formally "domicile" there – which as discussed above in connection with federal diversity jurisdiction (paragraph 58) distinguishes between temporary residence and the establishment of a more permanent form of residence – is the paradigmatic basis for that state to have general jurisdiction over a natural person. Incorporation in a state, often said to amount to "corporate domicile," is the paradigmatic basis for that state to have general jurisdiction over a corporation. Beyond these paradigms, however, much remains that is uncertain about the predicates for general jurisdiction over a particular defendant.

The US Supreme Court first articulated the test for general jurisdiction as whether the defendant has "continuous and systematic" contacts with the forum state.[1] In its only other decision squarely addressing the concept of general jurisdiction, the *Helicopteros* case, the Supreme Court added that such continuous and systematic contacts must also be "sufficient."[2] This case involved a Colombian corporation that chartered helicopters. Over a seven-year period that corporation had expended more than USD 4 million in Texas to purchase helicopters and to train its pilots in their operation. As presented to the court, the *Helicopteros* case involved an attempt to sue the corporation in Texas on a cause of action unrelated to these purchases of helicopters and related services. The Supreme Court held that these "purchases and related training trips" were "not a sufficient basis" for Texas to exercise general jurisdiction over the corporation.[3]

1. *Perkins v. Benguet Consol. Mining Co.*, 342 U.S. 437, 445-446 (1952).
2. *Helicopteros Nacionales De Colombia, S.A. v. Hall*, 466 U.S. 408 (1984).
3. Id., at 417.

95. In order to gauge what might be a sufficient level of contacts to support general jurisdiction, one must take account of the awesome power over a defendant that general jurisdiction entails. Remember that the point of general jurisdiction is to permit the forum to adjudicate any claim whatsoever against the defendant, no matter how unrelated to anything that defendant has ever done in the forum state. It means that any plaintiff in the world, with respect to the alleged conduct of the defendant anywhere in the world at any time in the past, can call that defendant to defend its conduct in the courts of a state with general jurisdiction over that defendant.

It makes eminent sense that every defendant that lives within or exists under the law of an American state be thus subject to the unqualified jurisdictional power of at least that one "home" state, so that plaintiffs can resort to the courts of that home state to redress any alleged grievances against the defendant without any preliminary jurisdictional wrangling. And because for various reasons of domestic law many American corporations are formally chartered by one state (generally Delaware) but conduct most or all of their business elsewhere, it also makes sense for the state in which a corporation has its "principal place of business" (discussed above in paragraph

60 in the context of federal diversity jurisdiction) to have general jurisdiction over such a nominally "foreign" corporation.

It is not so obvious that there should be a multiplicity of states, other than the state of domicile or incorporation or some one other, "principal" state of corporate business, in which an individual or corporation is subject to general jurisdiction. Nonetheless, current constitutional law admits that possibility when the defendant's contacts with some other state are both "continuous and systematic" and, in some inchoate sense, "sufficient."

We think the formula for general jurisdiction should be restated to require a showing of "*purposeful* contact that is continuous, systematic, and *substantial*." The purposefulness requirement is uncontroversial. It is now well-established that only purposeful contacts are relevant to minimum-contacts analysis, and this was confirmed in the general-jurisdiction context by the *Helicopteros* case discussed above, in which certain other contacts between the defendant corporation and Texas were disregarded because they resulted from the "unilateral activity of another party or a third person."[1] The substantiality requirement goes beyond the vague sufficiency standard used by the US Supreme Court itself, in order to emphasize that "continuous and systematic" contact, even when purposeful, will be insufficient to justify general jurisdiction absent a very high level of sustained contact with the forum state.

It remains an open question just what level of continuous and systematic contact with a state will be substantial enough to permit that state to exercise general jurisdiction over a particular defendant. It is clear that some forms of affiliation to a particular state, such as domicile or incorporation, suffice per se to justify that state's power to adjudicate any claim whatsoever against the defendant, and that some other forms of pervasive or at least "substantial" affiliation may also suffice. A great deal of precedent appears to support the proposition that such an affiliation results when a corporation of one state so concentrates its activities in another state as to make that other state its "principal place of business," although it has been questioned whether in many such cases there was indeed no relationship between the litigation in question and the defendant's activities in the forum state.[2] For purposes of federal diversity jurisdiction, discussed above (paragraph 60), a corporation can have only one such "principal place of business." Whether the same is true for purposes of general jurisdiction within the constitutional law of state-court territorial jurisdiction is likely, but as yet not definitively established by the US Supreme Court.

1. Id.
2. *See* Mary Twitchell, "The Myth of General Jurisdiction," Harv. L. Rev. 101 (1988): 610. *See also* *Gator.com Corp. v. L.L. Bean, Inc.*, 341 F.3rd 1072 (9th Cir. 2003).

5. Specific Jurisdiction

If the defendant's purposeful contacts are insufficient to establish general jurisdiction, are they sufficiently related to the litigation in question to establish "specific jurisdiction?"

96. "Specific jurisdiction" extends only to the particular litigation in question. Unlike general jurisdiction, which opens the forum to anyone in the world to file any lawsuit whatsoever against the defendant, specific jurisdiction extends only to a lawsuit that "is related to or 'arises out of' a defendant's contacts with the forum."[1] This demand for some degree of "relatedness" raises an issue no less subtle and confused than that of "purposefulness," discussed above (paragraph 92) as the second step of our suggested six-step analysis. Here, as elsewhere, when the US Supreme Court speaks of "a defendant's contacts" it must be understood to refer only to the defendant's *purposeful* contacts. The court has not yet indicated whether the relatedness standard is met only when the litigation "arises out of" the defendant's purposeful contacts in some fairly direct sense that parallels the concept of proximate cause within the law of torts, or may be satisfied by some less direct connection or relationship between what the defendant did that amounts to purposeful contact with the forum state, and what the defendant did that has caused the plaintiff to file the particular lawsuit in question.

For instance, suppose defendant D's purposeful contacts with state X consist solely of marketing and selling in state X just one product: drug Z. The plaintiff is injured by using drug Z, but the particular dose of drug Z that caused plaintiff P's injury was purchased and caused injury in state Y. Other consumers purchased drug Z in state X, however, and (in other litigation) have alleged that they suffered resulting injury within state X. Is there a sufficient relationship between P's particular injury and the defendant's activities in marketing and selling drug Z in state X to permit state X to exercise specific jurisdiction of P's suit against D, which did not "arise out of" D's activities in state X, but rather from D's related activities in state Y?

The best answer to this question might entail a balancing test or "sliding-scale" approach to relatedness. By such an approach, the amount of relatedness required would be inversely proportional to the degree of the defendant's purposeful contacts with the forum state. With reference to the foregoing example, if D sold only a little of drug Z in state X, then state X would not have specific jurisdiction of P's merely "related" suit against D arising from D's sale and P's use of drug Z outside of state X. But if D sold a large volume of drug Z to consumers in state X, then X would have specific jurisdiction even as to P's suit for damages arising from the sale and use of the same product – drug Z – in state Y rather than state X.

1. *Helicopteros*, 466 U.S. at 414.

97. The US Supreme Court appeared to suggest such a sliding-scale approach to relatedness in *International Shoe*,[1] but in the later *Helicopteros* case appeared to treat the question as an open one.[2] Another case may shed some additional light on the "relatedness" standard, however. The *Keeton* case involved an allegedly defamatory article contained in a magazine of which several thousand copies were sold in the forum state.[3] The plaintiff's suit against the defendant sought to recover damages not merely for whatever harm resulted from those copies sold in the forum state, but from the much larger number of copies sold nationwide. Thus the full scope of the litigation did not arise directly from what the defendant did in the forum state, but there was a strong relationship between the fairly substantial acts of the defendant that caused injury in the forum state and its far more substantial acts elsewhere for which the plaintiff was also seeking redress in the forum state. The US Supreme Court upheld the specific jurisdiction of the forum state over the entire litigation, including the claim for nationwide damages, without commenting on whether the sale of only 10 or 15 copies of the offending magazine in the forum state would have been enough, instead of the sale of the 10,000 to 15,000 copies that actually occurred.

It is difficult to resist the implication that the magnitude of the defendant's acts in the forum state must have been relevant to the permissibility of the forum state having jurisdiction to award damages attributable to the defendant's related conduct in other states. On the other hand, it is possible that when the US Supreme Court decides to provide a definitive elaboration of the "relatedness" issue, it will decide that a marginal degree of relatedness, in proportion to the degree of the defendant's purposeful contacts with the forum state, should be taken account of in the final step of our suggested six-step approach. This step poses the ultimate question of whether the exercise of specific jurisdiction is circumstantially "reasonable." For this reason we recommend that a loose standard of "relatedness" be applied at the present, fifth step of analysis. If the defendant's purposeful contacts with the forum state have some plausible relationship to the conduct of the defendant at issue in a particular lawsuit, that should be deemed sufficient for the forum state to have specific jurisdiction over that lawsuit. Analysis must then proceed to the sixth and final step, next discussed, with any lingering concern over the marginal degree of "relatedness" addressed as part of its overall "reasonableness" calculation. (This relationship between "relatedness" and "reasonableness" is discussed specifically in paragraph 99 below.)

1. *International Shoe*, 326 U.S. at 319-320.
2. *Helicopteros*, 466 U.S. at 414.
3. *Keeton v. Hustler Magazine, Inc.*, 465 U.S. 770 (1984).

6. Reasonableness

Is it "reasonable" for the forum state to exercise its specific jurisdiction?

98. Over the first four decades of its application of the new "minimum-contacts" test of *International Shoe*, the US Supreme Court occasionally punctuated its analysis of the defendant's contacts with the forum state with references to a grab bag of other factors affecting its jurisdictional determination. Some of these additional factors were party-specific, such as the burden it might impose on the defendant to litigate the case in the plaintiff's chosen forum, and the burden that the plaintiff might face in litigating elsewhere. The other factors were systemic, looking to the particular interest of the forum state in adjudicating the dispute, the general interests of other states in enforcing their public policy, and the interest of the entire interstate judicial system in the efficient resolution of potential duplicative litigation.[1]

In 1985, the US Supreme Court clarified how such additional factors might affect the minimum-contacts calculus. The *Burger King*[2] case reformulated the approach of *International Shoe* to make the constitutionality of specific jurisdiction turn on two successive questions. *International Shoe* had fully incorporated subjective considerations of "fair play and substantial justice" into the single question of the defendant's "minimum contacts" with the forum state. *Burger King* added a second-tier of "reasonableness" analysis, reached only after an initial determination that the "minimum contacts" threshold has been satisfied.

Under *Burger King*, subjective concern for "fair play and substantial justice" remains relevant to the initial determination that minimum contacts exist. Such concern arises from the constitutional foundation for minimum-contacts analysis, which is an "individual's liberty interest" under the Due Process Clause of the Fourteenth Amendment "in not being subject to the binding judgments of a forum with which he has no meaningful 'contacts, ties, or relations'".[3] The purposefulness and relatedness requirements are not entirely objective; they also serve the subjective concern of the Due Process Clause for "fair play and substantial justice" by restricting specific jurisdiction to cases in which the defendants have "fair warning that a particular activity may subject [them] to the jurisdiction of a foreign sovereign."[4] The "foreseeability" that minimum contacts with a particular state will presumptively vest that state with territorial jurisdiction over the defendant is not an independent requirement, but rather the upshot of the purposefulness and relatedness requirements.

The *Burger King* court took pains to note that the case before it involved an assertion of specific rather than general jurisdiction.[5] It did not otherwise discuss the application of its reformulation to cases of general jurisdiction, and this has led to some confusion among the lower courts. In our view, however, the court's careful distinction of general jurisdiction as a separate analytical category makes clear that the demands of due process are fully satisfied by a determination that a defendant's purposeful contacts with the forum state are so continuous, systematic, and substantial that general jurisdiction exists. Such a pervasive level of contact necessarily provides the defendant with "fair warning" that it is subject to suit in the forum state, thus satisfying what the *Burger King* court identified as the fundamental prerequisite for state-court territorial jurisdiction over a nonconsenting defendant. If such pervasive purposeful contact were not sufficient, in and of itself, to justify the assertion of territorial jurisdiction with respect to any cause of action at all, it would render meaningless the *Burger King* court's express preservation of general jurisdiction as a separate analytical category. If general jurisdiction could be defeated by circumstantial appeal to "reasonableness" factors as they apply to particular cases brought against a defendant, it would no longer be genuinely "general" jurisdiction. We recommend thinking of general jurisdiction as based on "maximum contacts" such that due process requires no further analysis of the nature and quality of the contacts in question in relation to the particular cause of action brought against the defendant in the forum state.

1. *See World-Wide Volkswagen*, 444 U.S. at 292; *Burger King Corp. v. Rudzewicz*, 471 U.S. at 462, 477 (1985).
2. *See Burger King v. Corp. v. Rudzewicz*, 471 U.S. at 462.
3. Id., at 471-472 (quoting *International Shoe*, 326 U.S. 310 (1945)).
4. Id., at 472 (quoting *Shaffer v. Heitner*, 433 U.S. 186 (1977)).
5. Id., at 473 n. 15 (citing *Helicopteros Nacionales De Colombia, S.A. v. Hall*, 466 U.S. 408 (1984) and *Perkins v. Benguet Consol. Mining Co.*, 342 U.S. at 437.).

99. In cases depending on specific jurisdiction, however, *Burger King* equally clearly provides that a finding of sufficient purposefulness and relatedness for "minimum contacts" to exist does not definitively establish that due process permits the forum state to assert jurisdiction in the particular case in question. "Fair play and substantial justice" require not only the "fair warning" of the *likelihood* of suit in the forum state that the "minimum contacts" threshold assures, but also further analysis of the ultimate *reasonableness* of the forum state's exercise of jurisdiction in the particular case in question. This "reasonableness" requirement is presumptively but not conclusively satisfied by the threshold finding that the defendant has minimum contacts with the forum state. The additional factors deemed relevant to specific jurisdiction in previous cases are applicable only at this second stage of analysis.

Burger King is rather Delphic in its description of the balancing process deployed at this second stage to determine the circumstantial reasonableness of specific jurisdiction. The following account is more detailed than that offered by the US Supreme Court, but coherently elaborates every element that the Supreme Court mentions. The balancing process begins by placing, on the "reasonableness" side of the scales, the minimum contacts previously found to exist. This tilts the scales in favor of a finding of reasonableness, consistent with the court's clear indication that the threshold finding of minimum contacts makes the exercise of specific jurisdiction presumptively reasonable. Any of the additional factors may in a particular case weigh either in favor of or against the reasonableness of the forum state's exercise of jurisdiction. Even the factor that looks to the convenience interests of the plaintiff that would be served by permitting the suit to go forward in the plaintiff's chosen forum may in fact weigh against reasonableness, and hence against the plaintiff, if indeed the plaintiff would not be inconvenienced by suit elsewhere and has chosen to file suit in a less convenient forum simply to take tactical advantage of some procedural or substantive feature of the legal system of the forum state. In the ordinary case, however, some of the factors will incline the balance either way.

Even if all of the additional factors were to weigh against the reasonableness of jurisdiction, they might not be enough to overcome the initial presumption in favor of reasonableness: "where a defendant who purposefully has directed his activities at forum residents seeks to defeat jurisdiction, he must present a *compelling* case that the presence of some other considerations would render jurisdiction unreasonable."[1] But it is at least possible for a defendant to succeed in making such a compelling showing of unreasonableness if the additional factors weigh heavily in the defendant's favor. This is most likely to occur when the only weight on the reasonableness side of the scales is provided by the presumptive weight of the defendant's minimum contacts with the forum state, and that presumptive weight is not great because the minimum-contacts threshold has barely been satisfied. These minimum contacts may be of scant presumptive weight because they are marginal in amount. But if we are right in our analysis above of what the *Keeton* case suggests about the relationship of "relatedness" and reasonableness (paragraph 97), they may also be of scant presumptive weight because they are only marginally related to the litigation in question.

In the ordinary case, where consideration of the additional factors is likely to add at least some weight in favor of the reasonableness of the plaintiff's choice, such additional factors as favor the plaintiff may be dispositive in establishing the reasonableness of jurisdiction despite only a marginal finding of the requisite minimum contacts. This is the sense of the US Supreme Court's observation that the additional factors may "sometimes serve to establish the reasonableness of jurisdiction upon a lesser showing of minimum contacts than would otherwise be required."[2]

1. Id., at 477 (emphasis added).
2. Id.

E. *Recent Decisions*

100. Two cases decided since *Burger King* cast more light on the reformulation of *International Shoe*'s minimum-contacts test as an important but nonexclusive component of the overall process of determining the constitutionality of a particular assertion of state-court territorial jurisdiction. Both were decided by fractured courts in which no majority of justices agreed upon key issues presented to the court. As such, they also demonstrate that this area of federal constitutional law is in disarray, and is likely to remain volatile for the indefinite future.

101. In its 1987 decision in the *Asahi* case,[1] the US Supreme Court ruled 8-1 that the previous list of additional factors pertinent to *Burger King*'s reasonableness determination – the sixth step of our proposed framework of minimum-contacts analysis – was not an exhaustive list. There remains a standing possibility that some new factor will be added to the grab bag as dispositive of a particular case. In *Asahi*, the Supreme Court identified two new additional factors and gave them dispositive weight: the "international context" of litigation implicating both the interests of foreign nations and the foreign-relations policies of the United States, and the "unique burdens" placed upon an alien defendant who must defend itself in a foreign legal system.[2] Thus it was held unreasonable for California to exercise its jurisdiction to adjudicate an indemnification dispute between two alien corporations, one Japanese and one Taiwanese. This holding was based on the assumption that the party challenging California's jurisdiction, the Japanese manufacturer of a component sold to the Taiwanese manufacturer and in turn incorporated by the latter manufacturer into a product that was sold and caused injury in California, did indeed have the threshold minimum contacts with California necessary to advance analysis to the "reasonableness" tier. On this point, competing wings of four justices each were deeply divided, one wing asserting that the Japanese manufacturer's "mere awareness" that its component might make its way to California was insufficient to establish any "purposeful" contact at all, the other wing asserting that in a "stream of commerce" case mere awareness of the ultimate market for a component part ought to be sufficient to establish purposeful contact with that market.

1. *Asahi Metal Indus. Co. v. Superior Court*, 480 U.S. 102 (1987).
2. Id., at 114.

102. In its 1990 decision in the *Burnham* case,[1] the US Supreme Court could agree only on its judgment, without any opinion commanding a majority of the justices. The case nonetheless has great significance because the differing rationales offered by competing wings of four justices each collectively established the virtually per se constitutionality of "tag jurisdiction," as noted above (paragraph 93) in connection with the third step of our suggested six-step approach. Thus the fundamental constitutional tenet of *Pennoyer*, that a state may exercise territorial jurisdiction over a nonresident individual with respect to any lawsuit whose process is served upon that nonresident while personally present within the state, remains a fixture of modern American constitutional law.

Three justices, with the partial concurrence of a fourth, thought that such a historic form of territorial jurisdiction was per se consistent with due process, and as such was a form of jurisdiction not subject to minimum-contacts analysis. Four justices insisted that minimum-contacts analysis still applied in this situation, the individual's voluntary presence in the state at the time of service constituting the vital prerequisite of purposeful contact. But the willingness of this group of four justices to uphold such jurisdiction as presumptively reasonable, without any inquiry into the relatedness of the defendant's conduct at issue in the litigation to the defendant's conduct in voluntarily entering the state, can only be termed disingenuous. In fact it was a defensive move by three of the justices[2] to provide the fourth[3] with a basis for upholding "tag jurisdiction" without furnishing the fifth vote for a majority opinion rejecting an ahistorical conception of "due process" that would embarrass her in the far more prominent debate then raging among the justices of the US Supreme Court over the degree to which the Due Process Clause limits state power to proscribe abortions.[4]

Despite its dubious pedigree, *Burnham* makes clear that "tag jurisdiction" is virtually immune from constitutional challenge. As such, some commentators mistakenly classify it as establishing a distinct form of general jurisdiction over natural persons. Although "tag jurisdiction" resembles general jurisdiction in one respect – there need be no showing that the litigation relates in any way to the reason for the defendant's transient presence in the forum state at the time of service of process – it differs from general jurisdiction in other, more significant ways. First, the transient presence of the defendant, although necessarily purposeful in at least the minimal sense that it must be voluntary,[5] is hardly "continuous" or "systematic," let alone "substantial." Second, the jurisdiction acquired by the forum state is not literally "general." It does not extend beyond the specific lawsuit whose process was served upon the defendant while present within the state.

Suppose that A of Texas causes vehicular injury to B of Ohio and C of California while all three are vacationing in Florida. Both B and C can sue A by invoking either the general jurisdiction of Texas over A, its domiciliary, or the specific jurisdiction of Florida over A for injuries caused by A incident to A's purposeful contact with Florida by entering it and driving on its highways. But C would prefer to bring suit against A in C's home state of California, and may do so by means of "tag jurisdiction" if C, aware of A's likely presence in California, files suit there and serves process on A after A enters California. If this were sufficient to give California general jurisdiction over A, B could then also file suit in California and assert jurisdiction over A without any independent requirement of service upon A while A is present in California. But this is not the case. Whether B will be able to invoke California's jurisdiction over A depends entirely (absent some other purposeful contact of A with California that is somehow related to the Florida accident) on B's own success in serving process on A while A is present in California.

1. *Burnham v. Superior Court*, 495 U.S. 604 (1990).
2. Justices Brennan, Marshall, and Blackmun.
3. Justice O'Connor.
4. *See Planned Parenthood v. Casey*, 505 U.S. 833 (1992); *Webster v. Reproductive Health Services*, 492 U.S. 490 (1989).
5. *Burnham*, 495 U.S. at 628-629; 638-639. (The four justices purporting to uphold "tag" jurisdiction as "generally" permissible on minimum-contacts grounds insisted on the defendant's "voluntary

presence in the forum.") *See also* id., at 628, where the fourth justice who concurred partially in the alternative, historical approach limited his concurrence to cases in which "presence in the forum state is intentional."

F. *Summary of Six-Step Approach*

103. It is time now to summarize the practical application of each step, in sequence, of our suggested six-step approach to determining in any case whether a state court's exercise of territorial jurisdiction will be sustained in the face of a defendant's due-process objection.

1. Contact

104. Has the defendant had contact of any kind with the forum state? If not, analysis ends at this first step. The defendant's motion to be dismissed from the case must be granted. While any defendant may waive the right to object to territorial jurisdiction on due-process grounds, either by consent or by conduct (see below, paragraphs 115-118), the present exercise assumes that the defendant has properly asserted a due-process objection. No state can exercise territorial jurisdiction over an objecting defendant in the absence of some form of contact between the defendant and that state. If there is some such contact, analysis proceeds to the second step.

2. Purposefulness

105. If there are contacts between the defendant and the forum state, do any of them constitute "purposeful" contacts? If not, analysis ends at this second step. The defendant's motion to be dismissed from the case must be granted. Due process always requires some form of purposeful contact between the defendant and the forum state. If there is any such purposeful contact, analysis proceeds to the third step.

3. Tag Jurisdiction

106. Is the defendant a natural person whose purposeful contact with the forum state includes voluntary presence within the forum state at the time of service of process, resulting in "tag jurisdiction" over that defendant limited to the particular lawsuit with whose process the defendant was thus served? If so, analysis ends at this third step. The defendant's objection to jurisdiction must be overruled, and the case may proceed in the courts of the forum state. If the purposeful contact identified at the second step does not involve in-state service of a voluntarily present natural person, analysis proceeds to the fourth step.

4. General Jurisdiction

107. Are the defendant's purposeful contacts with the forum state so substantial that the defendant is subject to that state's "general jurisdiction?" If so, analysis ends at this fourth step. The defendant's objection to jurisdiction must be overruled, and the case may proceed in the courts of the forum state. If the purposeful contact identified at the second step is not of this pervasive character, analysis proceeds to the fifth step.

5. Specific Jurisdiction

108. If the defendant's purposeful contacts are insufficient to establish general jurisdiction, are they sufficiently related to the litigation in question to establish "specific jurisdiction?" If not, analysis ends at this fifth step. The defendant's motion to be dismissed from the case must be granted. If the defendant's purposeful contact with the forum state does bear some plausible relationship to the litigation in question, analysis proceeds to the sixth step.

6. Reasonableness

109. Is it "reasonable" for the forum state to exercise its specific jurisdiction? If not, the defendant's motion to be dismissed from the case must be granted. But "unreasonableness" will be established only in an unusual case. Only a compelling showing of circumstantial unreasonableness in light of a grab bag of contingently applicable additional factors can overcome the presumptive reasonability of exercising specific jurisdiction over a defendant who has the requisite minimum contacts with the forum state. But the defendant has the standing opportunity to make such a showing, and the list of applicable additional factors is not static. The strength of the showing the defendant must make is sensitive to either the substantial or marginal nature of the minimum contacts between the defendant and the forum state. If the contacts themselves are slight, or if their relationship to the litigation is tenuous, there is a greater chance of establishing the unreasonableness of specific jurisdiction notwithstanding the marginal finding at the fifth step that the requisite minimum contacts exist. Ordinarily, however, the sixth step will result in overruling the defendant's objection, permitting the case to proceed in the courts of the forum state.

V. State "Long-Arm" Statutes

110. The constitutional principles just elaborated (paragraphs 88-109) determine whether a state *may* assert territorial jurisdiction over a particular defendant, at least with respect to a particular lawsuit. It does not follow that a state *will* assert territorial jurisdiction whenever that is constitutionally permissible. We have discussed the relevant constitutional principles first because they form the canvas upon which most of the law regarding state-court territorial jurisdiction has been painted. But in every case the statutory law of the state in question must also be examined to determine how fully it implements such territorial jurisdiction as the state is constitutionally free to assert.

As noted previously (paragraph 83), state jurisdictional statutes that authorize the assertion of territorial jurisdiction over nonresidents are called "long-arm" statutes. This terminology arises from the metaphorical image of the process of a state court reaching out (like a long arm) to grab defendants from other states. But a more artistic metaphor better serves our purpose of explaining the relationship between the federal constitutional law of state-court territorial jurisdiction and the local statutory law of each state authorizing the assertion of territorial jurisdiction. If federal constitutional law is the canvas upon which the full scope of permissible state-court territorial jurisdiction has been painted (however abstract, confusing, and perhaps inartistic that modern image may be), then the local statutory law of each state forms the frame around that canvas.

111. Some state long-arm statutes frame that image without any matting or obscuration whatsoever. As such, they incorporate the full scope of territorial jurisdiction permitted by the federal Constitution as the test for whatever territorial jurisdiction the courts of those states may exercise. California's long-arm statute exemplifies this approach. It provides simply: "A court of this state may exercise jurisdiction on any basis not inconsistent with the constitution of this state or of the United States."[1] Other state long-arm statutes are more detailed. For instance, New York's long-arm statute provides in pertinent part:

> Personal jurisdiction by acts of non-domiciliaries.
>
> (a) Acts which are the basis for jurisdiction. As to a cause of action arising from any of the acts enumerated in this section, a court may exercise personal jurisdiction over any non-domiciliary, or his executor of administrator, who in person or through an agent:
> (1) transacts any business within the state or contracts anywhere to supply goods and services in the state; or
> (2) commits a tortious act within the state, except as to a cause of action for defamation of character arising from the act; or
> (3) commits a tortious act without the state causing injury to person or property within the state, except as to a cause of action for defamation of character arising from the act, if he
> (i) regularly does or solicits business, or engages in any other persistent course of conduct, or derives substantial revenue from goods used or consumed or services rendered, in the state, or
> (ii) expects or should reasonably expect the act to have consequences in the state and derives substantial revenue from interstate or international commerce; or
> (4) owns, uses or possesses any real property situated within the state.[2]

1. Cal. Civ. Proc. Code §410.10 (West 2004).
2. N.Y.C.P.L.R. §302(a) (McKinney 1990).

112. When a state's long-arm statute takes this "laundry list" approach, seeking to enumerate specific factors that are determinative of territorial jurisdiction in a particular case, the possibility exists that territorial jurisdiction may be unavailable in that state with regard to a particular defendant in a particular case simply because the case and the defendant's conduct do not fall within one of the jurisdictional categories specified in the statute. Thus the statute obscures part of the broad canvas of federal constitutional law, making the full scope of state-court territorial jurisdiction *pro tanto* unavailable to courts within that state, in the same restrictive way that the insertion of a mat within the frame of a painting or photograph renders part of the full image invisible. No state long-arm statute can expand the territorial jurisdiction of courts within that state beyond the outer limits permitted by the federal Constitution. But a restrictive state long-arm statute can give courts within that state less jurisdictional power than they would have under an unrestrictive statute.

Just how restrictive a particular state long-arm statute may be is often a difficult question of state law, as to which the state's court of last resort has the final say. New York's highest court, the NY Court of Appeals, has construed the long-arm statute quoted above to indeed foreclose the New York trial courts from asserting territorial jurisdiction in some circumstances in which the two-tiered federal "minimum contacts" plus "reasonableness" test would be satisfied. But other state courts of last resort have construed the facially restrictive language of similarly detailed long-arm statutes as nonetheless conferring on their trial courts the full scope of jurisdictional power permitted by the federal Constitution. The trend nationwide is away from the New York approach and toward the California approach, but most often this has occurred by judicial construction rather than by legislative amendment. The best that can be said is that state long-arm statutes may – but generally do not – operate to restrict the territorial jurisdiction of particular state courts, and that the language of these statutes is often not a reliable guide to their effective meaning.

Whatever the scope of a particular state's long-arm statute, the territorial jurisdiction thereby conferred on its courts is generally not obligatory. All states recognize the common-law doctrine of *forum non conveniens*, sometimes as codified or qualified by statute but generally as a matter of decisional law. This doctrine permits a court voluntarily to relinquish the territorial jurisdiction that it might otherwise exercise. The fundamental prerequisite for the dismissal of litigation on *forum non conveniens* grounds is the existence of an alternative forum in which the litigation might proceed more conveniently or efficiently.[1] The plaintiff's choice of forum is entitled to considerable deference, but can be overcome upon a strong showing that the alternative forum is superior in light of such private and public factors as the convenience of witnesses, access to evidence, the relative burdens on the parties, and the relative interests of the original and alternative forums.[2]

1. The US Supreme Court recently held that a federal court has discretion to dismiss a case on *forum non conveniens* grounds even if it has not definitely established the court's subject-matter and personal jurisdiction. *See Sinochem Int'l Co. v. Malaysia Int'l Shipping Corp.*, 127 S. Ct. 1184 (2007).
2. *Gulf Oil v. Gilbert*, 330 U.S. 501 (1947). The federal Constitution neither imposes the doctrine of *forum non conveniens* upon the states nor regulates their invocation of it. In *Gilbert*, the US Supreme

Court was merely stating its view of the doctrine as a matter of common law. Nonetheless, *Gilbert* has become the leading American case on the dimensions of the doctrine of *forum non conveniens*, and its principles are widely if voluntarily followed by most state courts.

VI. The Territorial Jurisdiction of Federal District Courts

A. Constitutional Scope

113. The territorial jurisdiction of the federal district courts is limited by the Due Process Clause of the Fifth Amendment to the federal Constitution. Although the US Supreme Court has not yet ruled on the issue, several lower courts have held that the same "minimum contacts" plus "reasonableness" test applies to federal courts under the Fifth Amendment as applies to state courts under the Fourteenth Amendment. With respect to the "minimum contacts" prong of this test, the political structure of the federal court system makes this test far less constraining in the federal context. Although Congress has chosen to establish federal judicial districts on a state-by-state basis, this is a purely administrative decision that is not constitutionally required. All federal district courts are part of the same nationwide judicial system, created by the same national sovereign: the federal government. Thus, a defendant whose activities within the United States as a whole amount to "minimum contacts" may constitutionally be subjected to the territorial jurisdiction of the United States. It would not appear to be a matter of constitutional significance just where within the United States the particular district court in which the defendant is subject to suit is located, but it is at least arguable that the exercise of territorial jurisdiction by a district court at a particularly inconvenient location within the United States might implicate the "reasonableness" prong of due-process analysis.

B. Statutory Restriction

114. The lack of any definitive constitutional law regarding the scope of the territorial jurisdiction of the federal district courts is reflective of a statutory environment that is much different from that of the state courts. Whereas the governing jurisdictional statutes generally if not always extend the territorial jurisdiction of state courts as far as federal constitutional law will permit, the opposite is true of the jurisdictional statutes applicable to the federal district courts. By legislative choice rather than constitutional command, in the great majority of cases federal district courts may exercise no greater territorial jurisdiction than the courts of the state in which they sit.

Although this restriction of the territorial jurisdiction of federal trial courts was mandated by statute for much of the history of the United States, since 1938 it has resulted from an enabling statute that delegates procedural rulemaking power to the US Supreme Court. Pursuant to that statute,[1] the legislation restricting the territorial jurisdiction of the federal district courts is Rule 4 of the Federal Rules of Civil Procedure. The text of Rule 4 is regrettably complicated, but its effect is well understood. In almost all cases the territorial jurisdiction of a federal district court is determined by reference to the territorial jurisdiction of the state courts within which it sits. Thus, in the ordinary case a federal district court follows exactly the same process of analysis as a court of the state in which it sits. If a defendant objects to its territorial jurisdiction, the federal district court looks to the long-arm statute of the state in which the district court is located. Unless a more restrictive analysis is mandated by that statute, the federal district court determines the scope of its territorial jurisdiction by evaluating the defendant's contacts with the state in which it sits under the same "minimum contacts" plus "reasonableness" test as would a state court.[2]

This general régime reserves to Congress the power to extend the territorial jurisdiction of the federal district courts beyond state lines in particular cases.[3] Federal district courts may exercise nationwide territorial jurisdiction in, for example, cases brought under the federal antitrust and securities statutes.[4] Rule 4 itself provides for two other, quite limited exceptions to the normally state-by-state scope of federal territorial jurisdiction. In any type of case, whether based on federal or state law, a federal district court may reach beyond state lines – but only within a radius of 100 miles from where the court sits – to assert territorial jurisdiction over additional defendants whose joinder is required for just adjudication of the main litigation.[5] This is the only form of "ancillary territorial jurisdiction" expressly authorized by federal law. Finally, and more rarely applicable, is Rule 4(k)(2), a recently added provision permitting a federal district court to exercise nationwide territorial jurisdiction in any federal-question case in which a particular defendant is not subject to the territorial jurisdiction of any state.[6] Although this provision should be of concern to foreign litigants, at whom it is clearly targeted, the "negation" clause (making it applicable only upon a showing that no state has territorial jurisdiction of the defendant) is so difficult to satisfy that so far it has had virtually no effect.[7]

1. 28 U.S.C. §2072.
2. In a case asserting personal jurisdiction over the defendant, the provision that generally confines the territorial jurisdiction of a federal district court to that of the state in which it sits is Rule 4(k)(1). The assertion of in rem jurisdiction by a federal district court is similarly restricted. Although the restriction may be overridden by a contrary statute, Rule 4(n)(1), in rem jurisdiction, is otherwise governed by Rule 4(n)(2). It provides that a federal district court may exercise in rem jurisdiction only as to the property of a defendant who is not subject to its personal jurisdiction, and only to the extent that in rem jurisdiction could be asserted by a court of the state in which the federal district court sits.
3. Fed. R. Civ. P. 4(k)(1)(C).
4. *See* 15 U.S.C. §25 (antitrust cases); 15 U.S.C. §§77v(a), 77aa (securities cases). This is not an exhaustive list of cases eligible for nationwide territorial jurisdiction, but these are the most common kinds of such cases. Federal courts may also exercise nationwide territorial jurisdiction under Rule 4(k)(1)(c) in interpleader cases under 28 U.S.C. §1335. Interpleader cases are cases in which multiple claimants to a common fund are citizens of different states. Federal jurisdiction in interpleader cases based on state rather than federal law is also facilitated by a special grant of diversity jurisdiction that suspends the normal requirements of "complete" diversity and an amount in controversy that exceeds USD 75,000. Federal district courts have subject-matter jurisdiction under 28 U.S.C. §1335 over any interpleader case in which citizens of more than one state have conflicting claims to property worth at least USD 500. Only "minimal" diversity is required, making it immaterial that some of the conflicting claimants may be citizens of the same state.
5. Fed. R. Civ. P. 4(k)(1)(B), which applies only to "necessary parties" whose joinder to the main litigation is required by Rule 19, and to third-party defendants who may be impleaded under Rule 14 by existing parties seeking indemnification or contribution to offset their potential liability in the main litigation.
6. This provision was added in 1993 to allow suit under federal law of a defendant who has "minimum contacts" with the United States as a whole but whose contacts are so diffuse that they are

insufficient to bring that defendant within the territorial jurisdiction of any particular state within the United States.

7. An excellent overview of Rule 4(k)(2)'s history and problems of application is provided in *United States v. Swiss American Bank, Ltd.*, 191 F.3d 30 (1st Cir. 1999).

VII. Territorial Jurisdiction Based on Consent or Waiver

115. Because the constitutional restriction of the territorial jurisdiction of both state and federal courts is conceived of primarily as a function of the right to "due process" of a particular defendant, it is universally recognized that a court may assert jurisdiction over a defendant otherwise beyond the territorial jurisdiction of that particular court if the defendant waives the right to object. Such a waiver may result from consent in advance of suit, from voluntary submission after suit, or from other forms of conduct that give rise to a constructive waiver of the right to object.

116. Advance consent is generally manifested by the appointment of an agent for service of process within the state in question, but this is an archaic tradition that reflects the pre-*International Shoe* focus of American constitutional law on the supposed "presence" of the defendant within a state seeking to assert territorial jurisdiction. A contract by which the parties subscribe to a "forum selection clause," thus agreeing in advance to submit to the territorial jurisdiction of the chosen forum, is fully sufficient to create territorial jurisdiction by consent without regard to the normal calculus of the defendant's contacts with that forum, and may (depending on its wording) also bar the plaintiff from invoking the territorial jurisdiction of any other forum. As with any other contractual provision, a forum selection clause may be disregarded as "unconscionable" if it is objectively unreasonable and one party had overweening bargaining power over the other. But the US Supreme Court has shown great reluctance to invalidate forum selection clauses on such "contract of adhesion" grounds.[1]

1. *See Carnival Cruise Lines, Inc. v. Shute*, 499 U.S. 585 (1991).

117. Voluntary submission after suit is manifested by the defendant's entering a "general appearance" in response to the service of process. While many – probably most – general appearances result from the knowing and intelligent decision of a defendant to proceed with the litigation in the plaintiff's chosen forum, thus challenging the merits of the plaintiff's complaint without wasting time and money on a threshold objection to the forum's territorial jurisdiction, this is the point at which the line between actual consent and constructive waiver becomes blurred. Although there are important variations in form, all American courts recognize that anything *other* than a general appearance must conform to some special procedure for entering an appearance in response to the service of process while asserting – and hence preserving – the defendant's objection to the territorial jurisdiction of the forum.

Such an appearance is called a "special appearance." In some states whose procedural systems retain major elements of the "code-pleading" system pioneered by New York in 1848 – including such important states as California, Illinois, and Texas, in addition to New York – a special appearance is defective if the defendant raises any issue other than the trial court's lack of jurisdiction.[1] In such states any such misstep in the entry of a special appearance converts that appearance into a general appearance, and thus submits the defendant to the territorial jurisdiction of the court by constructive waiver rather than by actual consent. In the federal district courts and the majority of states (although not of the larger states) whose procedural systems are modeled on the Federal Rules of Civil Procedure,[2] a special appearance requires only that the defendant object to the trial court's territorial jurisdiction when *first* appearing in response to the service of process. Under the federal model of procedure, then, an objection to territorial jurisdiction can be combined with any other preliminary objection to the court's power to proceed, such as a venue objection or an objection to the form and manner of service of process, or even with an answer disputing the merits of the complaint filed by the plaintiff. But this is still in substance a special-appearance rule, because the failure to contest the court's territorial jurisdiction in the first motion or pleading filed by the defendant constructively waives that objection whether or not the defendant intended to consent to the jurisdiction of the court.[3]

1. Some code-pleading states will permit a specially appearing defendant to challenge simultaneously the trial court's subject-matter and territorial jurisdiction, but others will not. A particular jurisdiction may permit some other form of objection, not going to the merits of the dispute, to be combined with an objection to territorial jurisdiction. But such omnibus motions by a specially appearing defendant are always unwise, since the subsidiary ground is not waived if withheld until after the defendant's objection to territorial jurisdiction has been decided. The need for caution when entering a special appearance in a code-pleading state cannot be overemphasized.
2. *See* Oakley & Coon, *supra*, at 1369-1378.
3. Fed. R. Civ. P. 12(h)(1).

118. The federal courts have recognized that constructive waiver may result from conduct of the defendant other than the failure properly to raise an objection to territorial jurisdiction in the defendant's first appearance. A defendant may always resist the territorial jurisdiction of a particular court by entering no appearance at all, allowing judgment to be rendered by default, and collaterally attacking that judgment as jurisdictionally invalid when the plaintiff seeks to enforce the judgment in some other forum. But once having invoked by special appearance the power of the forum to determine the scope of its own territorial jurisdiction, the defendant is bound by the procedural rules of the forum as they apply to the determination of the jurisdictional dispute. The trial court may properly sanction a substantial breach of its procedural rules by holding that the defendant has thereby waived its jurisdictional objection. In the leading case on this point, the US Supreme Court held that a federal district court could exercise territorial jurisdiction over foreign defendants who refused to comply with its orders requiring discovery of facts pertinent to the jurisdictional dispute.[1]

1. *Insurance Corp. of Ireland, Ltd. v. Compagnie des Bauxites de Guinee*, 456 U.S. 694 (1982).

§3. Resolution of Jurisdictional Conflicts

I. Authoritative Tribunals

119. There is no special court within the American system just for the resolution of jurisdictional conflicts. Issues of state law that govern the subject-matter jurisdiction, territorial jurisdiction, and venue of state courts are resolved by each state's court of last resort. Issues of federal law that govern the subject-matter jurisdiction, territorial jurisdiction, and venue of the federal courts are resolved by the US Supreme Court.

Issues concerning the venue of state courts are not of federal constitutional significance, and the US Supreme Court has no role in resolving such issues. The US Supreme Court only occasionally addresses the scope of the subject-matter jurisdiction of state courts, and then only because some federal statute has conferred exclusive subject-matter jurisdiction of particular cases on the federal courts, and thus has *pro tanto* limited the subject-matter jurisdiction of state courts. Many cases within the subject-matter jurisdiction of state courts nonetheless implicate matters of federal law, including the many cases in which state courts have concurrent jurisdiction with federal courts. The US Supreme Court frequently reviews judgments of state courts that turn, on the merits, on some issue of federal law. But such review generally extends only to whether the state court's determination of federal law was correct, not to whether the state court had the subject-matter jurisdiction to make that determination.

Issues concerning the territorial jurisdiction of state courts frequently implicate the limits on state power imposed by the Due Process Clause of the Fourteenth Amendment of the federal Constitution, and sometimes arise in the context of the affirmative duty to give effect to valid judgments of other domestic courts imposed upon state and federal courts by the federal Constitution's Full Faith and Credit Clause, by the accompanying Full Faith and Credit statute, and by the federal Constitution's Supremacy Clause, which requires states to respect the supremacy of federal law by, inter alia, enforcing valid federal judgments. As the ultimate arbiter of these principles of federal constitutional law, the US Supreme Court not only resolves conflicts over territorial jurisdiction among state courts and between state and federal courts, but also plays a highly influential role in shaping the scope of the territorial jurisdiction of both state and federal courts.

II. Procedural Incidents

120. The special procedures for raising objections to territorial jurisdiction are described above (paragraphs 117-118) in connection with the creation of territorial jurisdiction by consent or waiver. Only judgments rendered by default, with no appearance by the defending party, can be "collaterally" attacked in subsequent proceedings that question the validity of an earlier final judgment on grounds of a lack of territorial jurisdiction.

121. It is widely held to be a universal rule of American law that subject-matter jurisdiction cannot be conferred by waiver, estoppel, or consent. This rule is qualified in practice, however, by the preclusive effect, discussed below (paragraph 122), of a court's actual or even implied determination that it has subject-matter jurisdiction of a particular case. It may be true, as an abstract matter of law in a world of perfect information, that a particular court lacks subject-matter jurisdiction of a particular case. But if the parties fail to raise that issue before the judgment in the case becomes final after appeal or after the opportunity for appeal has lapsed, the judgment cannot thereafter be collaterally attacked. Similarly, if the issue is litigated but the parties conduct the litigation poorly, leading to an erroneous determination by the court that it has subject-matter jurisdiction, an ensuing final judgment will again stand unimpeachable after all appeals have been concluded or the opportunity for appeal has lapsed. Thus the parties can by their conduct of the litigation contribute to an erroneous assumption or determination of jurisdiction that cannot later be undone. In a very real if functional sense this means that subject-matter jurisdiction can be conferred by acts of the parties that amount to waiver or estoppel.

If this were not the case, litigation could go on forever and no judgment could ever be said to be conclusive. Its validity and hence its enforceability could always later be challenged. Several special procedural incidents serve as a partial antidote against judgments being entered by courts that lack subject-matter jurisdiction, yet acquire conclusive effect through the neglect or inattention of the parties. First, despite the generally "adversarial" character of American litigation, the issue of a court's subject-matter jurisdiction is not left to the parties to raise or not, as they see fit. Every American court has the power – and in the federal system, the solemn obligation – to consider *sua sponte* whether it has subject-matter jurisdiction of a particular case. Second, there is no time limit for either the parties or the court itself to question a potential lack of subject-matter jurisdiction, other than the time at which a judgment becomes final and no longer appealable. Third, default judgments can be collaterally attacked after they have become final, on the ground that they are invalid for lack of subject-matter jurisdiction.

In this latter respect, a lack of venue is treated differently from a lack of territorial jurisdiction or subject-matter jurisdiction. Despite some superficial similarities between the essentially geographical allocation of venue and territorial jurisdiction, a judgment rendered by a court of improper venue is not regarded by American law as therefore "invalid." The only basis upon which a default judgment can be attacked collaterally is for lack of validity. Thus a default judgment is not subject to collateral attack on venue grounds, no matter how indisputable it may be that the court rendering that judgment lacked proper venue.

If a venue objection cannot be collaterally attacked after a court without proper venue enters a default judgment, the question arises of the plight of a defendant who fails to enter an appearance in which a dispositive venue objection could have been raised but for the plaintiff's failure to serve process on that defendant. The answer to this question lies in the American conception of the "validity" of a judgment. A default judgment may be attacked as invalid on any of *three* grounds:

(1) lack of subject-matter jurisdiction;
(2) lack of territorial jurisdiction; and

(3) lack of notice to the defendant of the commencement of the lawsuit.

This means that a default judgment rendered even by a court of proper subject-matter and territorial jurisdiction can be rendered nugatory upon collateral attack for lack of proper notice. Although a lack of proper venue does not of itself render a default judgment invalid, the ability to attack collaterally the validity of a default judgment for lack of proper notice to the defendant ensures that a court without proper venue cannot enter a binding judgment simply because the defendant was never given the chance to appear and object to the lack of proper venue.

In order to preserve a venue objection, a defendant must not only enter an appearance in response to service of process, but must also raise a venue objection at the outset of the proceedings. In code-pleading states, a venue objection must be raised as soon as any objection to territorial jurisdiction entered by special appearance has been overruled. In the federal courts and states with similar procedural systems, a venue objection must be raised in the defendant's first appearance. In all courts, state or federal, a venue objection is waived if not raised at the proper time.

III. Preclusive Effect

122. It is well established in American law that a court's determination that it has territorial jurisdiction is binding on the parties unless reversed on appeal, even if that determination is erroneous. In the leading *Baldwin* case,[1] the US Supreme Court dealt with the preclusive effect of a determination of territorial jurisdiction by a federal district court. Within the American legal system, the preclusive effect of a judgment is determined by reference to the preclusion law (i.e., the doctrine of res judicata) of the particular court system that rendered the judgment. Thus *Baldwin* settles only the preclusive effect of a determination of territorial jurisdiction by a federal court, but is binding on any court, state or federal, in which that determination of territorial jurisdiction might be questioned. *Baldwin* does not require the court system of any particular state to give similar preclusive effect to jurisdictional determinations by their own state courts, but in this respect state preclusion law closely follows federal preclusion law.

This is what leads to the rule that the judgment of a court that lacked territorial jurisdiction can be collaterally attacked only if it was a default judgment. If the defendant entered an appearance, the issue of territorial jurisdiction was either waived (in which case territorial jurisdiction exists as a matter of actual or constructive consent) or it was unsuccessfully contested, in which case the defendant is precluded by res judicata principles from relitigating the issue in another lawsuit in the same or any other forum.

By an interesting process of extension, this rule giving preclusive effect to the unsuccessful litigation of a waivable ground for objecting to a court's jurisdiction has been applied as well to the putatively nonwaivable issue of a lack of subject-matter jurisdiction, and even when that issue was never actually litigated before the judgment in question became final and no longer appealable. First, the US Supreme Court held that the actual litigation of a challenge to a federal district court's subject-matter jurisdiction was conclusive on the parties, treating this as an ordinary matter of preclusion law.[2] Then the court held that any federal judgment in which the parties could have raised an objection to the court's subject-matter jurisdiction, but failed to do so, was binding on those parties – even if the court itself determined in a later case that the statute purporting to vest the federal court with subject-matter jurisdiction in the earlier case was unconstitutional, and no such subject-matter jurisdiction ever existed as a matter of law. "The actual existence of [such a jurisdictional] statute, prior to such a determination [of its unconstitutionality], is an operative fact and may have consequences which cannot justly be ignored."[3] The court supported this conclusion by again invoking ordinary principles of preclusion law, deeming it an elementary application of res judicata that any defense to a judgment, even the defense of lack of subject-matter jurisdiction, is waived if not asserted in the earlier proceeding.

The underlying theory at work in these preclusion cases involving jurisdictional issues has come to be called "jurisdiction to determine jurisdiction." As discussed above (paragraph 121), some such theory is necessary to protect the finality of judgments, especially in a court system of such inherently limited jurisdiction as the federal system. The US Supreme Court's use of preclusion doctrine to establish that federal courts have inherent jurisdiction to determine or assume (however erroneously) that they have subject-matter jurisdiction has been widely followed by state courts, but not as universally as the parallel holding of the *Baldwin* case regarding the preclusive effect of a determination of territorial jurisdiction.

1. *Baldwin v. Iowa State Traveling Men's Ass'n.*, 283 U.S. 522 (1931).
2. *Stoll v. Gottlieb*, 305 U.S. 165 (1938).
3. *Chicot County Drainage Dist. v. Baxter State Bank*, 308 U.S. 371, 374 (1940).

Chapter 2. International Jurisdiction

§1. Rules Applicable in the Absence of a Treaty

123. The previous discussion of the territorial jurisdiction of American courts, state and federal (paragraphs 77-118), is fully applicable to the international assertion of territorial jurisdiction against foreign defendants. As noted in the discussion of the *Asahi* case (paragraph 101), the international context of litigation and the special burdens imposed on foreign litigants when summoned before the courts of another country have been recognized as factors that may be dispositive of the "reasonableness" of an assertion of territorial jurisdiction against a foreign defendant even when that defendant otherwise has "minimum contacts" with the forum state. These factors are equally significant in cases in which the federal courts have by special statute been granted nationwide territorial jurisdiction, which may be exercised against foreign litigants on the basis of their "minimum contacts" with the United States as a whole.

As previously noted (paragraph 114), Federal Rule of Civil Procedure 4(k)(2) is recent but rarely applicable legislation that grants the federal district courts such nationwide territorial jurisdiction with respect to foreign defendants. The FSIA, previously discussed in connection with the subject-matter jurisdiction of the federal district courts (paragraphs 67-68), also vests the federal district courts with nationwide territorial jurisdiction over a certain class of foreign defendants: foreign states, broadly defined to include state-owned corporations.[1]

The doctrine of *forum non conveniens*, previously discussed with respect to state courts' voluntary relinquishment of territorial jurisdiction (paragraph 112), has special significance in the federal courts with respect to the international assertion of territorial jurisdiction. As a domestic matter, the federal courts' power to invoke the doctrine of *forum non conveniens* has been superseded by the federal interdistrict transfer statute, 28 U.S.C. §1404, discussed above (paragraph 85). The doctrine retains currency in the federal courts when there is an available and more convenient forum available in the courts of a foreign country, and the mere fact that foreign law may be less favorable to the plaintiff will not prevent dismissal by a federal district court on *forum non conveniens* grounds if the foreign court is otherwise a clearly preferable alternative forum.[2]

1. U.S.C. §§1330(b), 1608. *See Seetransport Wiking Trader Schiffarhtsgesellschaft MBH & Co. v. Navimpex Centrala Navala*, 989 F.2nd 572 (2nd Cir. 1993).
2. *Piper Aircraft Co. v. Reyno*, 454 U.S. 235 (1981).

§2. International Treaties

124. The United States is a signatory to the 1964 Hague Service Convention, a treaty that has been signed by more than thirty other countries.[1] As a federal treaty, it preempts any conflicting state law, and is thus binding on state courts. The Hague Convention does not deal directly with territorial jurisdiction, but rather governs the manner in which the process of American courts may be served abroad on defendants within other signatory countries. Because the Hague Convention stipulates special procedures for the entry of default judgments against such defendants, and for relief from such judgments, and because a default judgment can in any event be attacked collaterally as invalid for lack of proper service of process (paragraph 121), with the Hague Convention as the controlling standard for the propriety of service of process, the Hague Convention provides a small measure of additional protection for foreign litigants against whom default judgments have been entered by American courts. Such judgments can be collaterally attacked not only for lack of territorial jurisdiction, but also for lack of proper notice. Because many American lawyers are unfamiliar with the provisions of the Hague Convention, the lack of proper notice may be easier to establish than a lack of territorial jurisdiction.

But the fact remains that if service is accomplished as required by the Hague Convention, a default judgment cannot then be resisted on service-of-process grounds. It can still be attacked collaterally as invalid for lack of territorial jurisdiction, but by then the merits will have been conclusively determined, by default, adversely to the defendant. A default judgment of one American court cannot be attacked collaterally in any other American court except as "invalid" for lack of proper subject-matter jurisdiction, territorial jurisdiction, or notice (paragraph 121). The only way to preserve the right to litigate the merits of the lawsuit, while also preserving the right to contest the often uncertain question of the territorial jurisdiction of the forum, is to enter an appearance in the American court after receiving proper service of process under the Hague Convention.

Further diluting the protective effect of the Hague Convention as to a foreign defendant sued in an American court is the fact that the Hague Convention does not always require service in the home country of that defendant. The US Supreme Court has held that a foreign litigant who has an agent for service of process within the United States may be served through that agent in the normal fashion provided by the procedural law of the court, state or federal, in which the foreign defendant has been sued, in full compliance with the Hague Convention but without recourse to its provisions for service of process outside the United States.[2]

1. *See Volkswagenwerk Aktiengesellschaft v. Schlunk*, 486 U.S. 694 (1988).
2. Id., at 707-708.

Part III. Actions and Claims

Chapter 1. Actions

§1. Types of Actions

125. Modern American civil procedure features just one type of action, the "civil action." In this respect, the historical trend has been toward simplification. The original thirteen states formed from British colonies incorporated the British system of procedure, which featured myriad "forms of action" at common law – derived from the medieval writ system – in addition to more specialized types of actions unique to courts exercising equitable or maritime jurisdiction.[1] Although vestiges of the older system remain in a few states, the federal courts and most state courts adjudicate civil disputes in one omnibus form, the "civil action," that embraces what used to be called "actions at law," "suits in equity," and all other sorts of proceedings, cases, and controversies subject to judicial resolution. These older terms survive in common legal parlance, however, as popular synonyms for what is formally a "civil action."

The older terms are also preserved in the language of the federal Constitution. Article III of the Constitution, ratified in 1788, limits the jurisdiction of federal courts to the adjudication of "cases" and "controversies" that fall within one of several categories of litigation likely to affect issues or parties of federal significance. It is generally thought that a "case" in this constitutional sense embraces both criminal and civil litigation, while a "controversy" refers generically to what is now termed a "civil action." The Eleventh Amendment of the Constitution, ratified in 1798, preserves the sovereign immunity of states from federal jurisdiction of "any suit in law or equity" brought by individuals against states. These words have long been given an expansive construction that bars the exercise of maritime as well as legal or equitable jurisdiction, and hence have a meaning that is coextensive with the modern term of "civil action."

Modern litigation features two extraordinary forms of "civil action" that are functionally distinct enough from the ordinary civil action to warrant special attention. These are civil actions for declaratory rather than coercive relief, and civil actions in which certain parties conducting the litigation are deemed to do so on behalf of a much larger class of absent parties who are intended to be bound by any judgment by or against their representatives. Our discussion below begins with the ordinary civil action, and extends to the special features of declaratory-judgment actions and class actions.

1. *See generally* Bodenheimer, *supra*, at 10-11, 51-58.

I. Ordinary Civil Actions

A. Definition

126. An ordinary civil action is a proceeding in a formal adjudicatory tribunal (a court) in which at least one initiating party presents at least one claim that the claimant (the plaintiff) has suffered or is threatened with an injury attributable to some actual or prospective act or omission by at least one opposing party (the defendant) in violation of a legal duty owed by the defendant to the plaintiff, and prays for some form of judicially enforced civil remedy that will either undo or compensate for any harm that has already occurred, or will forestall the anticipated future harm.

In some instances a civil action will seek "exemplary" or "punitive" damages, generally in addition to compensatory damages, that seek prospectively to deter similar breaches of legal duty by the same or similarly situated defendants. Civil actions may be brought by governmental entities seeking not only to enforce the essentially private rights of those entities as commercial or proprietary rights-holders, but also to enforce the collective legal rights of the public. Civil actions that seek to deter future legal violations or to vindicate public rights thus overlap to some extent with criminal prosecutions.

The essential distinction between civil actions and criminal prosecutions with respect to natural persons is that criminal prosecutions seek to deprive individuals of liberty or even life (when capital punishment is sought) as a punishment for past acts that were made criminal by laws existing at the time the acts occurred. The line between civil and criminal liability is often hard to discern when injunctive relief or sanctions for contempt of court are imposed against a defendant, when fines or penalties are exacted that serve both a compensatory and punitive function, or when the defendant is a corporate entity that must be sanctioned by some punishment other than the individual imprisonment that paradigmatically can be imposed only by the criminal law. Whether particular remedies sought in a nominally civil action should be deemed criminal in nature may occasionally present close questions, and the special procedural protections guaranteed to criminal defendants by the federal Constitution invest these questions with fundamental importance. But by and large, the character of litigation as civil or criminal can be easily determined by reference to the source of the legal duty allegedly breached by the defendant, with the presumption being that a legal duty gives rise only to civil liability unless by statute the duty is expressly made subject to criminal sanctions.

It is important to note that while the civil action is the means for enforcement of civil liability as to a particular claim, more than one claim may and commonly is asserted and adjudicated in the litigation of a single civil action. It is thus the claim and not the civil action that is the fundamental unit of litigation in American civil procedure. Most civil actions involve the litigation of clusters of claims reciprocally asserted by the opposing parties, and many civil actions involve often complex clusters of claiming and defending parties. The liberal American rules for "joinder of claims" and "joinder of parties" will be discussed below in paragraphs 146-153.

The formal name in federal practice for the fundamental unit of litigation that is presented for adjudication by means of a civil action is a "claim for relief." This terminology originated with Rule 8 of the Federal Rules of Civil Procedure, which became effective in 1938. This term was intended to avoid the ambiguity that had developed over the meaning of the parallel term – a "cause of action" – used by the system of "code pleading" pioneered by New York in its 1848 Code of Civil Procedure, and widely emulated by other states. Today both terms are used interchangeably by lawyers and judges, even within the federal system. Our references to the litigation of one or more "claims" by means of a civil action should be understood to refer to both "claims for relief" (the preferred federal nomenclature) and "causes of action" (the term still used in the statutes governing the pleading of civil actions in many states).

B. Initiation

127. Typically, a civil action begins when it is filed. For example, the Federal Rules of Civil Procedure provide in Rule 3 that "[A] civil action is commenced by filing a complaint with the court." In virtually all civil actions, the complaining party (generally denominated by the plaintiff) must initiate litigation by means of a civil action commenced within a certain time specified by the particular statute of limitations applicable to the claim or claims asserted by the plaintiff. Many claims seek relief for the violation of a substantive legal duty imposed by state law, and hence are governed by state rather than federal statutes of limitation. When a state statute of limitation specifies the time allowed for the litigation of particular claims, it may require more than that the litigation be commenced by the filing of a civil action within the time allowed. Many state statutes of limitation require that within the time allowed the plaintiff must not only file a civil action but also effectively serve the defendant with process compelling the defendant to appear in court to defend against the claim asserted in that civil action. In such states the "commencement" of a civil action is generally conceived of as requiring both filing and service of process.

(Just what law, state or federal, governs a particular claim, and when state law governs, just which state's law is controlling, is a perennially complex issue in American civil litigation. The issue may arise both with regard to the nature and source of the substantive legal duty allegedly breached by a defendant, and with regard to the separate issue – which falls at the intersection of what might be classified as "substantive" or "procedural" – of the time allowed for the litigation of that claim under the applicable statute of limitations. In American jurisprudence, this "choice of law" issue is left to the field of "Conflict of Laws" and is outside the scope of "Civil Procedure".)

II. Declaratory-Judgment Actions

128. Declaratory-judgment actions require separate elaboration because in one key respect they do not fall within the definition of an ordinary civil action. The declaratory-judgment plaintiff does not complain of some actual or threatened harm resulting from violation of a legal duty owed to the plaintiff. Such a plaintiff seeks instead a judgment that declares the legal rights of the parties in advance of action detrimental to one party or the other, and thus determines whether contemplated action can be taken from potential legal liability.

A declaratory judgment is a form of transformational relief, which attempts to determine or confirm the parties' legal relationships with regard to each other.[1] During the eighteenth and nineteenth centuries, American courts generally lacked power to grant transformational relief. The principal exception concerned suits in equity to quiet title. If two or more parties claimed conflicting interests in real property, any of the parties could bring a suit to quiet title. Absent the availability of such transformational relief, the parties could have altered the status quo only by acting at their legal peril, e.g., by committing a possible trespass on the disputed real property and hoping that subsequent legal action to redress that possible wrong would retrospectively resolve the competing claims to title against the party claiming trespass.[2]

There are many situations outside of the real-property context in which there is an analogous need to determine the relative legal rights of adverse parties by means less costly than a suit for coercive relief by a putative rights-holder who may deter socially efficient conduct merely by threatening suit to enforce a claim of legal right that a court might ultimately find lacking in merit. For instance, suppose A holds a patent on a particular technology for manufacturing color television monitors of such high quality that A can sell the monitors for USD 400. B develops a competing technology that will allow B to sell a monitor of equal quality and with an equal profit margin for USD 200. But it will cost B USD 100 million to build a plant capable of producing its USD 200 monitors, and it is possible (but not certain) that a court will find that B's technology infringes A's patent. B cannot afford to risk that USD 100 million investment if there is a substantial chance that A will win a suit to enjoin production of B's monitor, and A is unlikely to bring such a suit before B's investment of USD 100 million is unrecoverable, since A benefits from the deterrence of B while the probability of A's litigative success remains inchoate. The result is that society loses its chance to buy monitors of comparable quality for half of A's market price, unless B can force A's hand by seeking transformational relief that allows B, merely for the cost of suit rather than the cost of a possibly futile USD 100 million investment in a manufacturing facility, to determine whether B's product is indeed an infringement of A's patent.

To respond to such compelling situations, most jurisdictions in the United States have passed statutes broadly authorizing courts to grant transformational relief. The Federal Declaratory Judgment Act[3] is representative. Subject to the constraint that the dispute between the parties must be an "actual controversy" rather than a feigned dispute – a qualification necessary to bring declaratory-judgment actions within federal constitutional "standing" requirements, discussed below[4] – 28 U.S.C. §2201 authorizes the federal courts to "declare the rights and other legal relations of any interested party seeking such declaration, whether or not further relief is or could be sought."

1. Fleming James, Jr et al., *Civil Procedure* 5th edn (2001), §1.12 at 32.
2. Id., at 27.
3. 28 U.S.C. §§2201-2202. *See also* Fed. R. Civ. P. 57.

4. *See, e.g.*, *Aetna Life Ins. Co. v. Haworth*, 300 U.S. 227, 240 (1937).

III. Class Actions

129. Like declaratory-judgment actions, class actions are sufficiently different in kind from ordinary civil actions to require independent elaboration. Although an ordinary civil action may entail the joinder of multiple claiming or defending parties, a class action may bring before the court claims by or against a multitude of absentees who have party status only in a sense so abstract as to be metaphorical. Most class actions are brought by plaintiff classes, but it is possible for a group of defendants to be sued as a class, and even for a class of plaintiffs to sue a class of defendants.

A typical class action is commenced by one or more "named" plaintiffs who sue one or more defendants on behalf of a group of similarly wronged persons too numerous to permit these additional plaintiffs to be joined in an individual capacity. The threshold for the minimum size of the class represented by the named plaintiffs varies from court to court and class to class, but generally is between forty and one hundred class members. Many classes are much larger than this threshold, and may number in the thousands or even millions. The named plaintiffs are often several in number, chosen so that if there are minor differences in interests among class members, each of the individuals serving as named plaintiffs will be eligible to represent subclasses of absentees whose interests are identical to some but not all of the named plaintiffs.[1]

1. *See* James, *supra*, at §10.20 at 641.

130. There are a number of reasons why American civil procedure has been sympathetic to class actions.

First, class actions serve judicial economy where many individuals have suffered in common some injury serious enough to make it likely that, absent a class action, a flood of individual lawsuits would be filed.

Second, even if the number of individual lawsuits that would be filed absent a class action could practicably be handled by courts on a case-by-case basis, if the aggregate liability is likely to exhaust the assets of the defendant, a class action permits a fair proration of the available assets among all members of the injured class.

Third, class actions may be the only effective means of redress of widespread injury that in the aggregate involves a serious breach of legal duty but individually is too minor to make it practicable for the injured parties to litigate their claims one by one, especially when the resources of a large, institutional defendant are such that individual plaintiffs are likely to be overwhelmed by the sheer disparity in litigative resources. A successful class action may result in a huge judgment when the small amount of damages owed to individual class members is multiplied by the size of the class, and the prospect of creating such a "common fund" out of which the costs of suit may be paid – including an award of fees to counsel for the plaintiff class – may be the only rational basis for plaintiffs and their counsel to invest the time and money needed for expensive and protracted litigation against a well-financed defendant.

Fourth, class actions create incentives for law-abiding conduct by defendants who might otherwise deem themselves effectively immune from civil litigation that would be too expensive for any individually injured party to pursue.

Fifth, class actions are a useful device for collective litigation by members of large organizations that lack juridical status as entities with the capacity to sue or be sued institutionally – such as partnerships, labor unions, investment groups, and trade associations.[1]

After a significant revision of the original Rule 23 in 1966, parties hoping to bring a class action find themselves relatively unfettered by technical barriers to doing so, whether proceeding in a state or a federal court.[2] Federal class-action practice under Rule 23 of the Federal Rules of Civil Procedure has been widely copied by state courts, and provides a useful guide to the mechanics of bringing and maintaining a class action. Moreover, it is Federal Rule 23 and not some state analogue that will govern most large class actions in the future. As discussed above (Part II, paragraph 55), the Class Action Fairness Act of 2005 significantly expanded federal diversity jurisdiction over interstate class actions in order to concentrate such litigation in federal court.

1. *See* id., at 641-644.
2. *See generally* id., §10.22 at 650-652 (describing the difficulties engendered by the provisions of the 1938 version of Rule 23).

131. Rule 23(a) sets forth four fundamental prerequisites for the maintenance of a class action, each of which must be satisfied before a civil action will be permitted to proceed as a class action.

The "numerosity" requirement of Rule 23(a)(1) demands that the class be too large for individual joinder of class members to be feasible. As previously noted, this threshold is set by most courts at between forty and one hundred class members.

The "commonality" requirement of Rule 23(a)(2) requires the existence of at least one question of law or fact common to all members of the class. This is a toothless requirement, since it is virtually inconceivable that any rational party would seek to represent a class in the absence of such a common question.

The "typicality" requirement of Rule 23(a)(3) demands that the named party have claims or defenses typical of the class. It is essential that the party seeking to act on behalf of a class adequately represent the interests of the class, and the "typicality" requirement focuses on the status of the representative party as such. If that party is likely to have conflicts of interest with class members, or to have suffered an injury different in kind or degree than that allegedly suffered by class members, Rule 23(a)(3) may disqualify the party as an adequate class representative.

The "adequacy" requirement of Rule 23(a)(4) parallels the "typicality" requirement of Rule 23(a)(3), but focuses more broadly on the capacity rather than the interests of the representative party in asking whether the representative party is likely to be able to "fairly and adequately protect the interests of the class." Rule 23(a)(4) thus invites scrutiny of the ability and resources of the legal counsel for the representative party and hence for the class, since it is counsel – rather than the representative party – who in most cases will finance and control the actual conduct of the litigation on behalf of the class.

132. A putative representative party who satisfies all four of the conjunctive requirements of Rule 23(a) must surmount one more hurdle in order to proceed with the litigation as a class action. Rule 23(b) describes disjunctively three types of permissible class actions. A proposed class action must be shown to fall within one of these three alternative categories.

Rule 23(b)(1) provides that a class suit may go forward if separate actions by some class members would create a risk of exposing the opposing party to incompatible standards of conduct or prejudicing the interests of other class members.

Rule 23(b)(2) conditions class status on a showing that the action seeks injunctive relief or declaratory relief that will necessarily have a class-wide impact.

Rule 23(b)(3) is the most amorphous of the three categories, and hence the one that gives rise to the most procedural litigation over the propriety of permitting a particular action to proceed as a class action. It permits a representative plaintiff to sue for damages on a class-wide basis, even though there may be significant differences among class members as to the likelihood and degree of the liability owed by the defendant, provided that the court makes two key findings. First, that questions of law or fact common to all class members "predominate" over questions affecting only individual class members, and second, that a class action is "superior" to alternative methods for the fair and efficient adjudication of the controversy. Rule 23(b)(3) concludes with a nonexhaustive list of four factors to be considered by the court in making its "predominance" and "superiority" findings: the interest of class members in pursuing separate actions; the extent and nature of other pending litigation by or against the class; whether it is desirable to concentrate litigation affecting class members in one forum; and the difficulty likely to be encountered in the management of a class action by the court and the parties.

133. Rule 23(c)(1) instructs the court to issue an order as soon as possible after commencement of a putative class action that determines whether the criteria of Rule 23(b) are met, and hence whether the action may be maintained as a class action rather than as an ordinary civil action between only the named parties. This is conventionally referred to as an order granting or denying "certification" of a class action. Although Rule 23(c)(1) contemplates a speedy determination of whether an action may be maintained as a class action, this wish is seldom fulfilled. Because a class certification order is likely to change fundamentally the character of the litigation, vastly increasing the potential cost of an unsuccessful outcome to the party opposing a putative class, the class certification decision often comes only after years of expensive litigation devoted solely to this procedural issue.

By express terms of Rule 23(c)(1), a class certification decision is not a final order, and is subject to change as the litigation progresses. As a practical matter, however, the court's initial determination either to grant or deny class certification is generally dispositive of the litigation. In the typical situation where the putative representative parties seek to represent a much larger class of additional, unnamed plaintiffs, denial of class certification will result in the named plaintiffs' voluntary dismissal of litigation that would be too expensive to continue solely on their own behalf; on the other hand, the granting of class certification will impose hydraulic pressure on the defendants to negotiate a settlement rather than risk a catastrophic judgment holding them liable for the full amount of the aggregated claims of the entire class. Because so much turns on the class-certification stage of a putative class action, a 1998 amendment added a new subsection to Rule 23. New Rule 23(f) gives the courts of appeals discretion to grant immediate review of an order granting or denying class certification notwithstanding its interlocutory character.

134. The remaining provisions of Rule 23 deal with the complex administrative problems posed by class actions.

Rule 23(c)(2) distinguishes for notice purposes between actions certified under Rule 23(b)(3) as opposed to Rule 23(b)(1-2). Rule 23(c)(2) requires the court to direct to the members of a Rule 23(b)(3) class "the best notice practicable under the circumstances," including individual notice to all the members who may be identified through "reasonable efforts."[1] Specifically, the notice must advise the recipient that each class member has the right to "opt out" of the class, that any member not opting for exclusion from the class will be included in and bound by any judgment for or against the class, and that any member of the class who does not request exclusion may enter an appearance through counsel. By contrast, Rule 23(c)(3) provides that in class actions certified under 23(b)(1) or 23(b)(2), the trial court's judgment shall bind all members of the class as described by the judgment without any requirement of prior notification of class members, although Rule 23(d)(2) permits the trial court in its discretion to require such notification.

Rule 23(c)(4) allows the court to certify classes for particular issues only or to divide a class into subclasses, which are viewed as distinct classes for treatment under other provisions of the rule.

Rule 23(d) gives the court exceptional powers to manage the conduct of a class action, vesting significant control of the litigation in the trial court rather than the parties or their counsel. The trial court is expected to use these exceptional powers to make sure that the parties actually before the court serve and protect the represented class, and any broader interests of the public that may be implicated by the class action.[2] Class actions thus have unique status in American litigation, blending the traditional Anglo-American "adversarial" system of party-controlled litigation with a more European "inquisitorial" approach in which the parties respond to judicial initiatives.[3]

Rule 23(e) prevents the class action from being dismissed or compromised without court approval. This allows the court to police the fairness of proposed settlements. The threat of class-wide liability generally leads the named parties to negotiate a settlement mutually advantageous to the named parties (and their counsel), and once such a settlement has been reached, the named parties are no longer adversaries but become united in their interest to win judicial approval of the settlement. Serious questions may arise as to a conflict of interest between the named parties and the represented class, which may stand to receive only token benefits from the proposed settlement.[4] The court is allowed to order that notice of the proposed settlement be sent to all class members, affording them an opportunity to object to the terms of the settlement.

1. *See Mullane v. Central Hanover Bank & Trust, Co.*, 339 U.S. 306 (1950) (describing what represents reasonable efforts).
2. *See* Abram Chayes, "The Role of the Judge in Public Law Litigation," Harv. L. Rev. 89 (1976): 1281.

3. *See* Judith Resnik, "Managerial Judges," Harv. L. Rev. 96 (1982): 376.
4. *See* John B. Oakley et al., "Summing Up Procedural Justice: Exploring the Tension between Collective Processes and Individual Rights in the Context of Settlement and Litigating Classes," U.C. Davis L. Rev. 30 (1997): 787.

§2. Parties to an Action

I. Capacity to Sue and Interest in the Litigation

135. Juridical capacity – the capacity to sue or be sued – is a prerequisite for a person or entity to be party to a civil action. When a civil action that is not a class action is brought by or against a party with undoubted juridical capacity who represents the interests of some other person or entity who may be burdened or benefited by the judgment sought in the civil action, issues of whether the "real party in interest" should be joined to the litigation may arise.

136. In federal practice, issues of "real party in interest" status and juridical capacity are governed by Rule 17 of the Federal Rules of Civil Procedure.

Rule 17(a) sets forth a list of common types of representative parties, such as executors, trustees of express trusts, and parties otherwise statutorily authorized to sue for the benefit of others, and empowers them to proceed with litigation without joinder of those whose interests they represent. In other situations, Rule 17(a) provides liberally that representative litigation may proceed if within a reasonable time after an objection is raised by a "real party in interest," the defect is cured by ratification of the litigation by the real party in interest, or by joinder or substitution of the real party in interest on a "nunc pro tunc" basis (now for then) that treats the newly added real party in interest as having been joined from the outset of the litigation. This allows "real party in interest" problems to be cured even when the applicable statute of limitations would bar the commencement of new litigation brought by the real party in interest. Nonetheless, the determination that an absentee is a real party in interest may sometimes require dismissal of a federal civil action if the real party in interest's citizenship destroys the diversity of citizenship upon which federal jurisdiction depends.

Rule 17(b) provides generally that the juridical capacity of an individual or corporation is to be determined by reference to the law of the state in which the individual is domiciled or the corporation was organized. In other cases (those involving unincorporated associations and parties acting in a representative capacity), juridical capacity is determined by reference to the law of the state in which the federal district court (i.e., the trial court) is located. Notwithstanding any contrary state law, however, partnerships and unincorporated associations (typically labor unions) have the capacity to sue and be sued in federal court in order to enforce a substantive right granted by federal law in favor of, or against, such an entity. Federal law also governs the juridical capacity of receivers appointed by federal courts to hold and manage property.

Rule 17(c) supplements Rules 17(a-b) by providing specially for suits by or against an infant or incompetent to be maintainable by a previously appointed fiduciary of the infant or incompetent, or by a guardian ad litem specially appointed by the federal court in which the litigation is pending.

137. A final requirement imposed on a party seeking to prosecute a civil action is that the party have "standing" to sue. As a matter of state law, "standing" issues are generally subsumed within the law of juridical capacity and "real party in interest" status. In the federal courts, however, "standing" issues have an added jurisdictional dimension that is discussed in detail in the next subsection.

II. Jurisdictional "Standing" Requirements

A. Federal Courts

138. Article III, §2 of the federal Constitution provides that the judicial power of the United States shall extend to various types of "cases" (such as those arising under federal law) and "controversies" (such as those between citizens of different states). Nothing significant turns on the distinction between a "case" and a "controversy,"[1] but the threshold restriction of federal judicial power to the adjudication of either a "case" or a "controversy" has led the US Supreme Court to fashion an important preliminary requirement for any exercise of jurisdiction by a federal court. This "case or controversy" requirement excludes from federal jurisdiction any dispute that is not "justiciable." Cases or controversies that do not present a federal court with a concrete dispute between adverse parties that is capable of judicial resolution are deemed nonjusticiable, which is another way of saying that the dispute is not a "case or controversy" of the sort that the Constitution permits federal courts to adjudicate.

1. It is likely that the framers of the Constitution used "controversy" to refer to lawsuits of a civil nature, and "case" as a broader term that would include both civil suits and criminal prosecutions.

139. There are many strands to the federal justiciability doctrine. Some turn on the nature of the dispute. If a lawsuit involves a potential injury to one party that might not come to pass, the suit may not qualify as a presently justiciable "case or controversy" because it is not yet "ripe" for adjudication. If a lawsuit involves a dispute that is resolved by external events before it can be adjudicated – such as a dispute over the legality of a strike that ends while the litigation is still proceeding – it may be dismissed because it has become "moot" and is no longer justiciable. If a lawsuit seeks relief that would intrude unduly on the prerogatives of the legislative or executive branches of government, it may be dismissed as a nonjusticiable "political question." The most frequently litigated of these justiciability doctrines, however, concerns not the character of the dispute but rather the characteristics of the parties in relationship to the dispute. This type of justiciability concern is called "standing," which demands that a plaintiff seeking federal judicial relief have a sufficiently concrete and personal stake in the litigation to justify adjudicating the dispute at the behest of that particular plaintiff. Although this is sometimes a relative test, turning on the issue of whether some other potential plaintiff might be more directly affected by the judgment sought, it is not necessarily so. Some lawsuits may involve claims of illegality that are justiciable in terms of the issues they present, but involve alleged harm so abstract and general that no plaintiff has suffered individualized injury sufficiently concrete to confer standing to sue to redress the illegality.

140. Federal standing doctrine is generally thought to be in an unsatisfactory state: a congeries of details that are voluminous, convoluted, and arguably contradictory. Nevertheless, a few generalizations can be hazarded.

First, plaintiffs must satisfy a discrete set of requirements that are grounded specifically in the constitutional "case or controversy" requirement. These constitutional requirements are the product of judicial interpretation, and to that extent are subject to reinterpretation, but in principle the constitutional core of federal standing doctrine is not subject to judicial or legislative abrogation.

Second, the elements of constitutional standing may be summarized as requiring a showing by a particular plaintiff of "actual injury redressable by the court."[1] This succinct six-word formulation has been further parsed into three prongs constituting a "triad of injury in fact, causation, and redressability"[2] and requiring the plaintiff to show individualized, concrete injury (injury in fact) that was caused by the defendant (causation) and that would be redressed by the judgment sought (redressability). Otherwise, resolution of the dispute by the federal courts would not be genuinely judicial, but would instead engage the federal courts in issues of a theoretical or political nature in violation of the limited powers granted to the federal judiciary by Article III of the Constitution.

Third, this set of minimum constitutional requirements for standing to sue in federal court is supplemented by additional "prudential" standing requirements that are imposed as a matter of federal judicial discretion. Sometimes a lack of "prudential" standing entails only a stiffening of the core constitutional standing requirements, but there are at least two distinct doctrines of prudential standing: a general prohibition of "third-party standing" that is invoked when a plaintiff relies on the violation of the legal rights of third parties (*jus tertii*) as the grounds for redressing harm suffered by the plaintiff,[3] and a general requirement that a plaintiff who seeks relief from the violation of some statutory duty show that the sort of injury suffered by the plaintiff was within the "zone of interests" that the statute in question was intended to protect.[4] Because such prudential standing requirements are judicially conceived rules of self-restraint that are not directly grounded in the Constitution, they are subject to being overridden when Congress expressly instructs the federal courts to exercise their jurisdiction to the full extent permitted by the Constitution.[5]

1. *Simon v. Eastern Kentucky Welfare Rights Org.*, 426 U.S. 26, 39 (1976).
2. *Steel Co. v. Citizens for a Better Environment*, 523 U.S. 83, 103-104 (1998).
3. *See Craig v. Boren*, 429 U.S. 190 (1976).
4. *See Association of Data Processing Serv. Organizations., Inc. v. Camp*, 397 U.S. 150 (1970).
5. *See Trafficante v. Metropolitan Life Ins. Co.*, 409 U.S. 205 (1972) (holding that Congress authorized third-party standing in suits under the Fair Housing Act of 1968).

B. State Courts

141. The foregoing describes the standing requirements applied by federal courts. State courts are free to fashion their own standing requirements, which in general are more liberal than those applied by federal courts. Leading examples of states whose courts enforce less stringent standing requirements than those of the federal courts are California,[1] Illinois,[2] and New York.[3] Pennsylvania conforms more closely to the federal model of standing, but with some exceptions.[4] Texas state courts impose particularly strict standing requirements.[5]

American judicial federalism has produced an interesting resolution of a potential paradox with respect to the adjudication of federal claims by state courts. On the one hand, the Supremacy Clause of Article VI of the federal Constitution has been construed to require state courts to adjudicate federal claims on an equal footing with claims based on state law.[6] On the other hand, the standing requirements of Article III of the federal Constitution have been construed to limit only the jurisdiction of the federal courts, and not the jurisdiction of state courts to adjudicate federal claims. This makes it possible for a plaintiff who would lack standing to assert a federal claim in a federal court to sue upon the same federal claim in the courts of a state that as a matter of state law has more liberal standing rules than apply in federal court – for instance, in California, Illinois, or New York, as discussed in the previous paragraph. The potential paradox is that the US Supreme Court might be unable to review the application of federal law in such a suit, since if the plaintiff lacks standing according to the federal criteria, no "case or controversy" might exist that would bring the suit within the judicial power of any federal court, the US Supreme Court included.

One resolution of this paradox would be to impose on all state courts the standing requirements of Article III of the federal Constitution with respect to any state court's adjudication of issues of federal law.[7] This would significantly curtail the traditional operation of some state courts, however,[8] and the US Supreme Court has devised a different and somewhat Solomonic resolution. If a plaintiff without standing to sue in federal court seeks judicial relief on federal grounds in a state court and loses, this possible underenforcement of federal law is unreviewable by the US Supreme Court.[9] But if such a plaintiff prevails in state court by winning a judgment that turns on an issue of federal law, this possible overenforcement of federal law is deemed to threaten cognizable injury to the defendant, who then has the requisite standing as a matter of federal law to seek review in the US Supreme Court.[10]

1. *See, e.g., National Audubon Society v. Superior Court*, 33 Cal. 3rd 419, 658 P.2nd 709 (1983); *Torres v. City of Yorba Linda*, 13 Cal. App. 4th 1035 (1993).
2. *See In Re Marriage of Rodriguez*, 131 Ill. 2nd 273, 545 N.E.2nd 731 (1989).
3. *See, e.g., Axelrod v. Sobol*, 78 N.Y.2nd 112, 575 N.E.2nd 388 (1991); *Dairylea Coop., Inc. v. Walkley*, 38 N.Y.2nd 6, 339 N.E.2nd 865 (1975).
4. *See Sprague v. Casey*, 520 Pa. 38, 550 A.2nd 184 (1988).
5. *Anderson v. Anderson*, 620 S.W.2nd 815 (Tex. Civ. App. 1981).
6. *See Howlett by Howlett v. Rose*, 496 U.S. 356 (1990).
7. *See* William A. Fletcher, "The "Case or Controversy" Requirement in State Court Adjudication of Federal Questions," Calif. L. Rev. 78 (1990): 263.
8. A substantial number of states permit their courts to render "advisory opinions" on the legality under state or federal law of proposed action by other branches of state government, a practice long deemed prohibited by the "case or controversy" limitation of federal judicial power under the rule of *Hayburn's Case*, 2 U.S. (2 Dall.) 408 (1792). *See* Richard H. Fallon, Jr, Daniel J. Meltzer & David L. Shapiro, *Hart and Wechsler's: The Federal Courts and the Federal System*, 5th edn (2003), 98.
9. *See Tileston v. Ullman*, 318 U.S. 44 (1943).
10. *See ASARCO, Inc. v. Kadish*, 490 U.S. 605 (1989).

§3. VEXATIOUS LITIGATION

142. Vexatious litigation is treated by American courts as a serious procedural irregularity amounting to misconduct. A judicial finding that litigation has been filed or conducted vexatiously will generally result not only in dismissal of the lawsuit (or of the particular claim or defense involved), but also in the imposition of sanctions on the party or attorney (or both) responsible for the misconduct. Because the vexatious character of litigation is tied so closely in American practice to the imposition of sanctions, our principal discussion of vexatious litigation is deferred until our discussion of litigious misconduct (paragraphs 164-168).

In some instances – most obviously when the vexatious litigant is an incarcerated person filing a pro se complaint without benefit of counsel – the threat of sanctions will provide little disincentive against vexatious litigation. Federal statutes, recently stiffened (28 U.S.C. §§1915-1915A), give a federal court substantial discretion to dismiss such suits as vexatious with far less than the normal opportunity in a counseled action to challenge such unilateral judicial action.

Chapter 2. Pleading and Joinder of Claims and Defenses

§1. Definitions

I. Claims

143. A claim is the fundamental litigative unit of a civil action.[1] Every claim in this strict and fundamental sense is bipolar and unilateral. A claim is bipolar because it consists of the assertion by a single claiming party against a single defending party that by virtue of certain facts (which may or may not be in dispute) there exists a legal relationship between the parties that entitles the claiming party to some form of judicial relief from the defending party. A claim is unilateral because the claiming party's right to relief from the defending party is separate and distinct from any reciprocal claim the defending party may have to judicial relief as against the claiming party.

In an ordinary civil action the claiming party seeks some coercive relief to redress or prevent the breach of a legal duty owed to the claiming party by the defending party, but in a declaratory-judgment action the claiming party may seek only a declaration of legal rights as between the parties, and this often takes the form of a declaration of nonliability of the claiming party to the defending party. Thus a potential defending party in an ordinary civil action for coercive relief can preemptively initiate a reciprocal declaratory-judgment action in which the potential defending party becomes the claiming party by asserting a claim for declaratory relief that, if granted, will bar the declaratory-judgment defending party from later seeking coercive relief as a claiming party in an ordinary civil action.

1. *See* John B. Oakley, "Federal Jurisdiction and the Problem of the Litigative Unit: When Does What "Arise Under" Federal Law?," Tex. L. Rev. 76 (1998): 1829, 1832.

144. As previously discussed (paragraph 126), our use of the term "claim" is a shorthand reference to what Rule 8 of the Federal Rules of Civil Procedure refers to as a "claim for relief," and is synonymous with the term "cause of action" used by many state systems of civil procedure.

In the simplest of civil actions, a single plaintiff asserts a single claim against a single defendant, and no other claim is asserted in the action by either party. Even in an apparently simple action with just one plaintiff claiming against just one defendant, however, it is often difficult to determine whether the plaintiff is asserting just one claim, or several. The difficulty arises from the fact that a given set of facts, such as an automobile accident in which the plaintiff's vehicle is struck by the defendant's vehicle, may give rise to several different theories of liability or to a right to several different types of remedies.[1] As a general matter, the law of preclusion or res judicata permits the plaintiff to sue the defendant only one time for relief from injuries arising out of a particular out-of-court transaction or occurrence.[2] Any legal theory bearing on the plaintiff's right to relief or the nature of that relief that is not adjudicated in the plaintiff's first lawsuit with regard to a particular claim is nonetheless barred from subsequent adjudication. Therefore the plaintiff has an incentive to assert every plausible theory of relief and seek every available remedy, and will often subdivide the complaint into separate sections independently asserting alternative factual contentions, alternative legal theories, and alternative prayers for particular kinds of relief.

Rule 8(d) of the Federal Rules of Civil Procedure refers to these alternative contentions as alternative "statements of a claim" but this terminology is not frequently used in most pleadings or in common parlance. It is commonplace for complaints to set forth what are referred to as multiple "claims" or "causes of action" when these are formally just alternative statements of the same claim or cause of action.

1. Suppose the defendant was allegedly driving too fast. Was that merely careless, constituting negligence and creating liability for compensatory damages? Or was it reckless (as it would be if the defendant had been engaged in an illegal "drag racing" competition with another vehicle), creating liability for punitive as well as compensatory damages? In addition to being held liable for damages, should the defendant be enjoined from engaging in such reckless conduct again?
2. This general statement is subject to considerable qualification, as discussed below in Part IX's more extensive discussion of res judicata principles. The modern term in American law for res judicata is "preclusion doctrine," and the preclusive effect of a previous judgment is dependent on the "scope of the claim" that was previously adjudicated as defined by the court system responsible for that adjudication. There is considerable local variation among state courts in how a "claim" is defined for preclusion purposes, but the "transaction or occurrence" test is the most common, and is also the test used by the federal courts to determine the preclusive effect of a prior federal judgment.

145. The next section will discuss the law of joinder of claims, which governs the extent to which plaintiffs and defendants may join genuinely distinct claims (not simply alternative statements of the same claim) together to expand the scope of a civil action beyond its minimum dimensions.

II. Defenses

146. Defenses are contentions of fact or law that negate the liability asserted by a claim against a defending party. The most common defense consists simply of a denial of the truth of the facts alleged by the claiming party as the basis for the claim. Any fact alleged by the claiming party is deemed admitted unless denied by the defending party. Defenses that depend upon the truth of facts not alleged in the claim against which the defense is interposed are called "affirmative defenses." Affirmative defenses are waived if not asserted in the responsive pleading of the defending party. Rule 8(c)(1) of the Federal Rules of Civil Procedure sets forth an alphabetically organized, nonexhaustive list of such affirmative defenses:

> accord and satisfaction, arbitration and award, assumption of risk, contributory negligence, discharge in bankruptcy, duress, estoppel, failure of consideration, fraud, illegality, injury by fellow servant, laches, license, payment, release, res judicata, statute of frauds, statute of limitations, waiver, and any other matter constituting an avoidance or affirmative defense.

147. Rule 12(b) of the Federal Rules of Civil Procedure sets forth seven jurisdictional or procedural defenses that may be asserted either in the defending party's responsive pleading or by preliminary motion. These defenses include:

(1) lack of subject-matter jurisdiction;
(2) lack of personal jurisdiction;
(3) improper venue;
(4) insufficient process, referring to some defect in the contents of the process served on the defending party;
(5) insufficient service of process, referring to some defect in the manner in which process was served on the defending party rather than the contents of what was received by the defending party;
(6) failure to state a claim upon which relief can be granted, referring to the legal insufficiency of the claim even if the facts alleged in support of the claim are assumed to be true; and
(7) failure to join a party under Rule 19, the Federal Rule of Civil Procedure governing joinder of parties deemed necessary to the just adjudication of a civil action.

Of the above defenses, (2)-(5) are waived if not raised in the first instance by the defendant, while (6) and (7) may be raised at any time until the end of trial, and (1) may be raised at any time before a judgment has become final and no longer appealable.

The process by which claims and defenses are asserted in the pleadings of the parties to a civil action is discussed in more detail in Part IV.

§2. DISTINCTIONS

148. The federal courts and (with some local qualifications) most state courts have highly liberal rules encouraging the aggregation of multiple claims in a single civil action. This encourages judicial economy by avoiding an unnecessary multiplicity of litigation. Instead of adjudicating claims on a piecemeal basis, one claim at a time, courts are able to dispose of many claims in a single judgment. This also reduces the risk that factually related claims might be adjudicated in factually inconsistent ways in trials held before different triers of fact.

149. There are two fundamental rules that define this liberal American joinder policy.

First, *unlimited* joinder of *claims*. There is no limit whatsoever to the joinder of additional claims between existing parties to a civil action. Second, *extensive* joinder of *parties*, virtually to the limits of rationality. Existing parties to a civil action can join to that action claims against additional parties subject only to the minimal constraint that these claims against new parties have some tenuous connection to the issues framed by the claims between existing parties.

These two fundamental rules apply at all stages of the pleading of claims in a civil action, but with important practical variations that make it useful to distinguish between the joinder of claims and parties in the initial pleading – the complaint – by which one or more plaintiffs commence a civil action against one or more defendants, and the subsequent joinder of additional claims and parties in pleadings – answers, replies, and third-party complaints and answers – that are filed in reaction to the initiation of a civil action by the filing of a complaint.[1]

The rule of unlimited joinder of claims is paralleled by a more obvious rule permitting unlimited joinder of defenses, as exemplified by Rule 8(d)(2) of the Federal Rules of Civil Procedure. As a practical matter, it is mandatory for a defending party to join all available defenses in the pleading by which that party responds to the claiming party, because any defense (whether a denial or an affirmative defense) is waived if not so asserted.

1. Rule 7 of the Federal Rules of Civil Procedure describes the pleadings that may be filed in a civil action. The practice and sequence of pleading is discussed in more detail in Part IV.

150. One final point is of particular importance in understanding the joinder of claims and parties in civil actions adjudicated in the federal courts. This discussion deals only with the permissible and occasionally mandatory scope of *joinder* of claims and parties. Because federal courts are courts of limited jurisdiction, a particular federal court adjudicating a particular civil action may lack the subject-matter jurisdiction necessary to adjudicate some claims even if those claims and the parties to those claims have been properly joined as a procedural matter. Federal jurisdiction is "claim-specific"[1] and does not necessarily extend to every claim that the liberal federal joinder rules permit to be joined to a civil action. The supplemental jurisdiction of the federal courts, discussed above (paragraphs 69-72), facilitates the liberal joinder of claims and parties in federal civil actions but is not coextensive with the full range of joinder opportunities that may be procedurally permissible.[2]

1. *See* John B. Oakley, *Reporter's Memorandum, supra*, at 599-656.
2. *See* John B. Oakley, "Integrating Supplemental Jurisdiction and Diversity Jurisdiction: A Progress Report on the Work of the American Law Institute," Ind. L. J. 74 (1998): 25.

I. Joinder in the Complaint

A. Claims

151. As previously discussed (paragraph 144), if a plaintiff (driver A) commences a civil action by filing a complaint asserting a claim against a defendant (driver B) seeking judicial relief on account of a collision between the automobiles of A and B, A may and as a practical matter must (to avoid later preclusion by res judicata principles) join in the complaint as many alternative statements of the claim as A wishes to assert. A may thus seek relief both on grounds of negligence and on grounds of recklessness, and may seek different kinds of relief, such as compensatory damages, punitive damages, and an injunction against future recklessness by B that threatens injury to A.

But suppose A has some other claim against B, unrelated to their automobile accident. Now that A has assumed an adversarial position vis-à-vis B, may A join that unrelated claim to the same civil action that involves the automobile accident? As a matter of pleading policy, Rule 8(d)(2) of the Federal Rules of Civil Procedure permits A to join in the complaint not only alternative statements of the claim for relief based on the automobile accident, but also any separate and independent claims A may wish to assert against B. As a matter of joinder policy, Rule 18 of the Federal Rules of Civil Procedure likewise so provides: "A party asserting a claim to relief … may join … as many claims as it has against an opposing party." By authorizing such an unlimited joinder of claims, Rules 8 and 18 thus permit what might otherwise be several different civil actions between the plaintiff and the defendant to be aggregated into a single civil action that adjudicates several different claims at one time.

The unlimited joinder of claims permitted by Rules 8 and 18 is nominally voluntary, leaving it to the discretion of the plaintiff to choose how many claims are asserted in a given complaint against a particular defendant. As discussed below in Part IV and Part IX, however, if there is any room for doubt whether certain claims arising out of the same transaction or occurrence may in fact not be genuinely separate claims, but merely alternative statements of the same claim, the joinder in the complaint of all related claims or statements of claim that a particular plaintiff may be entitled to assert against a particular defendant may be a practical necessity. Joinder of all related claims avoids the risk that at a later date some claims may be barred by the doctrine of res judicata or "claim preclusion."

B. Parties

1. Permissive Joinder

152. Rule 20 of the Federal Rules of Civil Procedure controls permissive joinder of parties as plaintiffs and defendants. Rule 20(a) provides that multiple parties may join as plaintiffs or be joined as defendants in the same civil action provided only that at least one claim asserted by or against each party arises "out of the same transaction, occurrence, or series of transactions or occurrences" and further that at least one "question of law or fact common to all these persons will arise in the action." These transactional-nexus and common-question requirements slightly limit the permissibility of joinder of parties, and contrasts with the unlimited rule governing joinder of claims between parties.

Rule 18's permission for unlimited joinder of claims and Rule 20's slightly limited permission for broad joinder of parties may be invoked in tandem. Suppose that in the civil action previously hypothesized as arising out of an automobile accident (paragraphs 144, 151), plaintiff A invokes Rule 20 to join in the complaint claims against two defendants: defendant B, the other driver, and defendant C, the owner of the car that B was driving at the time of the collision with A. Rule 20 permits the joinder of A's claim against C, on the ground that the substantive law makes an owner of an automobile vicariously liable for any harm caused by its operation; C may be sued in the same civil action as A's claim against B, the actual driver whom C permitted to use the automobile. Once both B and C are properly joined as defending parties in A's complaint, A can invoke Rule 18 to join in the same complaint additional, unrelated claims against either B or C. For instance, A could join a second claim against B for an unrelated breach of a contract by B to pay rent on property owned by A and leased by B. A could also join a second claim against C for an unrelated incident in which C fraudulently induced A to purchase securities owned by C. This joinder of unrelated claims against B and C is permissible under Rule 18 once it has been established that B and C can both be joined as parties under Rule 20 by the assertion against them of related claims arising out of the automobile accident that pose the common question of whether B was at fault in causing the accident.

Because such interactive use of Rules 18 and 20 may permit the joinder of parties and claims that serves no useful purpose of judicial administration, the trial court has discretion under Rules 20(b) and 42(b) of the Federal Rules of Civil Procedure to order separate trials of particular claims or issues, and under Rule 21 to sever any claim. These provisions allow a trial court to reconstruct a single civil action that has become too unwieldy by converting that action into two or more separate actions. If a particular party has been improperly joined, that claim should be severed or (if the civil action has been filed in a federal court that lacks jurisdiction over the severed claim) dismissed, dropping the party from the action. The original action, however, may not be dismissed because of the misjoinder of a particular party.

2. Compulsory Joinder

153. Rule 19 of the Federal Rules of Civil Procedure controls the joinder of necessary parties. This is a form of compulsory joinder. A necessary party is one whose absence will prevent complete relief,[1] will impair or impede that person's ability to protect interests related to the subject of the action,[2] or expose the parties already before the court to double, multiple or otherwise inconsistent obligations.[3]

Rule 19(a)(1) stipulates two preconditions to adding a necessary party. First, the party to be joined must be subject to service of process. In other words, the court must be able to exercise personal jurisdiction over the party. Second, joinder of the party cannot deprive the court of its subject-matter jurisdiction. In addition, a necessary party can resist joinder by asserting a valid venue objection. If a court determines that a party is necessary but cannot be joined for lack of territorial jurisdiction, subject-matter jurisdiction, or proper venue, the court must then consider whether the action may continue according to the standards of Rule 19(b).

If a necessary party cannot be joined, Rule 19(b) directs the court to "determine whether, in equity and good conscience, the action should proceed among the existing parties or should be dismissed." Rule 19(b) sets forth a nonexhaustive list of factors that the court should consider in making this determination:

(1) the extent to which a judgment rendered in the person's absence might prejudice that person or the existing parties;
(2) the extent to which any prejudice could be lessened or avoided by:
  (a) protective provisions in the judgment;
  (b) shaping the relief; or
  (c) other measures;
(3) whether a judgment rendered in the person's absence would be adequate; and
(4) whether the plaintiff would have an adequate remedy if the action were dismissed for nonjoinder.

These amorphous standards have given rise to a great deal of litigation.[4] In many cases, a necessary party's absence is not raised until trial or appeal, when courts are faced with the distasteful choices of either issuing an incomplete award, dismissing the action, or adding the necessary party and beginning the litigation process over again.[5] Necessary-party questions take on greater importance in federal courts, especially in diversity cases where the joinder of a necessary party may be foreclosed for lack of diversity of citizenship. State courts generally have unrestricted subject-matter jurisdiction, and face obstacles in joining a necessary party only for lack of territorial jurisdiction. Even then an alternate state forum is usually a prerequisite to dismissal.[6]

1. Fed. R. Civ. P. 19(a)(1)(A).
2. Id., 19(a)(1)(B)(i).
3. Id., 19(a)(1)(B)(ii).
4. *See generally* Jack H. Friedenthal et al., *Civil Procedure*, 4th edn (2005), §6.5; James, *supra*, §10.12.
5. James, *supra*, §10.11 at 610-611.
6. Id., at 610.

3. Interpleader

154. Interpleader is a specialized form of compulsory joinder of parties. It is used by a party (the "stakeholder") in possession of property (the "stake") to which two or more (often many more) parties have or may assert conflicting claims. The stakeholder may take the initiative by commencing a civil action in which the stakeholder as plaintiff "interpleads" all of the rival claimants by filing a "complaint in interpleader" naming them jointly as codefendants. The court in which a complaint in interpleader is filed typically issues an injunction that bars the interpleaded defendants from commencing conflicting litigation against the stakeholder, thereby forcing all defendants to resolve their claims among themselves and between them and the plaintiff-stakeholder in a single civil action. This avoids the possibility that the stakeholder might otherwise be exposed to inconsistent liabilities if each claimant were allowed on a piecemeal basis to seek a judgment against the stakeholder.

Rule 22 of the Federal Rules of Civil Procedure and parallel provisions under the law of most states liberally authorize the filing of complaints in interpleader. Old restrictions on interpleader have generally been abolished, allowing the stakeholder to interplead defendants whose claims are merely contingent, and also allowing the stakeholder to assert in the interpleader litigation a claim to ownership of all or part of the stake in its own right.

The benefits of modern interpleader practice would frequently be unavailable in cases involving claimants residing in different states if constrained by the normal limitations on state-court territorial jurisdiction, which as a general matter also limit the territorial jurisdiction of the federal district courts (see paragraph 114). Such interstate disputes often arise in connection with the obligations of insurance companies.[1] The Federal Interpleader Act of 1936 cured this problem by specially vesting the federal district courts with subject-matter jurisdiction of interpleader litigation in which any one interpleaded defendant is of diverse citizenship with respect to any other interpleaded defendant, and in which the stake is worth at least

USD 500.[2] The same Act also permits such a suit to be filed in any district in which at least one defendant resides,[3] and vests the district court with nationwide territorial jurisdiction.[4]

1. *See, e.g., State Farm Fire & Casualty Co. v. Tashire*, 386 U.S. 523 (1967).
2. 28 U.S.C. §1335.
3. 28 U.S.C. §1397.
4. 28 U.S.C. §2361.

II. Joinder in Reaction to a Prior Pleading

155. The previous subsection on "Joinder in the Complaint" dealt with the joinder of claims and parties in the plaintiff's complaint, the initial pleading that commences a civil action. As suggested by the generic references therein to the joinder options of a "claiming party" with respect to a "defending party," the rules governing joinder of claims and parties are of general application, and are not limited to joinder of additional claims and parties in the complaint alone. As discussed more fully in Part IV, Rule 7 of the Federal Rules of Civil Procedure describes a total of seven pleadings that are permitted in a civil action:

(1) a complaint;
(2) an answer to a complaint;
(3) an answer to a counterclaim;
(4) an answer to a cross-claim;
(5) a third-party complaint;
(6) an answer to a third-party complaint, and, if ordered by the trial court;
(7) a reply to an answer.

The liberal rules governing joinder of claims and joinder of parties apply to all of these pleadings, but some forms of joinder are particularly associated with responsive pleadings, that is, pleadings filed in reaction to an earlier pleading.

A. Counterclaims

156. A counterclaim is asserted by a defending party against a claiming party in response to the pleading of a claim against the defending party. In most instances, counterclaims are asserted by defendants in response to claims pleaded against them in the complaint that commences a civil action. Rule 13 of the Federal Rules of Civil Procedure describes two types of counterclaims, requiring the joinder of one type but merely permitting the joinder of the other type at the option of the pleader.

Any transactionally related counterclaim that a defending party has against a party that has asserted a claim against the defending party must be asserted in the pleading by which the defending party responds to the claim asserted by the claiming party. This is called a "compulsory counterclaim." Rule 13(a) describes a compulsory counterclaim as one that "arises out of the transaction or occurrence that is the subject matter of the opposing party's claim." Any compulsory counterclaim that is not thus joined to a civil action will be precluded from later adjudication. The compulsory counterclaim imposed in the federal courts by Rule 13(a) is a virtually universal feature of state practice as well. The preclusive effect of the failure to assert a compulsory counterclaim is part of the general American law of res judicata.

Rule 13(b) also permits a defending party to assert any other claim against an opposing party, even though it is unrelated to the claim asserted against the defending party by that opposing party. In this respect, Rule 13(b) simply restates the unlimited joinder of claims authorized by Rule 18. The importance of Rule 13(b)'s separate treatment of such unrelated counterclaims is that it makes clear that unrelated counterclaims are "permissive counterclaims." Only transactionally related counterclaims are made compulsory, on pain of preclusion, by Rule 13(a). Permissive counterclaims may be asserted without preclusion in later litigation if the defending party chooses not to join them to the civil action that is already under way.

By way of example, suppose that in the car-crash litigation previously hypothesized (paragraphs 144, 151), defendant B maintains that the collision was caused by the negligent driving of A. If B wishes to assert a claim against A for compensation for the injuries that B suffered in the accident, that is a compulsory counterclaim that B must assert in B's answer to A's complaint. If B fails to assert this compulsory counterclaim and later seeks relief from A on this ground in a separate civil action, B's belated suit will be precluded as a violation of the compulsory-counterclaim rule. It will make no difference that B might successfully have defended against A's suit by establishing that A was the negligent driver who caused the accident. The compulsory-counterclaim rule will still preclude any later litigation by B of a claim against A that is transactionally related to any claim asserted by A against B in earlier litigation.

B. Cross-Claims

157. When two or more parties have been joined in an action, Rule 13(g) of the Federal Rules of Civil Procedure permits one coparty to assert a claim against another coparty, provided that the claim arises out of the same transaction or occurrence as the claims that have been filed jointly against the coparties. Such a claim between coparties is called a "cross-claim."

Although a transactional relationship is required for the joinder of an initial cross-claim, the joinder of such a cross-claim is not compulsory. But once a cross-claim with the requisite transactional relationship to the main litigation has been asserted by one coparty against another, the relationship between the coparties changes. The coparty against whom the cross-claim was asserted is now a defending party with respect to the cross-claim, and must comply with Rule 13(a)'s compulsory-counterclaim rule. Moreover, either coparty can then assert additional cross-claims against the other coparty, because once Rule 13(g)'s requirement of a transactional relationship has been satisfied by the initial assertion of at least one properly related cross-claim, Rule 18 and Rule 13(b) permit unlimited joinder of additional cross-claims between the coparties.

For example, if as previously hypothesized (paragraph 152) plaintiff A commences a civil action by filing a complaint arising out of an automobile accident in which factually related claims are asserted against both defendant B (the other driver) and defendant C (the owner of the car driven by B), B and C are coparties by virtue of their joinder in A's complaint. If C wishes to assert a claim against B for the damage caused to C's car in B's collision with A, C may (but need not) do so by filing a cross-claim against B under Rule 13(g) as part of C's answer to A's complaint. If C wishes to assert a claim against A for the same damage, C *must* do so by filing a counterclaim against A under Rule 13(a) as part of C's answer to A's complaint. The joinder of C's counterclaim against A is required because it arises from the same transaction or occurrence as A's claim in the complaint against C, and therefore is defined as a "compulsory counterclaim" by Rule 13(a). The joinder of C's cross-claim against B requires the same sort of transactional relationship as requires the joinder of C's compulsory counterclaim against A, but the cross-claim provision of Rule 13(g) lacks the compulsory feature of the counterclaim provision of Rule 13(a).

Suppose further that B believes that the accident may have been caused by the failure of the brake system of C's car, and that this failure is attributable to C's negligent maintenance of the car. B thus has a claim that may properly be asserted as a cross-claim against C, since it is transactionally related to A's claim in the complaint against B. Rule 13(g) permits but does not require that B assert this cross-claim against C, *provided that C has not previously asserted a cross-claim against B.* If C initiates an adversarial relationship between C and B by filing a cross-claim against B, however, Rule 13(g) no longer governs the status of B's negligence-maintenance claim against C. Once C files a cross-claim against B, B becomes an opposing party with respect to C, and Rule 13(a)'s compulsory-counterclaim rule requires that B assert the negligent-maintenance claim against C in response to C's cross-claim against B.

C. *Impleader of Third Parties*

158. If a complaint asserts that two codefendants are jointly liable to the plaintiff, as would be the case in the car-crash hypothetical (paragraph 152) if A's complaint jointly named both B and C as defendants, the codefendant that is only secondarily liable (such as C, if the accident was caused by B's poor driving rather than C's poor maintenance of the vehicle driven by B) can seek indemnification from the codefendant that is the primarily liable party by the assertion against that codefendant of a cross-claim under Rule 13(g). But in many instances a defending party will have a claim for indemnification against a so-called "third party" who has not yet been joined to the litigation. This would be the case in the car-crash hypothetical if plaintiff A's complaint asserted a claim only against the owner of the other car, defendant C, and did not join in the complaint a claim against B as the driver of C's car.

The joinder of third-party defendants for purposes of indemnification is important not only to avoid a multiplicity of lawsuits arising from the same out-of-court transaction or occurrence, but also to avoid the risk of inconsistent results. Suppose that in A's suit against C, A wins a judgment for damages based on the trier of fact's conclusion that B was the negligent driver, and that the substantive law makes C vicariously liable to A for injuries caused by B as a permissive driver of C's car. If C then sues B in a separate civil action seeking indemnification from B, B (who has not yet had an opportunity to contest A's version of events) may convince a different trier of fact that the accident was A's fault. These inconsistent verdicts will result in C having to pay a judgment to A without recourse from B, even though the only basis for C's liability was the fault of B that was determined inconsistently in the two lawsuits.

In some instances third parties can be joined or "impleaded" into litigation already underway between other parties by naming them as additional defending parties to a counterclaim or cross-claim pursuant to Rule 13(h) of the Federal Rules of Civil Procedure and analogous state provisions. But most instances of the impleader of third parties require resort to Rule 14 of the Federal Rules of Civil Procedure and its state-court analogues.

The essential preconditions to the impleader of a third party under Rule 14 are that the impleading party must be a defending party, and must assert a claim against the impleaded third party that seeks indemnity or contribution (i.e., partial indemnification) from the impleaded third party in the event that the impleading defending party is held liable to some other party in the litigation. Because the third party is a stranger to the litigation until formally impleaded into the litigation, impleader requires the filing and service of a complaint against the third party. This is called a "third-party complaint," and with respect to that complaint the impleading party is the "third-party plaintiff" and the impleaded third party is the "third-party defendant."

Although a claim for indemnity or contribution is required by Rule 14 as a precondition to the impleader of a third-party defendant, Rule 18 permits other claims against the third-party defendant to be joined in the third-party complaint. Once a third party has been impleaded into a civil action by the filing of a third-party complaint under Rule 14, all of the other joinder rules applicable to defending parties – such as the rules requiring assertion of compulsory counterclaims and permitting the assertion of permissive counterclaims and cross-claims – are fully applicable to the third-party defendant. The third-party defendant can even invoke Rule 14 to create a daisy chain of litigation by impleading a new party (a fourth-party defendant) who may be liable to the third-party defendant (now fourth-party plaintiff) for some or all of any liability that the third-party defendant owes to another defending party (the third-party plaintiff) further up the daisy chain.

D. *Intervention*

159. In some cases, a stranger to litigation may have an interest in the litigation that it desires to protect by becoming a party to the litigation. Rule 24 of the Federal Rules of Civil Procedure is reflective of virtually universal American practice by broadly authorizing the joinder of third parties at their own request. This is called "intervention," in distinction to the involuntary impleader of a third party by third-party complaint under Rule 14. There are two types of intervention.

Rule 24(a) governs "intervention of right." It requires the trial court to grant a timely application[1] to intervene if the proposed intervenor has been granted a right to intervene by statute, or (in the more typical situation) "when the applicant claims an interest relating to the property or transaction that is the subject of the action, and is so situated that, disposing of the action may as a practical matter impair or impede the movant's ability to protect its interest, unless existing parties adequately represent that interest." This general provision for intervention as of right contains three elements:

(1) the interest of the applicant must relate to the specific property or transaction at issue in the pending litigation;
(2) the applicant must face at least practical impairment of that interest, even if the applicant would not formally be bound by a judgment in a civil action to which it is not a party; and
(3) the conduct of the litigation by existing parties must not be likely vicariously to protect the interest of the applicant.

Rule 24(b) covers "permissive intervention." It applies when the applicant relies on a statutory right to intervene that is conditional rather than absolute, or (more typically) when the applicant wishes to assert a claim or defense that involves some question of law or fact in common with the issues already raised in the litigation into which the applicant seeks to intervene. This is a very loose test, and the trial court has virtually plenary discretion to grant or (as happens in most cases) to deny an application for permissive intervention.[2]

1. The "timeliness" requirement is quite liberally construed by the federal courts but more narrowly by some state courts.
2. Although permissive intervention is discretionary with the trial court, once that discretion has been exercised to permit intervention, the new party is vested with all of the rights to influence the future course of the litigation that are possessed by the other parties. Trial courts are therefore inclined to view the grant of an application for permissive intervention as potentially lifting the lid of Pandora's box. A popular alternative that maintains plenary judicial control over the conduct of a proposed permissive intervenor is to deny leave to intervene but to permit the proposed intervenor to enjoy quasi-party status, subject to the day-to-day discretion of the trial judge, as a "litigating *amicus curiae.*" While not without value, this has been criticized as a "bastard form of intervention" that reduces "the litigating *amicus* to the puppet of the judge" with "no appeal as of right should the judge err." John B. Oakley, "The United States as Participant in Public Interest Litigation: Recent Developments," U.C. Davis L. Rev. 13 (1980): 247, 255-257.

III. Consolidation and Severance of Claims and Parties

160. The unlimited joinder of claims and liberal joinder of parties authorized by Rules 18 and 20 of the Federal Rules of Civil Procedure may be exercised interactively, and in conjunction with the specific provisions for joining counterclaims, cross-claims, claims against third parties, and claims by or against intervenors. The net effect may be to permit such an abundant joinder of claims and parties that a single civil action may become too complex for unitary adjudication, thereby performing a disservice to the goal of efficient judicial administration that liberal joinder is intended to encourage. As an antidote to joinder run riot, the trial court has discretion under Rules 20(b) and 42(b) of the Federal Rules of Civil Procedure to order separate trials of particular claims or issues, and under Rule 21 to sever any claim. These provisions allow a trial court to reconstruct a single civil action that has become too unwieldy by converting that action into two or more separate actions.

If a particular claim or party has been improperly joined, that claim or party should similarly be severed and adjudicated separately, but if the federal court lacks jurisdiction with respect to that claim or party, the claim should be dismissed and the party dropped from the action. The rest of the action, however, may not be dismissed because of the misjoinder of a particular claim or party.

Rule 42(a) confers on the trial court a parallel power to conduct a joint hearing or trial of similar matters pending in separate civil actions, or even to consolidate separate civil actions into one collective civil action.

Modern joinder rules and these ancillary rules permitting judicial severance and consolidation operate like the "cut and paste" functions of a modern word-processing computer program. Parts of a single document can be rearranged, or turned into separate documents; separate documents can be combined into a single document. With reference to modern American joinder practice rather than modern methods of word processing, the civil action is the "document" and particular claims and parties are the parts of that document that are subject to virtually infinite rearrangement.

By and large, the process of constructing a particular civil action by the "pasting" of various claims and parties into that action is left to the initiative of the litigants, while the process of "cutting down" the scope of an unwieldy civil action is left to the initiative and discretion of the trial judge. A great deal of attention has been focused of late, however, on the potential benefits of court-ordered aggregate adjudication or at least pretrial administration of large numbers of similar cases, especially with regard to "mass torts" (such as the exposure of hundreds or even thousands of individuals to a toxic substance such as asbestos). The use of class actions for this purpose has thus far proved to be problematic.[1] Present law allows the mass consolidation of ordinary civil actions only if they are pending in federal rather than state courts, and then only for purposes of pretrial proceedings absent consent by the parties to plenary consolidation for all purposes including trial and judgment.[2]

1. *See, e.g., Ortiz v. Fibreboard Corp.*, 527 U.S. 815 (1999).
2. *See* 28 U.S.C. §§1404, 1407, as construed in *Lexecon, Inc. v. Milberg Weiss Bershad Hynes & Lerach*, 523 U.S. 26 (1998).

Chapter 3. Sanctions

§1. Procedural Irregularities

I. Formal Requirements

161. Affirmative duties imposed by procedural rules are in general enforced by termination of the litigation of the claim in question. For instance, the Federal Rules of Civil Procedure permit a claim to be dismissed for breach of the rules by the claiming party (Rule 41(b-c)), and permit entry of a default, and ultimately a default judgment, with respect to any claim that a defending party fails properly to defend (Rule 55(a-b)). Rule 37 sets forth an extensive array of sanctions that are applicable exclusively to violations of Rules 26-36 regarding pretrial disclosure and discovery of evidence. These include not only dismissal or entry of a default with respect to the particular claim (or even the entire civil action) as to which there was a breach of the disclosure and discovery rules, but also an array of other sanctions including an award of costs, fee shifting, a limitation of the right to establish or dispute certain contentions, and even an order holding a recalcitrant party in contempt of court.

II. Time Limits

162. Many procedural rules permitting or requiring that a party take certain action also impose a time limit for taking that action. In general, the failure to act permissively within the stipulated time results only in a loss of that procedural opportunity. For instance, Rule 38(b) of the Federal Rules of Civil Procedure requires any party desiring jury trial of an issue of fact to serve upon the other parties a written demand for jury trial no later than ten days after the service of the last pleading directed to the issue as to which jury trial is desired, and to file proof of such service with the court. Rule 38(d) provides that a failure to serve and file the demand for jury trial within this period waives the right to jury trial. The failure to perform some required act within the specified time period is generally enforced like any other procedural default, by involuntary dismissal of the relevant claim under Rule 41 (sanctioning the claiming party) or entry of default as to that claim under Rule 55 (sanctioning the defending party). Rule 4(m) of the Federal Rules of Civil Procedure provides specially that if a defendant is not served within 120 days of the filing of the complaint, then the court shall dismiss the action without prejudice unless the plaintiff shows good cause for the delay in service.

III. Statutes of Limitations

163. The substantive law that makes a claim actionable will also generally provide that the claim is extinguished if a civil action to enforce the claim is not commenced within a stipulated period of time. This time period is almost universally (if somewhat loosely) referred to as a "statute of limitations," whether or not it is internal to the substantive law that creates the claim, or is independently provided by statute, rule of court, or decisional law applicable to a particular class of claim, such as claims for personal injury, claims for breach of contract, and so forth. Failure to commence a civil action to enforce a claim within the time allowed by the applicable statute of limitations is an affirmative defense that if properly asserted will entitle the defending party to a judgment as a matter of law even if it is unequivocally clear on the merits that but for the delay in suit the claiming party would be entitled to a judgment against the defending party.

The relatively simple concept that the litigation of most claims must commence within the period prescribed by the applicable statute of limitations is greatly complicated in practice by certain idiosyncratic features of American civil procedure, which are made even more arbitrary and unpredictable by the confused nature of American principles of choice of law.

First, some (but relatively few) claims, especially those grounded not in statute but in common law principles traditionally enforced by courts exercising equitable jurisdiction, may be subject not to a statute of limitations but rather only to the doctrine of "laches." Instead of providing a complete defense to the delayed litigation of a claim, laches provides only a conditional defense that requires the defending party to show prejudice attributable to the claiming party's delay in commencing the litigation.

Second, statutes of limitations generally refer to particular types of legal theories (tort claims, contract claims, fraud claims, etc.) or particular types of injuries (personal injuries, property damage, competitive injury, etc.) rather than to particular claims conceived of as a litigative unit whereby a particular claiming party seeks to establish a right to relief from a particular defending party with respect to some out-of-court transaction or occurrence. This may mean that more than one statute of limitations may apply to the litigation of a particular claim, depending upon the legal theory underlying a particular statement of that claim in the complaint or other pleading asserting the claim. For instance, a consumer injured in the course of driving a defective automobile may sue the manufacturer of the automobile, stating the claim in several alternative ways: as predicated on the manufacturer's negligence (a theory of relief based on the law of torts); as predicated on the manufacturer's breach of a warranty (a theory predicated on the law of contracts); as seeking relief for injury to the consumer's person; and as seeking relief for injury to the consumer's property. If the applicable statutes of limitations distinguish between tort and contract actions and between injuries to person and injuries to property, the same claim may or may not be barred depending on just what period is specified by each of the statutes of limitations that may be applicable depending upon how the consumer's pleading states the claim asserted against the manufacturer.

Third, there is virtually no uniformity in the statutes of limitations applicable in particular states to particular types of common litigation. A claim that must be litigated within one or two years in some states may remain open to litigation for as many as six years in other states.

Fourth – and of particular significance in view of the third point – it is well established for purposes of federal constitutional regulation of interstate choice of law that statutes of limitations are "procedural" rather than "substantive." This means that any state may apply its own statute of limitations even to a claim that is governed by the substantive law of some other state. Suppose, for instance, that the consumer previously mentioned purchased the car in question in Illinois and was injured in New York, where the consumer resides, and that the manufacturer is a corporation organized in Delaware but the car was manufactured in Michigan. If the consumer brings a civil action against the manufacturer in Mississippi, it is likely that the state courts of Mississippi must apply the substantive law of Illinois, New York, Delaware, or Michigan, since the US Supreme Court limits the choice of the substantive law in such a case to a choice among the laws only of those states that have "a significant contact or aggregation of contacts" with the parties and the events giving rise to the litigation.[1] But even if the civil action in Mississippi would be barred by the statutes of limitations applicable to such a claim under the law of every one of these states, Mississippi is free to apply its own, longer statute of limitations to permit the consumer's suit to proceed in its own courts, even while it looks to the substantive law of one of these other states to determine if the consumer does indeed have any right to relief from the manufacturer.[2]

Fifth, the liberal rules governing state-court territorial jurisdiction (discussed above in paragraphs 86-109) – especially the rules permitting "tag jurisdiction" over individuals and "general jurisdiction" over corporations – make it easy for a forum-shopping plaintiff to bring suit in a state with an unusually long statute of limitations solely to gain the benefit of that statute of limitations, even though the particular claim in question is wholly unrelated to any activity by the defendant in the forum state.

Sixth, if the suit of such a forum-shopping plaintiff upon a state-created claim is filed originally in federal court or is removed to federal court by the defendant, the federal court has no power to make an independent choice of the applicable statute of limitations and must instead apply the limitations law of the state in which it sits.[3]

1. *Phillips Petroleum Co. v. Shutts*, 472 U.S. 797, 821-822 (1985).
2. *See Sun Oil Co. v. Wortman*, 486 U.S. 717 (1988).
3. *See Guaranty Trust Co. v. York*, 326 U.S. 99 (1945).

§2. LITIGATIVE MISCONDUCT

164. In federal practice, the courts have three methods of punishing parties for violations of procedural rules so serious as to amount to misconduct. First, a court may impose a variety of sanctions against parties who make unfounded or vexatious representations to the court, or who violate the discovery and disclosure rules, pursuant to Rules 11 and 37 of the Federal Rules of Civil Procedure. Second, a court may sanction attorneys or any other persons pursuant to 28 U.S.C. §1927 for unreasonably or vexatiously increasing the cost of litigation. Third, the court has inherent power to punish misconduct by equitable fee-shifting or by holding wrongdoers in contempt of court. A similar array of sanctioning devices is available to most state courts.

I. Rule 11 Sanctions

165. Rule 11(b) of the Federal Rules of Civil Procedure requires that any attorney (or any unrepresented party conducting litigation *pro se*) certify that every written representation of fact or law presented to the court, including pleadings, written motions, affidavits, and all other litigation documents, has been determined by the attorney or party after "an inquiry reasonable under the circumstances" to satisfy the following standards:

(1) it is not being presented for any improper purpose, such as to harass, cause unnecessary delay, or needlessly increase the cost of litigation
(2) the claims, defenses, and other legal contentions are warranted by existing law or by a nonfrivolous argument for extending, modifying, or reversing existing law or for establishing new law;
(3) the factual contentions have evidentiary support or, if specifically so indentified, will likely have evidentiary support after a reasonable opportunity for further investigation or discovery; and
(4) the denials of factual contentions are warranted on the evidence or, if specifically so identified, are reasonably based on belief or a lack of information.

Rule 11(c)(4) provides that breach of these standards may result in nonmonetary sanctions, penalties payable to the court, or an award of attorney's fees to the other party for costs incurred because of the impermissible conduct. Rule 11 has twice been amended in recent years, in 1983 and 1993, first to make its effect more draconian and then to mitigate its sanctions so as to avoid undue deterrence of optimistic advocacy of contentions of fact or law that are later determined to be insupportable.

Rule 11(d) specifically exempts from Rule 11 the regulation of the pretrial disclosure and discovery process that is separately governed by Rules 26-37 of the Federal Rules of Civil Procedure. The sanction provisions of Rule 37 are discussed above in paragraph 161 of this chapter.

II. Sanctions Under 28 U.S.C. §1927

166. Under §1927, an attorney or any other person may be subject to sanctions, including paying excess costs, expenses and attorneys' fees, for "unreasonably and vexatiously" multiplying the proceedings of any federal court. Because Rule 11 covers only the process of filing and advocating written papers presenting contentions of fact or law, §1927 has a complementary role to play in punishing and hence deterring what a psychologist might call a "passive-aggressive" approach to civil litigation, unduly prolonging the proceedings through pettifogging conduct and recurrent delay. Such tactics might otherwise be particularly attractive to parties with weak cases but large litigation budgets who hope to force a voluntary dismissal or discounted settlement by waging a war of attrition against a less wealthy opponent.

The federal courts are not of one mind on whether §1927 is merely a complement to Rule 11, or a sterner alternative, and this split in authority has assumed greater importance in light of the 1993 amendment of Rule 11 that softened its sanctioning provisions. Associated with this debate is a split among the federal courts of appeals concerning the proper standard for bad-faith conduct that may be sanctioned under §1927.[1] Courts that wish to make stern use of §1927 apply an objective standard for determining bad faith, permitting punishment of what are determined to be bad deeds even when committed with a pure heart. Courts that apply §1927 more leniently, and primarily as a complement rather than an alternative to Rule 11, demand a showing of subjective bad faith, i.e., willfully vexatious conduct. A third line of authority takes the middle road of sanctioning misconduct without a showing of subjective bad faith, but only if the misconduct is objectively reckless rather than merely unreasonable.

1. *See* Janet Josselyn, "The Story of Sirens – Sanctioning Lawyers Under 28 U.S.C. §1927," B.C. L. Rev. 31 (1990): 477.

III. Inherent Sanctioning Powers

167. As discussed below in Part VI (paragraph 218), the so-called "American Rule" (as opposed to the fee-shifting "English Rule") leaves each party ordinarily liable for its own legal fees regardless of the outcome of the litigation. The judgment-winner may, and generally does, receive reimbursement for "costs" but these do not include attorney's fees. The US Supreme Court has held that federal courts have inherent power to alter the American Rule, however, as a sanction for misconduct that has increased the expense of litigation. In *Alyeska Pipeline Service Co. v. Wilderness Society*,[1] the Supreme Court restricted use of this inherent sanctioning power to situations in which a court has first exhausted its express sanctioning powers, the sanction is assessed against the losing party, and that party has acted in bad faith. These restrictions were eased, however, in *Chambers v. NASCO, Inc.*,[2] which held that a federal court's inherent sanctioning power is not necessarily a last resort and may be deployed as an alternative to sanctions under Rule 11 and §1927. This power may be exercised against a prevailing as well as a losing party, and is justified if the sanctionable conduct was undertaken in bad faith even if the rest of the litigation was otherwise conducted in good faith.

1. *Alyeska Pipeline Serv. Co. v. Wilderness Soc'y*, 421 U.S. 240 (1975).
2. *Chambers v. NASCO, Inc.*, 501 U.S. 32 (1991).

IV. State Sanctioning Provisions

168. The sanctioning provisions available to state courts vary considerably from jurisdiction to jurisdiction. From a nationwide perspective, states may be organized into three general groups whose sanctioning policies reflect the three-way split among federal courts of appeals regarding the proper standard for sanctioning "bad-faith" conduct under 28 U.S.C. §1927. Some states prefer underdeterrence to discouraging access to courts, and thus set a high threshold for sanctionable misconduct by requiring a showing of subjective bad faith. Other states set a low threshold by assessing bad faith according to an objective standard. A third group of states uses a hybrid standard that in principle requires only an objective showing of bad faith but procedurally limits the scope of sanctions for such bad faith.[1]

1. *See* Byron C. Keeling, "Toward a Balanced Approach to "Frivolous" Litigation: A Critical Review of Federal Rule 11 and State Sanctions Provisions," Pepperdine L. Rev. 21 (1994): 1067, 1095-1102. The author classifies particular states as follows: the "high threshold" standard is applied in California, Connecticut, Florida, Maine, Massachusetts, New Mexico, Pennsylvania, and South Carolina; the "low threshold" standard is applied in Arkansas, Delaware, District of Columbia, Georgia, Idaho, Iowa, Kansas, Minnesota, Missouri, Montana, Nevada, North Carolina, North Dakota, Oklahoma, Oregon, Rhode Island, South Dakota, Tennessee, Virginia, Vermont, Washington, West Virginia, and Wyoming; the "hybrid" standard is applied in Alaska, Arizona, Alabama, Colorado, Hawaii, Illinois, Indiana, Kentucky, Louisiana, Maryland, Michigan, Mississippi, Nebraska, New Hampshire, New Jersey, New York, Ohio, Texas, Utah, and Wisconsin.

Part IV. Proceedings

Chapter 1. Initial Proceedings

169. A civil lawsuit in the United States is commenced by the filing of an initial pleading by a plaintiff, known in the federal and most state systems as a complaint (see paragraph 127). Some states use other terminology, such as a declaration, to describe this initial plaintiff's pleading. Upon the filing of a complaint, a plaintiff may seek preliminary relief, including a seizure of defendant's property or injunctive relief, to make post-trial relief as meaningful and helpful as possible. Such preliminary relief, issued during the pendency of pretrial and trial proceedings, is discussed in paragraphs 213-216.

Chapter 2. Proceedings Leading to Judgment

§1. Adversary Proceedings

I. Introduction of the Claim

A. Notice

170. For a defendant to be properly subject to the jurisdiction of a court, a number of requirements must be satisfied. Many of these requirements have already been discussed in Part II. For example, lack of subject-matter jurisdiction, territorial jurisdiction, or proper venue can be a basis for a defendant to seek dismissal of an action (and in the case of subject-matter jurisdiction, a basis for the court to dismiss on its own.) For over a century, the US Supreme Court has also made clear that a defendant must have received adequate notice of the lawsuit against him before any adverse judgment can be binding. Whether a case is brought in federal or state court, notice must be adequate in two respects:

(1) it must satisfy the requirements of due process in the United States Constitution; and
(2) the form of the notice must satisfy the applicable federal or state statutory requirements for service of process.

1. The Constitutional Test

171. The due process clauses of the Fifth and Fourteenth amendments to the Constitution of the United States impose on federal and state courts, respectively, a requirement that notice to a defendant of an action against him must be given before a valid and enforceable judgment may be entered. The constitutional requirement for notice is the same under the Fifth and Fourteenth amendments, although describing that requirement has not always been easy. In the nineteenth century, in cases such as *Pennoyer v. Neff*[1] (described more fully in paragraph 87), the US Supreme Court embraced different notice requirements for in rem and in personam actions. With regard to in rem actions, where ownership and control of property lie at the heart of the litigation, notice was adequately effectuated merely by attaching the property in question prior to any other judicial proceedings, on the theory that attachment would notify the defendant because generally people keep an eye on their property. With regard to in personam jurisdiction, in which a judgment would not be limited to a defendant's in-state property, notice was accomplished by serving the defendants with notice of the lawsuit while he was physically present in the jurisdiction; this was required for the court to exercise personal jurisdiction. Thus, in the era of *Pennoyer*, physical presence in the jurisdiction – of the defendant's property or his person – worked to satisfy both personal jurisdiction and notice requirements under the

Constitution. The two were thus bound up together in an inquiry focused on territorial presence.

1. *Pennoyer v. Neff*, 95 U.S. (5 Otto) 714 (1877).

172. As personal jurisdiction in the twentieth century has moved away from strict notions of physical presence in the court's jurisdiction (see discussion of *International Shoe* and its progeny in paragraphs 88-102), notice has emerged as a separate and distinct constitutional question. If personal jurisdiction could be established in personam without personal service of the defendant in the forum state, how could we be sure the defendant knew or could have known of the lawsuit such that his failure to appear could result in a judgment against him? And, in a similar vein, would attachment of property (including intangible property such as bank accounts or debts) – which was no longer even necessary for personal jurisdiction under modern minimum-contacts analysis – fairly put twentieth-century defendants, who own real and intangible property in a wide variety of locales, on notice that their property was in danger of being lost?

In 1950, in a series of cases beginning with *Mullane v. Central Hanover Bank & Trust Co.*,[1] the US Supreme Court answered these questions by holding that due process requires fair notice of a pending lawsuit against a defendant, separate from the basis for and inquiry into personal jurisdiction. More specifically, the court held that due process requires "notice, reasonably calculated, under all the circumstances, to apprise interested parties of the pendency of the action and afford them an opportunity to present objections. ... The means [of notice] employed must be such as one desirous of actually informing the absentee might reasonably adopt to accomplish it."[2] On the facts of the *Mullane* case, which involved a statutory accounting device by which people's interests in trust accounts in a bank would be settled, this constitutional requirement meant:

(1) trust interest holders whose names and addresses were known had to be sent notice of the proceeding by at least ordinary mail;
(2) defendants who were known but whose current addresses were unknown may not have to be individually notified, especially since their interests were likely to be represented by interest holders who were in fact notified and who participated in the litigation; and
(3) unknown interest holders were entitled – as a constitutional matter – to no more than notice by publication, that is, notice in the local newspapers that the settlement proceeding had been initiated for specified trusts at the bank.

The *Mullane* constitutional standard, which remains the governing framework a half-century later, thus focuses on the importance of actual notice and the opportunity to be heard, but it also takes into account the cost and difficulty of actual notice, and relies in some instances on the virtual representation and virtual participation that comes from having other defendants with similar interests already in the case.

Notwithstanding the flexibility inherent in the *Mullane* standard, the US Supreme Court has made clear in the past few decades that the minimal constitutional standard has some bite. In *Greene v. Lindsey*, for example, the court invalidated default judgments obtained by a group of Kentucky public housing officials against tenants they sought to evict, on the ground that the notice of the eviction proceedings given to the tenants was constitutionally inadequate.[3] The public housing officials had fully satisfied the mechanics of service of process required by state law (see paragraph 174 below for a discussion of these technical requirements) in that they posted notice of the eviction on the doors of the premises at issue, having unsuccessfully tried once to serve defendants or their responsible teenage children in person. The court held that due process required more efforts to actually notify the evictees – either multiple efforts at personal service and/or backup service by mail.

More recently, in *Jones v. Flowers*,[4] the US Supreme Court applied and elaborated the due process notice principles articulated in *Mullane* to hold that when a state sent a certified letter to a homeowner at the home address to notify him of an impending tax sale caused by delinquent property taxes, and the state was made aware that the letter went "unclaimed," the state was then under an obligation to pursue other reasonable means of notice. Such other means might include sending a regular first-class letter to the home, which letter (unlike the certified letter) might stay there long enough to be picked up by the property owner, or posting a notice of tax sale on the property itself. Due process does not, however, require the state to search the local phone book and other government records to locate the current residence of the property owner.

1. *Mullane v. Central Hanover Bank & Trust Co.*, 339 U.S. 309 (1950).
2. Id., at 314-315.
3. *Greene v. Lindsey*, 456 U.S. 444 (1982).
4. *Jones v. Flowers*, 547 U.S. 220 (2006).

2. Statutory Requirements and Mechanics of Service of Process

173. In addition to satisfying the Constitution, a plaintiff's notice to defendant(s) must also comply with applicable federal or state (depending on which court the case is filed in) procedures for serving notice. The form and contents of the court papers served on the defendant must be correct, and the manner in which the defendant is presented with these papers must also be correct. The papers are referred to as the "process of the court," and the manner of their presentation is referred to as the "service of process" on the defendant. The papers served on a defendant at the commencement of a civil action ordinarily consist of a copy of a document known as a summons, which directs the defendant to appear (or respond in writing) if he wishes to be heard in the matter filed against him, and a copy of the complaint, which sets out the claim(s) against the defendant filed by the plaintiff. The service of process may be effected by one of several means.

The classic form of service is hand delivery by a process server to the defendant. Personal service of process was traditionally required by the common law. Personal service may be made by any adult not a party to the action. Professional process servers exist and are commonly used. In unusual circumstances, a plaintiff may prevail upon local peace officers to serve process personally on a defendant. Where a plaintiff is suing an entity defendant, local law identifies the agents or officers of the entity upon whom process may be validly served. When a copy of the summons and complaint are personally served upon a defendant, the process server returns the original summons and complaint to the court – so-called "return of service" – along with the details of when and where service was made.

174. Many states provide for alternative means of service of process that are less costly than personal service. One is known as "substituted service," which is personal service upon someone of suitable age and competence other than the defendant at the defendant's place of residence. A second important alternative to personal service on the defendant is postal service, i.e., service on the defendant by mail, which becomes effective only if the defendant returns by mail a receipt of acknowledgment of the service of process. If the defendant fails to return the acknowledgment of receipt, the plaintiff will have to effect personal service, but the defendant (who chooses to ignore postal service) will then be liable for the costs of personal service. Postal service to an out-of-state defendant is often acceptable under state laws even without return of an acknowledgment of receipt. Another form of service of process that many states recognize as legitimate under some circumstances is constructive service, such as service by publication in newspapers, where a more personal form of service is impracticable.[1]

Each state has its own rules for the form and service of process, and many of these rules can be technical and nit-picking. Before initiating civil litigation in state court, a practitioner must familiarize himself with the specific technical requirements.

1. *See Mullane v. Hanover Bank & Trust*, 339 U.S. 309 (1950).

175. The situation in the federal courts is similar, but has been moving in the direction of abandoning the technicalities. Rule 4(b) of the Federal Rules of Civil Procedure requires that the district court clerk issue a summons upon the filing of a complaint with the court by the plaintiff. Rule 4(c)(2) provides that copies of the summons and the complaint may be served personally by any person eighteen years of age who is not a party to the action. Where process is to be served by mail, Rule 4(d)(1)(G) allows even the plaintiff to effectuate the mailing. Rule 4(c)(3) sets out the procedure for making use of federal peace officers – i.e., US Marshals – when appropriate.

Rule 4 allows a plaintiff to decide between personal service on in-state defendants, substituted service, or postal service (in which case the defendant must acknowledge receipt, otherwise the plaintiff will have to choose another method and seek reimbursement from the defendant). In addition, regardless of whether the defendant is located in state or out of state, a plaintiff filing in a federal district court may make use of any other service method authorized by the law of the state in which the federal district is located. This incorporation of state law broadens rather than limits the service-of-process devices available to plaintiffs, who can choose among the various methods of service of process authorized either by the federal rules or by the applicable state's law.

The Federal Rules of Civil Procedure have special provisions concerning corporations, partnerships and similar entities, and federal and state governmental defendants. There are also special provisions in Rule 4 for out-of-state defendants who have been made parties under Rule 14's third-party or Rule 19's required-party provisions. In addition, under Rule 4 a plaintiff must effect "prompt service" on defendants. Rule 4(m), added as part of the 1983 amendments to the Federal Rules of Civil Procedure, mandates dismissal (without prohibiting refiling) of any action in which, without good cause, service of process has not been accomplished within 120 days of filing the complaint with the court.

A few other points concerning federal service of process should be mentioned. (Defendant's objections to service of process will be discussed below.) First, there are special substantive federal laws which authorize nationwide service of process for certain kinds of federal claims, regardless of the service of process provisions of the state law of the state in which a federal action is filed. Finally, if a nonresident defendant lives not in another state, but rather a foreign country, Rule 4(f) authorizes a variety of methods of service of process, including personal service, postal service, and service authorized by the country in which the defendant lives. If the defendant lives in a country that is a signatory to the Hague Service Convention, however, special rules apply.

B. Pretrial Law and Motion Practice

1. Complaint

176. The filing and serving of the complaint is the formal initiation of the civil lawsuit (see paragraph 127). The complaint, which is governed by Rule 8 in the federal courts, marks the beginning of a pleading process that serves many functions. As noted in Part III, the notice pleading system that prevails in the federal courts and most states is not followed in all American jurisdictions; therefore the following discussion may not be applicable to the exceptional states.

Under the modern pleading system exemplified by the Federal Rules of Civil Procedure, pleading seeks to achieve the following related objectives:

(1) demonstrate that the court has subject-matter jurisdiction over the claim (see Rule 8(a)(1));
(2) put the parties on notice of the nature of the opponents' claims and contentions;
(3) identify the questions of law that will arise in the action;
(4) identify the disputed issues of fact that arise in the action;
(5) narrow the issues for trial;
(6) provide a roadmap for discovery and for trial; and
(7) provide a record for the scope of judgment for use in the application of preclusion doctrines.

Rule 8 of the Federal Rules of Civil Procedure requires, among other things, the plaintiff who files a complaint to set forth a short and plain statement indicating that the plaintiff is entitled to relief, and to specify the relief sought. Rule 8's requirements are intended to be minimal and easily met. In the leading case of *Conley v. Gibson*, the US Supreme Court held that the short and plain statement requirement means only that the plaintiff give the defendant "fair notice" of what the plaintiff's claim is and the ground upon which it rests.[1] Facts need not be recited in great detail, nor must the facts be pleaded with any special or magic language. The pleader does, however, need to put the defendant on notice of the nature of his claim(s), and also demonstrate to the court that relief is available should the plaintiff succeed in proving his allegations. As the court elaborated in *Conley*, a complaint satisfies Rule 8 "unless it appears beyond doubt that the plaintiff can prove no set of facts in support of the claim which would entitle him to relief."[2] This is a very generous standard, and was originally intended to be so. The forms appearing at the end of the Federal Rules of Civil Procedure, which illustrate how to satisfy the Rules, show how minimal complaints can be and still satisfy Rule 8. Rule 8 also explicitly allows a pleader to allege facts in the alternative that may be inconsistent with each other. As long as every statement complies with Rule 11 (see paragraph 165) inconsistency is permitted.

In spite of the conscious decision modern pleading regimes have made in allowing minimalistic complaints, courts often seem to require a plaintiff to meet a higher standard. For example, *Bell Atlantic Corp. v. Twombly*[3] concerned the standard to be used under Federal Rules of Civil Procedure 8 and 12 in deciding whether to dismiss a lawsuit for failure to state a claim upon which relief can be granted. In *Twombly*, plaintiffs sought to bring a class action on behalf of telephone customers against local telephone companies, asserting that the companies ran afoul of federal antitrust laws by conspiring to divide up the national market into a system of local monopolies. The US Supreme Court held that the complaint should be dismissed because it did not include "enough factual matter (taken as true) to suggest that an agreement was made" among the various local telephone company defendants.[4] The Supreme Court noted that "antitrust discovery can be expensive" and that, accordingly, district judges should take "care to require allegations that reach the level suggesting conspiracy" before permitting a case to survive a Rule 12(b)(6) motion.[5] Reaching this level requires more than a formulaic recitation of the elements of the cause of action, but instead obligates a plaintiff to include enough "factual matter" to suggest that an agreement to conspire was plausible.

Whether *Twombly* really does reflect a change (and increase) in pleading standards, in antitrust cases, in conspiracy cases, in antitrust conspiracy cases, or perhaps in all cases (which seems somewhat unlikely given that the Supreme Court itself cited *Twombly* later in its term in *Erickson v. Pardus*[6] as authority for rejecting a requirement of heightened pleading in a prisoner case), is something lower courts will be grappling with in the next few years until the Supreme Court revisits these issues with more clarification.

Happily for plaintiffs, however, a district court that dismisses a complaint for failure to allege a claim with adequate specificity will almost always do so with leave to amend. Indeed, in many instances, failure to allow leave to amend a complaint at least once will constitute an abuse of the district court's discretion subject to appellate reversal.

1. *Conley v. Gibson*, 355 U.S. 41 (1957).
2. Id., at 45-46.
3. *Bell Atlantic Corp. v. Twombly*, 127 S.Ct. 1955 (2007).
4. Id., at 1965.
5. Id., at 1967.
6. *Erickson v. Pardus*, 127 S.Ct. 2197 (2007).

177. The Federal Rules of Civil Procedure, and specifically Rule 9, identify certain categories of complaints in which the allegations must be set forth with more particularity. Complaints alleging fraud or mistake are treated in this manner. This requirement reflects in part the view, emerging from the common law, that certain kinds of allegations, such as fraud, can cause reputational damage whether or not they are backed up by proof. Accordingly, to protect defendants against meritless accusations, Rule 9 requires a plaintiff to set forth in more detail the specifics of the fraud – the who, what, where, when, and how. Some might argue that today other kinds of cases, such as sexual harassment cases, might merit special pleading requirements because of the damage inflicted by the accusations themselves. Similar arguments have been made that other kinds of lawsuits, such as shareholder-derivative actions or civil-rights suits against government officials, are too easily brought and should be subjected to some kind of heightened pleading requirement. Indeed, even in the absence of specific language in the Rules, some lower courts have overtly applied such heightened requirements to certain kinds of actions. The US Supreme Court recently addressed the validity of heightened pleading in the context of civil-rights claims, and held that Rule 9 exhausts the kinds of complaints that should be subject to more specific pleading, and that until Rule 9 is changed no heightened requirements outside the Rule are permitted. It remains to be seen how faithfully lower courts will be in heeding this message.

Another rule that arguably limits Rule 8's breadth is Rule 11, discussed earlier in Part III (paragraph 165), which authorizes federal courts to impose sanctions on lawyers and parties for submitting papers to the court that lack an objective basis in fact or in law. Federal notice pleading permits the statement of a claim in vague terms. There is no requirement that the pleader possess knowledge of all the facts that back up his claim, or that he disclose all the knowledge he does have. Rule 11 prohibits, however, a pleader from making factual allegations he knows are false or which he cannot reasonably expect to embrace as true after opportunity for reasonable investigation. Rule 11 also authorizes sanctions for the advancement of legal theories that are not well grounded under current law, or which have absolutely no reasonable chance of being accepted as a change in law.

There is undoubtedly some tension between Rule 8's minimal requirements and Rule 11's triggers for sanction authority. The tension may not be as great as might first appear. Rule 8 governs what a pleader must say; Rule 11 governs what a pleader must reasonably know or believe. Logically, then, the rules taken together may require that a plaintiff know more than he must disclose. But a more satisfactory answer to the tension between Rules 8 and 11 acknowledges that they are products of two very different times and two very different attitudes. Rule 8 was an integral part of the original Federal Rules of Civil Procedure, promulgated in 1938 as a self-conscious reaction to, and rejection of, the stylized system that code pleading had become. Under the notice pleading envisioned under Rule 8, as the court explained in *Conley*, the complaint was not intended to be a meaningful screening device to rid the federal judicial system of meritless litigation. Discovery, judgment on the pleadings, and summary judgment, all discussed below, were intended to fulfill that function more directly.

The 1938 version of Rule 11 was essentially toothless. The history of modern Rule 11 dates to 1983, when it was substantially amended in response to a prevailing sense that it had become too easy to initiate a lawsuit in federal court and to impose costs on the opposing party and to the system that invited the defendant to agree to settlement of a frivolous lawsuit for its "nuisance" value. The 1983 amendment of

Rule 11 was thus designed to correct what was perceived as an overly generous front door embodied by Rule 8. While modern Rule 11 was surely never intended to take things back to the pleading world before 1938 (and for that reason does not really speak to the form a complaint must take, but rather its substantive plausibility), it nonetheless sought to strike a slightly different balance than that represented by the original Rules.

Interestingly enough, it took only a decade after the 1983 amendment of Rule 11 for a sense to emerge that the balance that had been struck was itself in need of correction. Throughout that decade, from 1983 until 1993, Rule 11 litigation – that is, collateral litigation concerning whether Rule 11 had been violated – seemed to be occupying far too many resources. This wave of Rule 11 proceedings led to the further amendment of Rule 11 in 1993, producing the revised Rule 11 that is currently in effect. The 1993 amendment effected a number of changes, but two warrant particular mention here.

First, current Rule 11 directs courts, in deciding what sanctions to impose for a Rule 11 violation, to focus not on compensating the party victimized by the violation, but rather on specially deterring similar violations by the party responsible for the violation, and generally deterring similar conduct by future litigants. The preferred enforcement mechanisms are now fines paid to the court (rather than to the opposing party) and non-monetary sanctions (such as training). This shift from compensatory to deterrent sanctions has reduced the incentives for parties to claim to be Rule 11 victims entitled to Rule 11 damages from their adversaries.

Second, alleged Rule 11 violators against whom proceedings have been initiated by motion of an opposing party now have twenty-one days (after being notified of the proceedings) to withdraw the papers alleged to have been filed in violation of Rule 11. If the allegedly offending papers are withdrawn during this so-called "safe harbor" period, Rule 11 proceedings cease. If the federal district court itself initiates Rule 11 proceedings against an offending party, that party is not entitled as of right to invoke this twenty-one-day "safe harbor" provision, but similar leeway may be provided to the offending party in the discretion of the trial judge.

2. Responses to the Complaint

178. A person against whom a claim has been asserted may have one or more defenses that, if proven true, would vitiate the defendant's liability to the plaintiff. As previously listed and discussed in Part III (paragraph 147), Rule 12(b) sets forth a number of specific procedural defenses that may be asserted either in the defendant's answer – the document in which the defendant admits or denies the truth of the plaintiff's allegations – or (if the defendant makes one) by means of a single pre-answer motion. These defenses include: lack of personal jurisdiction; improper venue; insufficiency in the form of process (what was served on the defendant) or the manner in which process was served; lack of subject-matter jurisdiction; failure to state a claim upon which relief may be granted; and failure to join an indispensable party under Rule 19. Of these defenses, all but the last three are waived if they are not raised by defendant in the answer or the initial pre-answer motion (if one is made), whichever comes first. Subject-matter jurisdiction, discussed in depth in paragraphs

51-76, is so important that a court has a standing duty to consider whether it is lacking at any time in the lawsuit, even if no party has asserted a jurisdictional objection. In addition to these objections available to the defendant, the defendant may also move for the plaintiff to clarify the complaint if it is too vague to be understood, or move to strike inflammatory language from the complaint, although both of these motions are rarely successful.

Perhaps the most important and often-used Rule 12 defense is a motion to dismiss for failure to state a claim upon which relief may be granted. If this motion is made early in the lawsuit, before an answer, it is brought under Rule 12(b)(6). The same defense can be raised later on (indeed at any time before or during trial) although it is then brought in the form of a motion for judgment on the pleadings under Rule 12(c). The idea behind a 12(b)(6) motion is simple but important; the defendant concedes for purposes of the motion that the plaintiff's factual allegations are true, but argues that the applicable substantive law simply does not recognize a claim for relief under the alleged facts. For example, if a plaintiff sues a defendant invoking Title VII, a federal anti-discrimination statute governing the employment setting, and alleges that he was terminated from his employment because of his height, the defendant could successfully bring a 12(b)(6) motion or a motion for judgment on the pleadings, because even if the plaintiff's height was the motivation for his termination (a fact the defendant assumes for purposes of the motion), Title VII simply does not prohibit height-based discrimination. Rather, it prohibits discrimination based on race, ethnicity, sex, or religion. Thus, a 12(b)(6) motion is really concerned with the meaning of substantive law as applied to a set of facts alleged by the plaintiff in the complaint – facts which for the purposes of evaluating the motion are assumed to be true. If the plaintiff's allegations simply do not (and cannot after opportunity for amendment to add new facts) constitute something for which the substantive law affords relief, dismissal is warranted. State courts also permit attacks on the legal sufficiency of a claim by motions similar to those authorized in federal court by Rules 12(b)(6) and 12(c). In many states the term used to describe such a motion is a "general demurrer."

179. Assuming there is no defect in jurisdiction or process, and that the plaintiff's allegations on their face constitute a tenable claim for relief, a defendant will have to take a position on the facts of the case. The vehicle a defendant uses for this is known in the federal system as the answer. A federal answer contains a number of distinct elements. First, it may include the preliminary objections (e.g., lack of personal jurisdiction, etc.) described above (see paragraph 178). Second, it contains admissions and denials of the allegations in the complaint, ordinarily on a paragraph-by-paragraph basis.[1] Third, the answer may contain new matter, that is, affirmative defenses available to the defendant. Fourth, the answer may contain a counterclaim against the plaintiff or a cross-claim against another defendant making affirmative allegations of liability owed to the answering party.

Under Rule 8(b), the defendant's answer must admit or deny the allegations of the complaint. If the defendant is without knowledge or information sufficient to form a belief as to the truth of an allegation by the plaintiff, the defendant can and should deny the allegation on this basis. Any allegation not denied by the defendant is deemed admitted. If the defendant intends to deny only part of an allegation, he should identify the specific part he seeks to deny. The defendant's denials and admissions, like the plaintiff's allegations, are subject to Rule 11's requirement of objective reasonableness given the information available to the party at the time a representation is made. The Federal Rules of Civil Procedure also allow a plaintiff to seek recovery for the costs of proving facts which the defendant denies, but such compensatory relief is discretionary and very unusual.

1. *See* Fed. R. Civ. P. 8(b).

180. Affirmative defenses, also called avoidances, are defenses to liability that do not constitute a denial or rebuttal of the plaintiff's allegations, but rather introduce new material that affirmatively absolves defendant. Generally speaking, a defendant bears the burden of persuasion at trial on any matter constituting an affirmative defense. Such defenses include expiration of the statute of limitations, preclusion of the plaintiff's claim, waiver of the plaintiff's claim, and contributory negligence on the part of the plaintiff. Rule 8(c) requires that the defendant "affirmatively state any avoidance or affirmative defense." Rule 8(c) and its state-law counterparts provide lists of affirmative defenses, but such lists are illustrative rather than exhaustive. If an affirmative defense is not specifically included in the defendant's answer, the defendant waives the defense and is not permitted to introduce evidence at trial regarding the waived defense.

To identify affirmative defenses not specifically listed by Rule 8(c), courts have employed one or both of two tests. First, they have asked whether the defendant's theory is logically or analytically distinct from the plaintiff's allegations or the elements of the plaintiff's cause of action. In this regard, courts have asked whether the evidence the defendant needs to prove his position diverges from the evidence that bears on the plaintiff's allegations. For some defenses, this logical-essence approach works easily.

For example, it is clear that a defense of expiration of the statute of limitations is logically unrelated to the plaintiff's allegations of the elements of his cause of action. Thus a defendant who asserts only a limitations defense may not contest at trial the truth of the facts that the plaintiff has alleged as the substantive basis for the defendant's alleged liability. However, this logical-essence test does not always resolve issues posed by other defenses. For example, if a defendant asserts an easement in response to a trespass claim by plaintiff, is this defense logically unrelated to plaintiff's claim of trespass, such that it must be pleaded affirmatively or otherwise is waived? Or does the presence of an easement destroy the plaintiff's ability to prove the crucial allegations and elements of ownership and lack of permission to enter, so that a denial of the truth of the plaintiff's allegations will permit the defendant to assert at trial not just that the plaintiff does not own the property in question, but also (or alternatively) that an easement existed giving the defendant the right to enter the property regardless of who its true owner might be?

Because there is no obvious answer to this question, courts have sometimes made use of a second and different approach to defining an affirmative defense and determining whether an arguable affirmative defense has been waived if not affirmatively asserted in the defendant's answer. This approach focuses on fair notice to the plaintiff. If the purpose of requiring the affirmative declaration of a defense is to adequately inform the plaintiff of the defendant's theories of the case, then whether or not the defendant should be permitted to prove a particular point at trial depends upon how reasonably predictable it was for the plaintiff to believe that such issue would arise. This notice approach focuses less on the abstract definition of what a defense is, and more on the whole process by which the plaintiff has learned of the defendant's positions. This process would include not just the defendant's answer, but also the course of any discovery (discussed below in paragraphs 182-189) that followed the pleading phase of the litigation. If, in the above example, the plaintiff learned of the defendant's theory of an easement early in discovery, courts following the fair-notice approach would likely permit the defendant to prove an easement at trial, whether or not an easement was specifically mentioned in the answer.

3. Amendments to the Pleadings

181. Rule 15 of the Federal Rules of Civil Procedure covers the question of amendments to pleadings, including complaints, answers and replies to counterclaims. A number of basic questions arise concerning amendments. One, of course, is will the court allow the party to amend the pleading? Another is, if the statute of limitations of a particular claim or defense has expired before an amendment is attempted, will the proposed amendment relate back in time to the date on which the original pleading was filed and thus avoid the statute of limitations problem?

Amendments can be made once as a matter of course – that is, without leave of court or permission by the opposing party – at any time before a responsive pleading is served, or, if the pleading is one to which no responsive pleading is permitted and the action has not been placed on the trial calendar, the party may amend that pleading as a matter of course within twenty days after it was served on the opposing parties. Pleadings can also be amended before trial, and even after trial, if the amending parties obtain written permission from all other parties.[1]

If the conditions mentioned in the above paragraph do not exist, amendment can be obtained only by leave of court. Rule 15(a) states that leave "shall be freely given when justice so requires." But deciding when justice so requires is not always simple. Caselaw establishes a presumption of amendability before trial, but the presumption can be overcome by a demonstration of prejudice by the party opposing amendment. Sometimes prejudice takes the form of increased trial-preparation costs, and sometimes it takes the form of an inability to pursue relief against more appropriate parties, as when a defendant, after the statute of limitations has expired, amends his answer to deny that he was the one present to cause plaintiff's injuries. Balancing prejudice to the non-amending parties and fairness to the party seeking amendment is a delicate trial court task that appellate courts usually do not second guess. Rule 15(b) allows amendment to be made during or after trial over the objection of the non-amending party under a similar prejudice analysis, although amendments after the start of trial are harder to justify.

As to the second question, an amendment relates back to the filing of the initial pleading when, under the terms of Rule 15, it arises out of the same "conduct, transaction or occurrence" set forth in the original pleading. The transaction test is similar to the tests used regarding joinder of parties and compulsory counterclaims (see paragraphs 152-156). It also uses similar language to the tests employed for supplemental jurisdiction (see paragraph 70) and preclusion (see paragraphs 278-282 below). Like the tests employed in these other areas, the Rule 15 relation-back test is somewhat flexible, and should be applied with an appreciation of its underlying purpose – namely, notice and fairness to the non-amending party. Lower-court cases under Rule 15(c)'s relation-back language are not all easy to harmonize.

1. Fed. R. Civ. P. 15(a).

II. Progress of Proceedings

A. Discovery

182. Discovery is the formal process by which parties obtain information from their adversaries or other witnesses who may have information bearing on the litigation. Modern discovery practice goes back to the major reforms embodied in the Federal Rules of Civil Procedure promulgated in 1938. By liberalizing pleading and de-emphasizing its role in narrowing legal and factual issues for trial, the drafters of the Federal Rules relied on discovery to accomplish much of these ends. The federal discovery model, which is discussed here, has proven successful enough to be copied by most of the state jurisdictions, including some that do not fully embrace the liberal notice pleading standards described above in paragraphs 176-177.

Discovery is designed to serve a number of related purposes. It enables parties to find out information necessary to prepare for trial. It helps narrow the issues in the case by eliminating from the litigation those issues that are not contested. It produces a record and locks parties into certain positions so that opposing parties do not face moving targets later in litigation. It preserves information that may be used directly at trial if the source of the information is no longer available at the time of trial. Perhaps most importantly, discovery allows parties to adduce evidence that can be used in summary-judgment proceedings that obviate the need for a more costly trial. In addition to these legitimate uses of discovery, it can be – and unfortunately often is – used strategically to drive up the costs of litigation to the opposing parties, to wear down adversaries and/or enhance settlement positions. The following paragraphs describe briefly the scope of discoverable materials, the mechanics of the devices used to discover information, and the problems of and response to the expense and abuse of discovery.

Consistent with these premises, and the desire to "make a trial less a game of blind man's bluff and more a fair contest with the basic issues and the facts disclosed to the fullest practicable extent,"[1] discovery rules in federal court grant litigants broad powers to obtain discovery from other parties and non-parties. Indeed, recent amendments to the Federal Rules of Civil Procedure mandate an initial exchange of information between the parties in most ordinary civil litigation commenced in federal court (see below, paragraph 187). In addition to these "initial disclosures," parties can and do undertake significant additional discovery, which is governed by Rules 26-37. Federal Rule 26(b)(1) sets out the broad standard for discoverability: "any matter which is relevant to any party's claim or defense" and which "appears reasonably calculated to lead to the discovery of admissible evidence" is presumptively discoverable.

A number of points about the breadth of Rule 26(b) are in order. First, Rule 26(b) exempts from its coverage privileged information, and information that, while not privileged, is protected for some other policy reason, such as encouraging lawyers to vigorously prepare their own case. For a discussion of the law of privilege and related protections, see Part VII concerning Evidence. Second, note that the fact for which discovery is sought need not be admissible in and of itself, so long as it "appears reasonably calculated to lead to the discovery of admissible evidence."[2] Thus, a question that will not yield an answer that itself is admissible, but which has "lead value" and might identify another witness who may provide admissible information, is permissible under Rule 26.

The scope of permissible discovery will obviously depend upon the nature of the case and the substantive law under which a plaintiff is suing. If a plaintiff sues a law firm for violating Title VII by refusing to hire her as an associate attorney because she is a woman, obviously her questions concerning the treatment of other female associate candidates are within Rule 26, inasmuch as they might bear on the defendant's gender-discriminatory mind set. Questions concerning defendant's treatment of disabled persons, however, even if they bear on whether defendant is a callous person, would not be relevant notwithstanding the breadth of Rule 26. If, however, the plaintiff's suit claimed she was illegally discriminated against both because she is a woman and because she is disabled (in violation of the Americans with Disabilities Act), the substantive law governing the case is more expansive, and so correspondingly is the scope of permissible discovery.

Discovery concerning a party's treatment of persons other than the opposing party is often problematic. In the Title VII hypothetical in the previous paragraph, we observed that the plaintiff could discover the defendant's treatment of other female associate-attorney applicants, on the plausible theory that discriminatory intent may be demonstrated by a pattern or practice. But how far could we carry this reasoning? Most courts would probably allow the plaintiff to inquire about the defendant's treatment of female attorneys who were in fact hired, on the ground that discrimination against female associates is logically related to discrimination against female-associate candidates. But would courts allow discovery of a law firm's treatment of female employees who are not attorneys? Certainly, stereotypical gender attitudes toward secretaries may correlate to stereotypical gender attitudes toward women attorneys. And yet it is not clear that discovery ought to be permitted as to the defendant's employment practices relating to secretaries. Rule 26's minimal requirements may have been met, but discovery may be denied under Rule 26(c)'s provision for a "protective order." Rule 26(c) recognizes that 26(b)'s breadth might create injustice, and therefore allows a court to prevent discovery even of relevant material if such discovery would impose undue burden, embarrassment, or other harm on the party from whom discovery is sought.

Two other aspects of Rule 26(b) warrant mention. First, sometimes it is not necessary to satisfy the normal Rule 26 relevancy requirement as a predicate for discovery. For policy reasons, parties are sometimes allowed to discover information that has no evidentiary or lead value. For example, among the required "initial disclosures" is the existence of insurance policies that may reimburse opposing parties if they are found to be liable. The existence of such policies is not admissible or particularly likely to lead to something admissible. But knowledge of such policies may facilitate settlement, so public policy concerns justify disclosure, as Rule 26(a)(1)(A)(iv) confirms.

Second, the general principles of Rule 26(b) do not ordinarily make discoverable facts known or opinions held by an expert retained or specially employed by a party in anticipation of litigation or to prepare for trial, unless the party has identified the expert as one who may testify at trial. This special protection of the confidentiality of consultations with non-testifying experts provides an incentive for litigants to seek candid advice from experts even if it reflects negatively on their case. The limitation of discovery from experts could be viewed as part of the larger problem of "trial preparation" or attorney "work-product" protection, discussed in paragraph 259 below under the rubric of privilege, but it bears mention here that Rules 26(a)(2) and 26(b)(3)-(5) deal explicitly with the matter.

1. *United States v. Procter & Gamble Co.*, 356 U.S. 677, 682-683 (1958).
2. Fed. R. Civ. P. 26(b)(1).

1. Depositions

183. Depositions are governed by Rules 27-32, especially Rule 30 and Rule 45 which govern subpoenas to persons who can be deposed. The oral deposition is a self-executing discovery device which usually requires no court order and becomes compulsory upon a party simply by sending notice that a deposition has been scheduled. Depositions are not limited to parties and may be taken from "any person" under Rule 30(a). The deposition can thus be used to obtain information from bystanders and other witnesses who may have information about the litigation. The deposition consists of a live question-and-answer session between the witness (the deponent) and the lawyer of the party who noticed the deposition. A variant on the traditional oral deposition is the so-called deposition on written questions, which in some ways is more like interrogatories, discussed below in paragraph 184. The live deposition session is conducted under oath, as would be trial testimony, and is recorded by a court reporter. If disputes about the propriety of questions arise during a deposition, they must either be resolved by the persons present at the deposition, or the deposition must be stopped in order for the court in which the action was filed to hear and rule on the disputed questions. Depositions can be very expensive, given the cost of a lawyer's time, but they provide a good way to uncover important information, because the deposing attorney can adjust her line of questions to account for the answers to prior questions.

Parties must attend a deposition and be examined upon proper notice under Rule 30(b)(1). No formal subpoena or other process is necessary to compel the attendance of a party witness. By contrast, non-party witnesses can be compelled to attend only by use of a subpoena. Rules 30(a) and 45(d) govern the subpoena power and what witnesses can be forced to do and bring with them. Under Rule 30(b)(6), a corporation served with a deposition may designate an appropriate officer or person with knowledge of the relevant matters on which the deposition is to be held, which is specified in the notice of the deposition.

Non-party witnesses who must be subpoenaed under Rule 45 can be forced to attend a deposition only:

(1) where they reside;
(2) where they are employed;
(3) where they transact business;
(4) where they were served with notice of the deposition;
(5) within 100 miles of where they were served with notice of the deposition; or
(6) another convenient place fixed by the court.

Corporations can be deposed only where they conduct business. Protective orders under Rule 26(c) are available to deponents who feel unduly burdened by being deposed.

Depositions may be taken at any time after the commencement of the action. Although no time is specified, courts usually insist upon a minimum notice of about a week.

2. Interrogatories

184. Interrogatories, which are governed by Rule 33, consist of sets of written questions propounded by a party to other parties in the litigation. Unlike depositions, interrogatories may be served only on other parties, and not upon non-party witnesses. Like deposition answers, written answers to the interrogatories are made under oath.

Interrogatories are less expensive to create and execute than depositions, because they do not involve as much lawyer time. But because written questions cannot take account of the answers given to other questions, they are not as flexible and valuable as depositions. Still, interrogatories have often proved especially useful in making initial inquiries into the basis of the claims, contentions and pleadings of other parties, and for identifying witnesses and other persons with relevant information, so that future decisions about deposing people and seeking documents through document requests, described below in paragraph 185, can be made more intelligently. Because interrogatories are relatively inexpensive to propound and serve, and for that reason may be abused, many courts limit the number of interrogatories a party can serve on other parties.

3. Requests to Produce Documents and Other Tangible Things and for Entry onto Real Property

185. Requests to produce documents and other tangible things, as well as requests to enter onto real property, are governed by Rule 34. Like interrogatories, they are, strictly speaking, available only to parties, and not non-party witnesses. But a party wishing to inspect items in possession of non-parties may obtain a subpoena under Rule 45 (with or without noticing a deposition) and specify which items must be brought to the deposition.

Disputes under Rule 34 often arise over requests for document production that require the availability of continuing access by one party to another party's documents or other records. Today, most courts are willing to grant continuing access – not just a one-time right to inspect.

In the early twenty-first century, there has been much discussion and wrangling over access to electronically stored information – so-called "e-discovery." After several years of deliberation, the drafters of the Federal Rules of Civil Procedure were able to implement formal amendments to the Federal Rules of Civil Procedure to address e-discovery. As of December, 2006, Rules 16, 26, 33, 34, 37 and 45 were all amended to try to address discovery problems posed by the proliferation of electronic data.

Much of the pressure for change was brought about by the dramatic surge in e-mail activity since the mid-1990s. E-mails have figured prominently in the high-profile convictions of the auditing firm Arthur Andersen and others accused in civil and criminal proceedings alleging wrongdoing in connection with financial institutions. Going beyond e-mail, perhaps more than 90% of business documents are created electronically and never printed out.

Electronic documents have raised many discovery problems, including those concerning format. When hard copies are produced during discovery, their format usually does not become an issue. But stores of information that are electronic exist in and can be accessed in many different forms, and sometimes produce usable material only when properly queried. Finding and unraveling information stored on emergency backup tapes can be harder still.

To address these concerns, Rule 26 was amended to ensure that electronically stored information is included among the required initial disclosures (see paragraph 187) and to require discussion of e-discovery, particularly the form of production, if this type of discovery is contemplated in the action as part of the mandatory discovery plan parties must undertake before the outset of formal discovery. Rule 34 was also amended to differentiate between "documents" and "electronically stored information," which might suggest that the requesting party must specify whether both or only one is sought. The amended rule also permits the requesting party to indicate the preferred form of production for electronically stored information. If no such preference is indicated, the responding party may produce in either the form in which the information is maintained, or in a form that is electronically searchable.

4. Physical and Mental Examinations

186. Rule 35 authorizes requests for physical and mental examinations of parties, when relevant to the subject matter of the case. Because of the obvious privacy concerns involved, this discovery device – unlike the others discussed – is available only after a court has made a specific finding that an inspection is appropriate (that is, "good cause" exists) and grants leave accordingly. Like interrogatories and document requests, it is available only as to parties, but it applies to both plaintiffs and defendants.

5. The Adversarial Nature of Discovery, the Problem of Discovery Abuse, and the Disclosure Idea

187. As noted earlier, responding to discovery can be costly, and parties sometimes make use of that reality to impose costs on other parties for illicit tactical reasons.

Much of the problem derives from the fact that discovery is ordinarily regulated by the parties themselves without judicial supervision. The Federal Rules of Civil Procedure, however, allow a party to invoke the power of the court when another party is either improperly making discovery requests or refusing to answer legitimate requests or questions. Ordinarily, a party who feels wronged seeks either a protective order under Rule 26(c) or an order to compel under Rule 37. If a party violates a court order, he can be sanctioned in a variety of ways (see paragraphs 161-168). Because judicial involvement is cumbersome and expensive, the extent of compliance with the letter and spirit of discovery rules is often determined through private negotiation between the parties.

Criticism of the party-directed nature of discovery caused significant amendment to the Federal Rules over the last few decades. Generated by a belief that discovery, far from assisting the parties in reaching a fair resolution, often tends to dominate modern litigation and inflict disproportionate injuries on parties and the court system, amendments to the Federal Rules of Civil Procedure adopted in 2000 sought to eliminate some of the adversarial nature of the discovery process. In particular, they now provide for mandatory "initial disclosures" by each party of important information and witnesses, regardless of whether opposing parties have sought such information affirmatively. Specifically, Rule 26(a)(1) now requires parties to disclose, soon after an action is initiated, the names of all known witnesses, copies or descriptions of all documents and things "relevant to disputed facts alleged with particularity in the pleadings," the computation of any damages claimed, and existence of any liability insurance agreements. Rule 26(a)(2) also requires disclosure of important information concerning expert witnesses who may testify at trial. After the initial round of disclosures, the parties then can make use of the discovery devices described above, but are limited in the extent to which they can make discovery requests without court permission. For example, leave of court or stipulation by the parties is required if a party seeks to take more than ten depositions.[1]

1. Fed. R. Civ. P. 30.

6. Duty to Supplement Responses

188. As discussed above, one of the main goals of modern discovery is to obtain the fullest knowledge possible of the issues and facts of a case prior to trial (see paragraph 182). In furtherance of this goal, most jurisdictions and the federal courts require parties to supplement or correct responses to discovery requests when new information is obtained. Rule 26(e) of the Federal Rules of Civil Procedure states that a party is under a duty to supplement or correct information provided through mandatory disclosure if the party discovers that some material aspect of the information is incomplete or incorrect and has not been made known to the other party. This should be done at appropriate intervals during the discovery period, and with special promptness as the trial date approaches.[1] Failure to perform this duty may lead to Rule 37 sanctions, including exclusion of undisclosed information at trial. Any changes in an expert's deposition or report must also be disclosed at least thirty days before trial. In addition, responses to interrogatories, requests for production and requests for admission must be corrected or supplemented if additional or corrective information surfaces. While there is no specific time period in which a party must supplement or correct these types of responses, it should be done in a timely manner. Determining whether a party has violated Rule 26(e) and whether sanctions are warranted is left to the discretion of the trial judge.

1. *See* Fed. R. Civ. P. 26(e), Advisory Committee's Note to the 1993 Amendments.

7. International Discovery

189. When evidence is sought in an international context the discovery process becomes more complicated. Issues of international comity and judicial sovereignty are of central importance. Many countries, especially those with a civil law system, object to the broad scope of US discovery. They view the US pretrial discovery process and its potential for unlimited document production as intrusive judicial acts that violate state sovereignty.[1] To avoid violating judicial sovereignty, discovery efforts in another country must comply with foreign laws. A litigator must take into account both the laws of the United States and those of the foreign country.[2] There are two main methods of obtaining evidence in a foreign setting. A party may proceed according to the Federal Rules of Civil Procedure or the procedures set out in international treaties, such as the Hague Convention on the Taking of Evidence Abroad in Civil or Commercial Matters.

A party may obtain discovery from a party or non-party through the Federal Rules of Civil Procedure. When discovery is sought from a party to the action, the federal rules are generally enforceable. The failure of a party to comply with standard requests for evidence through interrogatories, document productions, or depositions may result in the court issuing sanctions under Rule 37 or compelling the party to return to the United States to be deposed. Typical sanctions include the imposition of fines which continue until compliance with the order. Where good faith is lacking, a court may even consider issuing a default judgment. A party may rely upon the federal rules when a non-party person with discoverable evidence is willing to cooperate and such voluntary cooperation does not violate the laws of the foreign country in which the person is located. This is the most effective method of gathering evidence abroad because the foreign government is not involved and deposition testimony can be taken in a manner that is compatible with US discovery and evidentiary standards.

According to Rule 28(b) of the Federal Rules, taking a deposition in a foreign country can be accomplished in four ways:

(1) pursuant to any applicable treaty or convention,
(2) pursuant to a letter of request,
(3) on notice before a person authorized to administer oaths by the law of the United States or the foreign country where the examination is held, or
(4) before a person commissioned by the court.

When a witness is willing to appear voluntarily, a party may rely on either the notice or commission method to obtain deposition testimony. A deposition upon notice may be taken before individuals authorized to administer oaths by either US law, such as US consular officers, or foreign law. Additionally, a US court may issue a commission to a foreign official, a private person or a US consular officer. Some countries forbid both of these options; therefore a party must seek evidence through a letter of request.

A letter of request is issued by the US court in which the action is pending to a foreign court asking for that court's assistance in obtaining evidence. The letter of request will not be issued unless the person sought to be examined is subject to the foreign court's jurisdiction. It is not necessary to establish that the sought-after evidence cannot be obtained through any other method. Foreign courts honor letters of request in their discretion, on the basis of comity, but are not bound to comply with any request. Many countries will not honor letters of request seeking pretrial discovery; therefore it should be clearly specified, when true, that the evidence requested is intended to be used in the trial of the case. A major benefit of obtaining evidence through this method is that a foreign court honoring the request has the ability to compel an unwilling witness to attend a deposition. Because this method employs the courts of a foreign country, it is unlikely that judicial sovereignty will be violated.

The Hague Evidence Convention provides additional methods for obtaining evidence in signatory countries.[3] The goal of this multilateral treaty is to "improve judicial cooperation in civil and commercial matters."[4] To facilitate this process, the Convention provides three methods of requesting information in a foreign country:

(1) through a letter of request from a judicial authority to a foreign state's central authority,
(2) by consular agents upon permission of the foreign state, or
(3) by duly appointed commissioners upon permission of the foreign state.

The procedures for utilizing the letter of request, notice and commission methods are similar to the procedures set out in Rule 28(b) of the Federal Rules of Civil Procedure discussed above. Unlike non-contracting countries, signatory countries are bound by the treaty to honor appropriate letters of request. The treaty specifies, however, that a "[l]etter shall not be used to obtain evidence which is not intended for use in judicial proceedings, commenced or contemplated."[5] This language clearly reflects the aversion other countries have toward America's broad scope of discovery. One advantage of utilizing the treaty's letter-of-request method is that a party may request special procedures or methods to be followed when obtaining the sought-after evidence. Under the Hague Convention, the judicial authority executing a letter of request applies its own laws as to the methods and procedures to be followed. It will, however, follow a request for a special method or procedure if it is not incompatible with the internal law of the country or impossible to perform.[6] Often such requests are ignored when made of non-contracting countries.

The procedures set out in the Hague Convention are not the exclusive means for obtaining discovery in signatory countries. In its decision in *Societe Nationale Industrielle Aerospatiale v. United States District Court*, the US Supreme Court held that the treaty establishes "*optional procedures* that … facilitate the taking of evidence abroad," and therefore does not divest a district court of its power to compel a foreign national party to produce evidence physically located in a signatory country.[7] This ruling allows US courts to use direct discovery as a first resort in most matters. However, the court did direct district courts to take into account "the particular facts, sovereign interests, and likelihood that resort to the [Hague Convention] procedures will prove effective" when determining whether to apply the treaty's methods.[8] In addition, the court stated that courts should "exercise special vigilance to protect foreign litigants from the danger that unnecessary, or unduly burdensome, discovery may place them in a disadvantageous position."[9] Nonetheless, some critics argue that in the years following the *Aerospatiale* decision, lower courts have not given appropriate weight to concerns of international comity.[10]

The US Supreme Court has recently had occasion to discuss an American statute that addresses the converse situation – when litigants in a foreign proceeding seek to obtain discovery in the United States. *Intel Corp. v. Advanced Micro Devices, Inc.*,[11] involved 28 U.S.C. §1782(a), which is the "product of congressional efforts, over the span of nearly 150 years, to provide federal-court assistance in [the] gathering of evidence for use in foreign tribunals."[12] Adopted in 1964, the current version of §1782(a) provides that a federal district court "may order" a person "resid[ing]" or "found" in the district to produce documents or provide testimony "for use in a proceeding in a foreign or international tribunal ... upon application of any interested person." The *Intel* controversy arose after Advanced Micro Devices (AMD), one of Intel's worldwide competitors in the microprocessing market, filed a complaint with the Directorate-General for Competition of the European Commission. "The Commission exercises responsibility over the wide range of subject areas covered by the European Union treaty; those areas include the treaty provisions [and regulations] governing competition."[13] In its complaint, AMD alleged that Intel had abused its dominant position through a variety of anti-competitive devices. After filing, AMD urged the Directorate-General for Competition to attempt to obtain documents Intel had produced in a private antitrust lawsuit that had been brought against it in federal district court in Alabama. When the Directorate-General did not actively seek the documents from the US courts, AMD filed a petition under §1782(a) in the Northern District of California, where both AMD and Intel are headquartered, for an order forcing Intel to produce the same documents on file in the Alabama federal court.

The district court denied the petition. The Ninth Circuit reversed the district court and remanded the case. The US Supreme Court affirmed the judgment of the Ninth Circuit. In giving meaning to §1782(a), the Supreme Court made a number of potentially significant holdings:

(1) A person need not hold formal "party" or "litigant" status in a foreign proceeding to be an "interested person" who is entitled to seek assistance under §1782(a). AMD qualifies under the statute;
(2) the Commission is, for purposes of 1782(a), a "tribunal" when it acts as a first-instance decisionmaker, even though another, more formally judicial, tribunal, may review the Commission's disposition of the complaint;
(3) the "proceeding" for which a person wants discovery under §1782(a) need not be "pending" or "imminent," but rather must only be "in reasonable contemplation;"
(4) there is no requirement under §1782(a) that the sought-after evidence would have to be discoverable had it been located in the foreign jurisdiction;

(5) there is similarly no requirement in §1782(a) that the information sought be discoverable in an analogous action filed in the United States.

For these reasons, the Supreme Court held that the district court in California had the power to grant AMD's request. Whether there were sound reasons – relating to the potential need for informational secrecy, among other things – to decline or limit the scope of the request were issues left to the district court on remand.

1. *See* David Epstein et al., *International Litigation: A Guide to Jurisdiction, Practice and Strategy*, 3rd edn (1999), §10.03.
2. Some countries have enacted privacy laws or blocking statutes which make it illegal to disclose certain types of information. The US Supreme Court held that the existence of such privacy laws or blocking statutes does not automatically divest the district court of its power to order a party subject to its jurisdiction to produce evidence. *Societe Internationale Pour Participations Industrielles et Commercilaes, S.A. v. Rogers*, 357 U.S. 197, 211 (1958).
3. Signatory countries include Anguilla, Argentina, Aruba, Australia, Barbados, Bulgaria, Cayman Islands, China, Cyprus, Czech Republic, Denmark, Djibouti, Estonia, Falkland Islands, Finland, France, French Guiana, French Polynesia, Germany, Gibraltar, Guadeloupe, Guernsey, Hong Kong, Isle of Man, Israel, Italy, Jersey, Latvia, Luxembourg, Macao, Martinique, Mexico, Monaco, the Netherlands, Norway, Poland, Portugal, Saint Pierre and Miquelon, Singapore, Slovak Republic, South Africa, Sovereign Base Areas of Akrotiri and Dhekelia, Spain, Sweden, Switzerland, United Kingdom, United States, Venezuela. 28 U.S.C. §1781 note (Convention on the Taking of Evidence Abroad in Civil or Commercial Matters).
4. Convention on the Taking of Evidence Abroad in Civil and Commercial Matters.
5. Convention on the Taking of Evidence Abroad in Civil or Commercial Matters, 18 Mar. 1970, Ch. 1, Art. 1, 23 U.S.T. 2555, T.I.A.S. No. 7444.
6. *See* id., at Ch. 1, Art. 9.
7. *Societe Nationale Industrielle Aerospatiale v. United States District Court*, 482 U.S. 522, 538-540 (1987) (emphasis added).
8. Id., at 544.
9. Id., at 546.
10. *See* Epstein, *supra*, at §10.12; Joseph P. Griffin & Mark N. Bravin, "Beyond Aerospatiale: A Commentary on Foreign Discovery Provisions of the Restatement (Third) and the Proposed Amendments to the Federal Rules of Civil Procedure," Int'l Law. 25 (1991): 331.
11. *Intel Corp. v. Advanced Micro Devices*, 542 U.S. 241 (2004).
12. Id., at 247.
13. Id., at 250.

B. Summary Judgment

190. Summary judgment is an important device for testing the factual sufficiency of legally sufficient claims, i.e., claims that have survived (or could survive) a Rule 12(b)(6) motion to dismiss. Summary judgment is about proof. It attempts to weed out claims that are not supported by sufficient proof, thereby avoiding the delay and expense of a trial when a reasonable finder of fact at trial (be it judge or jury) could not find in favor of the party against whom summary judgment is sought.

Summary judgment is governed in federal court by Rule 56. While many state systems emulate the federal model, and are doing so increasingly, state summary-judgment practice may diverge from Rule 56's approach. Because of the importance of the summary judgment device, we will present some of the state models that diverge from Rule 56 after we discuss the federal standards.

Before 1986, federal courts tended to view summary judgment as a disfavored procedural shortcut. When hearing such motions, trial judges were required to draw even implausible inferences from circumstantial evidence in favor of the non-moving party in order to prevent invading the province of the finder of fact (most often the jury). A trilogy of important US Supreme Court cases in the mid-1980s, however, rejuvenated summary judgment and made it the most important device for disposing of factually weak cases without a full-blown trial.[1]

1. *See Anderson v. Liberty Lobby, Inc.*, 477 U.S. 242 (1986) (holding that the inquiry involved in a ruling on a motion for summary judgment necessarily implicates the substantive evidentiary standard of proof that would apply at the trial on the merits); *Celotex Corp. v. Catrett*, 477 U.S. 317 (1986) (holding that the moving party need merely point out by specific reference to the relevant discovery items that no evidence exists to support an essential element of the claim; the burden then shifts to the non-moving party to show evidence beyond the pleading that creates a genuine issue of fact); *Matsushita Elec. Indus. Co. v. Zenith Radio Corp.*, 475 U.S. 574 (1986) (holding a court is to grant summary judgment if inferences drawn from circumstantial evidence by non-moving party are implausible).

1. Federal Summary-Judgment Standards

191. The key operative language of Rule 56 provides that summary judgment may be rendered in favor of the moving party "if the pleadings, depositions, answers to interrogatories, and admissions on file, together with the affidavits, if any, show that there is no genuine issue as to any material fact and that the moving party is entitled to judgment as a matter of law."[1] This deceptively simple text embodies a number of related inquiries.

The first step is to identify the "material facts" in the case. Whether a particular fact is material to a case depends upon the substantive law and the legal theories of the parties applied to the case. As was true with "relevance" under Rule 26's broad discovery standard, a fact that is material to one lawsuit will not necessarily be material to another. A fact is material only if its resolution might have some bearing on the case under the applicable substantive law. Thus, for example, the question of whether the defendant had a valid driver's license on the day he injured the plaintiff would be material if the plaintiff is suing him in tort for physical damage arising out of an automobile collision, but would not be material if the claim were based on the defendant's termination of plaintiff's employment in an alleged violation of the plaintiff's contract of employment.

The next question is whether there is a "genuine issue" as to any material fact. If there is a genuine issue, and the fact is material, Rule 56 precludes summary judgment. A genuine issue is more than a conflict in the allegations concerning the material fact. As noted earlier, summary judgment – unlike a 12(b)(6) motion testing legal rather than factual sufficiency – is focused not just on the allegations, but rather on the evidence supporting these allegations. An issue is "genuine" only if it is contested by the parties and there is enough evidence available for presentation at trial such that a finder of fact could reasonably resolve the conflict either way. If the inferences that could plausibly be drawn from the evidence (i.e., the inferences that could be drawn from the discovery responses, etc.) suggest that the contested issue of fact could be resolved only in one direction at trial, there is no "genuine" issue as to that material fact, even though the parties allege different things concerning it. In other words, one cannot defeat summary judgment merely by pointing to allegations in the pleadings that contest the position of the moving party; instead, to create a genuine issue of material fact, a non-moving party must point to evidence on which a reasonable trier of fact could reject the moving party's characterization of the fact.

In assessing what a reasonable finder of fact could decide at trial, the US Supreme Court has made clear that burdens of proof matter. If a party bears a burden of proof at trial as to a fact (e.g., plaintiff bears the burden of proving causation in negligence cases), then that party cannot defeat summary judgment merely by pointing to a lack of evidence to support the other side's position. Having a burden of proof means that in the absence of any proof at all on a question of fact, that question must be resolved against the party with the burden. Unless the non-moving party affirmatively points to some evidence in its favor, a reasonable finder of fact would have no choice but to decide against it, such that there would be no "genuine" issue under Rule 56. Indeed, even if a non-moving party adduces some tiny bit of evidence in support of its factual position, this may not necessarily create a "genuine" issue. If the moving party's evidentiary demonstration is impressive, a "mere scintilla" of opposing evidence might not be enough for a finder of fact to come out in favor of the non-moving party on that issue. The key question is always: Could a reasonable juror decide only one way?

Just as that question takes into account who has the burden of proof, it also takes into account how high that burden is. The preceding paragraph assumed that the party bearing the burden had to discharge that burden by a preponderance of the evidence. In some settings the burden is greater: a party may have to prove a fact by "clear and convincing evidence." If that is so, to avoid summary judgment a non-moving party bearing such a high burden will have to produce a greater amount of evidence than would suffice under a lesser burden of proof – enough evidence for a jury to reasonably conclude that his proof of the fact was "clear and convincing."

Things are slightly different when the party moving for summary judgment is the one bearing the burden of proof. In such a case, to prevail, the moving party must show that the evidence is so credible and overwhelming that a reasonable jury would have no choice but to resolve the contested fact in his favor. If a party seeking summary judgment has a burden to prove a fact by clear and convincing evidence, the motion is even tougher going. The party opposing summary judgment can defeat it merely by demonstrating that a reasonable jury could reject the moving party's evidence and resolve a contested fact in the non-moving party's favor. The non-moving party may do this either by pointing to evidence that supports his own position, or by merely pointing to holes in the moving party's evidence that a finder of fact might seize upon to reject it, although this is not true when the moving party is the one bearing the burden of proof at trial.

Two final observations concerning Rule 56 warrant mention. First, because summary judgment, unlike a 12(b)(6) motion or a motion for judgment on the pleadings, concerns proof and not just allegations, summary judgment may not be appropriate if the non-moving party has not had adequate opportunity to conduct discovery in order to adduce the evidence necessary to support its positions. Rule 56(f) explicitly recognizes this possibility. Second, Rules 56(a) and (b) make clear that parties may move for partial summary judgment in the same manner that they may seek complete summary judgment. Partial summary judgment resolves certain claims or issues in the case, but does not resolve the whole case – some issues remain that will require trial. Summary judgment thus can streamline trials in some cases, while wholly eliminating the need for trial in other cases.

1. Fed. R. Civ. P. 56(c).

2. State Summary-Judgment Standards

192. Though several states have followed the lead of the federal courts, many (including some of the most populous) have stayed with the more traditional approach of disfavoring summary judgment. California has recently moved very close to the federal approach, as have Ohio and Massachusetts, among others.[1]

In 1993, California Code of Civil Procedure §437(c) was amended to remove the requirement that the moving party must negate an essential element of the cause of action or the affirmative defense of the non-moving party. In *Union Bank v. Superior Court* it was held, consistently with the federal model, that a party seeking summary judgment may prevail without affirmatively disproving claims of the opposition.[2] The court further stated that the moving party may rely on the non-moving party's factually barren discovery responses to shift the burden onto the non-moving party. Once the burden has been shifted, the non-moving party must set forth the specific facts which prove the existence of a triable issue of material fact.

Through a series of cases, Ohio has also embraced the federal law on summary judgment. In *Hodgkinson v. Dunlop Tire & Rubber Corp.*, the Ohio Court of Appeals extensively quoted the *Celotex* decision and held that Ohio Civil Procedure Rule 56 did not always require the moving party to support his or her motion with affidavits or other similar materials negating the opponent's claim.[3] The Court of Appeals showed a complete reliance on *Celotex* and *Anderson* in its 1992 decision in *Barney v. Chi Chi's*.[4]

The Massachusetts Supreme Court adopted the *Celotex*[5] summary-judgment standard in its decision in *Kourouvacilis v. General Motors*.[6] In this case, the defendant moving party showed that the plaintiff had no reasonable expectation of establishing an essential element of her claim. While the party moving for summary judgment has the burden of affirmatively demonstrating that there is no genuine issue of fact on every relevant issue raised by the pleadings, this burden may be discharged by showing that there is an absence of evidence to support the non-moving party's case. Following the federal summary-judgment standard, the Massachusetts Supreme Court enabled a party to more easily secure summary judgments.

1. Other states moving toward the federal standard include Hawaii, Maryland, Missouri, Nebraska, and South Carolina.
2. *Union Bank v. Superior Court*, 31 Cal. App. 4th 573 (1995).
3. *Hodgkinson v. Dunlop Tire & Rubber Corp.*, 38 Ohio App. 3rd 101, 526 N.E. 2nd 89 (Ohio Ct. App. 1987).
4. *Barney v. Chi Chi's, Inc.*, 84 Ohio App. 3rd 40, 616 N.E. 2nd 269 (Ohio Ct. App. 1992).
5. *Celotex Corp. v. Catrett*, 477 U.S. 317 (1986), discussed above in para. 190.
6. *Kourouvacilis v. General Motors Corp.*, 410 Mass. 706, 575 N.E. 2nd 734 (Mass. 1991).

193. Important states that have not followed the federal approach include New York and Texas. In both states, the moving party has the burden of setting forth evidence disproving the other side's case, regardless of who will bear the burden of proof at trial. The approach makes summary judgment much harder to obtain.[1]

In New York, the party moving for summary judgment has the burden of setting forth evidence from which it must clearly appear that no material and triable issue of fact is presented. Anything less requires denial of the motion, even if the opposing party's papers do not raise a triable issue of fact. In *Harper v. Murphy Overhead Doors*, the plaintiff successfully opposed summary judgment despite failing to present any admissible evidence linking the defendant to the defective garage door that had injured the plaintiff.[2] Nevertheless, when making a motion for summary judgment, the moving party bears the initial burden of making a prima facie case that establishes, by submission of competent evidence, its entitlement to judgment as a matter of law.[3] Only then does the burden shift to the party opposing the motion to produce evidentiary proof in an admissible form to establish the existence of such facts which require a trial of the action.

Texas standards for granting a summary judgment do not reflect any of the changes set out in the federal trilogy. It has been observed that Texans have an enthusiasm for trial by jury that is virtually unrivaled elsewhere in the country.[4] Summary judgments are to be denied when there is the slightest doubt as to the facts. In their zeal to protect a litigant's right to trial by jury, the courts of Texas allow insupportable claims to go to trial.[5] To get a summary judgment in Texas, plaintiff or defendant must conclusively prove all the essential elements of his cause of action or affirmative defense. Texas courts will not grant a summary judgment based on failure of the non-movant's evidence to support his claims. Moreover, every reasonable inference from the evidence must be indulged in favor of the non-movant, with any doubts being resolved in his favor. If this burden is met, then the non-movant cannot stand on his pleadings and must produce evidence that raises a genuine issue of material fact.

1. Other states that make motions for summary judgment harder to win include Illinois, Florida, Pennsylvania, Kentucky, and Alabama.
2. *Harper v. Murphy Overhead Doors*, 131 A.D.2nd 966, 516 N.Y.S. 2nd 547 (N.Y. App. Div. 1987).
3. *Cheeseman v. Inserra*, 174 A.D.2nd 956, 571 N.Y.S.2nd 358 (N.Y. App. Div. 1991).
4. *See* Sheila Leute, "The Effective Use of Summary Judgment: A Comparison of Federal and Texas Standards," Baylor L. Rev. 40 (1988): 617.
5. Id., at 631.

C. *The Trial*

194. The full-blown courtroom trial in American civil justice is obviously an important and complex event, worthy of the many volumes that have been written on it alone. For present purposes, however, a very brief overview, followed by a short discussion of the right to a trial by a jury (rather than a judge) under the Seventh Amendment to the United States Constitution, is sufficient to convey the essential flavor of an American civil trial.

1. Trial Process Overview

195. The formal beginning of the trial itself is ordinarily preceded by a trial-setting or "final pretrial conference" held between the lawyers and the judge a few weeks in advance of the trial. Federal Rule 16 authorizes pretrial conferences in federal courts. During the course of discovery and summary-judgment proceedings, a number of such conferences might already have been held. The final pretrial conference gives the judge a chance to review all the evidence that will be submitted at trial, and to have it labeled and prepared for admission into evidence. The judge also has the chance to anticipate objections the lawyers may make at trial to evidentiary rulings or jury instructions.

On the very eve of the trial, the lawyers for each side are likely to formally make one or more motions *in limine*. These motions generally focus procedures to be employed or evidence to be considered. For example, a party may move *in limine* to exclude all witnesses from the courtroom until they need to take the stand, or may move to suppress some piece of evidence thought to be highly prejudicial. These motions are made to and ruled on by the judge outside the presence of the jury, should there be one.

In the case of a jury trial, the last step prior to the formal beginning of trial is the *voir dire* examination of potential jurors. Persons will already have been selected randomly from the population to serve as potential jurors, and will then be examined to make sure they are fit. Federal practice tends toward examination by the judge rather than by the lawyers, but individual examination by the lawyers is sometimes permitted after the judge has finished. At the conclusion of the examination, the judge will excuse "for cause" any juror who he believes (or who one of the lawyers has convinced him) is unable to be fair, impartial and competent in discharging the duties of a juror. Disqualification may occur because the juror personally knows the parties or witnesses, the juror has a large financial stake in the outcome, or the juror may have biases she is unable to put aside. In the federal system and most states, each party is also given the chance to make a number of so-called peremptory strikes. These are opportunities to remove jurors without demonstrating good cause. These peremptory strikes, or challenges, can be used for any reason or no reason at all, except that they cannot be based on the race (and perhaps the gender) of the juror. Once the "for cause" and peremptory removals are completed, the jury is seated and the case is ready to proceed to the formal commencement of trial. If the case does not involve a jury, the *voir dire* step is omitted.

The plaintiff, or more specifically the party with the burden of proof, generally makes the first opening statement and at the end of trial makes the last closing argument. The opening statement is a preview of the evidence of the case, and a framework for organizing that evidence so that the finder of fact will understand how each piece of evidence introduced fits into the party's theory of the case. Defendant's lawyer usually follows by making an opening statement in which he presents his view of the evidence and witnesses, and gives his outline and theory of the case.

The plaintiff then proceeds to present her "case-in-chief," which consists of the testimony of witnesses called by the plaintiff and examined by her lawyer, including the presentation of real and documentary evidence which the plaintiff believes supports the facts she must prove to establish liability under the applicable substantive law. During the case-in-chief, the defendant and other parties have the opportunity to object to the introduction of evidence, and to have their lawyers cross-examine witnesses presented by the plaintiff.

At the conclusion of the plaintiff's presentation of her case-in-chief, the defense can and typically does make a motion for a directed verdict (now called in federal court a pre-verdict motion for judgment as a matter of law), arguing that the evidence presented by plaintiff is not sufficient to enable a finder of fact, acting rationally, to find in the plaintiff's favor on each of the required elements of plaintiff's claim. The directed-verdict standard is analytically identical to the summary-judgment standard described earlier in paragraphs 190-191. The difference between the two motions is that a directed-verdict motion focuses on the evidence that has been submitted, whereas summary-judgment motions focus on evidence that will be submitted should the case go to trial.

If no directed verdict is sought or granted, defendant proceeds to put on its case-in-chief, during which plaintiff's attorney has the right to object and cross-examine witnesses. Each side then can put on rebuttal evidence that responds to matters raised during the other side's presentation. At the conclusion of the defendant's case and the rebuttal presentations, one or both sides may move for a directed verdict, once again arguing that a rational trier of fact could come out only one way in the case.

If no directed verdict is issued, then the plaintiff makes her closing argument or summation to the jury, in which plaintiff's lawyer reviews the evidence presented and argues to the jury why the plaintiff should prevail on the basis of the facts and the law. The defendant responds with a summation of his own, and the plaintiff then gets to make a final short summation. Because the party bearing the burden of proof has, by definition, the harder task, she is given the first and last say to the finder of fact. If the case is tried without a jury, i.e., to the court, at this point the judge takes the case under submission and deliberates to produce findings of fact and conclusions of law that would resolve the case. In the case of a jury trial, though, the closing arguments are followed by the judge's instructions to the jury, setting out the legal framework within which the jury must evaluate the evidence, identifying the elements of the plaintiff's cause(s) of action and the defendant's defenses, and telling the jury to consider how the evidence is relevant to these elements and/or defenses. The jury then deliberates and produces a verdict, which may (depending on the judge and the parties' wishes) be either a general verdict, which just announces an outcome, or a special verdict, which breaks down the jury's findings into specific issues which, taken together, are used to determine the ultimate outcome.

2. Right to Jury Trial

196. The Seventh Amendment to the United States Constitution provides that "in suits at common law, where the value in controversy shall exceed twenty dollars, the right of trial by jury shall be preserved." ...This portion of the Seventh Amendment, known as the preservation clause, requires federal courts to respect the right of trial by jury in civil cases where that right would have existed at the time of the adoption of the Seventh Amendment in 1791. At that time, there were separate courts of law and equity, with (more or less) mutually exclusive jurisdiction. If the case was within the jurisdiction of a court of law, a jury trial was provided. If a case was within the jurisdiction of a court of equity, no jury trial right existed. Thus, determining access to jury trial was easy – it was a function of the court (legal or equitable) with jurisdiction over the case.

Now that law and equity have been merged into a single federal court system, the question of access to a jury trial has become much more complicated. At the risk of oversimplifying, current Seventh Amendment doctrine focuses on the nature of the plaintiff's claim, the nature of the remedy sought, the historical antecedents (if any) to the plaintiff's cause of action, and whether a historically analogous case would have been brought in a court of law or equity.

Where a right to jury trial exists, it must be invoked in a timely demand, on pain of waiver under Rule 38(d). There may be such a right to jury trial even if it is not guaranteed by the Constitution. Congress has the legislative discretion to mandate jury trial even in cases where the Constitution does not require it, and has occasionally done so.

It is very important to recognize that the Seventh Amendment is one of the few provisions of the Bill of Rights that has not been "incorporated" into the Fourteenth Amendment's guarantee of due process of law, and thus made applicable to the states. This means that state courts are generally not bound by the US Supreme Court's determination of when a jury trial is required in civil cases tried in the federal courts. (The only exception is when Congress has created a federal cause of action triable at the plaintiff's option in state court, and has mandated jury trial of that federally created cause of action.[1]) In almost all civil cases tried in a state court, whether a jury trial is required is determined solely by reference to state law. Most state constitutions, however, contain provisions that are analogous to a greater or lesser extent to the Seventh Amendment, so that jury trial is guaranteed in state courts to almost as great an extent as in federal court.

1. *See Dice v. Akron, Canton & Youngstown Railroad Co.*, 342 U.S. 359 (1952).

D. Judgment

197. The entry of a judgment is the judicial act that gives effect to a jury verdict or court decision. Rule 54 of the Federal Rules of Civil Procedure defines a judgment as "a decree [or] any order from which an appeal lies." The formal entry of a judgment is a significant event because it clearly establishes the time of judgment. Time constraints placed on making post-trial motions and filing an appeal begin running at the entry of judgment (see paragraph 271). Furthermore, the entry of a judgment signifies the final determination of an action. This element of finality is relevant to the preclusion doctrines, which require a judgment to be final (see paragraphs 279-284). In order for a judgment to take effect, Rule 58 requires that two formal steps be completed. First, the judgment must be set out in a separate document. Second, the court clerk must sign and enter the judgment in the docket as provided by Rule 79. A clerk may act without the direction of the court when there is a general verdict or a court decision that allows the party to recover only a sum certain, or costs or no relief at all, unless the court orders otherwise. When the decision grants other forms of relief or there is a special verdict or general verdict accompanied by answers to interrogatories, the court must promptly approve the form of judgment. The clerk can then enter the judgment.

E. Post-Verdict Motions

198. Of the post-verdict motions that a dissatisfied party can make to the trial court, two of the most important are a motion for judgment as a matter of law under Rule 50 and a motion for a new trial under Rule 59. A post-verdict motion for judgment as a matter of law under Rule 50 poses essentially the same issue as a Rule 50 pre-verdict motion (or motion for a directed verdict) – could a rational jury decide against the moving party on the basis of the evidence presented? The difference between the directed-verdict request and the post-verdict motion for judgment as a matter of law is one of timing; the latter is made after the jury verdict has been returned. In federal court and most state courts, a party must move for a directed verdict at the close of evidence to preserve the right to make a post-verdict motion for judgment as a matter of law after an adverse jury result. In many states and at common law, the judgment as a matter of law goes under the name "judgment notwithstanding the verdict," or "JNOV."

One might wonder why a judge would deny a directed-verdict motion and then consider granting a post-verdict motion for judgment as a matter of law. Wouldn't the judge be essentially reversing his denial of the directed-verdict motion? Yes, but there are sound policy reasons for a judge to deny a directed verdict even if he thinks it should be entered. By waiting for the jury to render its result, a judge who grants judgment as a matter of law but who is reversed by the appellate court can simply reinstate the jury verdict without the need for a new trial. If a judge grants a directed verdict and is reversed on appeal, a whole new trial is required because the jury never rendered a verdict. Thus, even if a judge thinks a rational jury could come out only one way, it makes sense for him to wait and see what the jury does, in case an appellate court disagrees with him on whether a jury could rationally reach a contrary verdict.

Another important post-trial motion is the motion for a new trial under Rule 59. Under this rule, a federal judge and state judges in state systems with analogous provisions have broad latitude to vacate the jury verdict and, instead of entering a contrary judgment, to grant a new trial. The grounds for a new trial may include erroneous evidentiary rulings that a judge has rethought, the discovery of new evidence, or simply a verdict that is "against the weight of the evidence." Importantly, a judge may grant a request for a new trial even though he does not believe the jury was acting outside the bounds of impartial rationality in rendering its verdict; he may grant a new trial if he simply disagrees with the result. Needless to say, most judges attempt to exercise this very broad power somewhat sparingly. Oftentimes, judges will use their power to grant new trials to get the parties to agree to modify the jury verdict to something the judge thinks is more fair. For example, a judge may give a prevailing plaintiff an option: accept less money than the jury awarded or endure the expense and uncertainty of an entirely new trial. Such a device is known as "remittitur," and has been held not to violate a party's constitutional right to a jury trial.

Chapter 3. Review Proceedings

§1. Appeal

199. There is a widely shared intuition in the United States that dissatisfied civil litigants should have the right to at least one level of appeal from judgments of the trial courts to the intermediate courts of appeal. After that basic agreement, however, philosophical and practical differences of opinion result in different implementations of appeal in the various judicial systems in the United States. In the brief review that follows, we touch on a number of questions, including when an appeal can be had, how an appeal is prosecuted, and what precisely appellate courts do when they conduct review.

I. Who May Seek Appellate Review

200. In order to appeal a case, one must have been a party below, and one must have been a losing party. Ordinarily, this simple description does not pose many practical difficulties, but complications do arise when a party in the lower court has pressed multiple claims and/or theories. Appellate courts sometimes have to decide whether a party who prevails on one theory in the lower court but who loses on another may seek an appeal on the losing theory. The answer generally given by American appellate courts is overtly pragmatic: if the relief sought in the lower court by the party trying to appeal (known in the federal system as the "appellant") was the same under the losing theory as that which was awarded under the theory that prevailed, then the party has not lost anything cognizable that would justify expenditure of appellate resources. This is true even where the appellate court thinks the trial court improperly rejected the losing theory.

On the other hand, if the losing theory would have allowed the appellant to obtain relief that in any meaningful way would be superior to the relief obtained, then appellate review may be had on that theory even though the appealing party was in some sense a winner below. For example, if a plaintiff sues a defendant to recover a money judgment on both a breach-of-contract theory and a fraudulent-tort theory, and if he prevails on the contract claim and loses on the tort claim, he may seek appellate review of the ruling on his tort claim, even if the amount of damages he seeks in tort is no greater than that awarded him in contract, because a money judgment for fraud may not be dischargeable in bankruptcy in the way a contract-damage judgment would be. This real-world difference in the value of the relief obtained would be sufficient for a "winning" party to appeal the rejection of one of his theories.

201. In addition to being a losing party, a person seeking to invoke the jurisdiction of the appellate court ordinarily must have raised the issue to be appealed by appropriate motion or objection in the trial court. If the issue has not been presented to the trial court in a timely fashion, it is said to be waived for appellate purposes. This requirement serves a number of purposes. First, it reflects a respect for trial courts by encouraging parties to present important issues for their review. Second, it serves efficiency by eliminating the need for an appellate court to correct an error that would have been cured by the trial court had it been given a chance. Most jurisdictions have exceptions to this requirement: for issues that were futile to raise before the trial court given its other rulings, or issues that are so fundamental that fairness requires an appellate court to examine them, even if the appellant had no good reason for not having given the trial court a chance to consider the issue. There is also an exception for defects of subject-matter jurisdiction, which can be raised at any time on appeal, whether pressed by appellant below or not. Indeed, an appellate court, like the trial court, is under an obligation to look for a lack of subject-matter jurisdiction on its own, whether or not the issue was raised by the parties in the trial court or on appeal.

Another apparent exception to this waiver doctrine is not really an exception but is sometimes described that way by courts. This pseudo exception is the rule that a party who *defends* the judgment of the lower court – in federal parlance the "appellee" – is free to make any arguments in defense of the lower court's result, whether or not those arguments were presented to the lower court. Thus, for example, consider again a case in which appellant appeals the trial court's rejection of his fraud claim against appellee. Appellant is limited to making only those arguments made in the trial court, but appellee is free to defend the dismissal of the fraud claim even on theories and under caselaw not presented to the trial court. This leeway given to the appellee is grounded in the same pragmatism that undergirds much of the structure of appellate procedure. First, if appellee knows the trial judge is going to rule in his favor on an issue, we do not want to create an incentive for appellee to "overlawyer" the case by raising more arguments than are necessary. Second, if after the appellate court corrected the erroneous reasoning of the trial court and sent the case back down for further proceedings there was yet another basis on which the appellee would prevail anyway, there is no use in the pointless exercise of an appellate remand. This is but one example of the general rule that appellate courts review the results, not the reasoning, of the trial courts.

II. When Appeal Can Be Had

202. In the federal system, 28 U.S.C. §1291 provides that appeals ordinarily lie only from "final decisions" of the district courts. Most, but by no means all, of the state jurisdictions follow a similar approach. A final decision is one that "ends the litigation on the merits and leaves nothing to do but execute the judgment."[1] Thus, under the federal model, the ordinary rule – subject to a number of statutory exceptions – is that no appeal may be taken from errors in the course of trial and the pretrial process until the litigation in the trial court has run its entire course and a final judgment has been entered. Thus, for example, if a party wants to appeal a discovery ruling, or a trial court evidentiary ruling, he must wait until the trial court proceedings are finished, and then appeal if he was a losing party in the case. Some states, including California and New York, follow a policy of allowing "piecemeal" appeal – that is, appeal of discrete issues in the case from the trial court to the appellate court even before the trial court is necessarily finished with the case.

The differences between the federal model and the piecemeal model reflect different views about the efficiency and fairness of the two approaches. On the one hand, the federal final-judgment rule may tend to preserve appellate resources, because some disputes – such as a dispute over discovery – will never be appealed if the party who lost on the disputed pretrial issue nonetheless wins the overall case at the trial level. Because a party who won the relief sought from the trial court is not a "losing" party in the case – even if he lost on some preliminary issues along the way – many disputes that are not immediately appealable never become appealable. On the other hand, the federal final-judgment rule may result in the increased expenditure of trial resources by courts and parties in some cases, because permitting piecemeal appeal may avoid wasting additional trial court time on further litigation of a case already infected by reversible error by the trial court. For example, if a trial court wrongly excludes a piece of evidence, and that erroneous ruling is not corrected by an appellate court until after the whole trial is over, the portion of the trial that took place after the erroneous evidentiary ruling is a waste that would have been avoided if the aggrieved party could have gotten an immediate appellate reversal of it. To some, this may seem inefficient, and unfair to the party who has to expend resources retrying cases.

1. *Catlin v. United States*, 324 U.S. 229, 233 (1945).

203. Even in the federal system, there are a great number of exceptions to the so-called final-judgment rule. One important exception is for cases that are final as a practical if not a technical matter. The US Supreme Court has described this exception as the "collateral-order doctrine." Under this doctrine, immediate review is allowed for the small class of prejudgment orders that "finally determine claims of right separable from, and collateral to, rights asserted in the action [and that are] too important to be denied review and too independent of the cause itself to require that appellate consideration be deferred until the whole case is adjudicated."[1] To fall within this exception, an order must satisfy what the court has characterized as a "three-prong" test:

(1) it must conclusively determine the question from which appeal is sought;
(2) the issue resolved must be important and completely separate from the merits of the action; and
(3) it must be effectively unreviewable on appeal from a final judgment.[2]

Examples of orders reviewable under this doctrine include: the trial court's denial of a motion to dismiss based on a defendant's assertion, as a government official, of absolute immunity from suit based on his official status; an order refusing under the *Erie* doctrine (paragraph 56) to enforce against a federal plaintiff a state law requiring the posting of security costs in a shareholder derivative suit; and an order requiring a class-action defendant to pay the cost of notice to the plaintiff class.

Another important exception to the final-judgment rule appears in 28 U.S.C. §1292(a), which allows appeals from interlocutory orders (that is, orders which are not final judgments) of the district court "granting, continuing, modifying, refusing or dissolving injunctions, or refusing to dissolve or modify injunctions." This exception is based on the potentially irreparable harm that may be caused by an erroneous injunction, or suffered if an injunction is erroneously denied.

A third important exception to finality permits the district court to certify that a particular ruling "involves a controlling question of law as to which there is substantial ground for difference of opinion" and that "an immediate appeal from the order may materially advance the ultimate termination of the litigation."[3] The court of appeals then has discretionary power to grant or deny review of the certified question.

1. *Cohen v. Beneficial Industrial Loan Corp.*, 337 U.S. 541, 546 (1949).
2. *Gulfstream Aerospace Corp. v. Mayacamas Corp.*, 485 U.S. 271, 277 (1988). Alert readers will note that the court's "three-pronged test" actually contains four prongs. The second of the court's prongs contains two distinct elements: the issue in question must be "important," and must also be "completely separate from the merits of the action." It is quite possible that a separable issue may not be sufficiently important to merit collateral-order review, or that an important issue may not be sufficiently separable from the merits of the underlying action to permit collateral-order review.
3. 28 U.S.C. §1292(b).

III. The Mechanics of Appeal

204. In most American systems, one takes an appeal by filing a "notice of appeal," which tells the appellate court and the parties that a formal appeal is forthcoming. This notice must be made within a specified period of time. In the federal system, this period is in most cases thirty days after the date of entry of the judgment or order appealed from. Extensions of time are available in most systems, but the leniency in granting and implementing extensions varies. For example, in a recent and controversial decision in *Bowles v. Russell*,[1] the Supreme Court held that a federal court of appeals had no jurisdiction to entertain an appeal from by a habeas corpus petitioner because the notice of appeal was filed two days late – even though it was filed one day *before* the date that the federal district judge had (mistakenly) told the petitioner that the notice of appeal was due.

After notice of appeal is filed, the appellant must prepare and file the record – which is an excerpted version of the full official record of the trial court that covers the matters on which appeal will be taken. The next step is the timely preparation of a brief setting forth the contentions and the arguments that warrant appellate reversal of the trial court's ruling. The appellee then files an opposing brief, setting forth arguments for sustaining the lower court, and the appellant then usually has the option of filing a short reply brief. Oral argument is generally permitted, and in some states is required unless waived by counsel – rarely done in an important case. In the federal system Rule 34 of the Federal Rules of Appellate Procedure permit a court of appeals to order a case heard without oral argument. Although Rule 34 implies that this is to be an exceptional procedure, in fact roughly half of the appeals decided annually in the federal system are decided *without* oral argument. When oral argument is heard, the appellate judges (in the federal system sitting as panels of three judges) not only hear the views of counsel for the parties but also ask counsel any questions the judges may have. The case is then submitted to the appellate court, and a decision is announced at a later date. The time between oral argument and decision varies greatly between courts, and may be a matter of weeks, months (the norm), or (rarely) years.

1. *Bowles v. Russell*, 127 S. Ct. 2360 (2007).

IV. The Scope of Appellate Review

205. Even after an appellate court has taken a case, it will not disturb the ruling by the trial court unless it falls within the description of reversible error. Whether an error is reversible depends upon (1) the standard of review applied by the appellate court, and (2) whether the error affected the result in the trial court.

An appellate court reviews errors of fact under a deferential "clearly erroneous" standard of review. This means that, as to findings of fact, an appellate court will not reverse even if it disagrees with the trial court's findings, unless the trial court's findings are *clearly* wrong. In other words, under this standard, an appellate court is not supposed to substitute its own factual findings for those of the trial court, but only to ensure that the trial court's findings fall within a range of reasonable discretion about what findings to make. Where there are two logically permissible views of the evidence, the trial court's choice between them cannot be clearly erroneous. This standard, at least in the federal system, applies whether the trial court's findings of fact are based on documentary evidence or live testimony.[1]

An appellate court's review of the trial court's interpretations of law, by contrast, is much less deferential. Review of claimed legal errors is "de novo" or "from the beginning." This means that an appellate court will displace a trial court's legal rulings if the appellate court would have come to a different ruling in the first instance, even if the trial court's rulings are not outside the range of reasonableness. Of course, even under this "de novo" standard, an appellate court will take into account the reasoning of the trial court, and will give due respect to the experience and judgment of the trial judge.

Even if a court of appeals applying the appropriate standard of review concludes that the trial court has erred, it will still not reverse the trial court unless the error is likely to have affected the result in the lower court. In civil litigation, the so-called "harmless error" rule (by which harmless errors are ignored) requires a party seeking appellate reversal to show a substantial probability that, but for the error, the judgment would have been more favorable to the appellant. This rule is but another illustration that appellate courts will not lightly overturn judgments, and that appellate courts are pragmatic in their focus on the result below rather than the reasoning of the lower court.

1. *See* Fed. R. Civ. P. 52(a).

V. Appealing from an Appellate Court

206. After an intermediate court of appeals has rendered its decision, usually acting through a three-judge panel, a party who is not satisfied with the result has several options for further review. First, a party may ask the entire intermediate appellate court (from which the three-judge panel was drawn) to hear the case in full, or "en banc." Such en banc review is available at the discretion of a majority of the judges of the intermediate appellate court. In the federal system this number ranges from six to twenty-eight judges. Usually, a case has to be very important or involve a legal ruling that conflicts with that of other appellate courts in order to warrant en banc review. If en banc review is granted, the three-judge panel decision is vacated, new briefs are written, new oral arguments are had, and the whole court of appeals decides the case (see also Part I, paragraphs 15 and 17).

A second option, which can be pursued after or instead of en banc review, is to seek review in the jurisdiction's court of last resort. In the federal system, this is the US Supreme Court. In most states, it is the state supreme court, although state terminology varies widely. Finally, if a decision of a state court of last resort turns on an issue of federal law, the losing party may seek review of that federal issue in the US Supreme Court.

Today, the US Supreme Court's docket is by statute almost entirely discretionary – except in rare cases there is no appeal as of right. The court's internal operating rules require that four of the nine justices on the court vote to hear a case before discretionary review is granted. The US Supreme Court does not sit primarily to correct mistakes of trial courts or courts of appeal. Instead, the court views its primary function as clarifying important and recurring questions of federal constitutional and statutory law. For that reason, discretionary review (exercised by granting the writ of *certiorari*) is reserved primarily for issues over which the lower courts are split, and cases that are otherwise of fundamental importance to the proper application of the US Constitution or Acts of Congress. Oftentimes, the court will decline to review an issue until it has percolated in the lower courts for a sufficient time, so that the court will have the full benefit of the insights of other courts before rendering its dispositive opinion.[1]

1. The jurisdiction and operating procedures of the US Supreme Court are also discussed in Part I (para. 16).

Part V. Incidents

Chapter 1. Judicial Disqualification

207. Traditionally, two terms have been used to describe situations where a judge is removed from hearing a case: recusal and disqualification. "Recusal" refers to situations where a judge decides to stand down voluntarily. "Disqualification," by contrast, describes occasions when a party to the litigation challenges, by statutorily or constitutionally authorized motion, a judge's participation. While historically distinct, the terms are used interchangeably by modern jurisdictions and governing statutes.[1] Accordingly, this chapter will discuss disqualification in the modern sense that includes recusal, providing an overview of federal and state provisions. Recusal in the narrow sense that deals only with judicial self-disqualification is also discussed above in Part I (paragraph 31).

1. *See generally* Richard E. Flamm, *Judicial Disqualification: Recusal and Disqualification of Judges* (1996), §1.

§1. Disqualification for Cause

208. Generally, American law provides two grounds for disqualification of a judge for cause: constitutional due-process concerns and statutory provisions. Due-process concerns stem from a fundamental guarantee to all litigants of a fair and impartial trial. Therefore, in cases where a judge's self-interest may prejudice his or her conduct during the course of trial, litigants may challenge that judge's continuing role in the proceedings. While the US Supreme Court has never explicitly so held, it has suggested that judicial partiality may violate due process in some circumstances.[1] Due-process justifications for disqualification stem from the Fifth Amendment (as to federal courts) and the Fourteenth Amendment (as to state courts). Both amendments require the government to provide equal protection of the law to all citizens. However, disqualification orders are rarely based expressly on due-process rights because all jurisdictions have supplemented the constitutional guarantee with statutory disqualification provisions.[2]

1. *See, e.g.*, *Tumey v. Ohio*, 273 U.S. 510, 523 (1927).
2. *See generally* Flamm, *supra*, §2.

I. Federal Provisions

209. In federal courts, comprehensive disqualification authority is found in 28 U.S.C. §455. Under §455(a), any federal judge must disqualify himself from any proceeding where his impartiality might reasonably be questioned. In practice, this provision has been applied under a reasonable-person standard. In *Potashnick v. Port City Construction Co.*,[1] for example, the Fifth Circuit held that a judge should recuse himself where his continued participation in a given case would cause the average person on the street to question his impartiality. The statute also provides specific circumstances under which a judge should consider disqualification in §455(b).

Section 455(b) sets out several alternative instances where a judge should disqualify himself. Disqualification is required where a judge has a personal prejudice or bias towards a party; has personal knowledge of the proceeding's evidentiary facts; has served as a lawyer in private practice in the matter before him; has worked with a lawyer currently associated with the proceeding; where either the judge or a lawyer he worked with is a material witness in the proceeding; where the judge, working as a government employee, participated as counsel, adviser, or witness in the proceeding; or where the judge has a financial or other interest that could be substantially affected by the outcome of the proceeding. Finally, the judge should consider disqualification, under §455(b)(5), when the judge, the judge's spouse, or a relation of either, is a party, lawyer, or witness in the proceeding. If the judge, the judge's spouse, or a relative divests themselves of any interest conflicting with §455(b) during the course of the proceedings, disqualification is not required.[2]

Section 455(b) lists several occasions that Congress felt were identifiable, per se violations of a judge's duty to be fair and impartial. This listing is non-exhaustive. Accordingly, if a party seeks the disqualification of a judge, yet cannot point to any facts suggesting a violation of §455(b), the party may always resort to §455(a) as authority for disqualification in any instance where the judge's impartiality might reasonably be questioned.[3]

A particularly detailed and thought-provoking, if controversial, explanation by a Supreme Court Justice of his decision not to recuse himself under §455(a) can be found in *Cheney v. United States District Court*,[4] where Justice Scalia attempted to justify his decision to hear a case involving Vice President Richard Cheney notwithstanding the personal relationship between the Vice President and Justice Scalia.

1. *Potashnick v. Port City Constr. Co.*, 609 F.2nd 1101 (5th Cir. 1980).
2. 28 U.S.C. §455(f).
3. *See* Flamm, *supra*, at §24.1.
4. *Cheney v. United States District Court*, 541 U.S. 913 (2004) (in chambers opinion of Scalia, J.).

II. State Provisions

210. While specific state provisions vary by jurisdictions,[1] forty-five of the fifty states have adopted the Model Code of Judicial Conduct, prepared by the American

Bar Association.[2] The remaining five states have adopted rules substantially based on the Model Code and are considering adopting the Model Code in toto. Accordingly, this section will discuss Canon 3 of the Model Code in order to provide an overview of state disqualification standards.

The American Bar Association originally formulated the Model Code in 1972 and its most recent version was completed in 1990. Closely paralleling 28 U.S.C. §455, the Model Code specifies a variety of circumstances in which a judicial officer "should" disqualify herself.[3] According to the Code, disqualification should occur in five circumstances very similar to the provisions of §455:

(1) When a judge has personal knowledge of the disputed evidentiary facts;
(2) When a judge has personal bias or prejudice concerning a party to the litigation;
(3) When the judge served as a lawyer in the matter, served as a lawyer with counsel now representing the parties, or when the judge or lawyer he has served with will be a material witness in the proceeding;
(4) When the judge, or the judge's fiduciary, spouse, or minor child has a financial or any other interest that would be substantially affected by the litigation's outcome; or
(5) Where the judge, his spouse, or their relatives is a party to the proceeding, is a lawyer to the proceeding, is known by the judge to have an interest that would be substantially affected by the outcome, or is a material witness to the proceeding.[4]

To effect the purposes of the Code, Canon 3(c)(2) imposes upon judges a duty to be reasonably informed of his, his spouse's, and his minor children's fiduciary interests.

1. For exhaustive treatment of state disqualification provisions *see* Flamm, *supra*, §27.
2. *See* Leslie W. Abramson, *Judicial Disqualification under Canon 3 of the Code of Judicial Conduct* (1992), 1.
3. In this respect the Model Code's hortatory language ("should") differs from the mandatory language ("shall") of the parallel provisions of 28 U.S.C. §455.
4. ABA, *Model Code of Judicial Conduct Canon*, (1990), 3C.

§2. Disqualification Procedure

I. Federal Practice

211. A federal judge is required by 28 U.S.C. §144 to disqualify herself *sua sponte* (on her own motion) in circumstances where her impartiality might reasonably be challenged. After a *sua sponte* disqualification order, the self-disqualified judge stops hearing the case and a different judge is assigned. Section 144 also provides that any party may challenge a judge's continuing involvement in the litigation by filing an affidavit demonstrating the judge's bias or prejudice against that party. The affidavit should support contentions of bias with facts and be accompanied by counsel's declaration that the affidavit is filed in good faith. Each party may file one such affidavit during any case.[1]

1. *See generally* Flamm, *supra*, §§24-25.

II. State Practice

212. While all states feature judicial disqualification procedures based in their constitutions, statutes, or rules of court, their provisions diverge markedly. As noted (paragraph 210), however, forty-five of the fifty states have incorporated the Model Code of Judicial Conduct into their respective disqualification laws. Accordingly, there is considerable congruence of general disqualification provisions.

Perhaps the most significant disparity concerns peremptory disqualification. A majority of states, like the federal courts, permit disqualification only for cause. "Cause" can be defined as a factual showing by one party that the judge's involvement constitutes a violation of the jurisdiction's disqualification standards. A substantial minority of states, however, allow for peremptory disqualification. These states afford parties at least one opportunity to disqualify a judge as of right, for any reason or for no reason. In California, for example, a party may file a peremptory challenge pursuant to §170.6 of the state's Code of Civil Procedure. Under that section, California litigants are afforded the "extraordinary" right to disqualify a judge without any showing of cause.[1]

Amongst these minority jurisdictions, however, there is disagreement whether the good faith of the moving party may be challenged. Accordingly, the practitioner is well advised to consider local disqualification provisions in conjunction with the general disqualification principles discussed in this chapter.

1. *See, e.g., Nissan Motors v. Superior Court*, 6 Cal. App. 4th 150 (1992).

Chapter 2. Preliminary Injunctions

213. Broadly speaking, courts are empowered to issue three types of injunctions: temporary restraining orders (TROs), preliminary injunctions, and permanent injunctions. The first two types are orders issued in the conduct of litigation, while the final type, the permanent injunction, is a form of judgment issued after full litigation of the merits of a civil action. This chapter deals with preliminary injunctions and TROs as part of the procedure for litigating a civil action in American courts. The law governing permanent injunctions is part of the substantive law of remedies, which is outside the scope of this work's discussion of American civil procedure. As with any other procedural matter, the procedures for granting or denying preliminary injunctions and TROs vary somewhat among the many American court systems – the federal courts, and those of the fifty states. Most of the states, however, follow rules that are patterned after the guidelines for issuing preliminary injunctions and TROs set forth in Rule 65 of the Federal Rules of Civil Procedure. Our discussion will therefore focus on Rule 65.

§1. Temporary Restraining Orders

214. A district court may issue a TRO without notice to the adverse party, or ex parte. Because judicial action affecting one's legal rights without notice to that party is rare and may implicate constitutional due-process concerns, a TRO without notice is of necessity an emergency action of limited duration. Moreover, a TRO applicant must demonstrate that the applicant's need of judicial protection is immediate and necessary to avoid irreparable harm or injury.

Rule 65(b) provides for a TRO under two conjunctive circumstances. First, a TRO applicant must compellingly demonstrate via affidavit or verified complaint that irreparable damage, loss, or injury will occur before the opposing party or its attorney can be heard in opposition. An example of proper circumstances of irreparable harm is provided by a district court case, *Merrill Lynch v. Bishop.*[1] In that case, the plaintiff sufficiently supported its motion for a TRO when it showed that the defendant employee's use of the plaintiff's client lists was in violation of an employment agreement. On the other hand, another district court failed to find a sufficient showing of irreparable harm where a plaintiff, asserting an environmental interest, sought to enjoin the destruction of forty acres of timber because the plaintiff had visited the site once only and the tract was but a fraction of 260,000 acres of forest.[2]

Second, a TRO applicant's attorney must certify to the court in writing what efforts the attorney has undertaken to notify adverse parties, accompanied by reasons why formal notice should not be required. While formal notice complying with Rule 4 is ideal, the Advisory Committee Note to the 1966 amendment of Rule 65 observes that the rule is designed to encourage efforts at notifying an opposing party no matter how informally. A telephone call to the opponent's counsel may suffice and is preferable to no notice at all. In a 1968 case, the US Supreme Court tacitly endorsed this practice, noting that its jurisprudence permits ex parte issuance of TROs but cautioning district courts that a TRO should not be issued without notice unless the movant's showing of irreparable harm is compelling and the movant has demonstrated that all reasonable efforts towards notice have been exhausted.[3]

Once the movant has satisfied Rule 65(b)'s initial requirements, the district court retains discretion whether or not to issue the TRO.[4] If the court decides to grant the TRO, it must endorse the order with the date and time of issuance. So issued, the order lasts for no longer than ten days unless good cause can be shown for an extension. Next, the district court must schedule an adversarial hearing to consider a preliminary injunction "at the earliest possible time."[5] The hearing date takes precedence over all other court matters except for older matters of the same character. Finally, Rule 65(b) provides that after two day's notice, or such shorter time as the court prescribes, the adverse party may move and appear for the purpose of dissolving the order, modifying the order, or both. In such an event, Rule 65(b) requires the district court to conduct a hearing on the adverse party's motion "as expeditiously as the ends of justice require."[6]

1. *Merrill Lynch, Pierce, Fenner & Smith, Inc. v. Bishop*, 839 F. Supp. 68 (D. Me. 1993).
2. *See Donham v. U.S. Department of Agriculture*, 725 F. Supp. 985 (S.D. Ill. 1989).
3. *See Carroll v. President & Commissioners of Princess Anne*, 393 U.S. 175 (1968). *See also Granny Goose Foods v. Brotherhood of Teamsters*, 415 U.S. 423 (1974); *Samson v. Murray*, 415 U.S. 61 (1974).
4. *See* Fed. R. Civ. P. 65(b) ("A temporary restraining order *may* be granted without written or oral notice to the adverse party or that party's attorney…") (emphasis added).
5. Fed. R. Civ. P. 65(b).
6. Id.

§2. Preliminary Injunctions

215. Rule 65(a) controls a district court's use of preliminary injunctions. The rule, in subparagraph 1, simply states that no injunction shall be issued without notice to the adverse party. Subparagraph 2 authorizes the court to consolidate any motion for a preliminary injunction into a trial on the merits, at its discretion. In practice, courts have generally applied the standards discussed above concerning a TRO in deciding whether to issue a preliminary injunction. More specifically, several courts have resorted to a multifactor test in determining whether to use their injunctive powers. An Eleventh Circuit case, *United States v. Jefferson County*,[1] is representative. In that case, white male firefighters of Jefferson County sought to enjoin the implementation of consent decrees designed to remedy racial and sexual discrimination within the county's fire department, arguing that if the decrees were to take effect, their interests would be adversely affected. In rejecting their motion for injunctive relief, the court enunciated four prerequisites that the movant must satisfy to gain injunctive relief. The movant must show a substantial likelihood:

(1) that he will ultimately prevail on the merits;
(2) that he will suffer irreparable injury unless the court grants injunctive relief;
(3) that prospective injury to the movant outweighs any harm to the adverse party; and
(4) that an injunction, if issued, would not violate the public interest.[2]

The US Supreme Court recently added a further limitation to a district court's power to issue injunctions. In *Grupo Mexicano de Desarollo, S.A. v. Alliance Bond Fund, Inc.*,[3] an investment group that had purchased unsecured notes issued by a Mexican toll-road operator alleged that the operator had defaulted on its obligations under the notes. The group sued for damages, and sought a preliminary injunction to prevent the notes from being assigned to the Mexican government. The district court issued the requested injunction and the Second Circuit affirmed. The US Supreme Court reversed the lower courts, holding inter alia that a district court lacked the power to issue a preliminary injunction regarding the disposition of assets incident to a mere damages action in which no lien or equitable claim had been asserted.[4]

Once the court decides to issue a preliminary injunction or TRO, Rule 65 imposes two further conditions. First, Rule 65(c) requires the applicant to post security in an amount the court deems proper to cover any possible damage the opponent may suffer as a result of a wrongful injunction. However, the rule exempts the United States, its officers, or its agencies from the security requirement. Second, the court, by dint of Rule 65(d), must set forth with specificity the reasons for the order, its terms, the acts the order seeks to restrain, and limit the order to litigant parties and their agents.

Finally, Rule 65(e) exempts from its conditions any injunctions authorized by Acts of Congress relating to employment or interpleader, and in actions under 28 U.S.C. §2284, i.e., those rare civil actions that must be heard and determined by a special district-court panel of three judges.

1. *United States v. Jefferson County*, 720 F.2nd 1511 (11th Cir. 1983).
2. *See* id., at 1519.
3. *Grupo Mexicano de Desarollo, S.A. v. Alliance Bond Fund, Inc.*, 527 U.S. 308 (1999).
4. It has since been held by a lower court that a district court may permissibly issue a preliminary injunction freezing a defendant's assets if the underlying claim asserts a right to *both* legal and equitable remedies. *See United States ex rel. Rahman v. Oncology Associates*, 198 F.3rd 489 (4th Cir. 1999).

§3. Injunctive Relief Incident to Arbitration

216. As a related matter, arbitration procedures (discussed generally in Part X) may allow arbitrators to issue TROs and preliminary injunctions.[1] However, arbitration participants seeking to enforce such orders must resort to the courts to do so. In such a case, the orders are treated under the Federal Arbitration Act as any other arbitration order or award.[2] Accordingly, commentators on the subject have noted that such treatment only delays the arbitration proceeding, undermining the privacy and efficiency of the arbitral process. Some commentators have thus suggested that counsel should consider avoiding arbitration where she would need to seek preliminary injunctive relief or a TRO.[3]

1. *See, e.g.*, American Arbitration Association, *Commercial Arbitration Rules* (1999), Rules 36, 45.
2. *See infra* para. 294.
3. *See, e.g.*, Mark A. Buckstein, "An Introductory Primer on Pre-Litigation: ADR Counseling for the Outside Lawyer," Disp. Resol. J. 52-Jan. (1997): 35.

Part VI. Legal Aid and Legal Costs

Chapter 1. Legal Aid

217. The charity of private lawyers provided all civil legal aid in the United States prior to 1965.[1] At that time, legal-aid societies had an annual budget of USD 4 million with which they employed around 600 lawyers.[2] But this amount represented just 2% of total expenditures for the employment of all attorneys in the country.[3] Legal-aid societies were a major source of employment for female and minority attorneys who could not obtain access to private law firms.[4] Many local bars expressed hostility to legal-aid societies; solo practitioners feared legal aid would harm their businesses.[5]

In 1965, private legal-aid societies were joined by the United States' first government-sponsored legal-aid program. The Office of Economic Opportunity established the Legal Services Program (LSP) that year as part of President Lyndon Johnson's "Great Society" programs. In the five years immediately after LSP's creation, the nation's total legal-aid civil caseload tripled and the total budget more than quadrupled.[6] The LSP passionately sought not just to provide basic legal services to the poor on a case-by-case basis, but also to reform the laws that affected poor people most. LSP fought for an extension of equal-protection and due-process rights in regard to public benefits, as well as increased access to the courts for the indigent.[7] In pursuit of these goals, the LSP managed to bring a total of 119 of its cases before the US Supreme Court for plenary review in just ten years, from 1965 to 1974.[8]

The LSP and its goals were met with resistance from governors of numerous states, including California, Arizona, Connecticut, Illinois, Louisiana, Montana, and the Dakotas, all of whom resisted state monetary contribution to LSP funding.[9] President Richard Nixon's administration sought to stop the growth of the LSP and to depoliticize the organization. In 1975, the LSP was dismantled and replaced by a new agency, the Legal Services Corporation (LSC).[10] Under President Jimmy Carter's administration, federally sponsored legal aid, now embodied by the LSC, enjoyed a sixfold budget increase. Additionally, more than 6,000 lawyers were now involved.[11]

Notwithstanding this growth, many commentators viewed the advent of the LSC as a sign that legal aid in the United States was becoming less relevant in important policy-making matters.[12] The LSC, unlike the LSP before it, was prohibited from engaging in "political" activities such as ballot measures, facilitating abortions, desegregation of schools, and the like. The focus of government-sponsored legal aid changed from expanding the rights of the impoverished to providing basic legal services to the poor.[13]

Funding for the LSC is based on the number of clients it serves. As a result, LSC lawyers end up managing huge caseloads even though they engage in very little actual courtroom litigation. About a million and a half cases were handled by legal-aid entities in 1991, but only a few ever reached trial; in 1987, 389 state court cases and 157 federal court cases were litigated by legal-aid lawyers.[14] The large caseloads legal-aid lawyers must handle necessitate quick processing and disposition. Most advice from legal-aid sources is given to clients over the phone. Cases are most often resolved through negotiated settlement, which is much faster than a trial. The adversaries of legal-aid clients enjoy the advantage of knowing that most legal-aid cases can never afford to proceed to trial.[15]

The high caseloads and limited budgets also create problems for legal-aid organizations to staff their lawyer ranks. Although legal-aid positions now attract top law school graduates, low pay and the frustration of spending so little time on each case lead to a high turnover rate for legal-aid attorneys.[16] Private firms do donate time, called pro bono work, to legal-aid organizations. However, in the larger firms with the greatest resources, the burden of taking care of legal-aid cases usually falls to the most junior, and inexperienced, staff members, who often use pro bono matters to gain experience to then be used in the for-profit work.[17]

The LSC has also suffered from being seen as a political body, even though its statutory mandate imposes limits on political activity. Many leaders of the Republican Party have viewed the LSC as taxpayer support for liberal ideologues. Consequently, during President Ronald Reagan's administration the LSC budget was reduced by one-third. Large numbers of the program's attorneys and staff members were laid off.[18] However, the LSC is still the largest source of local legal-aid budgets. To fill the void left by federal cuts, many state programs have been set up to divert to legal-aid programs the interest accrued by attorneys in trust accounts.[19] The US Supreme Court at one time held that the interest earned on client funds is the private property of the clients for purposes of the Fifth Amendment's Takings Clause.[20] The Supreme Court has since ruled, however, that clients are entitled to nothing as "just compensation" for any such takings, since they would have made no income on these funds had the state not pooled them to generate legal-aid resources.[21] The Court also ruled that these schemes are not barred by the Fifth Amendment's "public use" requirement inasmuch as generating income for legal aid is indeed a "public use."[22]

An individual client's eligibility for legal-aid assistance depends upon the income of the individual and the type of case for which she is seeking assistance. No legal aid is provided for personal-injury cases, on the theory that plaintiffs in those case are more likely to be able to find private attorneys who will take their cases for contingency fees, described below (paragraph 219). Cases where there is little or no chance of a contingency-fee arrangement with a private lawyer, such as family or landlord-tenant disputes, are given priority. Unfortunately, many persons who meet all these eligibility requirements still do not receive legal assistance due to the limited resources available.[23]

A consequence of turning otherwise qualified people away from legal aid has been a dramatic increase in the number of people trying to represent themselves. *Pro per* litigation, where a party acts as his own lawyer, has become especially common in California, where nearly two-thirds of family law cases are *pro per*. Aside from placing the indigent client at a disadvantage at trial, *pro per* cases place additional burdens on the courts. On account of their inexperience in the courtroom and lack of legal training, *pro per* litigants significantly slow down the court system. This is especially true when a *pro per* litigant tries to handle a complex case. Nor can the problem be fully solved by judges and clerks, who must maintain impartiality in the courtroom, and thus cannot actively assist *pro per* litigants.[24]

1. For a brief history of pre-1965 legal aid, *see generally* Earl Johnson Jr, *Justice and Reform* (1974).
2. Richard L. Abel, "Law without Politics: Legal Aid under Advanced Capitalism," U.C.L.A. L. Rev. 32 (1985): 474, 542.
3. Id.
4. Id., at 510-511.
5. Id., at 499.
6. Id., at 545.
7. *See generally* Johnson, *supra*, at 126-134 (discussing the development of law reform as the "priority management goal" within the LSP).
8. Allen Redlich, "Who Will Litigate Constitutional Issues for the Poor?," Hastings Const. L. Q. 19 (1992): 745, 752.
9. *See* Abel, *supra*, at 526.
10. Redlich, *supra*, at 757.
11. Abel, *supra*, at 546.
12. Id., at 546-550.
13. Redlich, *supra*, at 758.
14. Id., at 762.
15. Abel, *supra*, at 570-579.
16. Id., at 580; Redlich, *supra*, at 758.
17. *See* Abel, *supra*, at 580-581.
18. Id., at 547-548.
19. *See, e.g.*, Frances A. Koncilja, "Colorado Bar Association President's Message to Members," 24 Colo. Law. 24 (1995): 9 (discussing Colorado's attempts to fund legal aid via trust fund interest).
20. *See Phillips v. Washington Legal Foundation*, 524 U.S. 156 (1998). This decision was sensitive to the particular nature of the beneficial ownership of attorney trust funds under the law of Texas, the state in question. It is possible that similar programs set up under the property laws of other states might not be held to be unconstitutional takings of private property.
21. *Brown v. Legal Foundation of Washington*, 538 U.S. 216 (2003).
22. Id.
23. *See generally* John F. Vargo, "The American Rule on Attorney Fee Allocation: The Injured Person's Access to Justice," Am. U.L. Rev. 42 (1993): 1567. As of 2007, the maximum income of individuals eligible for legal aid was USD 12,763 if that person lived alone. Maximum eligible income rose gradually depending upon family size, e.g., USD 25,813 for a family of four, and USD 43,213 for a family of eight. These figures were slightly higher for residents of Alaska and Hawaii. *See* Alan W. Houseman, *Civil Legal Aid in the United States: An Update for 2007* (Center for Law and Social Policy, 2007), available at <www.clasp.org/publications/civil_legal_aid_2007.pdf> (last visited 6 Aug. 2008).
24. *See generally* Suzanne Northington, "Pro Per Behavior: Filings in Pro Per are Up – Way Up – in Family Court," Cal. Law. 14-May (1994): 29.

Chapter 2. Legal Costs

§1. ATTORNEYS' FEES

I. The American Rule

218. The "American Rule" is a term commonly used to refer to the convention in the United States that each party pays its own attorney's fees and court costs, regardless of which party wins the case.[1] Usually, but not always (see below), each client pays his lawyer at an hourly rate. Under the American rule, any damages award made to a victorious plaintiff fails to fully compensate plaintiff to the extent that the plaintiff must use part (or in some cases all) of the award to pay her attorney.[2] An alternative regime in which the losing party bears the litigation costs of both sides (sometimes known as the "English Rule") would ensure full compensation to victorious plaintiffs, and would also save a victorious defendant from being hurt by having to pay for a winning defense. Such a regime, however, would deter plaintiffs and defendants from asserting good-faith claims and defenses, respectively, when the possibility of attorney's fees in the entire case is too economically frightening. In this regard, one must remember that valid claims and winning defenses do not always prevail – all litigation has a certain element of unpredictability.[3] The American rule sacrifices full compensation for victorious plaintiffs and defendants, in order to preserve access to courts on the part of parties who have the ability to finance their own lawyers but no more.[4]

In reality, the American rule is less an iron-clad rule than a presumption that can be rebutted in certain conditions defined by statute and the common law.[5] For example, the filing of a frivolous paper in federal court can result in the imposition of the entire case's costs and fees against the offender, under Federal Rule of Civil Procedure 11 (see paragraphs 165, 177). The common law provides a similar exception; a plaintiff must pay the defendant's fees if the plaintiff brings a "malicious prosecution."[6] By federal statute, successful plaintiffs in civil-rights cases are generally able to recover their attorneys' fees.[7] Additionally, contracting parties can specify that the loser pay all fees and court costs should a dispute over the contract arise.[8]

1. *See* Vargo, *supra*, at 1569; *see also* Geoffrey C. Hazard, Jr et al., *Cases and Materials on Pleading and Procedure – State and Federal*, 9th edn (2005), 110-112.
2. *See* Hazard, *Pleading and Procedure, supra*, at 111.
3. *See* Vargo, *supra*, at 1608-1610.
4. *See* Hazard, *Pleading and Procedure, supra*, at 112.
5. *See, e.g., Serrano v. Priest*, 20 Cal.3rd 25, 569 P.2nd 1303 (1977) (awarding attorneys fees in public interest litigation via the equitable powers of the court); *see generally* Vargo, *supra*, at 1578-1590 (exhaustively detailing the exceptions to the American Rule allowing cost shifting).
6. Vargo, *supra*, at 1586.
7. *See* 42 U.S.C. §1988(b).
8. Vargo, *supra*, at 1578-1579.

II. The Contingency Fee

219. The contingency fee is a device attractive to parties (almost always plaintiffs) who are unable to finance their own side of a lawsuit, let alone the costs and fees incurred on the other side. The device essentially allows a party to borrow against the value of an expected recovery or saving. A lawyer agrees to represent the client in return for a portion of the recovery (or more rarely, a savings on the part of defendant who anticipates some liability) – usually 30%–35%. If the lawyer does not recover any award (or achieve any saving) for the client, the lawyer receives no pay for his or her work on that case. Consequently, most lawyers take contingency-fee cases only when the odds of a substantial recovery are high. In essence, contingency-fee lawyers serve as a pre-filing screening system for civil lawsuits. Stronger cases are taken on a contingent-fee basis and move forward. Weak cases with little or no likelihood of success are turned down if they cannot be resolved summarily, without protracted negotiation or litigation.[1]

The contingency-fee system is not without its critics. Some argue that it can encourage the under-lawyering of some cases. If a lawyer can settle a case early she can collect a fee with little expense, which translates into a high hourly rate and low risk.[2] Even if the client would win a much larger reward by taking the case to trial, the lawyer may generate more income per hour by settling early. Trial involves many hours of preparation, great expense, and the standing risk of an adverse judgment. A lawyer can settle multiple cases in the time it takes to try a single case. Thus, the contingency fee can encourage a lawyer to devote fewer resources to resolving a case than would be in the client's self-interest and may induce a lawyer to advise a client to settle when to do so serves the lawyer, but not the client.[3] Incidentally, the opposite effect is created by the hourly-fee approach, in which lawyers may be tempted to make more money by over-lawyering, spending unnecessary time on cases.[4]

Another way to look at the contingency fee is that it allows plaintiffs to pool their risks, in the same way that liability insurance allows potential defendants to pool their risks. However, in the case of the contingency fee, not all contribute to the pool; only winners pay. Since the fees from winners must cover the costs of all plaintiffs on contingency, winners' fees are higher than they otherwise would be. The ability to pool risks opens the courts to a greater number of claimants by providing legal representation to those who would otherwise be unable to afford the expense of asserting their legal rights.[5]

1. *See generally* id., at 1617-1619 (describing the operation and effect of typical contingency-fee arrangements).
2. For an exhaustive treatment of the "effective hourly rate" earned by attorneys while litigating cases on contingency fees, *see generally* Herbert M. Kritzer, "The Wages of Risk: The Returns of Contingency Fee Legal Practice," DePaul L. Rev. 47 (1998): 267.
3. *See* Angela Wennihan, "Let's Put the Contingency Back in the Contingency Fee," SMU L. Rev. 49 (1996): 1639, 1652-1662; the early settlement issue may be especially acute in class actions where a lawyer often receives "windfall fees". *See, e.g.*, Lester Brickman, "ABA Regulation of Contingency Fees: Money Talks, Ethics Walks," Fordham L. Rev. 65 (1996): 247, 276-283.
4. *See generally* David D. Rosenstein, "For Whom the Bill Tolls: Quantity, Not Quality, Becomes the Goal When Hourly Fees Prevail," A.B.A. J. 81-Nov (1995): 120 (discussing the drive to overbill clients to meet firm "billable hours" requirements).

5. *See generally* Lester Brickman, "Contingent Fees Without Contingencies: Hamlet Without the Prince of Denmark?," UCLA L. Rev. 37 (1989): 29, 42-44 (discussing the risk-allocation function of contingency fees); David Rosenberg, "Individual Justice and Collectivizing Risk-Based Claims in Mass-Exposure Cases," N.Y.U. L. Rev. 71 (1996): 210 (calling for greater aggregation of claims in mass-exposure toxic-tort cases to maximize the deterrent effect of litigation); *but cf.* Jonathan R. Macey and & Geoffrey P. Miller, "The Plaintiff's Attorney's Role in Class Action and Derivative Litigation: Economic Analysis and Recommendations for Reform," U. Chi. L. Rev. 58 (1991): 1 (suggesting reform in class-action contingency-fee structures to reduce the influence of a lawyer's economic interest in the outcome of the litigation).

Part VII. Evidence

Chapter 1. Introduction

220. The law of evidence in the United States is considered, and taught, as a body of law separate and distinct from civil procedure. Nonetheless, the law of evidence – namely, the rules governing the kinds of proof that can be submitted to or withheld from courts, and the weight that these proofs can or must be given – is obviously related to the rules of civil procedure. To give but one example, the right that procedural rules give the parties to compel disclosure of information from other parties as well as witnesses – so-called discovery rules – is shaped by the evidentiary rules concerning the kinds of things that ultimately can be considered at trial. Thus, for both the practitioner and the academic, anyone interested in the procedures of civil litigation will also need some basic understanding of the law of evidence. This chapter attempts to provide an entree for this understanding, and does so by using as a template the law of evidence as practiced in the federal courts in the United States. Readers should appreciate, of course, that like rules of procedure, rules of evidence in the United States vary from state to state; just as there are fifty-one procedural systems (those of the fifty states, plus that of the federal courts), so too are there fifty-one evidentiary systems. As with procedure proper, however, state evidentiary rules have been influenced by the federal model, which is codified in the Federal Rules of Evidence (FRE).

Chapter 2. Presumptions and Burdens of Proof

§1. DEFINITIONS

221. The burden of proof can be described as the duty borne by a party ultimately to convince the trier of fact (the jury or judge, depending on whether a jury trial is available) that all of the essential elements of his claim or defense are proved by the evidence presented. The burden of proof is sometimes also called the burden of persuasion. Under either terminology, a party who bears the burden but who fails to discharge it loses on the particular claim or defense at issue.

The burden of proof is to be distinguished from another burden often referred to in statutes and opinions – the burden of production (also called the burden of going forward). The burden of production is an initial burden to produce *some* evidence with respect to a particular fact or element in the proceeding, but not necessarily enough evidence that a finder of fact would be convinced as to that fact or element. A finder of fact may determine that a party who has discharged his burden of production has nonetheless failed to discharge his burden of proof. Generally speaking, if a party has the burden of proof on a particular element, he will also have the burden of production. There are many factors which influence which party the law places the burden of proof upon, including policy considerations such as the desire to encourage or discourage a particular type of litigation, and fairness considerations, such as which party has control over the evidence which bears on a fact or element.

Identifying who bears the *burden* of proof is to be distinguished from defining the *standard* of proof itself. In most civil cases in the United States, the standard of proof used is the preponderance-of-evidence standard; that is, a party who bears the burden of proof must adduce sufficient evidence to convince a finder of fact to conclude that a preponderance of the evidence weighs in his favor on the disputed fact or issue. The preponderance standard has, in turn, been defined to mean that a party who bears the burden must prove the disputed proposition asserted by that party is more likely true than not true. This preponderance standard is much less onerous than, for example, the standard used in most American criminal cases – the standard of "proof beyond a reasonable doubt." Under a reasonable-doubt standard, a finder of fact can believe that a criminal defendant is much more likely than not to be guilty, but nonetheless return a verdict of acquittal because not all reasonable doubt has been removed. In some civil lawsuits, for example those involving certain kinds of claims (like fraud or defamation), or certain remedies (like punitive damages), a standard of proof in between the preponderance and the reasonable-doubt standards is used, and is often called the "clear and convincing evidence" standard. In general, it is fair to say "the more important the rights at stake, the more important must be the procedural safeguards surrounding those rights,"[1] leading to application of a more demanding standard of proof.

1. *Murel v. Baltimore City Criminal Court*, 407 U.S. 355, 362 (1972) (quoting opinion from *Speiser v. Randall*, 357 U.S. 513, 520-521 (1958)).

§2. Applicability to Summary Judgment

222. For purposes of summary judgment, discussed in paragraphs 190-193, the party who bears the burden of proof at trial will bear the burden of proof at the summary-judgment stage as well. Thus, for example, a defendant who does not bear the burden of proof at trial can move for and obtain summary judgment without adducing any evidence at all, merely by demonstrating that the non-moving party – the plaintiff who bears the burden of proof – has not come forward with enough evidence of its own to discharge its burden under whichever standard of proof – the preponderance standard or the "clear and convincing evidence" standard – happens to govern the particular action. In this way, the burdens and standards of proof at trial track those applicable at the summary-judgment stage.

Chapter 3. Admissibility and Categories of Evidence

§1. Relevance and Prejudice

223. FRE 402 sets out a broad rule that no evidence can be admissible unless it is logically relevant, and that all logically relevant evidence is admissible, except as provided by the US Constitution, Act of Congress, or by the FRE or other rules prescribed by the US Supreme Court. Most of the important exceptions to the rule that relevant evidence is admissible are found in the FRE themselves.

The concept of logical relevance is itself defined in FRE 401, which says that relevant evidence is "evidence having any tendency to make the existence of any fact that is of consequence to the determination of the action more probable or less probable than it would be without the evidence." This test can be usefully broken down into two component questions:

(1) Does the proffered evidence make the existence of a fact more probable or less probable?
(2) Is that fact to which the evidence is relevant of consequence to the action? The answer to this second question obviously turns on the substantive law governing a dispute and the things that matter under the substantive legal standard.

Facts are of consequence to the action – or "material" – if they are legally significant. Material facts include those which themselves comprise the elements of a claim or defense, as alleged in the pleadings. They also include facts from which inferences can be drawn that amount to circumstantial evidence of the elements of the claim or defense, as well as facts which bear upon the credibility of witnesses and other evidence. In some courts, if the facts to be proved by particular evidence are not in dispute, the evidence may not be presented to the jury.[1]

> "Relevance" is a term used to describe both logical relevance within the meaning of Rules 401 and 402, and the ultimate judicial conclusion of whether a piece of evidence is relevant enough in light of other factors to be admitted – so-called legal relevance. Legal relevance is determined by application of FRE 403, which provides that judges have the discretion to exclude logically relevant evidence "if the probative value is substantially outweighed by the danger of unfair prejudice, confusion of the issues, or misleading the jury, or by considerations of undue delay, waste of time, or needless presentation of cumulative evidence."

Thus, evidence will be considered legally irrelevant and excluded under Rule 403, where – notwithstanding some logical relevance of the evidence – the trial judge believes, due to the emotionally charged component of the evidence, that there is a genuine risk that the emotions of the jury will be excited to irrational behavior, and that this risk is disproportionate to the probative or logical value of the offered evidence. In making a decision under FRE 403, the reviewing court must look at the evidence in a light most favorable to its proponent, maximizing its probative value and minimizing its prejudicial effect.

Courts have identified a number of different ways in which possible problems can arise such that evidence ought to be excluded under Rule 403. Three important ones are:

(1) Prejudice due to the inflammatory nature of some evidence: the jury is so emotionally aroused that it will use its verdict to react to the evidence.
(2) Prejudice arising from improper use of evidence: the evidence may be admissible on one point but not another and the danger is high that the jury will use it to deliberate on the wrong point.
(3) Prejudice arising from undue weight given to evidence: the evidence is relevant, but the jury will give it more weight than it is worth because of its emotional nature.

It is important to remember that all evidence is subject to Rule 403 discretion and may properly be excluded under it.

1. *United States v. Wasman,* 700 F.2nd 663, 665 (11th Cir. 1983).

§2. Specific Categories of Relevant Evidence

224. Rules 404-412 cover evidence that has repeatedly been found to be so prejudicial that it is routinely excluded from proceedings. These rules make a number of categories of evidence generally inadmissible, subject to important exceptions.

I. Character Evidence

225. Rule 404 prohibits the use of evidence about someone's "character" for the purpose of proving "action in conformity therewith on a particular occasion." However, if the character of the party is a genuine issue in the case – because the applicable substantive law makes it a question that legally matters or otherwise – evidence of that character may be admitted. Rule 404 also provides other exceptions to its blanket prohibition. Thus, a pertinent character trait of the accused in a criminal proceeding, evidence of a pertinent trait of character of the victim, and evidence of the character of a witness may all be presented under some circumstances. For example, the pertinent-trait doctrine would often permit a party to show a character trait for untruthfulness in an action for fraud. Moreover, evidence of other crimes, wrongs, or acts not admissible to prove the character of a party only to show general propensity for committing those acts may be admissible for other purposes, including motive, opportunity, intent, preparation, absence of mistake or accident, knowledge, and identity. However, the judge still has discretion under Rule 403 to exclude any unfairly prejudicial evidence. When character is admissible, Rule 405 permits character to be shown by reputation or opinion when the character trait is not an essential element of the claim. In those instances when the character trait is an essential element of the claim, the trait may be shown by evidence of specific instances of conduct, even if the conduct includes illegal activities.

Rule 406 draws a distinction between character evidence and evidence of habit. Under FRE 406, evidence of the habit of a person or of routine practices of an organization, whether there is eyewitness testimony to support the evidence or not, is admissible to prove the conduct of a person or organization on a particular occasion in conformity with the habit or routine practice. The difference between habit and routine practice is that "habit" is the frequently repeated specific behavior pattern of an individual, whereas "routine practice" refers to the behavioral patterns of an entity.

II. Subsequent Remedial Measures

226. Rule 407 prohibits evidence of changes or repairs made after the event in question has occurred, which if made "previously would have made the event less likely to occur," when the evidence is being offered to prove negligence or culpable conduct in connection with the event. The evidence may be offered for other purposes, including "proving ownership, control, or feasibility of precautionary measures, or impeachment," if any of these facts is disputed.

The policy behind Rule 407 is straightforward: society does not want to do anything that discourages parties from making repairs or changes after an accident. FRE 407 also reflects the belief that a change in design after an accident does not necessarily mean that the original design was defective, and that not all triers of fact will be analytically careful in this regard. In some jurisdictions, evidence of subsequent remedial measures will be admitted if the action is one involving strict liability, i.e., liability without fault. The federal courts do not follow that view.

III. Compromise and Offers to Compromise

227. Rule 408 prohibits evidence of "(1) furnishing or offering or promising to furnish or (2) accepting or offering or promising to accept a valuable consideration in compromising or attempting to compromise a claim which was disputed as to either validity or amount if the evidence is used to prove liability for or invalidity of the claim or its amount." Evidence of conduct or statements made in compromise negotiations are also inadmissible under this rule. For Rule 408 to apply, a legal claim must be involved, either in the future, or at the time of the attempted settlement. Moreover, liability for the claim or the amount of the claim must be in dispute. Rule 408 applies to attempted settlements with the opposing party, as well as to completed settlements made with others involved in the same occurrence.

Settlement evidence, like evidence of repair under Rule 407, may be admissible for purposes other than liability, including: proving bias or prejudice; negating a contention of undue delay; or proving an effort to obstruct a criminal investigation or prosecution.

Rule 409 provides that evidence of furnishing or offering or promising to pay medical and similar expenses caused by the injury is not admissible to prove liability for the injury.

IV. Liability Insurance

228. Rule 411 is designed to encourage the procuring of liability insurance undeterred by the fear that liability will be predicated on this very act. FRE 411 provides that "evidence that a person was or was not insured against liability is not admissible upon the issue whether the person acted negligently or otherwise wrongfully." The evidence may be admissible if offered for another purpose, such as proof of agency ownership or control (when in dispute), or bias or prejudice of a witness. The evidence may also be admitted where admission of liability comes by implication from a reference to the fact or effect of insurance, as when an alleged tortfeasor tells the injured party: "Don't worry. My insurance company will take care of everything."

§3. The Hearsay Rule and Exceptions

229. All American jurisdictions have rules governing the use of hearsay statements in judicial proceedings. "Hearsay" is defined as an out-of-court statement, offered to prove the truth of the matter asserted in the statement. Hearsay need not be an oral statement. Written assertions and nonverbal assertive conduct may also be considered hearsay. In most cases, evidence that meets the hearsay definition will be excluded from the proceeding.

The rationale for the prohibition is three-fold. First, live witnesses are required to take the oath, whereas out-of-court declarants are (in most cases) not under oath when they make their statement. Second, if the declarant gives testimony in front of the finder of fact, the finder of fact can evaluate the demeanor of the witness and use its observations to aid in measuring credibility. Finally, out-of-court declarants are not subject to cross-examination. During cross-examination, the witness may be probed concerning his veracity, the accuracy of initial perceptions, and the quality of his memory.

In order to challenge a statement as hearsay, the opponent of the evidence must show that the statement was offered for a purpose that implicates the credibility of the out-of-court declarant. If, for example, a statement is offered to simply show that certain words were spoken – i.e., that the statement was, in fact, made – it will not be excluded as hearsay, because the out-of-court declarant's credibility would not be implicated. Instead, the finder of fact can assess the credibility of the person who heard the statement being made. Examples of this include when a party wants to offer an out-of-court statement he heard as evidence of the declarant's mental state at the time in question, or where the mere speaking of words is a fact in itself that has legal operation, such as words that constitute an oral contract.

Thus, the rule against admitting hearsay is limited by the definition of hearsay itself. It is also limited by several explicit exceptions, many of which are codified in the FRE. Some of the important ones are discussed below.

I. Admissions

230. Under FRE 801(d)(2), the federal courts recognize a category of out-of-court statements that otherwise fall within the general definition of hearsay, but are nonetheless deemed not to be hearsay at all. In other jurisdictions the same types of statements are similarly admissible in evidence, but on a slightly different rationale. Instead of being defined as non-hearsay statements, they are treated as hearsay but are admitted into evidence as exceptions to the general rule of the inadmissibility of hearsay. This exceptional category includes admissions of a party opponent, prior guilty pleas, judicial admissions, vicarious admissions and statements of co-conspirators.

To be considered an admission of a party opponent, the statement must be offered into evidence against the party who made it. It is not required that the statement be against the interest of the party when it was made and the statement need not be based upon personal knowledge of the declarant.

Judicial admissions include the contents of a complaint or answer filed in the proceeding. Like admissions of a party opponent, they are offered against the party who made them. Admissions included in this category include inconsistent allegations made in the pleadings, allegations in earlier pleadings now superseded by amendment, and allegations against another party in the same or a related case. However, the modern trend is toward giving pleadings less weight and attention. Accordingly, some courts are reluctant to admit this evidence, believing that juries do not understand the purpose of pleadings and may misuse the evidence.

Vicarious admissions include statements made by agents of a party opponent. This may seem like an unusual exception because the statements being presented were not actually made by the party against whom they are offered. But this exception is primarily used in situations where the party opponent is a corporation or other organization which, technically, cannot speak. Most courts are willing to accept that statements made by employees of the organization are made for the organization, and allow introduction of the evidence as an admission by the organization.

The co-conspirator exception, to be applicable, requires that the statement be made by the co-conspirator of a party and that the statement be made during the course and in furtherance of the conspiracy. In determining the existence of the conspiracy, the judge is allowed to consider the statement at issue along with any other evidence to aid his decision.

II. Unavailability Exceptions

231. Under FRE 804(a), certain forms of witness unavailability will justify admission of hearsay by an out-of-court witness. These include death, physical or mental illness, refusal to testify, lack of memory concerning the incident, or witnesses who have been exempted from testifying on the ground of privilege, are beyond the subpoena power of the court, or are missing.

III. Declarations against Interest

232. FRE 804(b)(3) permits hearsay statements that are against a declarant's pecuniary, proprietary, or penal interest to be admissible against him. In order for a statement against the declarant's penal interest to be admissible, corroborating circumstances must clearly indicate the trustworthiness of the statement. Courts have been divided over whether to admit statements that accompany statements against interest. There are three primary views on these so-called collateral statements:

(1) Some courts allow in all collateral statements. The implicit assumption by these courts is that the declarant was in a "truth-telling frame of mind."
(2) Some courts allow in collateral neutral statements, but exclude self-serving statements.
(3) Some courts refuse to admit both self-serving and neutral statements.

In *Williamson v. United States*, the US Supreme Court adopted the most restrictive view for the federal courts and refused to admit both self-serving and neutral statements.[1] Justice O'Connor, announcing the opinion of the court, stated that "the fact that a statement is collateral to a self-inculpatory statement says nothing at all about the collateral statement's reliability."[2] Reliability is often cited as the central focus in decisions concerning hearsay statements.

1. *Williamson v. United States*, 512 U.S. 594 (1994).
2. Id., at 600.

IV. Dying Declarations

233. Declarations by a person who is dying are admissible under FRE 804(b)(2), provided that the declarant is unavailable at the time of trial, and the declarant believed that his own death was imminent at the time of the statement. Most courts also require that the declarant actually died as a result of the incident.

V. Comparability Exceptions

234. Comparability exceptions involve statements which, in light of the surrounding circumstances, are presumed to be reliable. The declarant need not be unavailable for the evidence to be admitted. These include excited utterances, statements of present sense impression, statements of recent perception, statements of physical condition, statements of present state of mind, statements of present and past recollection, business records, and public records.

VI. Excited Utterances

235. FRE 803(2) defines an excited utterance as "a statement relating to a startling event or condition made while the declarant was under the stress of excitement caused by the event or condition." Some jurisdictions also require that the statement be spontaneous and not made in response to questions.

Courts believe that the circumstances surrounding the statement lend special reliability because there is generally not enough time between the event and the statement to fabricate the content of the statement. It is also believed that if the declarant testifies in court, his perception may not be as clear as when the event occurred, such that the excited utterance is actually more reliable than the live testimony.

VII. Present Sense Impression

236. FRE 803(1) recognizes an exception for statements narrating a present sense impression. The statement must describe the event at issue and have been made almost simultaneously with the event described.

VIII. Statement of Recent Perception

237. A statement of recent perception is similar to a present sense impression, but the requirement of simultaneity has been relaxed, which allows the admission of the statement as long as the declarant made the statement while his recollection of the event was still clear. At least one jurisdiction prohibits these statements if made in contemplation of litigation. This exception was included in the proposed FRE, but Congress refused to approve it, unwilling to risk the increased likelihood of fabrication by the declarant.

IX. Statements of Present Physical Condition or State of Mind

238. FRE 803(c) permits a hearsay exception for statements of the declarant's existing state of mind, emotion, sensation, or physical condition. The rationale for this exception is that there is no danger of the declarant misperceiving or misremembering the facts asserted. However, statements of memory are specifically excluded from this exception. For statements of physical condition, under the federal rules, there is no requirement that the statement be made to a treating physician.

The exception for statements of physical condition has been narrowly construed to exclude certain accompanying statements that bear no relationship to the diagnosis or treatment of the condition. For example, a statement that declarant was struck by a car would qualify, but not an accompanying statement that the car was driven through a red light.

The rationale for statements of present state of mind is similar. Since the declarant is describing the state of his mind at the very minute he is making the statement, there is no danger that his memory will be incorrect. It is believed that if called as a witness at trial, the declarant is more likely to fabricate or misremember what his state of mind was on an earlier occasion because the significance of a particular state of mind would now be apparent. Furthermore, it is relatively easy to lie about a matter as personal and internal as one's state of mind on a past occasion.

X. Present and Past Recollection

239. Witnesses are permitted to review any writings before and/or during testimony to refresh their recollection on a factual issue. The writing need not have been made by the witness himself nor made immediately after the event in question. However, the witness must swear that he is genuinely refreshed by the writing and not using the document as a cloak for getting in evidence contained in an otherwise inadmissible document. FRE 612 states that if a witness uses a writing to refresh memory for the purpose of testifying, an adverse party is entitled to have the writing produced, inspect it, cross-examine the witness, and "to introduce in evidence those portions which relate to the testimony of the witness."

FRE 803(5) permits a witness to testify concerning the accuracy of a memorandum or record "concerning a matter about which the witness once had knowledge, but now has insufficient recollection to enable the witness to testify fully and accurately." In order for 803(5) to apply, the writing must have been made by the witness when the facts were still fresh in his memory, the witness must have firsthand knowledge of the incident, and the witness must testify that the record was accurate when made.

Introducing documents under FRE 803(5) differs from using writings to refresh memory in that under 803(5), the writing is actually replacing the live testimony with the hearsay contained in the document. The document itself is not allowed in unless offered by an adverse party, but it may be read into evidence.

XI. Business Records

240. FRE 803(6) provides an exception to the hearsay rule for records made in the regular course of business. In order to qualify under the exception, the record must have been made at or near the event and prepared in a trustworthy manner. The record must also have been one routinely made for the business and used in decision making. There is no requirement that the recordmaker be unavailable for trial. The rationale for this exception is that the person making the record knows that the business relies on the accuracy of the record and that the record will be used by the business in its future operations and decisions.

XII. Public Records

241. FRE 803(8) similarly provides an exception to the hearsay rule for records, reports, etc. of public offices or agencies setting forth activities of the office, matters observed pursuant to duty imposed by law, and statements and factual findings in civil actions and proceedings against the government.

Chapter 4. Administration of Evidence

§1. Types of Evidence

242. There are three basic types of evidence used in judicial proceedings: direct evidence, circumstantial evidence, and real evidence. "Direct evidence" is eyewitness testimony and other testimony that goes directly to the proposition to be established. If the direct testimony is believed, the proposition will be established. Direct evidence cannot be objected to as irrelevant.

"Circumstantial evidence" is evidence of circumstances that requires the finder of fact to draw an inference. Contrary to popular opinion, there is nothing inherently weak about circumstantial evidence. It simply requires the finder of fact to take the extra step and make an inference. Circumstantial evidence can be objected to as irrelevant. "Real evidence," when presented, permits the trier of fact to make his own determination. Real evidence is based on the juror's or judge's own perceptions, often using senses other than sight in making the determination. For example, a sample of intoxicating liquor may be given to the jury from which they will decide, based upon their own observations, if it is actually intoxicating liquor. Other examples of real evidence include photographs, bodily demonstrations, models, maps, and the results of experiments usually conducted out of court.

Evidence can be presented in many forms, including oral testimony, scientific data and analysis, documents, and physical objects. The finder of fact is also often allowed to actually visit the location where a relevant event occurred.

§2. Authentication and Identification

243. The FRE require authentication or identification of all proffered evidence as a prerequisite to their admission. FRE 901(a) provides that the requirement is satisfied "by evidence sufficient to support a finding that the matter in question is what its proponent claims."

Rule 901(b) provides a non-exclusive list of examples of authentication or identification in conformance with the requirements. Examples include testimony of a witness with knowledge, comparison by trier of fact or expert witness, existence of distinctive characteristics, public records and reports, ancient documents, and data compilations.

Some types of evidence are self-authenticating. Rule 902 furnishes examples of self-authenticating evidence, including public documents under seal or bearing an authorized signature, foreign public documents, certified copies of public records, newspapers and periodicals, official publications, and documents accompanied by a certificate of acknowledgment.

Most authentication and identification of documents and items is conducted during the pretrial proceedings. This prevents most inadmissible evidence from being shown to the jury. Authentication may be accomplished through a pleading, a stipulation, an interrogatory, or an agreement reached during a pretrial conference.

§3. Best Evidence Rule

244. The best evidence rule is the name given to the law's preference for the production of an original of a writing, recording, or photograph, where the contents of the item are material. The rule was developed at common law to prevent inaccuracy and fraud. FRE 1001 provides definitions of writing, recording, photograph, original, and duplicate. FREs 1002-1007 discuss the intricacies of the best evidence rule.

FRE 1002 requires that to prove the content of a writing, recording, or photograph, the original must be introduced. If the terms of the document are not at issue, the original is not required and either a duplicate or testimony concerning the document may be admitted. Under FRE 1004, if the original is required and not produced, secondary evidence may be admitted upon the showing that the original is lost or destroyed or otherwise not obtainable, the original is in the possession of the opponent, or the document is not closely related to a controlling issue. Secondary evidence may include a photocopy of the original, oral testimony as to its contents, deposition testimony, or proof by affidavit.

FRE 1005 permits certified copies of public records to be admitted into evidence without the need to show inability to obtain the original document.

FRE 1006 permits the contents of voluminous writings, recordings, or photographs which cannot be conveniently presented in court in their original state to be summarized and presented to the jury in the form of a chart, summary, or calculation.

FRE 1007 provides that if the proffering party can get the opposing party to testify as to the contents of the writing, either through deposition, or written admission, the offering party need not account for nonproduction of the original.

§4. Witness Competency

245. In order to give testimony, a witness must be considered competent. Competency is to be distinguished from credibility. Competency requires the witness to be able to possess the mental and physical capacity to perceive, record, recollect, and recount information, and is determined as a preliminary matter by the judge. Credibility goes to the weight the finder of fact assigns to the testimony of a particular witness. Things affecting the weight of testimony include personal interest in the result of the proceeding, age, moral incapacity, physical capacity at the time of the perception (including intoxication), conviction of a crime, and relationship to parties in the action.

Competency and credibility are both to be distinguished from admissibility. A witness may be both competent and able to give credible testimony, yet be barred from testifying to certain matters found inadmissible under the FRE or by the courts.

FRE 601, a general rule of competency, provides that "every person is competent to be a witness except as otherwise provided in these rules." This broad standard has been held to mean that in order to meet the minimum competency requirements the witness must be able to record, observe, and recollect information and understand his duty to tell the truth. Judges tend to resolve doubts involving the competency of a witness in favor of allowing the testimony.

Even witnesses that had been found by a court to be feeble-minded, in need of guardianship, or incompetent to stand trial may be found to be competent witnesses. However, the weight accorded the mentally deficient witness's testimony by the finder of fact will often be affected by his mental state.

246. FRE 602 is known as the "personal knowledge rule." It requires that witnesses testify only to matters of which they have personal knowledge. The witness may even use his own testimony to prove personal knowledge. Rule 602 requires that the witness actually observed, recorded, recollects and can recount impressions obtained through any of his senses that have any tendency to establish a fact of consequence. The purpose for the personal knowledge rule is to reduce testimony containing speculations, rumors, opinions, and inferences, which may be better left for the finder of fact to draw at the conclusion of all testimony.

The court may reject the testimony of a witness if no rational juror could believe what the witness claims to have perceived actually happened. However, this is a strict standard, and if there is any possibility that the jury will believe the witness' perception, the judge will admit the testimony.

FRE 603 requires that, before testifying, the witness declares that he will testify truthfully, by oath or affirmation. An oath requires that the witness swear that he will "tell the truth, the whole truth, and nothing but the truth. So help me God." The affirmation simply requires the witness to swear that he will tell the truth. The oath is intended to impress upon each witness the importance of the proceeding and telling the truth.

§5. Opinion Testimony

I. Lay Opinion

247. At common law, non-expert witnesses were not permitted to give any opinion testimony. Instead, as suggested above, they were permitted to speak only on those facts of which they had personal knowledge. However, this proved to be an unrealistic constraint and many judges found it difficult to identify the line between fact and opinion.

FRE 701 provides a guideline for judges in permitting opinion testimony. It prohibits the use of lay witness opinion testimony unless the testimony meets two requirements:

(1) That the opinion is rationally based on the perception of the witness; and
(2) that the opinion is helpful to a clear understanding of the witness' testimony or the determination of a fact in issue.

Determination of whether the opinion meets the two criteria is a matter for the trial judge's discretion and is unlikely to be overturned on appellate review absent clear abuse.

To meet the first requirement, the party must first lay a foundation establishing personal knowledge of the facts which form the basis of the opinion or inference. Then, the party must also show that the opinion is rationally based on those facts; that any normal person would draw those same inferences from the same set of facts. The second requirement is easier to fulfill. If the judge finds that the testimony will aid the trier of fact even in a small way, the testimony should be admitted.

There are at least three circumstances where lay witness opinion testimony has often been held to be admissible:[1]

(1) When an expression of the witness' personal knowledge could be conveyed in no other form.[2]
(2) When a witness formed an accurate total impression, although unable to account for all the details upon which it was based.[3]
(3) When an accounting of the details alone could not accurately convey the total impression received by the witness.[4]

Examples of the above include a witness' subjective opinion about a person's age based on objective appearances, a witness' testimony as to the speed of an automobile, or a witness' testimony that someone was intoxicated at a given time.

1. Michael H. Graham, *Modern State and Federal Evidence: A Comprehensive Reference* (1989), 316.
2. *People v. Reed*, 333 Ill. 397, 401, 164 N.E. 847, 849-850 (Ill. 1928).
3. *United States v. Freeman*, 514 F.2nd 1184, 1191 (10th Cir. 1975).
4. *Randolph v. Collectramatic, Inc.*, 590 F.2nd 844, 846 (10th Cir. 1979).

II. Expert Opinion Testimony

248. Rules 702-705 govern the use of expert testimony in judicial proceedings. Experts may testify in the form of an opinion as well as give factual testimony. With the increased use of scientific evidence in the courtroom, these rules are important in keeping admission of the testimony uniform within the federal courts.

Rule 702 has two requirements. The first is that all expert testimony assist the trier of fact in "understand[ing] the evidence or to determine a fact in issue." The second is that the witness is qualified as an expert by knowledge, skill, experience, training, or education.

The first requirement is relatively easy to meet. As in Rule 701, if the judge finds that the testimony will aid the jury in any way, the testimony will be admitted (subject to the second requirement). This permits expert testimony where, even though the subject is well known to the average juror, the expert is able to draw a more reliable inference than a juror would without the aid of the expert's testimony.

Whether the witness meets the second requirement is a matter for the judge under Rule 104(a). There is no general requirement that the expert possess academic degrees or specialized experience in a particular field. However, the expert witness must be sufficiently familiar with the theory or method to which he is testifying. For example, a family medical doctor may be found incompetent to testify regarding a special birthing technique when he has neither seen nor performed the technique.[1]

1. *Hartke v. McKelway*, 526 F. Supp. 97 (D.D.C. 1981).

A. The Frye/Daubert *Debate*

249. One major point of contention between jurisdictions has been the level of reliability that scientific evidence must meet before it can be admitted by the trial judge. Before adoption of the FRE in the 1960s, the test announced in *Frye v. United States*[1] was the guiding principle used to answer that question. The *Frye* test required that the proffered scientific evidence be a generally accepted theory among those in the scientific field to which it belongs. The court was generally not concerned with whether the technique used was reliable. It was assumed that this determination would be made by a consensus of those in the scientific field. This resulted in a substantial amount of relevant and reliable testimony being excluded because it was not yet a "generally accepted" theory. Although the federal courts no longer adhere to the *Frye* test, it still exists in a minority of states.

After the adoption of the FRE, the US Supreme Court announced in *Daubert v. Merrell Dow Pharmaceuticals, Inc.*,[2] that the *Frye* test is no longer applicable in federal courts. Under the newer *Daubert* test, the scientific evidence will be admitted if its proponent can show that the conclusion is based upon sound scientific methodology. The test is not the correctness of the conclusion, but the soundness of the methodology. Moreover, and importantly, judges are not merely to defer to the consensus of the scientific community, but rather undertake some inquiry of their own into the reliability of the evidence. Of course, the views of scientists will factor into this inquiry. Factors the trial court will consider include:

(1) Whether the technique has survived peer review by publication in journals;
(2) Whether there is any way to verify the results of the methodology;
(3) The rate of error of the methodology;
(4) Whether the methodology is generally accepted by the people in the scientific field to which it pertains; and
(5) Whether the opinion was developed expressly for the purpose of testifying or based on pre-existing or independent research.

1. *Frye v. United States*, 293 F. 1013 (App. D.C. 1923).
2. *Daubert v. Merrell Dow Pharmaceuticals, Inc.*, 509 U.S. 579 (1993).

B. Bases for Expert Testimony

250. Rule 703 permits expert witnesses to base their testimony on facts and data perceived by or made known to the expert at or before the hearing. One common basis for expert opinions is the personal observations of the expert witness. However, Rule 703 also permits testimony based on information "reasonably relied upon by experts in the particular field in forming opinions or inferences upon the subject" whether or not the outside information is itself admissible at trial. The facts and data relied upon may include documents, oral statements, treatises, and opinions or conclusions of others if that information is of the type the expert normally relies upon in reaching an opinion.

The court must make an initial inquiry into whether the information relied upon by the expert is of the type customarily relied upon by experts in the field. This may require the trial court judge to examine the expert outside of the presence of the jury and/or consult textbooks or other authorities on the field in question.

Expert witnesses can also base their testimony on hypothetical questions given at trial. Hypothetical questions require the witness to assume a certain set of given facts. Generally, the facts have already been presented or will soon be presented to the jury as evidence, and the party is simply asking the expert to render an opinion based on those facts.

§6. Impeachment of a Witness

251. Every time a witness gets on the stand, she is putting her credibility at issue. Methods used to impeach a witness' credibility include attacking capacity, character, and bias of the witness; presenting evidence of a prior inconsistent statement; and pointing out a specific error in testimony. There are three ways in which impeachment of a witness may be carried out. The first is during the cross-examination. The second is laying a foundation for the impeaching evidence during cross-examination and following up with extrinsic evidence. The third, and usually most controversial, is going directly to extrinsic evidence.

I. Capacity

252. Impeaching a witness by attacking the capacity of the witness to perceive and remember correctly includes showing senility of the witness, poor eyesight or hearing, intoxication of the witness at the time of perception, or that the witness was excited or preoccupied at the time of perception. In federal court, the impeaching party must first lay a foundation for the incapacity during cross-examination and is then permitted to introduce extrinsic evidence to support the allegation.

II. Character

253. As indicated earlier, character evidence is ordinarily inadmissible. The only character trait that may be shown for the purpose of impeaching a witness is a trait for dishonesty. This can be done using character witnesses testifying as to the principal witness' reputation in the community, the personal opinion of an acquaintance of the principal witness, or by evidence of specific bad acts of the principal witness. In order to testify concerning reputation, the reputation witness must have sufficient acquaintance with the principal witness and his community in order to ensure that the testimony adequately reflects the community's assessment. In testifying about a personal opinion regarding the principal witness, the opinion witness is allowed to base his testimony solely on his own impression of the principal witness. No foundation of long acquaintance with the principal witness is required. If presenting evidence of specific acts in federal court, and the act is one for which the principal witness has been convicted in a criminal trial, evidence of felonies or crimes of untruthfulness are always allowed to be introduced to impeach the witness. If the act is one for which the principal witness has not been convicted, the act shown must be one that reveals the trait of dishonesty.

Not every state follows these rules of impeachment concerning character traits. In some states, evidence of any felony conviction is admissible to impeach credibility, and at least one line of cases prohibits evidence of acts similar to the act in question from being used to impeach because of the danger of misuse by the jury. However, the trend is certainly moving toward admitting evidence of any prior "bad" acts, especially those involving dishonesty, to impeach.

III. Bias

254. There are many ways to show bias, including proving a relationship to one of the parties, possibility of financial gain or payment for testimony, and showing that the witness is exculpating himself by testifying against one party.

The admissibility of bias evidence follows naturally from the rules governing relevance. "A successful showing of bias on the part of a witness would have a tendency to make the facts to which he testified less probable in the eyes of the jury than it would be without such testimony."[1] Evidence of bias of a witness is so powerful and probative that when courts start to limit it in criminal cases, they have to worry about whether they are violating the constitutional right of the defendant to confront all witnesses against him.

1. *United States v. Abel*, 469 U.S. 45, 51 (1984).

IV. Prior Inconsistent Statements

255. In federal courts, under FRE 801(d)(1)(A), evidence of prior inconsistent statements can be used to impeach. Because the out-of-court prior statement is being used to impeach, rather than for the truth of the matter asserted, the rule against hearsay imposes no limit. If the prior inconsistent statement was made at a trial, hearing or deposition and was given under oath, a hearsay exception applies, so that the trier of fact can consider the statement not merely for impeachment purposes, but also as substantive proof of the truth of the matter asserted in the inconsistent statement.

Chapter 5. Privileges

§1. GENERALLY

256. In both federal and state courts, certain kinds of relevant and otherwise admissible evidence is excludable by a party who holds a privilege with respect to such evidence. The privileges in federal and state courts differ, and this section provides a brief overview of the privileges in federal courts, especially in cases involving federal substantive law. Ordinarily speaking, the party asserting a privilege bears the burden of proving its existence and applicability.[1]

FRE 501 describes the rules prescribing when and how privileges will apply in federal courts. When the case will be decided upon federal law, Rule 501 provides that the privileges will be governed by the "principles of common law as they may be interpreted by the courts of the United States in the light of reason and experience." When the trial is in federal court on the basis of diversity of the parties, the rules to be applied are those of the state law applicable to the issues in the case.

With regard to federal question cases – the subject of this overview – the US Supreme Court also proposed several privileges to Congress for codification as part of the FRE. Congress rejected codification of these proposed rules, but many courts continue to use these proposed rules in determining whether to recognize certain privileges when requested to do so. One benefit of the present system is that the federal courts are not restricted to the privileges recognized at the time the FRE were adopted, nor are they restricted by the states' recognition of privileges. Thus the federal courts can benefit from new and ever-changing perspectives and the use of balancing tests in allowing privileges.

1. *In re Bevill, Brester & Schulman Asset Management Corp.*, 805 F.2nd 120, 124 (1986).

257. The primary justification for a privilege is society's sense that the information protected by the rules of privilege is personal in nature and may expose the holder to undue embarrassment. Most often, the existence of confidentiality is presumed to foster relationships that society views as important and is prepared to promote over the goal of full disclosure of relevant information.

Dean Wigmore, in his treatise on evidence, identified four prerequisites for recognition of a privilege:

(1) The communications must originate in a confidence that they will not be disclosed;
(2) This element of confidentiality must be essential to the full and satisfactory maintenance of the relation between the parties;
(3) The relation must be one which in the opinion of the community ought to be sedulously fostered;
(4) The injury that would inure to the relation by the disclosure of the communications must be greater than the benefit thereby gained for the correct disposal of litigation.[1]

In federal courts, many privileges are decided on a case-by-case basis, balancing the importance of the privilege with the importance of having all relevant facts presented to the fact finder. Above all, it is important to remember that evidentiary privileges in litigation are not favored and ordinarily construed narrowly because they keep relevant information from the fact finder.[2] However, there are a few privileges that all federal courts recognize at least to some degree.

1. 4 John Henry Wigmore, *A Treatise on the System of Evidence in Trial at Common Law* (1905), §2285.
2. *See In re Zuniga*, 714 F.2nd 632 (6th Cir. 1983) ("Whatever their origins, exceptions to the demand for every man's evidence are not lightly created nor expansively construed for they are in derogation of the search for the truth," quoting *United States v. Nixon*, 418 U.S. 683 (1974)).

§2. Specific Privileges

I. Attorney-Client Privilege

258. The attorney-client privilege is one of the oldest privileges for confidential communications. The justifications for this privilege include:

(1) the acknowledgment that the privilege furthers a societal goal by encouraging full and frank disclosure between attorney and client by assuring the parties that neither can be required to disclose the information revealed to one another;
(2) the idea that legal actions work in such a way that in order for the attorney to function effectively, he must be able to blend his legal knowledge with the client's complete knowledge of the facts of the case; and
(3) recognition that legal rights and the litigation process is so complex that lawyers are essential to their proper exercise and conduct of litigation.

For the privilege to apply to communication between an attorney and his client, there are two preliminary requirements. First, the communication must relate to the attorney's status as a legal advisor. For example, if the attorney and the client are also business partners in a collateral relationship, only communication relating to their relationship as attorney-client and not communications relating to their business partnership would satisfy the requirement and thus be privileged.

Second, the communication must be intended to be confidential. This does not necessarily mean that only the attorney and the client may be present when the information is given, but presence of any third parties must be reasonably necessary to facilitate the communication between client and counsel. This may include, among others, the presence of associates, law clerks, secretaries, interpreters, and agents of either the attorney or the client. Whether the presence of third parties destroys the privilege is decided on a case-by-case approach after the court decides the reasonableness and necessity of the presence of the third party.

Where a privilege exists, the client is the holder of the privilege and may prevent the attorney (or other involved party) from disclosing the information sought.

259. The scope of the privilege is relatively clear. The privilege encompasses oral and written communications between the attorney and the client. However, it is not the information itself which is privileged, but rather the communication. So, while a client may not be asked what she told her attorney and the attorney may not be asked to reveal what he was told, the information may be elicited from the witness in other ways. For instance, a client may not refuse to answer a question by replying that "I told the same information responsive to that question to my attorney." Similarly, a person does not waive the privilege by merely revealing the information contained in the confidential communications to a third party; the communications themselves must be revealed.

The privilege may also include communications made by an agent of the client. For example, in a personal-injury case, an attorney will often refer the client to a medical doctor for the purpose of examining the client and reporting his conclusions to the attorney. The communication between the doctor and the attorney is privileged. Courts have analogized this situation to where there is an interpreter and hold that the doctor is merely interpreting the physical condition of the client for the attorney so that he may use it in preparing his case for litigation. Had the client himself described his condition to his attorneys, there would be no doubt that the communication would be privileged.

There are also important exceptions to the attorney-client privilege (as there are to all privileges). These exceptions may be applied differently by various courts and one should remember to research the scope of the privilege in each forum before beginning litigation. The first exception is that if the communications relate to legal services rendered by the attorney, and the attorney is defending a lawsuit by the client over those services, e.g., a malpractice suit, the information contained in those communications is no longer privileged. This is because the client has put the contents of the communication and the very relationship at issue by initiating a lawsuit. There is often no other way to prove liability or innocence of the attorney without exposing the contents of those communications.

Another important exception to the privilege is communications made in furtherance of a current or future crime or fraud.[1] For the crime-fraud exception to apply, there must be a prima facie showing that the communication was made in an attempt to further or conceal an ongoing or future crime, the communication must bear a reasonably close relationship to the crime, and the communication must have been made in an attempt to further the crime or fraud, not just relate to it.[2]

The Federal Rules of Civil Procedure and the FRE also cover the semi-privileged nature of certain information called "work product." "Work product" includes any notes, working papers, memoranda, written statements of witnesses, mental impressions, personal recollections, and similar materials prepared or formed by an attorney or his agent in anticipation of litigation or for trial. The major difference between work-product protection and the attorney-client privilege is that work-product protection can be penetrated in the interests of justice. To overcome the protection afforded work product, the party seeking disclosure of the work product must show that she has a substantial need for the information and that the opposing party possesses the only reasonably obtainable copy of that information. In ordering discovery of such materials, the court protects against disclosure of the mental impressions and legal theories of the attorney by removing them from the information provided to the seeking party.

Another aspect of the attorney-client privilege is its application in the corporate setting, where giving the privilege meaning is difficult because a corporation is not a natural person but a legal fiction and the employees of the corporation are not speaking to the attorney on their own behalf but on that of the corporation. Early applications of this privilege in a corporate setting used a "control group" test – which focused on communications made by certain key personnel with decision-making authority – to determine which communications were privileged and which were not. However, in *Upjohn Co. v. United States*,[3] the US Supreme Court held that the control group test was not sufficiently broad and, instead, the attorney-client privilege should also cover information given by employees to lawyers to enable them to give "sound and informed advice" to the client-corporation. The Court did not intend to imply that anytime an employee talks to the corporate attorney that the communication is privileged. It merely held that when the communication concerns matters within the scope of the employee's corporate duties, the communication will be privileged.

1. *In re Impounded Case (Law Firm)*, 879 F.2nd 1211 (3rd Cir. 1989).
2. *Charles Woods Television Corp. v. Capital Cities/ABC Inc.*, 869 F.2nd 1155 (8th Cir. 1989).
3. *Upjohn Co. v. United States*, 449 U.S. 383 (1981).

II. Clergy-Communicant Privilege

260. The federal courts have recognized the clergy-communicant privilege for over a century and virtually every state has recognized it in some form. The clergy-communicant privilege "recognizes the human need to disclose to a spiritual counselor, in total and absolute confidence, what are believed to be flawed acts or thoughts and to receive priestly consolation and guidance in return."[1]

The first requirement for information to be protected under this privilege is that the information must be disclosed to a member of the clergy in confidence. This is similar to the attorney-client privilege in that the presence of third parties will not vitiate the privilege only if their presence is essential to facilitate the communication process. The privilege is not limited to clergy members only. Communications with individuals who function as spiritual advisors or whose duties conform to those normally performed by members of the clergy will also be protected.

The second requirement for protection is that the information disclosed to the clergy member must be disclosed for the purpose of obtaining spiritual guidance and rehabilitation.

The holders of this privilege may be either the clergy member and the communicant or both, depending upon the court defining the privilege. Some courts find that the clergy member is a holder of the privilege because according to religious tenets, he is often forbidden from disclosing the information, and he should not be compelled to violate those tenets. The precise boundaries of the privilege are delineated on a case-by-case basis.

1. *In re Grand Jury Investigation*, 918 F.2nd 374, 382 (3rd Cir. 1990).

III. Spousal Privileges

261. There are two types of marital privileges recognized by both state and federal courts: the privilege for confidential communications between husband and wife, and the privilege against adverse spousal testimony. In order to claim either privilege, there must first be a valid marriage. In any state that recognizes common law marriages, they will also satisfy the valid marriage requirement.

The scope of the marital communications privilege is somewhat narrow, and similar in nature to the attorney-client or clergy-communicant privileges. The privilege covers only confidential communications made during the existence of the marital relationship. The communications must be confidential and not revealed to nor overheard by third parties. All private communications are presumed to be confidential, unless circumstances indicate otherwise. This privilege also does not attach when the communication is in the form of a writing.

The spouses must be married at the time of the communication, but it is not necessary that they be married at the time of the trial. The privilege survives the marriage such that if the couple is later divorced or separated, the privilege for the confidential communication endures. While some states limit its application to criminal proceedings, most states apply it in both civil and criminal trials.

The justification for this privilege is to foster candor and intimacy within the relationship of marriage. It is presumed that if the husband and wife are allowed to freely exchange confidences and tell each other their secrets, the marriage bond will be strengthened.

One major exception to this privilege is the "joint participants" exception. The exception applies when the spouses in question were joint participants in an illegal venture to which the confidential communication relates.

Another exception is similar to an exception to the attorney-client privilege. This exception provides that communications made for the purpose of committing a crime or fraud and enlisting the aid of the spouse in the scheme are not privileged.

The privilege against adverse spousal testimony provides that one may not be compelled to testify against his/her spouse. This privilege protects a marriage that is in existence at the time when the trial testimony would be used. It is intended to prevent the ongoing litigation from damaging an existing marital relationship. This privilege acknowledges that the marital relationship is more important than the result of a given case, and assumes – quite plausibly – that one spouse's testimony against another will have a harmful effect on the marital relationship. Importantly, the privilege applies whether or not the witness spouse obtained the information to which she is being asked to testify through confidential spousal communications.

Traditionally, the party spouse (the defendant) was the holder of the privilege. However, the modern trend is turning toward allowing witness spouses to waive the privilege and testify if they choose to do so. According to *Trammel v. United States*,[1] the justification for this change in attitude is the acknowledgment that if the witness spouse invokes the privilege, the motion is made to save the marriage, which conforms to the policy justifications for the privilege. If the party spouse is invoking the privilege, the assumed motivation is to save himself, not the marriage.

Additionally, while some courts allow the privilege to apply in both civil and criminal cases, many limit the operation of the privilege to criminal cases.

1. *Trammel v. United States*, 445 U.S. 40 (1980).

IV. Doctor-Patient Privilege

262. The extent to which federal courts will recognize a physician-patient privilege under current federal common-law principles is far from clear. We note, however, that most states have enacted statutory privileges for physician-patient relationships.

The justification for such a privilege is that the physician has a better chance of obtaining the full disclosure needed for proper treatment of injury and disease if the patient is assured confidentiality and protection against the embarrassment and invasion of privacy that a revelation might cause.

Where the privilege is recognized, the holder of the privilege is the patient and the physician cannot testify as to the privileged information without his consent. The scope of the privilege includes not only communications made by the patient to the physician, but also records of diagnoses and treatment provided to the patient and information obtained by the physician through examination and observation of the patient. The information protected is limited to information obtained by a medical doctor for the purposes of treating the patient; information such as a patient's name and address is therefore not privileged.

There are four major exceptions to this privilege. The most commonly seen exception is for actions in which the patient asserting the privilege is also the litigant and the patient has put his physical condition at issue in the proceeding. The privilege also does not operate in criminal cases, will contests, nor in civil actions involving a patient's wrongful conduct.

V. Other Possible Privileges

263. In general, federal courts are hesitant to recognize any new privileges because of their effect of hiding relevant information from the finder of fact. However, individual states often recognize new privileges. Some of these include a psychotherapist-client privilege, an accountant-client privilege, a banker-depositor privilege, a parent-child privilege, and social worker-client privilege.

Part VIII. Particular Proceedings

Chapter 1. Divisible Divorce

264. The federal courts of the United States do not generally hear cases on family law issues, such as divorce, child custody, and alimony.[1] Although neither the Constitution nor the federal diversity statute prevents the federal courts from hearing such cases, what is known as "the domestic relations exception" has developed out of legislative and judge-made law.[2] Several theories exist that explain and justify the development of this exception:

(1) It is necessary to preserve state's traditional function and protect federalism specifically because power over domestic relations is not allocated to the federal government.
(2) The jurisdiction of the federal courts is limited to that of the English chancery courts which did not hear domestic relations cases. Such cases were heard by ecclesiastical courts.
(3) States have developed a considerable expertise in the area of family law and have developed special systems, including family courts and social service agencies, to address family law issues.
(4) State rather than federal law governs the issue of marital status.[3]

Family law is considered to be a traditional area of state regulation. The state of domicile of either spouse may issue a valid judgment dissolving a marriage even if the defendant lacks minimum contact with the forum state. The state in which the acting spouse is domiciled may grant an annulment, judicial separation, and divorce. The state court's power, however, does not extend to awarding marital support or dividing marital property. A state's judgment awarding marital support is invalid unless the defendant has minimum contacts with the forum state, thereby giving the court personal jurisdiction over the individual.[4] The validity and enforcement of judgments determining child custody has been clarified in recent decades by the congressional enactment of the Federal Parental Kidnapping Prevention Act.[5] The statute requires states to give full faith and credit to the custody determinations of a sister state, provided that at the time of the custody determination, the sister state was the "home state" of the child, as statutorily defined to exclude domicile acquired by parental attempt to evade the terms of an earlier custody determination.[6]

1. Cases that fall under family law which involve other areas of law, such as torts and contract, have proceeded in federal courts on the basis of diversity jurisdiction.
2. The US Supreme Court declared, "We disclaim altogether any jurisdiction in the courts of the United States upon the subject of divorce, or any allowance of alimony" *Barber v. Barber*, 62 U.S. (21 How.) 582, 584 (1859). *See Ankenbrandt v. Richards*, 504 U.S. 689, 504 U.S. 689 (1992) (reflecting the continuing vitality of the domestic relations exception); Naomi R. Cahn, "Family Law, Federalism and the Federal Courts," *Iowa L. Rev.* 79 (1994): 1073; Michael A. Stein, "The Domestic Relations Exception to Federal Jurisdiction: Rethinking an Unsettled Federal Courts Doctrine," B.C. L. Rev. 36 (1995): 669.
3. *See* Naomi R. Cahn, "Family Law, Federalism and the Federal Courts," Iowa L. Rev. 79 (1994): 1073 (critiquing the traditional rationales for the Domestic Relations Exception).
4. *See Kulko v. Superior Court*, 436 U.S. 84 (1978).
5. 28 U.S.C. §1738A.
6. *See Thompson v. Thompson*, 484 U.S. 174 (1987).

Chapter 2. Admiralty Procedure

265. Historically, admiralty cases falling under federal maritime law were subject to special procedures. In 1966, the Federal Rules of Civil Procedure became applicable to most admiralty cases. Some special procedures, however, were added governing such issues as attachment and garnishment, in rem actions and the limitation of liability.[1] As mentioned earlier, federal jurisdiction over admiralty cases is only nominally exclusive; many cases are heard in state courts (see paragraphs 64-66). In state court, when only damages are sought, the proceedings are subject to the normal state procedures that govern suits for damages in torts and contract actions.

1. *See* Fed. R. Civ. P., Supplemental Rules for Certain Admiralty and Maritime Claims, Rules A-G (2007).

Chapter 3. Fast-Track Proceedings

266. In recent decades, American courts in the more populous states have faced an increasing wave of litigation flooding their dockets.[1] For example, the California legislature addressed this problem by implementing what was initially a pilot project, the Trial Court Delay Reduction Act.[2] The Act established experimental programs in select counties designed to increase the speed of the litigation process. Beginning on 1 January 1988, the project was originally intended to last for only three years. After a number of intermediate extensions, legislators gave the Act permanent, statewide application as of 1 July 1992.[3]

The Trial Court Delay Reduction Act attempts to process litigation in a more timely manner and to reduce the cost to litigants by providing simplified procedures. The Act applies to all civil actions and proceedings in trial courts, except for probate, juvenile and domestics-relations cases, as well as cases specially assigned to a judge or judges for all purposes.[4] Many courts in California follow an independent calendaring system by which successive phases of the same case are handled by different judges.[5] Judges are primarily responsible for carrying out the goals of the act. They are expected to take a more active role in eliminating delay in the progress and ultimate resolution of litigation. The statute provides that judges are to "assume and maintain control over the pace of litigation, to actively manage the processing of litigation from commencement to disposition, and to compel attorneys and litigants to prepare and resolve litigation without delay, from the filing of the first document invoking court jurisdiction to final disposition of the action."[6] The method used to persuade attorneys and litigants to comply with "fast track" proceedings is the use of sanctions.[7] The Act encourages judges to impose sanctions when they will achieve greater efficiency.[8] Judges have the power to dismiss actions or strike pleadings when less severe sanctions would not be effective.[9]

Judges, in consultation with the bar of their court's county, are responsible for developing and publishing the procedures, standards and policies to be used in their court's program. This includes rules governing the time for the conclusion of all critical steps in the litigation process, subject to certain minimal standards that must be observed statewide.[10]

The state of Texas has also taken measures to expedite the litigation process. Rule 190 of the Texas Rules of Civil Procedure provides that all cases must be governed by one of three tiers of discovery plans. Level One governs cases involving USD 50,000 or less, excluding costs, pre-judgment interest and attorney's fees. Any suit for divorce not involving children where the marital estate is more than zero but less than USD 50,000 also falls into this category. There are strict controls on the amount of discovery permitted in Level One cases. Level Two is the default level for all other cases. In these cases there are still presumptive limits on discovery, but the overall scope of discovery is more liberal than in Level One cases. Level Three is reserved for complex cases involving exceptional circumstances. These cases are exempted from any presumptive limits on discovery; instead, a discovery control plan is mandated which tailors the scope of discovery to the circumstances of each Level Three case.

As discussed in Part X (paragraph 298), the Civil Justice Reform Act of 1990 (CJRA) encouraged individual districts to pursue ad hoc procedural reform. This led to a proliferation of local rules for individual districts within the federal trial-court system that has been criticized as a "balkanization" of the nominally uniform and nationwide system of civil procedure specified in the Federal Rules of Civil Procedure.[11] For example, in the Southern District of California there are about eighty separate local rules, many having lengthy subparts. In addition, there are about 435 "General Orders" – many being the functional equivalent of local rules – that announce varying policies and procedures for the individual judges of that particular district court.[12]

A decade later, the pendulum of federal procedural reform began to swing the other way. The CJRA's encouragement of ad hoc local variations in procedural rules for federal cases was complemented by the 1993 amendments to the Federal Rules of Civil Procedure, which permitted individual districts to "opt out" of otherwise uniform federal discovery rules. While there was value in such local experimentation with best procedural practices, the loss of national uniformity in federal civil procedure was widely criticized. The Federal Rules of Civil Procedure that regulate discovery (see Part IV, paragraphs 182-188) were again amended in 2000, substantially reducing the degree of local disuniformity permitted under the Federal Rules.[13]

1. *See* Kerekes, Robert J., "The Crisis of Congested Courts: One Potential Solution," Seton Hall Legis. J. 18 (1994): 489, discussing ways to solve congestion in New Jersey courts through legislation similar to California's Trial Court Delay Reduction Act.
2. Cal. Gov. Code §68600 (West 1997).
3. Id., at §68620.
4. Id., at §68608.
5. Cal. Rules of Court, Rule 10.603 (2008).
6. Cal. Gov. Code §68607 (West 1997).
7. Id., at §68608(b).
8. Id.
9. Id.
10. *See* id., at §68616. For instance, California Civil Procedure Code §583.420 generally requires dismissal if the action is not brought to trial within three years of commencement of the proceedings. At the local level, counties may require that defendants be served within sixty days. *See* Cal. Code Civ. Proc. §583.420.
11. *See* Linda S. Mullenix, "The Counter-Reformation in Procedural Justice," Minn. L. Rev. 77 (1992): 375; Carl Tobias, "Civil Justice Reform and the Balkanization of Federal Civil Procedure," Ariz. St. L. J. 24 (1992): 1393.
12. *See* Walter W. Heiser, "A Critical Review of Local Rules of the United States District Court for the Southern District of California," San Diego L. Rev. 33 (1996): 555, 560.
13. The process of adopting these amendments began in 1998. *See* Elizabeth G. Thornburg, "Giving the "Haves" a Little More: Considering the 1998 Discovery Proposals," S.M.U L. Rev. 52 (1999): 229.

Part IX. Preliminary Seizure and Enforcement of Judgments

Chapter 1. Preliminary Seizure

§1. Introduction

267. Attachment is the legal process of seizing another party's property in accordance with a writ or judicial order for the purpose of securing satisfaction of a judgment yet to be rendered. At common law, attachment was thought of differently – the primary purpose of attachment was to support in rem jurisdiction over the property of an out-of-state defendant who could not be subjected to the forum state's in personam jurisdiction (see paragraphs 86-87). It had little or nothing to do with providing security for a plaintiff's damage claim. Today, attachment enables the plaintiff to prevent a defendant from disposing of property subject to seizure, thus ensuring the enforceability of any money judgment that may be obtained after trial. At least as a matter of federal constitutional law,[1] in rem jurisdiction based on the seizure of property can reach no defendant not also subject to the forum's in personam jurisdiction (see paragraph 88).

1. *See Shaffer v. Heitner*, 433 U.S. 186 (1977).

§2. Proceedings

268. Each state has its own rules and procedures for obtaining prejudgment attachment of a defendant's property. When in federal court, litigants are subject to Federal Rule of Civil Procedure 64, which effectively incorporates state law by making available to plaintiffs all the seizure remedies that are obtainable under the laws of the state in which the district court sits.

Generally, attachment of a defendant's property may be available in most actions where the plaintiff has requested, and if successful on the merits would receive, a judgment for money damages. The New York regulations on prejudgment attachments are representative. They provide that a plaintiff can seek an attachment order at any time prior to judgment, even without notice, if the plaintiff can show that he has a reasonable probability of succeeding on the merits and that the defendant has or is likely to move or encumber property located in New York with an intent to defraud creditors or frustrate potential judgments. The judicial order, specifying the amount to be secured, is delivered to the sheriff of any county in which the defendant owns property. Once the order is granted, the plaintiff usually must move for a confirmation hearing to confirm the attachment. It is at this point that defendant is permitted to challenge the attachment. Indeed, due-process-notice and opportunity-to-be-heard requirements guarantee that defendants have prompt and ample opportunity to contest attachments. In some cases, such as wage attachment, pre-attachment process is constitutionally required. In other settings, prompt post-attachment process may suffice. But courts will not authorize attachment unless the basis and need for attachment are plain and clear.

§3. Judicial Review

269. Appellate courts usually review trial court decisions to grant or deny prejudgment attachment under the clearly-erroneous and/or abuse-of-discretion standards (see paragraph 205). Most states provide that if the defendant posts a bond in the amount of the attached property, the defendant may remove an attachment from his property.

§4. Preliminary Injunctions versus Attachments

270. The prejudgment attachment is similar to the preliminary-injunction device explored in paragraph 215 in that both provide judicial relief before a judgment on the merits of a lawsuit has been entered. A preliminary injunction, unlike an attachment, operates on the person of the defendant; if he violates a preliminary injunction forbidding him from disposing of or moving property, he is subject to personal contempt. An attachment, by contrast, does not go to the person, but rather consists of a lien on the property that is attached.

Until recently, there has been a vigorous controversy concerning whether a court has the authority to issue a preliminary injunction when the only relief sought in a case is money damages. The US Supreme Court in the narrowly decided *Grupo Mexicano* case[1] (see paragraph 215) has ruled that federal courts lack this power, and that preliminary injunctions are appropriate only to grant intermediate relief of the same kind as that which may be granted at the conclusion of trial. While this ruling may make sense, it is not hard to understand why a plaintiff may want the flexibility of both an attachment and a preliminary injunction, even if money damages are the ultimate goal. One reason may be that attachment powers are limited to property in the state in which the court sits, whereas the personal injunction, and the contempt power standing behind it, may restrain a defendant even as to out-of-jurisdiction property. Another reason is that state law often makes certain kinds of property, such as a personal residence, immune from attachment. At least one lower court has distinguished *Grupo Mexicano* and declined to follow it in cases where *both* damages *and* equitable relief are sought.[2]

1. *Grupo Mexicano de Desarollo, S.A. v. Alliance Bond Fund, Inc.*, 527 U.S. 308 (1999).
2. *See U.S. ex rel. Rahman v. Oncology Associates*, 198 F.3d 489, 498 (1999).

Chapter 2. Enforcement of Judgments

§1. Entry of Judgment

271. Enforcement of a judgment begins with the entry of the judgment. When a judgment is entered as a result of a default, a separate set of procedures is followed. Default judgments are based on less than a fully contested adversary resolution of the merits of a dispute. The party against whom the default is entered has been unable (because of absence, or judicially imposed sanction or some other reason) to present its case. The actual procedure for obtaining default judgments is similar to that for obtaining summary judgment, discussed in paragraphs 190-193. Most of the evidence is presented through affidavit or other written documents, rather than live in-court testimony as would be the case in an ordinary trial. Rule 55 of the Federal Rules of Civil Procedure, which outlines the federal process for default judgment, involves essentially two steps. First, default is entered against a party by the other side filing an affidavit with the clerk who then makes an entry that one party is in default. Second, after entry of default, a judgment is obtained either by the clerk (when the amount sought by the non-defaulting party is fixed in the pleadings) or by a court (in other cases.) Parties against whom default has been entered who never appeared in the action are given no notice of the imminence of the default judgment, whereas parties who have appeared are given three days' written notice that the moving party is applying for judgment. When damages or other ancillary issues must be determined as a matter of fact, the court must hold a hearing, including a jury trial where required. The amount available to a moving party is limited to the upper limit prayed for in the pleadings.[1]

When judgment is entered after a claim has been litigated to decision on the merits, judgment enters automatically (that is, without court approval) only where there has been a general verdict. When a jury returns a special verdict or a general verdict accompanied by special interrogatories (see paragraph 195), the court must approve the form of judgment prior to its entry by the clerk.

1. Fed. R. Civ. P. 54(c).

§2. Enforcement of Domestic Judgments

I. Proceedings

272. Some judgments, such as declaratory judgments, are essentially self-enforcing in that they need no subsequent enforcement procedures in order for the party obtaining the judgment to enjoy its benefits. Such declarations essentially clarify the law for the parties and are sought when such clarification is all that is needed to resolve the dispute. Other similar devices, such as quiet-title actions and some accountings, trigger automatic action by government officials, which is all the prevailing party needs to accomplish his objectives.

Unfortunately, however, most often a losing party may have to be coerced into abiding by the judicial resolution of the lawsuit. Litigation in which injunctive relief is sought is directly coercive. One party's explicit goal is having the court order the other party to do something or refrain from doing something. Such judicial injunctions are enforceable ultimately through the court's power of contempt. If a party disobeys a direct judicial order, he can be tried, both civilly and criminally, for contempt. Civil contempt aims to bring the recalcitrant party into compliance by depriving him of the benefit of non-compliance and making non-compliance costly. So, for example, a judge could incarcerate a civil contemnor until he agrees to come into compliance. Criminal contempt is punitive and deterrent, and while available to judges whose orders are violated, must ordinarily be accompanied by criminal procedural safeguards.

Most civil judgments are not directly coercive; instead, they take the form of money judgments that merely authorize the winning party to take coercive steps if payment is not forthcoming. When the time comes for a judgment creditor to collect a money judgment, many tools are at his disposal. He may levy personal or real property, garnish wages, or file a motion requesting turnover of the judgment debtor's property. State law generally governs the use of these and other enforcement devices. In federal court, enforcement is governed by state law, except that any statute of the United States governs to the extent that it is applicable.

First, the judgment creditor must identify and locate assets of the judgment debtor which may be used to satisfy the judgment. Post-judgment discovery devices are available to assist the judgment creditor in his search. The devices available include subpoenas and examination of the judgment debtor under oath. If a judgment debtor fails to cooperate, he may be subject to civil contempt proceedings.

In order to levy on personal or real property, the judgment creditor must apply for a writ of execution to be issued by the trial court. The writ will direct the local marshal or sheriff to seize the property described. The property will then be publicly sold and the proceeds remitted to the judgment creditor. Property subject to seizure includes bank accounts, vehicles, real property that does not qualify as the debtor's principal dwelling, and other personal property. State statutes also provide homestead exemptions, allowing a debtor to retain equity in a principal residence.

Garnishment is a proceeding whereby a plaintiff's creditor seeks to subject to his claim the property or money of a third party, owed by the third party to the judgment debtor.[1] A common example of garnishment is when the judgment creditor receives a percentage of the judgment debtor's wages. The percentage of wages available for garnishment can be up to 25% of the judgment debtor's total wages. Garnishment is regulated by both state and federal statutes.

As an alternative to execution, levy, or garnishment, many state statutes permit a judgment creditor to seek a general turnover order. Where the judgment debtor has dominion and control over property in which the judgment creditor has an interest, the court may order the debtor to deliver personal property to local law enforcement authorities to satisfy the judgment.[2]

1. *Black's Law Dictionary*, 6th edn (1990), 680.
2. Dennis J. Drebsky, & Lynn M. Barry, *Enforcing Money Judgments*, 686 PLI/Comm 27 (1994).

II. Special Issues of Enforcement

A. Enforcing Judgments in Multiple Jurisdictions

273. Once a party wins a lawsuit and receives a money judgment in his favor, he may find that the defendant's assets are scattered throughout many jurisdictions, requiring multiple steps and procedures in order to have the judgment satisfied. Fortunately, this process has been made relatively simple in the United States.

The US Constitution makes it clear that "Full Faith and Credit shall be given in each State to the public Acts, Records, and judicial Proceedings of every other State."[1] This means that judgments of any court within the United States will be given the same effect had it been rendered in the court where enforcement of the judgment is sought.[2]

A winning party who wishes to enforce the judgment of one jurisdiction's court in another jurisdiction must first register the judgment with the court clerk in the enforcing jurisdiction. Once the judgment is registered, it will be enforced according to the rules and procedures of the enforcing jurisdiction. Local law will govern execution and other supplemental proceedings, such as time limitations on the life of the judgment and exemption of certain types of property from execution.

1. US Const. Art. IV, §1.
2. *See also* 28 U.S.C. §1738.

274. More than forty states have adopted the Uniform Enforcement of Foreign Judgments Act ("Enforcement Act") which provides the guidelines for enforcing another state's judgment. There are two basic provisions. First, only final judgments are covered. Second, the enforcing court is not permitted to re-examine the merits of the suit. This inability to question the merits of the suit is governed not just by statute, but also by the Constitution. That is, once the judgment is final according to the law of the rendering forum, the Full Faith and Credit Clause prohibits collateral attack in the enforcing forum. If the losing party wants to attack the judgment, he must do so in the original forum.

There are, however, a few exceptions. First, the enforcing forum need not grant full faith and credit to another forum's judgment that was procured by fraud. Many courts distinguish between external fraud and internal fraud in deciding whether to allow collateral attack on the basis of fraud. External fraud is fraud that was not and could not have been ruled on by the first forum. For example, fraud that deprived one party of his opportunity to appear and defend himself. Internal fraud is fraud that the rendering forum had the opportunity to rule on, such as the allegation of fraudulent evidence.

Another exception to the Full Faith and Credit Clause involves lack of jurisdiction. If the rendering court lacks either subject matter or personal jurisdiction, its judgment is void and not entitled to enforcement in the alternate court. Indeed, going back as far as *Pennoyer v. Neff* (see paragraph 87), a judgment rendered without personal jurisdiction cannot be enforced in any court without violating the Constitution. It should be noted, however, if jurisdiction is attacked (or waived) in the original litigation, and the original forum rules that it has jurisdiction, the enforcing forum may disallow relitigation of the jurisdictional claims. In other words, a party challenging jurisdiction ordinarily can challenge it in only one forum.

"The law is well-settled that a state may not refuse to enforce the judgment of another state on the ground that the original action could not have been brought in the state in which enforcement is sought."[1] There are two limits to this statement. "First, a state is not required to permit a suit to enforce a judgment brought by one who lacks capacity to sue under forum law."[2] Second, a judgment creditor seeking to enforce a judgment must seek relief of a type ordinarily available in the enforcing forum.[3]

Apart from these exceptions, there is also no general public policy exception to the Full Faith and Credit Clause regarding judicial judgments entered after litigation. An enforcing forum may not refuse full faith and credit to another forum's judgment simply because that judgment is based upon a claim that violates the public policy of the enforcing forum.[4] However, there is support for the proposition that "A judgment rendered in one State of the United States need not be recognized or enforced in a sister State if such recognition or enforcement is not required by the national policy of full faith and credit because it would involve an *improper interference with important interests of the sister State*."[5] It is not entirely clear what kind of state interests would justify non-enforcement.

1. William L. Reynolds, "The Iron Law of Full Faith and Credit," Md. L. Rev. 53 (1994): 412, 433 (summarizing *Fauntleroy v. Lum*, 210 U.S. 230 (1908)).
2. Id., at 434. *See also* Restatement (Second) of Conflict of Laws §117 cmt. d (1969).
3. *See* Reynolds, *supra*, at 434. *See also* Restatement (Second) of Conflict of Laws §117 cmt. d (1969).
4. *See* Reynolds, *supra*, at 436. *See also* Restatement (Second) of Conflict of Laws §117 (1969).
5. Restatement (Second) of Conflict of Laws §103 (1969) (emphasis added).

B. Enforcing Federal Court Judgments

275. Judgments rendered by federal district courts are similarly enforced in accordance with 28 U.S.C. §1963. Section 1963 provides the procedure for registration of the out-of-jurisdiction judgment:

> A judgment in an action for the recovery of money or property entered in any district court … may be registered by filing a certified copy of such judgment in any other district … when the judgment has become final by appeal or expiration of the time for appeal … . A judgment so registered shall have the same effect as a judgment of the district court of the district where registered and may be enforced in a like manner.

Prior to the existence of Section 1963, a judgment creditor was required to bring a separate action to enforce the judgment in the court where judgment was sought. The creditor would file a complaint in the "foreign" federal district, attaching a copy of the original judgment, and then move for summary judgment. The disadvantage of this method is that the enforcement action is considered a new suit, and the new district must obtain personal jurisdiction over the defendant, which was not always easy. This method is still available as an alternative to Section 1963.

The mechanics of Section 1963 are simple. The winning party requests a certified copy of the judgment. If no appeal has been filed within the required period, the clerk issues the copy. The clerk in the foreign court then registers the judgment by entering the pertinent provisions of the sister court's judgment on its own judgment docket.

Federal Rule of Civil Procedure 62 provides the procedures for obtaining a stay of proceedings to enforce a judgment. Rule 62(a) prohibits execution upon a judgment or any other enforcement proceedings until ten days after entry of the judgment. Rule 62(b) permits the court to stay the execution of any proceedings to enforce a judgment pending the disposition of a motion for a new trial, or to alter or amend a judgment or a motion for relief from a judgment made pursuant to Rule 60 (relief for clerical mistakes, inadvertence, excusable neglect, fraud, newly discovered evidence, etc.). Rule 62(d) permits an appellant to obtain a stay pending the appeal by giving a supersedeas bond. A supersedeas bond is a bond made in the proper amount which can be used to make the other party whole if the appeal is ultimately unsuccessful.

§3. Recognition and Enforcement of Foreign Judgments

I. Introduction

276. The United States is not a party to any treaty regarding the recognition and enforcement of foreign judgments, nor does the Full Faith and Credit Clause of the Constitution apply to judgments rendered outside the United States. But this does not mean that it is unduly difficult to get a foreign judgment enforced.

II. Rules Applicable in the Absence of a Treaty

277. Any discussion regarding the recognition of foreign judgments in the US must begin with *Hilton v. Guyot.*[1] In *Hilton*, the US Supreme Court held as a matter of federal common law that foreign judgments would be given full faith and credit in the United States

> where there has been opportunity for a full and fair trial abroad before a court of competent jurisdiction, conduct of the trial on regular proceedings, after due citation of voluntary appearance of the defendant, and under a system of jurisprudence likely to secure an impartial administration of justice between the citizens of that country and those of other countries, and there is nothing to show either prejudice in the court or in the system of laws under which it was sitting, or fraud in procuring the judgment, or any other special reason why the comity of the United States should not allow it full effect.[2]

But the Supreme Court also announced in *Hilton* a "reciprocity" limitation, which allows courts in the United States to refuse to recognize a foreign judgment if the nation in which the judgment originated would not recognize a judgment from a

United States court under the same circumstances. The reciprocity rule was an effort to give foreign nations an incentive to recognize US judgments. Most US courts have abandoned the reciprocity requirement, but many foreign civil law countries still require reciprocity before they will recognize a foreign judgment.

1. *Hilton v. Guyot*, 159 U.S. 113 (1895).
2. Id., at 123.

278. The Uniform Foreign Money Judgments Recognition Act ("Recognition Act") represents an effort to standardize the full faith and credit to be given judgments from foreign countries. The Recognition Act essentially clarifies and codifies many of the factors identified by the Supreme Court in *Hilton* as governing recognition of foreign judgments. Some states have adopted the Act, making their rules for recognizing and enforcing judgments very clear to potential claimants. In particular, the Act allows US courts to refuse to recognize foreign judgments if specific criteria are met.

Section 4 provides the grounds for mandatory non-recognition:

(a) A foreign judgment is not conclusive (and will not be recognized) if
  (1) the judgment was rendered under a system which does not provide impartial tribunals or procedures compatible with the requirements of due process of law;
  (2) the foreign court did not have personal jurisdiction over the defendant; or
  (3) the foreign court did not have jurisdiction over the subject matter.

  Section 4 also provides discretionary grounds, under which the court may choose not to recognize the judgment:

(b) A foreign judgment need not be recognized if
  (1) the defendant in the proceedings in the foreign court did not receive notice of the proceedings in sufficient time to enable him to defend;
  (2) the judgment was obtained by fraud;
  (3) the [claim] on which the judgment was based is repugnant to the public policy of this state;
  (4) the judgment conflicts with another final and conclusive judgment;
  (5) the proceeding in the foreign court was contrary to an agreement between the parties under which the dispute in question was to be settled otherwise than by proceedings in that court; or
  (6) in the case of jurisdiction based only on personal service, the foreign court was a seriously inconvenient forum for the trial of the action.

In reality, these criteria are seldom met absent clear violation of the United States standards. US courts are very willing to find personal and subject-matter jurisdiction, satisfaction of due-process requirements, and fair tribunals absent clear violations of those principles. Even the public policy exception, which, at the beginning, many felt was a broad loophole, is seldom used in refusing to enforce foreign judgments. In order for the public policy exception to apply, the foreign judgment must be "repugnant to fundamental notions of what is decent and just in the State where enforcement is sought."[1] This criterion is not met when the foreign law simply conflicts with the law of the enforcing state; it must actually violate notions of decency, justice, and public morality, which have proven very difficult to demonstrate.

Only final judgments of foreign courts will be recognized. Generally, if the foreign judgment is subject to appeal or modification in the rendering court, the US court will stay the enforcement proceeding pending the appeal or modification.

When no defense to enforcement is available, the foreign judgment brought for enforcement in a state that has adopted the Recognition Act will be enforced in the same manner as a judgment of a sister state, which is entitled to full faith and credit.

Some states have not adopted the Act, yet still may recognize and enforce foreign judgments. The Restatement (Third) of Foreign Relations Law deals with recognition of foreign judgments and provides rules substantially similar to those in the Recognition Act. The Restatement provides that "a final judgment of a court of a foreign state granting or denying recovery of a sum of money … is conclusive between the parties, and is entitled to recognition in courts in the United States."[2] Some states do not follow either the Act or the Restatement, and instead have their own set of rules, which often take into account the reciprocity factor identified by the US Supreme Court in *Hilton*.

Once a foreign judgment has been recognized by a US court, the procedure for enforcement is substantially similar to the process for enforcing judgments from sister states. Most often, the judgment is either registered in the enforcing court, or a new suit may be brought against the defendant and expedited by bringing a motion for summary judgment with a copy of the judgment sought to be enforced attached. Once the judgment has been recognized, generally all that is needed is registration with the enforcing court.

1. *Ackermann v. Levine*, 788 F.2nd 830, 841 (2nd Cir. 1986).
2. American Law Institute, *Restatement (Third) of Foreign Relations Law* (1986), §481(1).

Chapter 3. Preclusion

§1. Introduction

279. Preclusion law in the United States governs the preclusive effect given to prior litigation when subsequent litigation (including forms of litigation and other enforcement proceedings, discussed above) is initiated. The law of preclusion is often usefully divided into two subcategories: res judicata and collateral estoppel.

§2. Res Judicata

280. The general rule of res judicata, also known as claim preclusion, can be stated in general terms as follows: a valid, final judgment, rendered on the merits, constitutes an absolute bar to a subsequent action between the same parties, or those in privity with them, upon the same claim or demand. Where it applies, res judicata operates to bind the parties both as to grounds actually litigated and determined in the first suit, and as to those grounds that might have been, but were not, actually raised and decided in the first action. The first judgment, when final and on the merits, thus puts an end to the whole second cause of action.

The key questions under this doctrine include when a judgment becomes final for preclusion purposes, what privity means, and most importantly, what constitutes the same claim. The first two of these, while important, do not give rise to as much controversy as the last, so we shall say only a few things about the first two questions before focusing on the last one. As to finality, perhaps the most interesting question is whether the filing of an appeal makes a judgment non-final for preclusion purposes. The majority rule is that an appeal does not suspend the finality of the judgment, although a court considering the res judicata bar may use the discretion it typically enjoys in the law of preclusion to refuse to apply preclusion when it feels the underlying judgment may be upset. As to privity, most states define it narrowly. Ordinarily speaking, only parties themselves are precluded by earlier litigation. Exceptions are based upon special relationships, including sometimes the husband-wife relationship, the parent-child relationship, organizational relationships and the indemnitee-indemnitor relationship.

281. Different states use different tests to identify what constitutes the same claim. Most state claim preclusion law, as well as federal preclusion law (which comes not from the Federal Rules but rather federal common law decisions) makes use of a "transaction" or occurrence test. Under this test, a cause of action pled in the current action is precluded if the facts which constitute it arose out of the same transaction or occurrence that served as the basis for the earlier already concluded litigation. A second test, used by some states, focuses on the "primary rights" being asserted in the two actions. Each primary right is distinct from other primary rights, and may be sued on separately. A third conceptual contender is the so-called "same evidence" approach. Two causes of action constitute the same claim for purposes of res judicata if the same evidence is used to prove them both.

To see how these three competing approaches work, consider an automobile accident in which the plaintiff suffers both damage to his person and to his vehicle. Under the prevailing transaction approach, the plaintiff must sue to redress both kinds of injuries in the same lawsuit. If he chooses to sue to redress only the injuries to the vehicle in the first lawsuit that goes to final judgment, he will be barred from later bringing an action against the same defendant for injuries to his body (unless they were not apparent at the time of the first action.) Under a primary-rights approach, he could bring two separate lawsuits, because personal injury and injury to property are defined as infringements of two separate primary rights. Under a "same evidence" approach, whether or not the second action is precluded might depend upon the evidence used to prove the two injuries. If the evidence largely overlaps, then preclusion might apply.

The term "transaction," which is of ultimate importance under the majority approach, is not, of course, self-defining. The Restatement (Second) of Judgments, which is used for guidance in many state and federal courts, defines "transaction" flexibly:

> What factual grouping constitutes a "transaction" … [is] to be determined pragmatically, giving weight to such considerations as whether the facts are related in time, space, origin or motivation, whether they form a convenient trial unit, and whether their treatment as a unit conforms to the parties' expectations or business understanding or usage.[1]

A few points should be made about this formulation. First, the reference to a "convenient trial unit" suggests that some of the considerations that were central to other res judicata approaches, such as the same evidence test, are blended into this pragmatic formula. Second, there is an obvious element of circularity in this test – a transaction is what is convenient to treat as a transaction. Nonetheless, the idea behind the test is a sound one. Modern litigation allows for generous joinder of claims and parties (see paragraphs 151-159) in order to resolve more, rather than fewer, elements of a dispute between various persons. Since these joinder rules are so generous, it is appropriate, efficient and fair to define res judicata effect more broadly than in earlier times. Moreover, although the scope of the transaction test may not be easy to predict in all its applications, the definition of the test gains coherence from its parallels to similar transaction formulas that govern joinder of parties and supplemental jurisdiction. Similarly, while counterclaims are not governed, as a formal matter, by principles of res judicata, Rule 13(a)'s compulsory-counterclaim requirement for federal courts uses a similar transactional test. We should note, however, that some states do not have compulsory-counterclaim rules that are as broad as Rule 13(b).

1. American Law Institute, *Restatement (Second) of Judgments* (1980), §24.

§3. Collateral Estoppel

282. The general rule of collateral estoppel, or issue preclusion, can be phrased as follows: A person is "estopped" or precluded from relitigating any issue of law or fact if the issue was actually litigated, was necessarily determined, and was essential to a valid and final judgment entered previously in litigation to which that person was a party, provided the estopped party had a full and fair opportunity and adequate incentive to litigate the issue conclusively, and subject to additional fairness constraints that arise when the party asserting the estoppel is not a party to the prior action.

There are some elements common to both claim and issue preclusion. The rules for what counts as a valid and final judgment on the merits are largely the same for the two doctrines, as are the rules for determining the parties bound by the earlier action. The key difference is that while claim preclusion forecloses whole causes of action, issue preclusion prevents relitigation of discrete issues – not just of law but of fact as well – whether or not those issues are central to the later litigation. Also, claim preclusion forecloses not only theories that were litigated, but also those that were not, although they are part of the same claim and could have been litigated in the earlier action, whereas issue preclusion forecloses only issues that were in fact litigated, fought over, and indeed necessary to the prior judgment. Finally, under certain circumstances, issue preclusion may be invoked by someone who was not a party to the earlier action; claim preclusion by definition may be invoked only by someone against whom the earlier claim was brought by definition, only someone against whom the earlier claim was brought may invoke claim preclusion.

A few of these points should be highlighted. To begin with, collateral estoppel is an incomplete bar. The second suit is not barred in toto, but issues identical to those already litigated in another suit may not be relitigated. Sometimes this will have the effect of barring the second action, but it need not be so as a logical matter. For example, if a party in an earlier action is determined to be a negligent driver, he may be precluded from relitigating the issue of his negligence in a subsequent lawsuit. Whether or not that ends the entire second lawsuit depends on what importance the substantive law places on that negligence question.

As noted above, an issue's relitigation can be precluded only if it was actually litigated and decided in the first action. Admissions or stipulations do not count for these purposes. The system wants to make sure a finder of fact ruled on an issue before resolution of that issue is forever taken for granted. Sometimes, we cannot know whether an issue was actually decided because of the opacity of a general jury verdict. For example, if A sued B for negligence in an automobile accident and a jury returned a verdict for B, we do not know that the jury found A to be contributorily negligent (even if that theory was argued). It might be that the jury found no contributory negligence, but found B free of negligence himself (or some other fact which would bar recovery). When faced with an opaque verdict, the system rejects issue preclusion.

Indeed, actual resolution of an issue is not enough. The resolution must have been central to the first action. In the above hypothetical, if the jury, by special verdict, found *both* contributory negligence by A *and* lack of negligence by B, *neither* would be central to its result, and thus neither would be entitled to preclusive effect in most jurisdictions. Because each finding was (or at least may have been) in some sense unnecessary to the ultimate resolution, the system does not place as much faith on each finding and denies its preclusive effect.

The Restatement (Second) of Judgments, followed to a greater or lesser extent in many United States jurisdictions, makes a series of additional exceptions to the general rules of issue preclusion. Among them are:

(1) The party against whom preclusion is sought could not, as a matter of law, obtain appellate review of the earlier action.
(2) The issue is one of law and a new determination is warranted to take account of an intervening change in the legal context or to avoid inequitable administration of the laws.
(3) A new determination is warranted because the procedures employed in the first action are not as elaborate as those in the second action.
(4) The party against whom preclusion is sought had a much smaller incentive to fight over the issue in the first action than in the second.

283. A major development in the law of issue preclusion over the last twenty-five years has been the decline in the requirement of mutuality. At common law, issue preclusion could be invoked only by one who was a party to the first action. The theory was that if someone was not going to be bound by an adverse result in the first action (as non-parties would not be), then fairness required that this person not be able to benefit from the first action either. But recently the US Supreme Court has held that so long as the party against whom the estoppel is sought was a party to the first action and had full and fair opportunity and incentive to litigate the issue, then he has had his day in court, and can be held to issue preclusion, even by someone who had no stake in the earlier action. Thus, for example, if A sues B for an automobile accident and loses because the jury found A to be contributorily negligent, when A sues C arising out of the same accident, C can invoke issue preclusion to prevent A from contesting his negligent conduct in the accident. This use would be termed "non-mutual defensive issue preclusion." It is non-mutual because the person invoking it (C) was not a party to the earlier action, and it is defensive because the person invoking it in the second action is using it as a shield, or defense.

The US Supreme Court has even allowed non-mutual offensive collateral estoppel, where the party asserting estoppel is a plaintiff suing a defendant who has lost on an issue in an earlier litigation. Because the defendant has had his day in court, due process is not offended. Offensive non-mutual issue preclusion can pose problems, however. Imagine two automobile accident victims, A and B. A sues the defendant C, and B declines to join A. If A loses, B will not be bound or precluded by A's loss because B has not had her day in court as due process requires. But if A wins, and B invokes non-mutual offensive collateral estoppel in her follow-on suit against C, her strategic behavior will have been rewarded. The court has made clear that where a party sits on the sideline in the earlier action merely to take advantage of possible issue preclusion, courts may decline to apply collateral estoppel.

§4. INTER-SYSTEM PRECLUSION

284. Since the rules of preclusion are common law rules, each court system will have its own, partially idiosyncratic system for determining preclusion. When inter-system preclusion is sought (i.e., the court in the second action is from a different system than the court in the first action), complexities arise.

The Constitution's Full Faith and Credit Clause and Congress' implementing statute, 28 U.S.C. §1738, require that each state court give the same preclusive effect to sister state judgments as they would have in the sister state (see paragraph 86). In other words, federal law requires that the preclusion law and principles of the state in which the first action was decided determine the preclusive effect of that first action. Thus, even if state A does not recognize non-mutual collateral estoppel, state A must give non-mutual preclusive effect to a judgment from state B if state B permits non-mutual collateral estoppel.

The US Supreme Court has read the Full Faith and Credit statute to require federal courts to enforce state court judgments just as they would be enforced in the state rendering the judgment. Thus, federal courts have the same duty as state courts to give preclusive effect to judgments from a sister state under the preclusion law of that sister state. The Supreme Court has also read the Supremacy Clause of Article VI of the Constitution to require state courts to give preclusive effect to federal judgments according to the federal common law of preclusion. Under this federal common law of preclusion, however, sometimes state-law preclusion principles are incorporated into federal common law and applied to determine the effect of a federal judgment, as where the federal court's subject-matter jurisdiction was based on diversity of citizenship.[1]

1. *See, e.g., Semtek Intern, Inc.v. Lockheed Martin Corp.*, 531 U.S. 497 (2001).

Part X. Arbitration

Chapter 1. Introduction

285. Arbitration is one of many forms of "Alternative Dispute Resolution" (ADR) in the United States. A proper understanding of arbitration use and function in the US requires a brief description of the goals of ADR, a short history of arbitration, and a discussion of other ADR methods.

§1. Goals of Alternative Dispute Resolution (ADR)

286. The goals of ADR are as varied as the methods. While there is some skepticism whether ADR is truly superior to traditional litigation, the growing popularity and employment of ADR attests that ADR does offer some advantages over litigation. Some of these benefits are discussed below.

I. Efficient Resolution of Disputes

287. Typically, the ADR process lasts one day or less, compared to years for litigation. Due to informal discovery and evidence procedures in most ADR proceedings, both sides can present their cases quickly and receive adjudication just as rapidly.[1]

1. *See* Miriam R. Arfin, "The Benefits of Alternative Dispute Resolution in Intellectual Property Disputes," Hastings Comm/Ent L. J. 17 (1995): 893, 899.

II. Lower Costs

288. Because most ADR methods take substantially less time to complete than does litigation, parties save on legal costs. While in some instances a lawyer may not even be required, shorter proceedings lead to fewer billable hours even when a lawyer is employed. Another cost-saving aspect relates to appeals. If the ADR outcome is binding on the parties and forecloses appeal of the award (paragraph 294), both sides potentially save time and money. This benefit can easily be underestimated unless the full financial and emotional costs of appellate litigation are duly appreciated.

III. Privacy and Confidentiality

289. Most ADR methods are conducted outside of the public eye. This is particularly helpful when parties are attempting to hide embarrassment over the suit or keep trade secrets away from the public and competitors. Furthermore, in most cases, neither the parties nor the arbitrator/mediator can be compelled to testify as to what happened in the proceedings.[1]

1. *See* id., at 901.

IV. Certainty and Finality of Resolution

290. ADR methods that are binding are generally non-appealable. One exception to this is the use of private judging in California and Texas, sometimes referred to as the "rent-a-judge" model of ADR (see below, paragraph 312). Judgments given in these situations are entered and treated as if they were awarded in a judicial court of law and are therefore appealable. This is sometimes perceived as the "short line to appellate court," used primarily by those who can afford to pay for their own judge and courtroom.

V. Flexibility of Procedures and Formation of Resolutions

291. Proponents of ADR believe that legally correct solutions are not always the best solutions. ADR resolutions can be easily tailored to meet the needs of the parties, especially when the parties are engaged in an ongoing relationship (e.g., lessee/lessor, landlord/tenant).[1] The parties involved can stipulate to traditional or unusual procedures concerning presentations of evidence, witness' testimony, production of documents, limitations on discovery, and often set time limits for presentation of their case to the neutral party. The parties are also allowed, in many situations, to choose the neutral third party who will arbitrate/mediate the case. This allows the parties to choose someone who is an expert in a particular industry, rather than a judge, who is generally an expert in the legal field only.[2]

1. *See* Carrie Menkel-Meadow, "When Dispute Resolution Begets Disputes of Its Own: Conflicts Among Dispute Professionals," UCLA L. Rev. 44 (1997): 1871, 1872.
2. *See* Suzanne J. Schmitz, "Using ADR for Your Client: An Illinois Lawyer's Guide," Ill. B.J. 85 (1997): 64, 68.

VI. Promotion of Success of Future Relationships between the Parties

292. When the parties have ongoing relationships, use of alternative methods of dispute resolution is believed to cool tempers and enable the parties to resume their relationship. The awards often also contain procedures to be used when future disputes arise, making future formal dispute resolution unnecessary.[1]

1. *See* Arfin, *supra*, at 901.

Chapter 2. Historical Background

§1. Traditional Hostility

293. Many courts have historically exhibited substantial hostility towards arbitration and other ADR techniques. Judges believed that only courts were properly equipped to resolve disputes efficiently and accurately. In fact, as recently as 1953, the US Supreme Court refused to enforce a pre-litigation agreement to arbitrate a dispute arising under the Securities Act of 1953. The Supreme Court believed that the issues involved under the act were too complex and important to entrust to an arbitrator.[1] It was not until the late 1960s that courts regularly enforced arbitration agreements within contracts.

1. *See Swan v. Wilko*, 346 U.S. 427 (1953), overruled by *Rodriquez de Quijas v. Shearson/American Express, Inc.*, 490 U.S. 477 (1989).

§2. Statutory Development

I. Federal Arbitration Act

294. The United States Congress passed the Federal Arbitration Act (FAA) in 1925. Prior to its passage, the common law courts would enforce contractual arbitration obligations only if the agreement to arbitrate was integrated into the original agreement giving rise to the dispute. Thus, the courts would not enforce agreements to arbitrate contractual disputes formed after the original contract, severely restricting the use and benefits of such agreements.[1] In response to heavy lobbying primarily by business interests and legal scholars, the American Bar Association (ABA) began to draft the United States Arbitration Act early in the 1920s. Congress essentially rubber-stamped the ABA's 1923 proposal to create the FAA. The main goals of the FAA, as stressed by the same lobbyists at the congressional hearings, were to reduce the delay and cost associated with litigation.[2]

Sections 2, 3, and 4 of the FAA are the keystones to accomplishing these objectives. Section 2 supersedes the common law rule on arbitration agreements by requiring courts to enforce such agreements as they would any other contractual obligation.[3] Section 3 allows federal courts to stay any proceedings on a motion by either party for any issue referable to arbitration unless the applicant has defaulted in her duty to arbitrate.[4] This provision essentially creates a good-faith duty to participate in arbitration if the applying party has so contracted. Section 4 requires the federal courts to order referral to arbitration if the moving party can demonstrate that both parties have contracted to arbitrate the dispute before the court.[5] In the event that the parties' contract does not provide the procedure for an arbitrator's selection, Section 5 supplements the powers granted via Sections 2-4 by allowing the court to designate an arbitrator, arbitrators, or umpires, as the case may require.[6] Taken together, these provisions allocate substantial authority to the federal courts to enforce arbitration agreements and, collaterally, to free its own docket of disputes that rightly ought to be before an arbitrator.

Section 6 provides that stay of proceedings applications be heard as any other motions while Section 7 authorizes arbitrators to compel witness attendance and other discovery as well as provide for summons procedure.[7] Section 8 departs from the general FAA pattern of arbitration facilitation to the extent that it retains the federal courts' ultimate authority in libel cases.[8]

Once arbitration has been completed and an award rendered, Section 9 requires the courts to enter an order confirming the award if the application for confirmation is made within one year of the award and the award has not been modified, vacated, or corrected pursuant to Sections 10 and 11.[9] Section 10 empowers the court to vacate, upon application by either party, an arbitration in a limited set of circumstances: where the award was procured by fraud or corruption;[10] where the arbitrator was evidently partial;[11] where arbitrator misconduct has prejudiced the right of the parties;[12] and where the arbitrator so exceeded or imperfectly executed her powers that the award is not mutual, final and definite.[13] Section 10(a)(5) further allows the court, in its discretion, to order a rehearing before another arbitrator if the time for arbitration has not lapsed. Section 11's provisions relate to modification and correction. Upon application by a party, the court may modify an arbitration award where there is an evident miscalculation of figures,[14] where the arbitrator has ruled on a matter not submitted to her,[15] or where the award is imperfect in a matter of form not affecting the merits of the controversy.[16] By limiting the court's powers of modification to merely technical matters, the twin aims of the FAA, reducing litigation costs and delay, are served by preventing parties from relitigating the dispute's substantive issues by an application for modification.

As noted above, despite congressional enthusiasm for arbitration in lieu of litigation, the courts were reluctant to broadly interpret the FAA's provisions. In *Swan*, the US Supreme Court held that arbitration could not adequately meet the policy aims of the 1933 Securities Act.[17] A similar view was taken by the Second Circuit in 1968 with respect to the antitrust laws.[18] Despite its averments that its decision was in no way influenced by distrust of arbitration, the court held that congressional intent in creating the antitrust statutes was to obtain legally accurate results and therefore antitrust disputes were ill-suited for arbitration where legal accuracy may be compromised to obtain the advantages of arbitration.[19]

Alongside the "litigation explosion" has developed a gradual judicial endorsement of ADR, as seen in the landmark decision of *Shearson/American Express, Inc. v. McMahon*.[20] In an action brought by consumers under §10(b) of the 1934 Securities Exchange Act (Exchange Act) and the Racketeer Influenced and Corrupt Organizations Act (RICO), the US Supreme Court reversed in part and affirmed in part a Second Circuit holding that the Exchange Act claim could be adequately arbitrated while the RICO claims could not. The court held both types of actions arbitrable under an arbitration clause contained within the purchase contract. Noting that decisions like *Swan* were premised on a perceived legislative intent to prohibit waiver of a judicial adjudication of certain claims arising under §12(2) of the Exchange Act, the court could discern no such intent from the legislative histories of either §10(b) of the Exchange Act or RICO. Absent such intent, the court concluded, the federal policy of rigorously enforcing valid arbitration agreements embodied within the FAA must be given effect. With its decision, the court finally gave the FAA the broad application that the language of 9 U.S.C. §2 seems to require.

1. *See* Mette M. Kurth, "An Unstoppable Mandate and an Immovable Policy: The Arbitration Act and the Bankruptcy Code Collide," U.C.L.A. L. Rev. 43 (1996): 999, 1003.
2. *See* id., at 1003-1006.
3. 9 U.S.C. §2 (arbitration agreements "… shall be valid, irrevocable, and enforceable, save upon such grounds as exist at law or in equity for the revocation of any contract").
4. Id., §3.
5. Id., §4.
6. Id., §5.
7. Id., §§6-7.
8. Id., §8.
9. Id., §9.
10. Id., §10(a)(1).
11. Id., §10(a)(2).
12. Id., §10(a)(3).
13. Id., §10(a)(4).
14. Id., §11(a).
15. Id., §11(b).
16. Id., §11(c).
17. *Swan v. Wilko*, 346 U.S. 427, 438 (1953).
18. *See American Safety Equip. Corp. v. J.P. Maguire & Co.*, 391 F.2nd 821 (2nd Cir. 1968).
19. Id., at 827.
20. *Shearson/American Express, Inc. v. McMahon*, 482 U.S. 220 (1987).

II. The New York Convention

295. Adopted by the United Nations in 1958, the Convention on the Recognition and Enforcement of Foreign Arbitral Awards (the New York Convention) entered into force in the United States in 1970.[1] The Convention mainly concerns the validity and enforceability of international commercial arbitration awards. Because Congress has absolute authority to regulate international commerce, the Convention applies to all US jurisdictions.

1. U.S.C. §201.

III. Uniform Arbitration Act[1]

296. While the FAA and the New York Convention operate at the federal level, the Uniform Arbitration Act (UAA) functions at the state level. Since its creation in 1955, thirty-four states and the District of Columbia have enacted the main provisions of the UAA.[2] Like the FAA, the UAA applies to written arbitration agreements entered into before, during or after contract formation. Unlike the FAA, which is limited to commercial contracts, the UAA applies to contracts concerning all matters, including employment contracts.[3]

Additional similarities between the FAA and the UAA include provisions for stay of proceedings, award vacation, award modification, and entry of award. The UAA goes beyond the FAA in its specificity. For example, UAA Section 7 authorizes arbitrators to compel discovery, issue subpoenas, and conduct discovery; Section 10 provides for arbitrator's fees and expenses to be part of the award; while Section 18 contains a venue provision, which has no parallel in the FAA.

To supplement the UAA, the Journal of Dispute Resolution annually prepares an article tracing recent developments in construction and implementation of the act.[4] In the interest of uniformity among state practices concerning the UAA, the Journal of Dispute Resolution reviews and documents emerging issues like the validity of arbitration agreements, overarching state laws that pre-empt the UAA, waiving ADR rights, and the potential prejudicial effects of arbitration awards.[5]

1. For the full text of the UAA *see* Howard M. Holtzmann & Donald Francis Donovan, "United States," in *International Handbook on Commercial Arbitration U.S.A.*, eds Pieter Sanders et al. (1998), Annex IV-1-6.
2. Dan Coughlin et al., "Recent Developments: The Uniform Arbitration Act," J. Disp. Resol. 1993 (1993): 397. For a complete listing of the location of arbitration provisions for each state *see* Holtzmann, *supra*, at Annex V.
3. "Unif. Arbitration Act" §1, 7 U.L.A. §1 (2000).
4. Coughlin, *supra*, at 397.
5. *See generally* id.

§3. Modern Attitudes

297. Courts today view pre-litigation arbitration agreements as a simple matter of contract: private parties voluntarily forgoing their right to litigate in exchange for a mutually agreeable resolution forum. Accordingly, the federal courts employ a presumption in favor of enforceability.[1] In essence, this presumption means that an arbitration clause will be enforced absent any traditional reasons for non-enforcement of a contract such as illegality, unconscionability or overreaching. In *Graham Oil Co. v. Arco Products Co.*, for example, the Ninth Circuit declared void an arbitration clause that subverted the intent of congressional legislation, the Petroleum Marketing Practices Act (PMPA).[2] Congress enacted PMPA in order to remedy gross disparity of bargaining power between petroleum franchisers and franchisees.[3] In *Graham*, the court found that the franchiser ARCO had inserted into the franchise agreement an arbitration clause that directly contradicted provisions of PMPA allowing for exemplary damages and attorney fees that were intended to remedy franchiser overreaching.[4] Accordingly, the court held that while there is indeed a firm federal policy in favor of enforcing arbitration agreements, such clauses could not be enforced in contravention of remedial statutory mandates.[5]

The Ninth Circuit's result in *Graham* mirrors US Supreme Court rulings in favor of arbitration agreements delivered in a series of decisions in the 1980s.[6] Unsurprisingly, as the US Supreme Court has consistently refused to allow the legal fallibility of arbitration awards to play a role in determining whether an arbitration agreement is enforceable, the lower federal courts have become advocates of the "ADR revolution."[7] The federal courts' enthusiasm for ADR can be seen by the incorporation of ADR into the litigation process via so-called "court-annexed ADR" (§313) Thus, traditional judicial hostility to ADR has transformed into acceptance and employment.[8]

1. *See, e.g., Quackenbush v. Allstate Ins. Co.*, 517 U.S. 706, 728 (1996); *see also Moses H. Cone Mem. Hosp. v. Mercury Constr. Corp.*, 460 U.S. 1, 24-25 (1983).
2. *Graham Oil Co. v. Arco Products Co., A Division of Atlantic Richfield Co.*, 43 F.3rd 1244 (9th Cir. 1994).
3. Id., at 1246.
4. Id., at 1247-1248.
5. Id., at 1248.
6. *See* Martin J. Newhouse, "Some Reflections on ADR and the Changing Role of the Courts", B. B.J. 39-Apr. (1995): 15, 15-16.
7. Id.
8. Id., at 17; *See* Developments, "The Paths of Civil Litigation," Harv. L. Rev. 113 (2000): 1752, 1851-1875.

I. Legislation

298. Recent legislative and executive action has further solidified ADR's position as a viable alternative to litigation.

In 1990, Congress enacted significant legislation bolstering ADR. The Civil Justice Reform Act (CJRA)[1] required each district to draft a plan to reduce litigation costs and delays. At the courts' discretion, ADR may be incorporated as part of the plan. All of the districts involved in Phase I of the act's implementation as pilot districts used some form of ADR in their plans.[2] The remaining districts completed their plans by December of 1993, with at least seventy-five of the ninety-four districts implementing the objectives of the CJRA by deploying some form of ADR.[3]

Another recent federal enactment is the Administrative Dispute Resolution Act (ADRA).[4] The ADRA authorizes and encourages federal agencies to use ADR in their enforcement and administrative functions. The agencies are not required to use ADR but must adopt a policy concerning implementation of the Act. So far, many agencies have complied, many of which incorporate ADR as part of their ADRA implementation policy. Incorporating agencies include the Equal Employment Opportunity Commission, the Securities Exchange Commission, the Department of Labor, and the US Air Force.[5]

Finally, in 1991, the first President Bush issued an executive order requiring federal agencies to work towards settlement, including via ADR.[6] The Justice Department, among others, has complied with the order by formulating and executing a number of directives encouraging ADR.[7]

The Clinton administration also endorsed ADR use in the public sector. Vice President Gore strongly recommended ADR in his National Performance Review, spurring President Clinton to issue an executive order directing federal agencies to explore consensual methods for rulemaking. President Clinton also established the National Partnership Council to provide training in ADR techniques to agency employees. Increased presidential interest in ADR can in part be attributed to the growth in lawsuits against federal agencies, spurred in part by flawed rulemaking processes that invite litigation by special-interest groups.[8]

1. 28 U.S.C. §473(a)(6).
2. S. Gale Dick, "ADR at the Crossroads," Disp. Resol. J. 49-Mar. (1994): 47, 48.
3. Id.
4. 5 U.S.C. §581.
5. Dick, *supra*, at 48.

6. Exec. Order No. 12778, 56 Fed. Reg. 55, 195 (1991).
7. Dick, *supra*, at 49.
8. Department, *ADR in the News*, 49-Mar. Disp. Resol. J. 3 (1994).

II. Other

299. Outside of the government sector, private institutions are gradually incorporating ADR as an alternative to litigation. For example, in 1993 the ABA established the ABA Section of Dispute Resolution, fifteen years after establishing the Standing Committee on Dispute Resolution to aid its members in ADR training and education. Nearly 700 corporations and 1,500 law firms have signed pledges with the Center for Public Resources to consider ADR before litigation. Additionally, the American Arbitration Association (AAA) reported that by 1992 it had processed more than one million cases.[1] In order to increase its ability to resolve disputes in an increasing variety of disputes, the AAA has been actively producing new rules and procedures to cover emerging arbitration arenas like health care and employment. This activity reflects growing use of ADR in consumer services and employment industries.[2] With ADR firmly positioned in the mainstream, ADR use and popularity can only increase.

1. Dick, *supra*, at 50.
2. Id., at 52.

Chapter 3. Types of ADR

§1. Negotiation

300. Negotiation is the most common dispute-resolution method, but is often overlooked as a formal ADR method. This is so despite the fact that most settlement agreements are reached via negotiation. Most often, there is no neutral third party assisting the parties in coming to an agreement, a significant distinction from most other types of ADR. Negotiation works best when participating parties frankly discuss the facts, issues, and solutions to their dispute. Compromise is the key to successful dispute resolution: settlement ultimately depends on the parties' ability to cooperate in order to reach agreement. While direct negotiation ought to be the first option to resolving disputes, most parties file suit first and negotiate later. Sophisticated business parties, however, recognize that large gains may be achieved by seeking negotiated resolutions before resorting to litigation.[1]

1. *See* Robert B. Fitzpatrick et al., "Alternative Dispute Resolution – Types of ADR Mechanisms," ALI-ABA C106 (1995): 565, 569 ("*ADR Mechanisms*" hereinafter).

§2. Arbitration

301. Arbitration is probably the best known alternative to litigation,[1] picking up where negotiation leaves off. Before arbitration proceedings begin, the parties must choose the arbitrator. Some prefer only one arbitrator, while others prefer three. Where panels of three are chosen, each party chooses one arbitrator and together the chosen arbitrators appoint a third neutral party. The parties are able to take many things into consideration when choosing the arbitrators, including familiarity with the industry, familiarity with this particular dispute, and presumed sympathy for one side or another. Parties define the procedures, which allows for maximum flexibility. There is usually limited discovery and rules of evidence may or may not be followed, depending on agreement of the parties. As discussed above (§294), if the parties opt for discovery, arbitrators have been empowered via the FAA and the UAA to compel that discovery. Regardless, there is often little presentation of direct evidence. Parties depend on written evidence and cross-examination is limited to the written testimony.

Once the proceedings have ended, the arbitrator usually has thirty days to render a written decision and award. It may or may not be accompanied by a written explanation or evaluation of the decision. However, evaluations often accompany awards given in non-binding arbitration hearings to aid in settlement conferences.[2] As mentioned above, arbitrators have been empowered to reach their conclusions via compulsory discovery.

While there are obvious parallels to adversary litigation,[3] arbitration differs in at least two important respects. First, the parties are usually involved in selecting the neutral individual(s) who will arbitrate the dispute. Second, arbitration procedures are flexible and adaptable to the unique needs and desires of each set of parties.[4]

Procedural flexibility leads to swifter resolution, lower costs, and possibly fairer results because the arbitrator may depart from the rule of law to formulate an equitable award.[5] In international disputes, procedural flexibility is especially attractive because the arbitrator can pick and choose among civil and common law rules to fashion an outcome that is acceptable to both parties, one or both of which may be suspicious of the rules of the arbitrating forum.[6]

1. Roger J. Patterson, "Dispute Resolution in a World of Alternatives," Cath. U. L. Rev. 37 (1988): 591, 592.
2. Robert B. Fitzpatrick, "Shouldn't We Make Full Disclosure to our Clients of ADR Options?," ALI-ABA SC59 (1998): 755, 765 ("*ADR Options*" hereinafter).
3. For an exhaustive discussion of the extent to which ADR procedure parallels civil procedure *see* Jack M. Sabatino, "ADR as "Litigation Lite": Procedural and Evidentiary Norms Embedded Within Alternative Dispute Resolution," Emory L. J. 47 (1998): 1289.
4. *See* Patterson, *supra*, at 593-594.
5. *See* Fitzpatrick, *ADR Options, supra*, at 766-767.
6. *See generally* Alan Scott Rau & Edward F. Sherman, "Tradition and Innovation in International Arbitration Procedure," Tex. Int'l L. J. 30 (1995): 89.

302. Arbitration can generally be classified into two varieties: binding and nonbinding.

I. Binding Arbitration

303. Binding arbitration is similar to the above description, except case presentations are somewhat more formal because of the binding nature of the proceeding. There may be live witnesses in addition to the written testimony, but there is still limited cross-examination and discovery. Many parties prefer binding arbitration because of its finality. The results of binding arbitration are seldom appealable absent a showing of fraud, undisclosed conflict of interest or overreaching by the arbitrator, or if the award itself goes against public policy.

II. Non-Binding Arbitration

304. Non-binding arbitration, on the other hand, is usually a very informal proceeding. The arbitrator may be more flexible in allowing certain types of evidence or in allowing the parties to go beyond the pleadings. Recalling that an arbitration award may be found void if the parties' constitutionally protected due-process rights are violated, non-binding arbitration can descend beneath this floor because the parties will not be bound by the outcome. The aim of non-binding arbitration is that if the parties do not accept the arbitrator's award, the arbitrator can then act as a mediator and facilitate resolution of the dispute in light of the evaluation given after all arguments have been presented.

At least one jurisdiction, however, has ruled that arbitration clauses allowing for non-binding arbitration are unenforceable. In *Schaefer v. Allstate*,[1] the Ohio Supreme Court refused to enforce a contractual arbitration clause that compelled arbitration but allowed de novo review of the dispute by the courts if the arbitrator's award exceeded a certain amount. The court reasoned that arbitration, by definition, must have a decision that is binding, regardless of outcome.[2] Any proceeding that resembles arbitration yet lacks a binding outcome, the court concluded, resembles mediation more than arbitration.[3]

One of the means recently employed by courts to reduce litigation delays and costs is court-annexed arbitration. It is very similar to private arbitration, except that the outcome is rarely binding over the objection of either party. If neither party requests review of the arbitrator's award within a certain period (e.g., thirty days) after the award date, the award does becomes binding. Further, if one party requests trial but does not improve his position by a certain margin (e.g., 10% greater than the arbitrator's award) then that party must bear his adversary's fees and costs for the trial. While court-annexed arbitration may not be conclusive, the courts have the power to compel pretrial arbitration in civil matters, either by rule or by statute.[4] Additionally, punitive rules like the ones above encourage parties to participate in good faith and maintain a reasonable conception of the worth of their claims.[5]

A final version of binding arbitration is "Last Offer Arbitration" (LOA), sometimes called "Baseball Arbitration." First, each party gives the arbitrator his proposal for a settlement agreement. Then, case presentations are given as in regular binding arbitration. The arbitrator then chooses between the original proposals based on what he perceives to be the most fair and reasonable. The arbitrator cannot choose any other amount but must choose between the amounts in the original proposals. Theoretically, this provides an incentive for both parties to be as reasonable as possible or the arbitrator will choose the other party's proposal.[6]

1. *Schaefer v. Allstate Ins. Co.*, 63 Ohio St. 3rd 708, 590 N.E. 2nd 1242 (Ohio 1992).
2. *Schaefer*, 63 Ohio St. 3rd at 713-714, 590 N.E. at 1246-1247.
3. *See generally* Kathryn L. Hale, "Nonbinding Arbitration: An Oxymoron?," U. Tol. L. Rev. 24 (1993): 1003 (discussing *Schaefer* and speculating on its impact on the Ohio ADR movement).
4. *See* Lucy V. Katz, :Compulsory Alternative Dispute Resolution and Voluntarism: Two-Headed Monster or Two Sides of the Same Coin?," J. Disp. Resol. 1993 (1993): 1, 20-45.
5. *See* Tom Arnold, "Vocabulary of ADR Procedures," ALI-ABA C976 (1994): 19, 46.
6. Id., at 47-48.

§3. Mediation

305. Mediation may be defined as negotiation with a third party, where the third party takes an active part in the negotiations. In contrast to an arbitrator who acts more like an impartial judge by hearing presentations and rendering an award, the mediator is a neutral person who facilitates communication between the parties. Acting as a "participant-observer," he may also evaluate the strengths and weaknesses of each side and attempt to persuade the parties to recognize the strengths of the opposing party's case in order to encourage compromise and settlement between the parties. Mediation may be an especially useful method where the parties have an ongoing relationship because there is the possibility of tailoring a resolution so that both sides come away winners. The mediator is generally not concerned with "justice"; however, the result is sometimes fairer than any resolution a court would devise.[1]

Mediation procedure involves very informal case presentations to the mediator, usually without formal "evidence," such as witness' testimony being presented. After the parties or their attorneys have presented a closing argument-like statement, the parties caucus while the mediator exercises so-called "shuttle-diplomacy," trekking between caucuses to find common ground and encourage compromise.[2] There is often little or no formal discovery before the sessions take place, yet participating attorneys should be forewarned to scrutinize local rules carefully lest they forego opportunities to introduce important documents or evidence.[3] The presence of representatives with settlement power is usually required at the mediation sessions.

Mediation is regarded as very successful, especially in cases where the parties are participating voluntarily. Most mediation participants, 75% or more, are satisfied with the process even when an agreement is not reached.[4] Studies have found that when compared to litigation, mediation may be superior in areas of compliance, cost, efficiency, and agreement stability.[5] In disputes involving parties in ongoing relationships, mediation has proven to be especially effective in fostering and maintaining beneficial future working relationships.[6]

Mediation may be less effective when participation is court mandated rather than voluntary.[7] It is also not generally appropriate for complex, fact-intensive disputes. In construction disputes, for example, attorneys surveyed felt that mediation was inappropriate for cases where the issues involved a novel point of law, where witness credibility was critical or where the opponent's veracity was uncertain.[8] Other instances where mediation may be inappropriate are criminal cases, disputes in which the state or the public has an interest in vindication, cases requiring constitutional interpretation, and potential mass torts where a plaintiff has yet to prevail.[9] Mediation may also be inappropriate where there is an imbalance of power between the parties and/or one or both parties are unwilling to transact in good faith.[10]

1. *See* Fitzpatrick, *ADR Options, supra*, at 764-766.
2. *See* id., at 764.
3. *See* Helen B. Culiner, "Practical Guidelines for Lawyers Representing Clients in Arbitration Proceedings Today," Disp. Resol. J. 49-Sep. (1994): 48, 52.
4. Lynn A. Kerbeshian, "ADR: To Be Or ...?," N.D. L. Rev. 70 (1994): 381, 385.
5. *See* id., at 385-397.
6. *See* Fitzpatrick, *ADR Options, supra*, at 765.
7. *See* Kebershian, *supra*, at 422-423.
8. Thomas J. Stipanowich, "Beyond Arbitration: Innovation and Evolution in the United States Construction Industry," Wake Forest L. Rev. 31 (1996): 65, 98.
9. Judith P. Meyer, "The Pros and Cons of Mediation," Disp. Resol. J. 52-Sum. (1997): 8, 14.
10. Id.

§4. Mediation-Arbitration Hybrids

306. The success of both arbitration and mediation has spawned a pair of hybrids as ADR participants attempt to tailor the process to their unique needs. First of the pair is "Med-Arb." Med-Arb is a hybrid method using aspects of both mediation and arbitration. Both parties agree that mediation will be attempted first, then, if no agreement can be reached, the mediator (or another neutral party) will become the arbitrator and decide the case according to the information acquired during the mediation sessions. The arbitrator's decision is usually somewhere between the last offers of each side. This process allows the neutral party to take an active role initially in resolving the conflict, a major benefit of mediation, then issue a final award, a main objective of arbitration. Further, the neutral party's active role can spur the disputants to greater reasonableness in their statements and positions in the caucus stage because they realize that outrageous or extreme statements may influence the final award.[1]

The other half of the hybrids pair is "MEDALOA" (*Med*iation *A*nd *L*ast *O*ffer *A*rbitration). MEDALOA obviously combines the features of mediation and LOA. After mediation efforts reach an impasse, each party presents a summation argument of its case and prepares a written final offer and gives it to the arbitrator. The arbitrator picks the offer which seems the most reasonable, and that becomes the award. Because it is presumed that the arbitrator will choose the most reasonable offer, parties have an incentive to be as reasonable as possible so that their offer will be chosen.

MEDALOA comes in two alternatives for two different situations. The first alternative is for impasse-breaking in small value disputes. Here, the procedure is virtually identical to the above description. Its main attraction is the relative speed by which a small dispute can be resolved. Even distrust of the mediator-turned-arbitrator is quickly and cheaply resolved by the neutral party contacting a likely arbitrator who will be agreeable to both parties. The second alterative arises in big value cases or where the impasse between the parties is significant. Here, the mediator becomes a mediator facilitator of the binding arbitration model and attempts to fashion a compromise award. The big value alternative is especially useful in disputes where initial arbitration would be unsafe, as in complex cases where the parties are unsure of the parameters of the dispute and how much of their resources ought to be devoted to the dispute. Having determined the parameters via mediation, the neutral party can then commence arbitration satisfactorily.[2]

1. *See* Arnold, *supra*, at 40-41.
2. Id., at 48-59.

§5. Conciliation

307. Conciliation is basically negotiation with the addition of a third party who may or may not be neutral. The third party facilitates communication and the expediency of the process but does not actively participate in resolving the dispute.[1] Most notably, Title VII of the Civil Rights Act of 1964 requires the Equal Employment Opportunity Commission to conciliate discrimination charges before filing a lawsuit or taking other final action.[2]

1. *See* Fitzpatrick, *ADR Options, supra*, at 763.
2. *See* 42 U.S.C. §2000e-5.

§6. Summary Jury Trial

308. Frequently used in the federal court system, summary jury trials (SJT) involve relatively formal case presentations by counsel to an advisory jury. In court-annexed SJT situations, the jury is empanelled from the regular jury pool and jurors may or may not be informed of their status as "advisory" jurors. Presentations are often limited to affidavit and documentary evidence, and legal arguments by counsel, unless the parties agree otherwise. Many SJTs take place in one half-day session (after discovery), which, if it results in settlement, is extremely cost-effective. The benefit of SJT is that it allows the parties to actually try the case in front of a jury. Once the jurors render their decision (which is usually non-binding), they are usually made available to the parties to answer questions. This allows the parties to gain insight into the value of their case without spending the time required to fully try a case and forces them to recognize the weaknesses of their side and the strengths of their opponent's arguments. In fact, "SJT is most effective when the parties are far apart and have divergent views of the facts and the evidence."[1] Because the goal of SJT is settlement, the parties or their representatives with settlement authority are usually required, as a matter of the forum's local rules, to attend the proceeding.[2]

There is considerable controversy over whether SJT is a worthwhile process. While some judges embrace SJT as a method of pretrial settlement,[3] others believe that when parties are forced to participate and will proceed to litigation whatever the result, SJT merely wastes valuable court time and resources. Much of the initial shine of SJT has been tarnished by the realization that SJT can only fully accomplish its purpose once discovery has been completed, usually a lengthy and expensive process.[4] However, since most SJTs are conducted in front of only six jurors and last less than one day, significant cost savings can be achieved if in fact settlement is facilitated through the process.[5]

Other opponents directly attack judicial authority to require participation in the SJT process, maintaining that the judges do not possess the requisite authority. In the 1993 decision *In re NLO, Inc.*, compulsory SJT was rejected as outside of judicial authority.[6] However, with the recent amendments to Rule 16 of the Federal Rules of Civil Procedure, explicitly authorizing the use of ADR in general and SJT in particular, as well as statutory support,[7] most commentators are willing to concede that the use of ADR, including SJT, is part of the federal court system, and that SJT is simply a type of pretrial conference.[8] Proponents assert that because SJT is not binding, it does not deny parties any rights, including the ultimate right to jury trial;[9] further, these advocates contend that even if settlement does not in fact occur after the SJT, the subsequent trials themselves proceed at a faster pace because the "rehearsal" provided a means to streamline the issues for trial.[10]

Another criticism of SJT concerns a belief that jurors will not take their duty as seriously when informed that they will be rendering an advisory opinion; opponents of SJT accordingly caution SJT advocates that if SJTs are used frequently, the entire jury pool may be tainted if jurors begin to believe a majority of decisions will be non-binding. However, studies have shown that jurors will take their duty at least as seriously as in traditional litigation, especially after they become aware that they will be required to answer questions concerning their verdict when the proceedings have finished.[11]

An additional, and perhaps more significant, controversy surrounding SJT is protection of work product and legal theories. During SJT, parties are required to exercise good faith in presenting their legal arguments. If the parties expect to continue to trial, they may be reluctant to expose their theories to the opposing party before the trial begins. Supporters of SJT contend that the new mandatory disclosure policies and generous sharing of information before trial already expose much of the information that the party hopes to protect until trial, and therefore it would be very unlikely that one party would be in possession of a piece of critical information just before trial that has not been made available to the other.[12] However, work-product concerns pervaded the Seventh Circuit decision in *Strandell v. Jackson County*,[13] which denied the district courts in its circuit the power to compel SJT participation. The court reasoned that the current work-product privilege rules reflect a careful balance between disclosure and confidentiality, a balance that may be upset by an SJT proceeding; thus, a district court cannot compel SJT participation in contravention of the work-product rules' policy.[14]

Despite the controversy surrounding SJT, many commentators agree that SJT does not meet the needs of every set of litigants. Therefore, some specific guidelines should be used when channeling cases into SJT. These include restricting SJT use to private disputes, limiting opportunities for work product and discovery abuse, considering the complexity of each case before referring it to SJT, ensuring full confidentiality of documents and other evidence, allowing opportunities for the parties to control and design their own SJT procedures, informing the jury of its advisory role in advance, and promoting the use of voluntary SJT.[15]

A final wrinkle in the SJT fabric is "Binding Hi-Low SJT": the SJT proceeds as above, except that the parties have agreed to a cap on the low and high recovery awards. The jury verdict will be binding if it is between the high and low caps. If the verdict comes in outside the agreed range, the amount awarded will be modified to reach the nearest cap. Because SJT was designed to be a non-binding process that allowed parties to evaluate probable outcomes to their suits, attorney and judicial support of the view that binding hi-low SJT ought to be employed, much less compelled, has been lukewarm at best. Generally, the SJT may only become binding by party stipulation out of respect for due-process rights.[16]

1. *See* Patterson, *supra*, at 596; Gladys Kessler & Linda J. Finkelstein, "The Evolution of a Multi-Door Courthouse," Cath. U. L. Rev. 37 (1988): 577, 589.
2. *See, e.g.*, US Dist. Ct. R. N.D. Ohio 16.8(4).
3. For example, the creator of SJT, Judge Thomas Lambros, referred over more than 90% ninety percent of his jury trial cases to the process. *See* Shelby F. Grubbs, "A Brief Survey of Court Annexed ADR: Where We Are and Where We Are Going," Tenn. B.J. 30-Feb. (1994): 20, 23.
4. Id.
5. *See* Thomas D. Lambros, "The Summary Jury Trial and Other Alternative Methods of Dispute Resolution: A Report to the Judicial Conference of the United States Committee on the Operation of the Jury System," F.R.D. 103 (1984): 461, 472.
6. *In re NLO, Inc.*, 5 F.3rd 154 (6th Cir. 1993).
7. *See* 28 U.S.C. §§473 (a)(6)(B), (b)(4) (requiring district courts, pursuant to CJRA, to consider SJT to reduce litigation delay and expense; district courts may also implement rules providing for compulsory attendance and sanctions if the courts choose to use SJT as part of their CJRA plans).
8. *See* Fed. R. Civ. P. 16(c)(9); *see also* Fed. R. Civ. P. 16 Advisory Committee's 1993 note.
9. Lucille M. Ponte, "Putting Mandatory Summary Jury Trial Back on the Docket: Recommendations on the Exercise of Judicial Authority," Fordham L. Rev. 63 (1995): 1069, 1091.
10. *See* Shira A. Scheindlin & David Ross, "The ADR Landscape," PLI/Lit 496 (1994): 437, 451.
11. *See* Bobby Marzine Harges, "The Promise of the Mandatory Summary Jury Trial," Temp. L. Rev. 63 (1990): 799, 809-810.
12. *See* id., at 808-809.
13. *Strandell v. Jackson County*, 838 F.2nd 884 (7th Cir. 1987).
14. Id., at 888.
15. *See* Ponte, *supra*, at 1095-1097.

16. *See* Ann E. Woodley, "Strengthening the Summary Jury Trial: A Proposal to Increase Its Effectiveness and Encouraging Uniformity in Its Use," Ohio St. J. on Disp. Resol. 12 (1997): 541, 598-602.

§7. Minitrial

309. Similar to advisory arbitration, a minitrial is a private affair and thus much less controversial than a SJT. Conceptually, a minitrial can be viewed as an arbitration where the parties prefer a trial-like proceeding. A minitrial involves a moderately formal case presentation, presented by counsel, involving affidavit, deposition, and documentary evidence. The entire proceeding frequently lasts only one or two days. The presentations are made to a neutral who is an expert in the industry and to party representatives with settlement authority. The ruling is non-binding and reasons customarily accompany the ruling, in an effort to spur settlement conferences between the parties.

Minitrials are intended to provide parties with a realistic view of their case and the likely outcome of the litigation. It is presumed that given this perspective, both sides will be more willing to settle and less unyielding due to unrealistic views. Like many ADR proceedings, the parties are given opportunities to tailor the proceedings to reflect their preferences. Formal rules of evidence and procedure may or may not be followed depending upon agreement of the parties. The goal of a minitrial is similar to mediation where there is an ongoing relationship between the parties and where the parties truly want to resolve the dispute amicably. If successful, the settlement reached will foster continued cooperation between the parties and may aid in resolving future disputes.[1]

1. *See generally* Kessler, *supra*, at 595-596.

§8. Fact-Finding

310. Combining elements of mediation and arbitration, fact-finding is a relatively simple process where the parties choose a neutral third party to investigate critical facts. When this method is used, the parties have already agreed that given a particular factual determination, they would resolve the case in accordance with those facts. The neutral party is generally an expert in the particular industry. It is presumed that once the disputed facts have been determined, the parties will be more likely to settle. The neutral party does not resolve the dispute, but only aids in the process.[1]

1. *See* Fitzpatrick, *ADR Mechanisms, supra*, at 574.

§9. Early Neutral Evaluation

311. Early neutral evaluation (ENE) is regularly used by the courts at an early point in the litigation process. It is a very informal process in which the parties are referred (usually by a court) to an outside neutral evaluator to discuss all aspects of the case. Formal rules of procedure and evidence are largely ignored and most of the sessions involve direct discussions between the evaluator and the parties. The evaluator listens to brief presentations by each party and offers his opinion as to the likely outcome of the case. The major purposes of ENE are similar to the purposes of pretrial conferences: to enhance communication, narrow issues, structure the discovery process, and promote settlement. As a facilitator of settlement, ENE works best when it is used shortly before trial. Shortly before trial, both parties can be assured that the case being evaluated will be substantially similar to the case that will be tried. Prior to full discovery, parties have no such assurance. Because the use of ENE is relatively uncontroversial, and because most parties truly gain from the process, many federal and state courts use ENE as a preliminary method of case evaluation.[1]

1. *See* Fitzpatrick, *ADR Options, supra*, at 773.

§10. Private Judging

312. Private judging is exactly what the name expresses: private parties hire a third party to act as a judge (oftentimes a retired judge), hire court reporters, acquire a "courtroom," and present their case as they would in a traditional forum. Usually, case presentations follow traditional formalities concerning procedural and evidentiary rules, including the presence of live witnesses. The private judge reports his decision to the proper court and judgment is entered on the decision as if the action had been decided in that court.[1]

At least two states, California[2] and Texas,[3] statutorily authorize the use of private judging and allow the decision to be subject to the normal appellate process. Because of the possibility for appeal, the process usually is procedurally identical to traditional courtroom litigation. Essentially a judgment of the court, the verdict rendered by the private judge must comport with due-process requirements and be legally accurate to be sustained on appeal. This aspect of private judging makes it unique among ADR techniques.[4]

Opponents of private judging have alleged that state encouragement of the "Rent-A-Judge" system entices judges to retire early so that they can earn substantial payments from the private sector. However, this is speculation and no research has been done to prove or disprove the allegation. Another criticism is that the existence of private judging creates a two-tiered system of justice where the "rich" are able to resolve their disputes quickly and efficiently, while those without substantial economic resources must endure the congested public court system. Proponents counter those assertions by pointing out that by allowing those who can afford to channel out of the public justice system to do so, more cases flow through the court's docket than otherwise would be able to, and at a faster pace.[5]

1. *See* Arnold, *supra*, at 65.
2. Cal. Code. Civ. Proc. §§638-644.
3. Tex. Civ. Prac. & Rem. Code §§151.001-151.013.
4. *See* Arnold, *supra*, at 65.
5. *See, e.g.*, Eric D. Green, "Avoiding the Legal Logjam – Private Justice, California Style," in *Corporate Dispute Management*, ed. Center for Public Resources (1982), 65, 79-81.

§11. Court-Annexed ADR

313. Judges are given considerable latitude in requiring parties to participate in ADR rather than going straight to traditional litigation. However, there are often restrictions. Cases worth more than a given dollar value (e.g., more than USD 100,000) or of a specific type (e.g., domestic violence disputes) are often not appropriate for ADR. Furthermore, many commentators doubt that forcing parties to participate in ADR affects the speed or cost of litigation when the parties are unwilling to settle from the beginning. However, participation in the ADR hearings, while mandatory, is never truly binding unless the parties agree otherwise.

When judges refer parties to court-annexed ADR, the neutral(s) is (are) usually members of the judiciary or lawyers specifically trained in mediation processes. This is different from private ADR, where the parties are allowed to choose their own neutral based on factors they feel are important.

While ADR initially developed as a voluntary, extrajudicial means for dispute settlement, ADR has become a component of the judicial system as well. As noted above, pursuant to the CRJA, many districts now employ ADR, including arbitration as part of their plans to reduce litigation delays and costs. Court-annexed ADR, however, diverges markedly from traditional ADR: where extrajudicial arbitration is voluntary, intrajudicial ADR is often compulsory and coercive.[1]

Most federal and some state courts have the authority to require the parties to participate in arbitration before the formal litigation process begins. While some commentators have challenged the courts' authority to order ADR, it is now well established that the federal courts may do so via their pretrial conferencing powers conferred in Federal Rule of Civil Procedure 16 (see paragraph 308). The decision is binding unless one party requests a trial de novo within a specified period of time (usually thirty to sixty days of the award).[2] However, the party requesting a trial must improve his position by a given amount at the trial or he will be required to pay the costs and attorneys' fees of his opponent for the trial. In cases where arbitration is court-ordered, both parties must participate in good faith. It is not uncommon for courts to order monetary sanctions on parties that fail to meet the good-faith standard.[3] Another sanction used by some courts is prohibiting evidence not presented in arbitration from being used during the trial. This usually succeeds at convincing the unwilling party to participate fully in the arbitration proceeding.[4]

While court-annexed ADR is generally conceded as a valid exercise of judicial authority, numerous validity issues abound. For example, many are concerned that court-compelled ADR may proceed in violation of constitutional rights like the right to jury trial, due process of law, equal protection of the laws, separation of powers, and First Amendment rights. The US Supreme Court has generally been hospitable to ADR methods since the 1980s, frequently going out of its way to find ADR procedures constitutionally non-offensive. In essence, the Supreme Court has held that ADR procedures of almost any type are constitutionally acceptable as long as the outcome is at some point subject to review.[5]

1. *See* Lucy V. Katz, "Compulsory Alternative Dispute Resolution and Voluntarism: Two-Headed Monster or Two Sides of the Same Coin?," J. Disp. Resol. 1993 (1993): 1.

2. Id., at 7-9.
3. Id., at 39-40.
4. Id., at 38.
5. *See* id., 22-31.

Chapter 4. Lex Arbitri

§1. Federal Lex Arbitri

314. The federal law of arbitration is, as noted above (paragraph 294), the FAA.[1] Because Congress has been given exclusive power over international commerce, any arbitration matter related to either foreign persons or foreign subject matter will be controlled by the FAA. Notably, the FAA, in Section 201, incorporates the New York Convention, which provides for international enforcement of arbitration awards and is discussed more fully below. Federal arbitration law is further supplemented by the Panama Convention. The Panama Convention is to the Western Hemisphere what the New York Convention is to the world. While closely paralleling the New York Convention, the Panama Convention differs from it most significantly in the area of enforceable awards by subject matter. This small yet important variance is also discussed below (paragraphs 319-321).

Section 2 of the FAA provides for the enforceability of arbitration clauses, yet invocation of Section 2 presupposes a valid contract. Thus, the validity of an arbitration clause is to be measured by common law contract principles before formal arbitration provisions can be applied. In federal courts, the contract principles applied will be determined by the forum state's choice-of-law doctrines.[2] Usually, the district court applies the law of the state in which it sits. Therefore, contract validity becomes a question of local law, which cannot be generalized.

While it has been traditionally held that the issue of whether a dispute is arbitrable is reserved for the public courts, the US Supreme Court indicated in *Prima Paints*[3] that if an arbitration clause within a contract is written so broadly that it can fairly be construed to be the intent of the parties to have any and all disputes arising out of the contract arbitrated, an arbitrator may permissibly resolve such issues, even substantive issues of validity. As noted above, the subject of the contract matters little in determining arbitrability. The 1987 *McMahon*[4] decision stood for the principle that as long as the agreement is voluntary, the parties are not waiving their statutory rights, but rather merely opting for a private, not public, adjudication forum. Since *McMahon*, however, at least one circuit has held that subsequent to *McMahon* Congress modified two statutes, Title VII (employment discrimination) and the Age Discrimination in Employment Act (ADEA), to require "knowing and voluntary" assent to arbitration in order for the agreement to be enforceable. The Ninth Circuit, in *Duffield v. Robertson Stephens & Co.*, held that employees could not, as a condition of employment, be forced to waive their statutory right to sue on Title VII or ADEA claims – and the US Supreme Court let that decision stand by refusing to review the case.[5] In light of the recent date of the decision, we are presently uncertain whether this decision (and the US Supreme Court's passive reactions) signals a retreat from a federal policy of rigorously enforcing arbitration agreements, or perhaps merely the delineation of a discrete set of claims to be held to a different standard of arbitrability. In this regard, we note that the Supreme Court has over the last half decade reaffirmed the broad proposition that questions of whether class-action treatment made a claim non-arbitrable was for the arbitrator rather than for a court to decide.[6] In general, we see little indication that the Supreme Court will diverge from its recent path of arbitrator empowerment.

1. U.S. Const. Art. I, §8, cl. 3.
2. *See* Joseph M. Lookofsky, *Transnational Litigation and Commercial Arbitration*, 2nd edn (2004), 758. For a thorough discussion of US choice-of-law doctrines, *see* Friedrich K. Juenger, "Conflict of Laws: A Critique of Interest Analysis," Am. J. Comp. L. 32 (1984): 1.
3. *See Prima Paint Corp. v. Flood & Conklin Mfg. Co.*, 388 U.S. 395, 406-407 (1967).
4. *Shearson/American Express, Inc. v. McMahon*, 482 U.S. 220 (1987).
5. *Duffield v. Robertson Stephens & Co.*, 144 F.3rd 1182 (9th Cir.), cert. denied, 525 U.S. 982 (1998).
6. *Green Tree Financial v. Bazzle*, 539 U.S. 444 (2003).

§2. State Lex Arbitri

315. As noted above, state lex arbitri varies from state to state. Due to their incorporation of the UAA, at least thirty-one states have somewhat similar rules governing arbitration. It bears noting, however, that the dramatic rise in the increased use of arbitration, and the resulting complaints about unfairness in some arbitration proceedings, has led to calls for reform in various states. A revised UAA, which increased discovery rights, remedial options, and arbitrator-disclosure requirements, had been adopted by at least ten states by 2005. In states that have not adopted the UAA, state lex arbitri is a matter of local statute and must be investigated individually. One general principle, however, can be stated with certainty. Because the FAA and the substantive body of law that accompanies it are federal rules concerning commerce, any state rule or decision concerning arbitration that does not comport with federal law is automatically superseded. One consequence of this policy is that state courts may have to follow federal decisions interpreting federal statutes, like Title VII, that have state parallels as part of their enforcement scheme. For example, the court in *Duffield* noted that the plaintiff's Title VII claims were nearly identical to her state law discrimination action (California's Fair Employment and Housing Act (FEHA) in this case). Accordingly, the arbitrability of her FEHA claims was to be determined by the extent to which her Title VII claims could be arbitrated.[1]

1. Id., at 1186, n. 3.

Chapter 5. Enforcement of Arbitration Awards

§1. Pre-Award Attachment

316. Unlike public courts, ADR tribunals usually do not have the power to authorize attachment of one or both parties' assets prior to adjudication. Because it may take several months to commence arbitral proceedings, pre-award attachment becomes a strategically important mechanism to prevent a party from hiding or ridding itself of assets. Accordingly, a party must resort to a traditional court and request pre-award attachment in order to ensure that there will be something against which to execute an award. One federal circuit, the Third, and New York State's highest court, have denied such requests on the grounds that an attachment request runs counter to the intent of arbitration agreements.[1] Most other courts, however, have held that pre-award attachment, rather than subverting the intent of arbitration, in fact furthers the aims of arbitration by ensuring awards will be enforceable and thereby enhancing the effectiveness of arbitration generally.[2]

One exception to this practice is where the parties have stipulated by contract to be bound by a set of arbitral rules that allow the arbitrator to grant interim protective measures. The AAA, for example, allows its arbitrators to issue orders to conserve goods by deposit with a third party, attach the defendant's property, or to sell perishable goods. Presumably, an interim award is the functional equivalent of a final award and may thus be enforced as any like award in the public courts.[3]

1. Charles N. Bower & W. Michael Tupman, "Court-Ordered Provisional Measures under the New York Convention," Am. J. Int'l L. 80 (1986): 21; *see, e.g., McCreary Tire & Rubber Co. v. CEAT S.p.A.*, 501 F.2nd 1032 (3rd Cir. 1974).
2. Holtzmann, *supra*, at 37.
3. Id.

§2. Enforcement

317. Whether the arbitration proceeding is foreign or domestic, forced compliance with awards is seldom necessary because the parties usually voluntarily comply with the awards. However, where necessary, procedures are in place to aid those who fall victim to losing parties who refuse to pay.

I. Domestic Awards

318. Enforcing arbitration awards is relatively simple. Absent unusual circumstances, the award can be confirmed as a court judgment. Once so confirmed, the winner can invoke the public court apparatus to collect payment. Domestic enforcement of arbitration awards is governed by the FAA, the UAA, or other parallel enforcement statutes that have been adopted in every state.[1]

The procedure is simple. The winning party files a motion in a court with appropriate jurisdiction and within a specified time frame, usually one year. However, this time period may vary from state to state. The court must affirm the award and enter judgment unless the losing party makes a timely motion that the award should not be confirmed. Under both the FAA and the UAA, this motion to vacate must be made within three months after announcement of the award.[2] Once the award is confirmed, it is executed using the same procedures employed for executing traditional judgments.

There are only a few situations in which a court will vacate a judgment conferred in arbitration proceedings; otherwise, the award is presumed to be valid unless the court agrees to vacate it. Circumstances permitting a court to vacate or modify an award include (under the UAA and roughly paralleled in the FAA): where the award was procured by corruption, fraud, or other undue means; where there was evidence of partiality or corruption among the arbitrators; where the arbitrators were guilty of misconduct by refusing to postpone the hearing upon sufficient cause, by refusing to hear pertinent and material evidence, or by engaging in any other misbehavior which prejudiced the parties; or where the arbitrators exceeded their powers or so improperly executed them that a mutual, final, and definite award on the subject matter was not made. Courts will not examine the merits of a decision unless it is obvious that the award exceeds the agreement of the parties. Instead, the courts limit themselves to a narrow review premised on the above circumstances.[3]

1. Joseph Colagiovanni & Thomas W. Hartmann, "Enforcing Arbitration Awards," Disp. Resol. J. 50-Jan. (1995): 14.
2. *See* Uniform Arbitration Act §12(b), 9 U.S.C. §12.
3. *See, e.g., Coast Trading Co. v. Pacific Molasses Co.*, 681 F.2nd 1195, 1197-1198 (9th Cir. 1982).

II. International Awards

319. There are numerous conventions and treaties under which arbitration awards are enforced. Because of the general US policy favoring arbitration, US courts are prone to enforce foreign awards with minimal inconvenience to the parties. The major conventions affecting international arbitration awards are the Convention on the Recognition and Enforcement of Foreign Arbitral Awards (the New York Convention) and the Panama Convention.

A. The New York Convention

320. International arbitration awards are usually enforced in the US under the 1958 United Nations Convention on the Recognition and Enforcement of Foreign Arbitral Awards (otherwise known as the New York Convention). Since 1958, more than sixty-eight nations have ratified or acceded to it. In 1970, the US acceded to the convention; the provisions under the convention were added to the FAA. Furthermore, Congress granted the US federal district courts original, but not exclusive, jurisdiction over actions arising under the convention.

The US operates under the New York Convention with two caveats. First, the federal courts will only enforce arbitration awards rendered by a forum in a signatory nation ("reciprocity"). Second, the federal courts will not give effect to arbitration awards relating to non-commercial transactions. In practice, the second caveat means that arbitration awards arising out of non-commercial contracts ancillary to commercial contracts will not be enforced.[1]

Because the US courts want to encourage the use of arbitration in the US and in foreign countries, Congress has made enforcement of international arbitration awards uncomplicated. The convention requires the US to recognize arbitral awards as binding and to enforce the awards according to the US rules of procedure. The party seeking confirmation of an award must, within three years of the decision, furnish the appropriate court with a written copy of the decision and a copy of the arbitration agreement.

Under the convention, there are seven grounds on which enforcement of an award may be challenged:

(1) The parties were under some incapacity, or the agreement is not valid under the law to which the parties have subjected it.
(2) The party against whom the award is invoked was not given proper notice of the appointment of the arbitrator or of the arbitration proceedings or was otherwise unable to present his case.
(3) The award deals with a dispute not contemplated by the terms of the submission to arbitration, or it contains decisions on matters beyond the scope of the submission to arbitration.
(4) The composition of the arbitral authority or procedure was not in accordance with the agreement of the parties.
(5) The agreement has not yet become binding on the parties.
(6) The subject matter of the dispute is not capable of settlement by arbitration under the law of the country.
(7) The recognition or enforcement of the award would be contrary to the public policy of that country.

All of these exceptions, including the possible "loophole" of the public policy exception, are consistently construed narrowly by the courts. This is consistent with the general US policy favoring arbitration.[2]

1. *See* David W. Rivkin, "International Arbitration," in *Commercial Arbitration For the 1990s*, ed. Richard J. Medalie (1991), 123, 135-155.
2. *See* Joseph T. McLaughlin, "Enforcement of Arbitral Awards under the New York Convention: Practice in U.S. Courts," PLI/Comm. 477 (1988): 275.

B. The Panama Convention

321. What the New York Convention is to the United Nations (UN) and the world, the Panama Convention is to the Western Hemisphere (see paragraph 314). It is essentially an agreement amongst North and South American states to recognize and enforce arbitral awards rendered in signatory forums. Significantly, the Panama

Convention recognizes all arbitral awards, regardless of subject matter. Where the New York Convention is limited, namely to commercial transactions only, the Panama Convention is expansive. Further, the Panama Convention does not distinguish between domestic and foreign awards. Thus, an arbitration award rendered in Uruguay that resolves a dispute between a Chilean buyer and a Honduran seller over the quality of services rendered in Mexico may be entered and enforced in the US or any other ratifying state.[1]

Another unique aspect of the Panama Convention is that it provides that if the parties do not select procedural rules for arbitration, the Rules of the Inter-American Commercial Arbitration Commission shall fill the gap.[2] In the event that a dispute is one that falls under both Conventions, the US implementing legislation for the Panama Convention provides that the Panama Convention shall apply.[3]

1. Rivkin, *supra*, at 135.
2. Panama Convention Art. 3.
3. 9 U.S.C. §305(2).

Chapter 6. Special Issues in ADR

§1. Negotiated Rulemaking

322. Often called "reg neg," negotiated rulemaking is a method of ADR which "brings together the interested parties to jointly participate in the process of developing rules to govern particular enterprises, endeavors, or relationships."[1] The goal of "reg neg" is to consider the concerns and conflicting interests involved in rulemaking before the rules are established in an effort to avoid subsequent legal suits once the regulations are passed. Additionally, "reg neg" attempts to diminish the influence special-interest groups exert on the rulemaking process, frequently turning the process into a "battleground" that is a "bonanza for lawyers."[2] In 1994, President Clinton issued an executive order directing federal agencies to explore consensual methods of dispute resolution, including negotiated rulemaking, where appropriate.[3]

1. *ADR in the News, supra*, at 3.
2. Id.
3. Id.

§2. Punitive Damages

323. Many commentators contend that arbitrators do not possess the authority to impose punitive damages upon parties involved in arbitration unless specifically authorized in the arbitration agreement. They claim that only the government may punish an offending party. Instead, they would require the winning party to file a separate claim for punitive damages in a judicial forum that is authorized by the state to impose punishment. While the FAA is silent on the issue of punitive damages, some arbitration associations, such as the AAA, expressly authorize imposition of punitive damages on the losing party. There is also some support for the proposition that if the underlying causes of action do not support punitive awards in a litigation setting, they should also not be awarded in an arbitration setting.[1]

Recently, in *Mastrobuono v. Shearson Lehman Hutton, Inc.*,[2] the US Supreme Court upheld an award of punitive damages granted by an arbitration panel. In *Mastrobuono*, the arbitration panel awarded compensatory and punitive damages to customers alleging that their securities brokerage firm had mishandled their account. The contract was governed by New York law, which prohibits arbitrators from awarding punitive damages; however, the arbitration clause provided that arbitration was to be governed by rules of the National Association of Securities Dealers which expressly permits awarding of punitive damages. The court, once again promoting full enforcement of arbitration agreements, held that the rules of the NASD govern the award of punitive damages and upheld the punitive damages awarded by the arbitrator.[3]

Justice Stevens, in his majority opinion, pointed out that the FAA "not only 'declared a national policy favoring arbitration', but actually 'withdrew the power of the states to require a judicial forum for the resolution of claims which the contracting parties agreed to resolve by arbitration'".[4] Furthermore, Justice Stevens cited *Volt Information Sciences, Inc. v. Board of Trustees of Leland Stanford Junior Univ.*,[5] which pointed out that "when a court interprets provisions in an agreement covered by the FAA, 'due regard must be given to the federal policy favoring arbitration, and ambiguities as to the scope of the arbitration clause itself resolved in favor of arbitration'".[6] In sum, the court held that where there the contract evinces no clear intent to avoid exemplary damages, punitive damages may be awarded by an arbitrator if appropriate.

It is as yet unclear whether *Mastrobuono* will be construed narrowly or broadly by the lower federal courts. However, given that ADR methods are currently held in favor by the US Supreme Court, a broad reading will be encouraged.

1. *See, e.g., Tinaway v. Merrill Lynch & Co.*, 692 F. Supp. 220, 226 (S.D.N.Y. 1988).
2. *Mastrobuono v. Shearson Lehman Hutton, Inc.*, 514 U.S. 52 (1995).
3. Id., at 61-62.
4. Id. at 56 (citing *Southland Corp. v. Keating*, 465 U.S. 1, 10 (1984)).
5. *Volt Information Sciences, Inc. v. Board of Trustees of Leland Stanford Junior Univ.*, 489 U.S. 468 (1989).
6. Id., at 476.

§3. MULTI-DOOR COURTHOUSE

324. Professor Sander of Harvard Law School has provided scholars with his image of the courthouse of the future: The Multi-Door Courthouse.[1] This vision has been temporarily incorporated into a few jurisdictions, like the District of Columbia, for example, and spurred experiments in others. Rather than providing resources solely to traditional litigation as a dispute-resolution method, the courthouse will have many dispute-resolution options or "doors" available to customers of the justice system.

One wishing to initiate an action would first meet with a screening professional, who would evaluate the case and refer it to the proper method of dispute resolution, whether that be mediation, minitrial, or full-fledged litigation, among other alternatives. Litigation would simply be one option among the myriad of dispute resolution alternatives available.[2]

At this time, several jurisdictions have experimented or are currently experimenting with the Multi-Door Courthouse scheme. While early results are generally positive, including reports of increased speed of resolution, reduced costs, and enhanced party satisfaction, much research will be required before the project can be introduced in all jurisdictions.[3]

1. Frank Sander, "Varieties of Dispute Processing," F.R.D. 70 (1976): 111, 130-131.
2. Id.
3. *See, e.g.*, Kenneth K. Stuart & Cynthia A. Savage, "The Multi-Door Courthouse: How It's Working," Colo. Law. 26-Oct. (1997): 13.

§4. NEIGHBORHOOD JUSTICE CENTERS

325. Another modern invention concerning ADR is the rise of Neighborhood Justice Centers (NJCs). Founded by the US Justice Department in 1978, the primary goal of the NJC program is to resolve simple private disputes within the community focusing on reconciliation rather than punishment. Most often, a community's NJC will handle landlord/tenant disputes, small claims actions between local community members, non-violent misdemeanors and similar neighborhood disputes. NJCs are designed to bring community values back into dispute resolution so that the disputes are being resolved taking those values into account rather than complex legal values. Instead of leaving clients confused or disappointed, most resolutions through NJCs leave clients hopeful for their future relationship with their opponent and satisfied with the result.[1]

The third party arbitrators and mediators in NJCs are usually members of the community who have been specially trained to mediate or arbitrate the disputes of others. They are often, but need not be, businessmen, lawyers, or other well-known community members. At this point, NJCs have little trouble finding enough volunteers willing to train and become neutrals; instead, most find that they have more volunteers than they can handle.[2]

There are, however, certain disputes that should not be dealt with on a community level. These include domestic violence disputes and disputes involving the greater public interest. These types of disputes often require a more binding judgment to change the actions of the offenders.

1. *See* Edith B. Primm, "The Neighborhood Justice Center Movement," Ky. L. J. 81 (1993): 1067, 1068-1069.
2. *See* id., at 1069-1070, 1072-1074.

§5. STATE OFFICES OF MEDIATION

326. While court-annexed ADR and NJCs have been around for quite a few years, it is only recently that states have begun sponsoring ADR centers. These centers provide dispute resolution to the state governments in an effort to manage, resolve, and prevent conflicts from occurring within the government and between the government and the public.[1]

In 1984, the National Institute for Dispute Resolution (NIDR) provided funding for six states that were to use the funds to set up ADR programs. Between 1989 and 1991, three additional states received funding for the same purpose. At this time, researchers have yet to report their full findings, but early reports are positive, demonstrating a successful track record of intervention and resolution. However, today, additional offices are being started by the states on their own initiative, revealing a trend of growing support for the ADR movement.[2]

1. *ADR in the News, supra*, at 3.
2. *See* Peter S. Adler, "State Offices of Mediation: Thoughts on the Evolution of a National Network," Ky. L. J. 81 (1993): 1013, 1014-1020.

Chapter 7. The Future of ADR

327. Those who are hopeful that ADR will take us to the next step in resolving contentious disputes recognize that in order for ADR meaningfully to change the legal world, attorneys, judges, and indeed all of society must become educated about the potential advantages it enjoys over traditional litigation. Only then will ADR be fully accepted as a true alternative to the public justice system and not seen as second-class justice. Prior to the existence of modern arbitration statutes, parties generally embarked upon the arbitration process as a result of an agreement to arbitrate after the dispute arose. Today, arbitration clauses are frequently found in contracts of many types including employment, banking, securities, real estate, health care, and insurance agreements.

Proponents also claim that the existence and acceptance of ADR is allowing disputants to take responsibility for resolving their own disputes, rather than relying on an already overworked judicial system to do it for them.[1] On the other hand, skeptics claim that it only creates more problems, wastes judicial resources, prevents public awareness of important societal failures, and creates a two-tiered justice system which mistakenly focuses on harmony rather than justice.

ADR commentators generally agree that the answers can be acquired only through more experimentation and research. This has proven difficult in the past due to the difficulty of creating "control groups" and "experimental groups" that are substantially identical. No two cases are exactly the same because of the "human factor," making it almost impossible to compare outcomes and confidently attribute that outcome to the dispute-resolution method used. Additionally, because ADR mechanisms are usually conducted in private, monitoring them has been next to impossible. As a result of these and other difficulties, numerous reports present completely opposite perspectives on the effectiveness of ADR. While some praise it as the savior of the court system, others find it no better, and sometimes worse, than the one that already exists.

Both sides also agree that there are some cases in which ADR should not be used. These include cases involving complex legal issues, where there is a great amount of public interest in the outcome, where one or both sides are seeking to create legal precedent, and where one or both sides hope to bind non-parties to the result.

All sides admit that ADR is here to stay. Not only are states, communities, and courts implementing ADR methods, but law firms are also creating specialized departments that handle ADR cases exclusively. Further, arbitration has become almost indispensable to international commercial transactions. The major questions remaining unanswered concern when ADR is appropriate to use and who should monitor that process. Court-annexed ADR may be expanded in the future because the supervision of the process would remain with the judges. ADR is not intended, nor should it be, a substitute for the judicial system. It works best when used as a supplement to the traditional system, working toward the same goals as the judicial system itself.

1. *See* Newhouse, *supra*, at 18.

Index

www.ingramcontent.com/pod-product-compliance
Lightning Source LLC
Chambersburg PA
CBHW071431230926
51846CB00001B/186
* 9 7 8 9 0 4 1 1 2 8 7 2 0 *